£15.00

ASLIB READER SERIES

Previously published titles in the *Aslib Reader Series*

No. 1 NATIONAL LIBRARIES — M. B. Line and J. Line

ISBN 0 85142 118 0 (hardback)
ISBN 0 85142 119 9 (paperback)

©Aslib 1979
3 Belgrave Square, London SW1X 8PL

Printed in Great Britain by Henry Ling Ltd., at the Dorset Press, Dorchester, Dorset.

ASLIB READER SERIES

VOLUME 2

THE SCIENTIFIC JOURNAL

EDITED BY
A.J. MEADOWS

Aslib

SERIES EDITORS: PETER J. TAYLOR & RUTH FINER

CONTENTS

Introduction   1

1. THE DEVELOPMENT OF THE SCIENTIFIC JOURNAL   3

The scientific periodical from 1665 to 1798   *Douglas McKie*   7

2. ECONOMICS OF JOURNAL PUBLICATION   19

General perspective   *Task Group on the Economics of Primary Publication*   23

Total cost of communicating scientific and technical information   *D.W. King, F.W. Lancaster, D.D. McDonald, N.K. Roderer, B.L. Wood*   29

Economic interaction between special libraries and publishers of scholarly and research journals   *Herbert S. White, Bernard M. Fry*   50

Subscription fulfillment   *Harry Florentine*   56

3. SOME BASIC PROBLEMS OF JOURNAL PUBLICATION   59

The future of scientific publishing — or, what will scientists be doing for Brownie points?   *Harold Wooster*   63

Proliferation and fragmentation of journals   *John Martyn*   68

Standardization in production of journals: a black and white case?   *Margaret Broadbent*   71

Research studies in patterns of scientific communication: III Information-exchange processes associated with the production of journal articles   *William D. Garvey, Nan Lin, Kazuo Tomita*   73

Some effects of delay in publication of information in medical journals, and implications for the future.   *David A.E. Shephard*   88

4. THE REFEREEING OF SCIENTIFIC JOURNALS   95

The scientific referee   *Frank T. Manheim*   99

The problem of refereeing   *A.J. Meadows*   104

Patterns of evaluation in science: institutionalisation,   *H. Zuckerman* 112
structure and functions of the referee system   *R.K. Merton*

5. THE CHARACTERISTICS AND INTERRELATIONSHIPS OF JOURNALS   147

The bibliography of operational research   *M.G. Kendall* 151

Networks of scientific papers   *Derek J. de Solla Price* 157

Interrelationships of scientific journals   *Francis Narin, Mark Carpenter* 163
                                       Nancy C. Berlt

Bibliographical citation characteristics of the   *Louis V. Xhignesse* 172
psychological journal network in 1950 and in 1960   *Charles E. Osgood*

Journal ranking and selection: a review in physics   *Alan Singleton* 186

6. AN ALTERNATIVE VIEWPOINT   219

Investigation of scientific journals as communication channels.
Appraising the contribution of individual countries to the
world scientific information flow.   *Z.B. Barinova et al* 223

Optimizing the structure of scientific publications   *Yu. A. Novikov* 248

The deposition of scientific works   *I.M. Basova* 256
(the experience of VINITI)   *I.F. Kusnetsova*

7. THE FUTURE OF THE SCIENTIFIC JOURNAL   269

Provisional scheme for central distribution of
scientific publications   *J.D. Bernal* 273

Evaluation of a dual journal concept   *Seldon W. Terrant* 279
                                       Lorrin R. Garson

An on-line scientific journal   *John Senders* 289

FURTHER READING   297

AUTHOR INDEX   299

This book consists of seven main sections on specific themes, each section consisting of a group of readings preceded by the editor's commentary. A list of annotated references to further reading following the structure of the main sections is also provided, together with an author index to all literature cited.

Professor Jack Meadows is Head of the Department of Astronomy and History of Science and Director of the Primary Communications Research Centre at the University of Leicester. Before moving to Leicester, he held appointments in the United States, in Scotland and the British Museum. He is author of six books and numerous articles on astronomy, the history of science and the communication of research.

INTRODUCTION

Journals represent the most important single source of information for the scientific research community. Their characteristics, and the problems they face, should therefore interest all who are involved with that community — librarians, information scientists, publishers, as well as the scientists themselves. But journals are not simply a convenient method of transmitting research results, something added onto the framework of science which could readily be replaced by another mode of communication. The scientific journal appeared in the seventeenth century, soon after the beginnings of modern science itself, and simultaneously with the origin of the scientific society. The development of science since then has continually been intertwined with the history of the printed journal. The journal has become an essential component in the organisation of science, in the apportionment of recognition to scientists, and in simply reaching agreement on what constitutes acceptable science. For this reason, historians and sociologists of science have also been forced to examine the role of the scientific journal, in their attempts to analyse how science functions. The papers collected together in this volume consequently come from a variety of sources, and have been written from a diversity of viewpoints.

A wide dispersal of relevant documents is one good reason for putting together a collection of readings. It is not, however, the main purpose behind the papers collected here; rather I have had the following two needs in mind whilst selecting material. In the first place, I have chosen mainly recent papers for re-publication, so that, it is hoped, the volume will provide an up-to-date picture of the scientific journal in the 1970s. Secondly, I have placed the selected items in a number of different categories which I believe to reflect *important* aspects of the development of scientific journals. This means that I have not covered some other aspects which seem to me to be of lesser significance. For example, modern methods of composition and printing have speeded up the production of journals, and, in some directions, reduced the production costs. I do not, however, see these developments as being of basic importance for the journal, and they are therefore barely touched upon in this volume.

The papers selected, together with the short introduction to each section, are put before you, therefore, as a thematic account of the scientific journal. They are intended to suggest possible lines of development in terms of which past, present, and future changes in journal production and usage may be considered.

1 THE DEVELOPMENT OF THE SCIENTIFIC JOURNAL

1. THE DEVELOPMENT OF THE SCIENTIFIC JOURNAL

Considerably more attention has been paid by historians to the early development of the scientific journal than to its progress during the past two centuries. The reason is clear enough; as is mentioned in the introduction, the origins of the journal are tied up with the origins of modern science, and the latter has long been a matter of major concern for historians. The one historical review reprinted in this section is therefore typical in covering the period up to 1800. No-one would suppose that the development of the journal finished at this point, or that interaction between the growth of science and the growth of journals ceased then. However, it might be supposed that no fundamental change has occurred since. I shall use this introductory piece to illustrate, by a couple of examples, that such an assumption is wrong.

By the latter part of the nineteenth century, it was becoming evident that retrieval of information from scientific journals might soon break down. The problem was that the amount of literature, particularly in chemistry, was growing beyond the point where the leisurely handling methods of the period could function efficiently. Consequently, an attempt was made to reorganise the journal literature — for example, by standardising bibliographical data and by introducing abstracts journals. These organisational revisions worked: with some later additions, such as the introduction of letters journals, they form the basis for the system that is still operating today. They also reflect a turning point in the growth of science, for they coincide in time with the growth of professionalisation of science.

Again, one of the striking changes in journal publication since the Second World War has been the increasing involvement of commercial publishers alongside the learned societies. This involvement reflects two new developments in scientific research. In the first place, it has been made possible by the vast growth of science, and therefore of the money available for producing journals. Secondly, it has arisen from the rapidly increasing specialisation of scientific research. Learned societies have traditionally been concerned with an entire, usually well-established, discipline. Commercial publishers observed that specialisation was leading to the establishment of new research fields within, or between, disciplines, and that these were not adequately catered for by the general-coverage, society journals. They therefore sought to make themselves indispensable in the newly-defined market of specialised and interdisciplinary journals.

We may expect that the development of science, and of scientific journals, will continue to progress in parallel in the future, as they have in the past. Later sections of this volume — especially Sections 5 and 7 — will indicate some of the directions such progress may take.

THE SCIENTIFIC PERIODICAL FROM 1665 TO 1798.

By DOUGLAS McKIE, D.Sc., Ph.D.

BEFORE the foundation of the scientific academies in the middle of the seventeenth century, there were no scientific periodicals ; and " natural philosophers " conveyed their ideas and accounts of their work and experiments to one another by means of letters which, from their scope and length, might be more appropriately described as dissertations. Much of this voluminous correspondence has survived ; and in it is to be found the give-and-take, and sometimes the cut-and-thrust, of scientific argument and debate. We need remind ourselves only of the extensive and historically important correspondence of Mersenne [1], from which today we obtain, or shall obtain when it has been completely published and studied, a real, or at least a deeper, knowledge of the history of physical science in the first half of the seventeenth century.

But the epistolary dissertation was not an ideal method for the communication of scientific fact and theory, even when it transcended frontiers. It was too personal. Men write to their friends, and not always, or not so often, to those who dispute their facts and reject their theories. Questions of priority were so easily raised ; and ciphers were used for secrecy. Moreover, the method could not spread new knowledge and new ideas either rapidly or widely : it was too slow and too limited within narrow personal circles.

With the foundation of the Royal Society of London and the Royal Academy of Science in Paris, the need for some better and wider means of communication became obvious and urgent. Conditions in England differed, however, from those in France. In England interest in scientific matters, in the new " philosophy," was actively centred in one group, which during the struggle between King and Parliament, met first in London, and then partly in London and partly in Oxford in separate assemblies, until their reunion in London after the Restoration to form " The Royal Society of London for the Improving of Natural Knowledge." But the *virtuosi* formed one group only [2]. In France, the very opposite conditions prevailed. In many French cities other than Paris there were independent groups of men interested in natural philosophy and meeting and joining in *conférences* and *sociétés* [3]. It was the fashion of the hour.

The foundation in 1666 of the Royal Academy of Science in Paris increased this interest in matters scientific, but there had already appeared in France in 1665 the first scientific journal, the ' Journal des Sçavans,' ancestor of all its kind [4]. Its editor, Denis de Sallo [5]

Reprinted from *Philosophical Magazine* Commemoration Issue, 1948, p. 122-32, by permission of the publisher.

(1626–69), was a friend of Colbert, Louis XIV's Minister and prime mover in the establishment of the Académie Royale des Sciences in Paris. Descended from an ancient and noble family of Poitou and educated at the Collège des Grassins, he became a lawyer. He was an omnivorous reader of all kinds of books and he kept two secretaries to compile notes and transcribe extracts from the books that he read. Overwork brought ill-health and enforced inactivity ; and de Sallo then thought that he might incorporate such material as he was led to abstract into a weekly journal of literary and scientific news, supposing that what had interested him would likewise interest others, especially the ever widening circle of amateurs of the " new philosophy."

The first number of the ' Journal ' was published in Paris on Monday, January 5, 1665. The reader was advised that the journal would contain details of new books, obituaries, news of experiments in physics and chemistry, discoveries in the arts and in science, such as machines and the useful and curious inventions afforded by mathematics, astronomical and anatomical observations, legal and ecclesiastical judgments from all countries, and " enfin, on taschera de faire en sorte qu'il ne passe rien dans l'Europe digne de la curiosité des Gens de lettres. qu'on ne puisse apprendre par ce Journal." The founders, so the reader was informed, had given much consideration to the problem of whether the journal should appear annually, monthly or weekly. They had concluded in favour of weekly publication in view of the fact that news ages quickly : " Mais enfin ils ont creu qu'il devoit paroistre chaque semaine ; parce que les choses vieilliroient trop, si on differoit d'en parler pendant l'espace d'un an ou d'un mois." They had been influenced also by the complaints of certain " persons of quality " that frequent issues of a journal were agreeable, whereas a whole volume of such items, from which the passage of time would have effaced the charm of novelty, might prove fatiguing [6].

De Sallo appeared as editor of the ' Journal ' under the pseudonym of the Sieur de Hédouville, but it is not certain whether he sought anonymity or whether the name was taken from an estate he is said to have owned in Normandy. He had help in his editorial labours from Chapelain and probably from the Abbé Gallois, and possibly from others ; and he allowed them complete freedom of opinion. However, this freedom led to criticism and raised an opposition that brought trouble upon the venture. After the appearance of the thirteenth number on March 30, 1665, de Sallo's privilege was withdrawn and the ' Journal ' was suppressed, this step being said to be due, however, not to the complaints of authors who considered themselves aggrieved, but to Jesuit irritation at disrespectful Gallican comment on a decree of the Inquisition. De Sallo declined to continue publication with a censor. However, his resolute stand for independence had impressed Colbert, who remained friendly towards him and continued to consult him on the many subjects on which he was well informed. Towards the end of his brief life of forty-three years, de Sallo was given a financial post by Colbert because his private means had become seriously depleted through his generosity, his love of gaming and his haphazard life. Such was our first scientific editor.

After its suppression in 1665, the 'Journal' resumed publication on January 4, 1666, under the editorship of the Abbé Gallois, and was continued in 1685 by the Abbé de la Roque, in 1687 by Cousin and from 1702 to July 1792 by a committee. It was suppressed during the Revolution and revived in 1816. From 1665 to 1792, a series of one hundred and eleven volumes were published. The 'Journal' was reprinted in Amsterdam and also in Paris. It was imitated in other countries and even in France.

Although we are considering here the rise of the scientific periodical, and necessarily excluding the serial publications of the scientific academies, some reference must be made to the ' Philosophical Transactions ' of the Royal Society of London. The Society had seen a copy of the ' Journal des Sçavans ' and had discussed its contents and the problem of publishing a similar work ; and they had concluded that something more " philosophical " was needed, excluding legal and theological items, but including more particularly accounts of the experiments made before the Society [7]. The first number of the ' Transactions ' appeared in London on March 6, 1665. It was edited by Henry Oldenburg, one of the two Secretaries of the Society. It was almost wholly scientific in content ; it did not cater for the interests of a widespread public of amateurs ; it was a monthly and not a weekly. It was the official organ of the Society and thus the first of its kind. Its appearance marked a new development ; for it was a medium for the publication of new observations and original work in science, mostly carried out by the Fellows of the Society, and it became the model on which all other published proceedings of the scientific academies have been fashioned. It reviewed books and gave space for the publication of differing scientific opinions by those engaged in similar experiments and studies. It was less amateur and more professional, if the latter term may be applied to the productions of an age when the professional scientist had not yet appeared on the scene.

However, although the ' Philosophical Transactions ' was the Royal Society's official organ, it was financially the private venture of Henry Oldenburg and it cannot be said to have yielded him much in the way of mere profit. Its continuance was no more secure than that of the ' Journal des Sçavans,' although for different reasons. It is also to be remembered that some stimulus towards its production is definitely to be ascribed to the appearance of the ' Journal des Sçavans,' since a discussion of the ' Journal ' by the Society led to the decision to publish the ' Philosophical Transactions '. The part played by Frenchmen in the foundation and development of the scientific periodical is inadequately recognized, as we shall see later on.

A word might be said in passing about Henry Oldenburg. He was born about 1615 in Bremen and died in Charlton, Kent, in 1677. He came to England about 1640 and, it is thought, remained here until 1648. In 1653 he came to England again to represent his native city on a matter of dispute with Cromwell and did not return to the Continent until 1657, when he acted as tutor and guardian to the Hon. Robert Boyle's nephew, Robert Jones, during a continental tour lasting until 1660. Returning to England, Oldenburg was appointed one of the two Secretaries of the Royal Society, the other being John Wilkins. Oldenburg carried on an extensive foreign correspondence on behalf of the Royal Society. Suspicion fell upon him during the Dutch War of 1665–67 and he was imprisoned in the Tower of London for two months. He was devoted to the new learning and enthusiastic in his labours to further the work of the Royal Society by " a commerce in all parts of the world with the most philosophical and curious persons to be found everywhere [8]."

The ' Journal ' and the ' Transactions ' gave two distinct models to scientific literature ; the former long influenced the development of the scientific periodical, until the rise of the journal specially devoted to one science only, while the latter became the pattern for the publications of the scientific academies that arose in greater numbers throughout Europe during the eighteenth century.

The ' Journal des Sçavans ' was imitated in Italy by the ' Giornale de Letterati di ' (Rome), which continued to appear with a change of title from 1668 to 1697. The ' Philosophical Transactions ' seem to have been the model for the famous ' Acta Eruditorum,' the learned scientific monthly which first appeared at Leipzig in 1682. Leipzig was the centre of the German trade in books and one of the most important functions of the ' Acta ' was the announcement of new works of scholarship. It contained articles on the work of Europe's leading scientists ; it included in its field medicine and mathematics, law and theology ; it was the first German scientific periodical. Fifty volumes were published from 1682 to 1731, with ten supplementary volumes, followed by the ' Nova Acta Eruditorum ' in forty-five volumes from 1732 to 1782 with eight supplementary volumes. The first editor was Otto Mencke (1644–1707), and he was succeeded by his son and then by his grandson until 1754, when the editorship passed out of the family [9]. The ' Acta ' will be remembered for many papers by Leibnitz, especially those dealing with his work on the calculus, which led to the controversy with Newton.

Mention might also be made of the ' Nouvelles de la république des lettres,' modelled on the ' Journal des Sçavans ' and edited by Pierre Bayle (1647–1706) during its first three years (Amsterdam, 1684–87). It was Holland's contribution to the cause of popular scientific periodical literature and continued until 1718.

The turn of the century in which the two types of scientific periodical had been established witnessed an important consequence of the reorganization of the Paris Academy of Science, namely, the publication of the first volume of the long series of ' Histoire et Mémoires ' of the Academy, with many supplementary volumes, a series modelled on the ' Philosophical Transactions.'

The eighteenth century brought great developments in the scientific periodical. Bolton [10] lists seventy-four new journals originating between 1725 and the close of the century, excluding purely medical journals but including all other periodicals containing scientific material. However, it is clear from his bibliography, that by far the greater number of these originated after the middle of the century. Indeed, only five of them appeared before 1750, namely, ' Raccolta, d'opuscoli scientifici e filologici ' (Venezia, 1728–57, 52 vols., continued as ' Nuova raccolta,' etc., Ferrara, 1755–87, 42 vols.). ' Le Pour et Contre' (Paris, 1733–40, 20 vols.), ' Bibliothèque Britannique, ou Histoire des ouvrages des savans de la Grande Bretagne ' (La Haye, 1733–47, 25 vols., followed by the ' Journal Britannique,' La Haye, 1750–57, 24 vols.). ' Göttingische Zeitung von Gelehrten Sachen ' (Göttingen, 1739–52, 14 vols., continued from 1753 to 1801 in 117 volumes under another title in association with the Göttingen Academy), and the ' Hamburgisches Magazin ' (Hamburg, 1747–67, 26 vols., continued as the ' Neues Hamburgisches Magazin,' Hamburg and Leipzig, 1767–81, 20 vols.).

These new periodicals doubtless contributed to the development of the scientific journal, but their number, namely five, in a half-century, or, if we take the actual first years of publication, five between 1728 and 1750, does not indicate any striking change as compared with the developments in this kind of literature during the pioneering second half of the seventeenth century. However, the pace rapidly quickened. Of the remaining sixty-nine periodicals to appear between 1750 and 1798, nine appeared between 1750 and 1759, six between 1760 and 1769, and nine between 1770 and 1779 ; but from 1780 to 1789, there were twenty new scientific periodicals and from 1790 to 1798 a further twenty-five. It was therefore only during the last two decades of the eighteenth century that the number of journals was greatly increased ; for forty-five of the sixty-nine new publications originated between 1780 and 1798.

Of the nine new periodicals originating between 1750 and 1759, probably the most important was the ' Commentarii de rebus in scientia naturali et medicina gestis,' a most useful and successful journal giving news of the work of the academies and details of new books. It was published in Leipzig, the first number appearing in 1752, and continued until 1798 in a long series of forty-one volumes, including supplementaries. With the ' Acta Eruditorum,' already mentioned, the ' Commentarii ' are a mine of valuable information for the historian of science. In passing, it might be noted that of the nine new periodicals published in this decade six were German, two French and one Dutch. The predominance of the German contribution is again evident during the period from 1760 to 1769, when of the six new periodicals that appeared, five were German, the other being Italian. None of these six calls for any special comment here.

From 1770 to 1779, nine further new periodicals were published, seven of which were German, one French and one Italian. This decade witnessed a most important and significant development in the first appearance of the specialized scientific journal both in physics and in chemistry, namely, the ' Observations sur la Physique ' [11], edited by the Abbé Rozier, and the ' Chemisches Journal ' of Lorenz Crell. The ' Observations,' however, although largely concerned with physics, dealt extensively with chemistry as well and included sections on natural history and the arts. But the contents tended to become more physical, although in the early years of the journal it was the medium for the publication of many of Lavoisier's classical papers in chemistry in their original unrevised form before they were re-presented and re-read to the Paris Academy of Science [12]. In the history of chemistry the journal is a most important source. In the development of the scientific periodical, its appearance is a landmark and the circumstances merit some consideration.

The full title of the journal was ' Observations sur la Physique, sur l'histoire naturelle, et sur les arts ' ; it was a monthly and the first number appeared in July, 1771. Eighteen numbers were published from that date to the end of 1772 in 12°. From January 1773, the format became 4° and continued so until the final issue of 1793. The first eighteen numbers are very rare and it had already become necessary to reprint them in 1777 in two 4° volumes under the title of ' Introduction aux Observations sur la physique,' etc. The volume for 1773, comprising the issues from January to June of that year, is numbered volume one ; and in all forty-three volumes, usually two every year, appeared up to 1793.

The " Avis " to the reader prefacing volume one (1773) [13] explained that the publications of the academies were written in the languages of the different nations and printed several years after the memoirs included in them had been read before the academies ; that during that interval facts that might prove of the greatest usefulness remained unknown ; and, moreover, that the publications of the Academies, having become very numerous and therefore very costly, were often beyond the means of those to whom they might be advantageous. The writer went on to draw attention to other causes of delay : " Il semble qu'à mesure que le nombre des Savans s'est accru, la Correspondance, entre ceux des Nations différentes, a été rallentie. Chacun a cru sans doute que les Académies nationales seroient suffisantes, & qu'on en tireroit tous les secours nécessaires. La Constitution de ces Compagnies, formées par les Souverains, ayant admis des Correspondans étrangers, sembloit prévenir cette illusion, & remédier à l'inconvénient qui en est la suite ; mais cette précaution, si sagement prise, n'a pas été justifiée par le succès.

"Il résulte de ce peu de communication, que les progrès des Sciences sont très-lents, que des Savans de deux Nations différentes, travaillent long-tems sur la même matiere, & qu'ils perdent un tems précieux pour acquérir une gloire qui devient à la fin problématique. Cet inconvénient est moindre que celui de travailler sur une matiere éclaircie par des travaux déja publiés, dont on n'a aucune connoissance. L'Auteur perd un tems qu'il auroit mieux employé pour le bien & la gloire de sa Patrie, si, en entrant dans la carriere qu'il vouloit parcourir, il eût eu sous les yeux le tableau actuel des connoissances physiques, & le terme où elles sont restées."

For these reasons it appeared necessary to publish a new journal: " Ces motifs ont fait desirer qu'un Ouvrage périodique, d'un débit sûr & animé, annonçât les découvertes que se font chaque jour dans les différentes parties des Sciences, soit par des Notices abrégées, soit par des Mémoires très-étendus, qui continssent le développement de toutes les preuves de ces découvertes, en traçant même la marche de l'esprit inventeur. On a pensé que ce moyen, le plus prompt pour la publication des découvertes nouvelles, accéléreroit également le progrès des Sciences, qui ne sont autre chose que la somme de ces découvertes.

" Telles ont été les raisons qui nous ont engagés à entreprendre ce Recueil ; & nous les présentons avec d'autant plus de confiance, aux savans Etrangers, que ce sera leur ouvrage. Il est écrit dans une Langue, aujourd'hui celle de tous ceux qui ont reçu quelqu'éducation en Europe. L'Académie Royale des Sciences de Paris sentoit depuis long-tems l'importance de ce Recueil. Plusieurs de ses Membres le proposerent l'année derniere à peu-près suivant le plan auquel nous nous sommes attachés. Des raisons particulieres en ont empêché l'exécution totale."

But the new journal was not for " leisured amateurs " seeking entertaining reading under the illusion that they were initiated into scientific pursuits of which, in fact, they had no real knowledge : " Malgré l'accueil favorable que cet Ouvrage a reçu ; malgré les éloges que les Savans lui ont donné, nous nous croyons obligés de circonscrire nos limites pour le rendre encore plus digne d'eux. Nous rejetterons en conséquence ci qui ne seroit que compilation indigeste, & dénuée de vues neuves & utiles. L'importance des matieres, la maniere dont elles seront présentées, nous décideront sur le choix des morceaux qui doivent être insérés dans ce Recueil. Nous n'offrirons pas aux Amateurs oisifs, des Ouvrages purement agréables, ni la douce illusion de se croire initiés dans les Sciences qu'ils ignorent." It was clear that the aims of the journal were serious and immediate and that popular science was not its object.

Moreover, the historical development of science was included in the plan : " Nous nous occuperons sur-tout de l'histoire des Sciences que nous embrassons dans notre plan ; & c'est dans ces vues, que nous nous attacherons à rapporter les faits de la même espece, & les raisonnemens différens qu'ils auront fait naître. Cette maniere de voir & de comparer, présente un fond inépuisable d'instructions, que nous saisirons avec le plus grand soin ; de sorte qu'on verra au premier coup d'œil, la suite des faits qui auront concouru à l'établissement d'une vérité importante [14]

" On ne sauroit trop inviter ceux qui veulent faire des progrès dans les Sciences, à rapprocher les connoissances transmises par les Savans de tous les siecles & de tous les pays. C'est un préalable nécessaire pour parvenir à de nouvelles découvertes, & ils doivent considérer, comme le premier pas qu'ils aient à faire, celui où les grandes Hommes, qui les ont précédés, ont terminé leurs travaux. La continuité des efforts des uns & des autres, forme cette union, & cet accord qui doit regner entre les Savans de tous les Pays pour étendre les limites des connoissances.

" C'est donc de cette réunion de travaux, de cette somme de connoissances que nous devons partir pour en acquérir de nouvelles, & pour donner à ce Recueil la consistance que son objet semble lui assurer. L'étendue de ce travail surpasseroit nos forces, si une société formée par des personnes uniquement occupées des Sciences utiles, ne daignoit concourir avec nous pour remplir le but que nous nous sommes proposé.

The journal was intended also to increase the circulation of scientific information of the first importance and the editor took Mersenne for his model : " Les vrais Savans n'ont pas la manie de faire des secrets de leurs découvertes ; amis de l'humanité, leur gloire est de lui être utile ; aussi, c'est à eux que nous offrons ce Recueil, comme un dépôt où ils ont droit de prendre acte de leurs découvertes. Nous les invitons à regarder notre Cabinet, comme celui du Pere Mersenne." And general and experimental physics, chemistry, medicine, agriculture and the arts and crafts were to be included in its province : " en un mot . . . . tout ce qui a rapport à l'observation & à l'expérience [15]." Memoirs written by authors in other languages would be translated into French or extracts would be published until further details would be forthcoming.

We have quoted at length from this historically important document because it reveals the state of affairs at this time with regard to the scientific periodical in general ; and its contents apply to the current situation and explain for a particular instance the circumstances that led to such an extraordinary increase in and development of scientific periodical literature during the last quarter of the eighteenth century.

The editor of the ' Observations ' deserves some mention. François Rozier was born at Lyon in 1734 and died there on the night of September 28–29, 1793. He was educated for the priesthood and revealed an unusual interest in scientific observation. Anxious to preserve his freedom, he resisted the attempts of the Jesuits to persuade him to join their Order. After his father's death in 1757, he managed an estate for his elder brother, agriculture being one of his constant interests and a subject on which he wrote extensively and became an authority as a result of the long experiments made on the estate that he superintended.

He became a friend of Rousseau and in 1771, now an Abbé, he acquired from Gautier d'Agoty an earlier journal called ' Observations sur l'histoire naturelle, sur la physique et sur la peinture,' which had first appeared in 1752 and had continued under changed and expanded titles not too successfully. Rozier was also a friend of the economist and physiocrat, Turgot, the Minister who in his short term of office brought about the reform of the French gunpowder-office under the organizing genius of Lavoisier. Rozier approved of the Revolution of 1789. He fell in the siege of Lyon, a devoted priest seeking by personal example to maintain the courage and assuage the sufferings of his people [16].

Until December of 1778, Rozier was sole editor of the 'Observations.' In 1779 he took as his assistant his nephew, J. A. Mongez, who was later sole editor from 1780 to 1785, when De la Métherie became editor. The 'Observations' proved a striking success, because it achieved all its aims. Under the last editor the phlogiston theory was favoured and the papers on chemistry were not of a high standard, as the phlogiston theory was already being superseded by the new chemistry of Lavoisier except among some of the German chemists [17].

Much the same circumstances led Lorenz Crell to produce his various journals of chemistry; and since, strictly speaking, the 'Observations sur la physique' included subjects other than physics, Crell may be regarded as the founder of the first specialized scientific periodical. From 1778 to 1781 he published six volumes of his 'Chemisches Journal,' then thirteen volumes of 'Die neuesten Entdeckungen in der Chemie' (1781–86), and two volumes of his 'Chemisches Archiv' (1783), eight volumes of 'Neues Chemisches Archiv' (1784–91) and one volume of 'Neuestes chemisches Archiv' (1798), while his 'Chemische Annalen,' etc. ran to forty volumes from 1784 to 1803 with a 'Beitrage' of six volumes from 1785 to 1799. A tireless correspondent and editor. In the meantime, however, the 'Annales de Chimie,' to be referred to presently, had been founded in 1789.

From 1780 to 1789 twenty new journals appeared. Some of these edited by Crell we have already mentioned. The others included eleven German and two French periodicals and the well-known English periodical, 'The Botanical Magazine, or Flower Garden Displayed' (London, 1787, and in continuation), under the editorship of William Curtis (1746–99), who said of it that, whereas his 'Flora' had brought him praise, the 'Magazine' had brought him pudding [18]. This beautifully illustrated journal with its one hundred and fifty volumes and nearly ten thousand coloured plates continues to the present day and is a splendid example of our periodical literature. Its editors have included Jackson, Hooker, Prain, Stapf and A. W. Hill.

But the most important journal to appear between 1780 and 1789, was undoubtedly the 'Annales de Chimie,' edited by de Morveau, Lavoisier, Monge, Berthollet, de Fourcroy, de Dieterich, Hassenfratz and Adet, the representatives in France of the new chemistry of Lavoisier. Born in the year of the Revolution, 1789, the 'Annales' outdistanced all its competitors. The 'Observations' under De la Métherie favoured the old theory and in any case became more physical in content : Crell's periodicals survived for some years. But the 'Annales,' of which ninety-six volumes appeared in Paris between 1789 and 1815 together with three volumes of ' Tables des matières ' (1801, 1807, 1821), became the leading journal of chemistry. It continued under the title of ' Annales de chimie et de physique ' in seventy-five volumes from 1816 to 1840 and later resumed its original name to continue to our own day, oldest survivor among chemical periodicals and a lasting monument to the great editors who launched it in the shadow of revolution. Lavoisier, its most distinguished editor and its enthusiastic founder, saw only the first few years of its success as he fell a victim to the Terror in 1794.

The last decade of the century was remarkable for the publication of twenty-five new journals, thirteen German, three French and five English. Notable among these was Gren's ' Journal der Physik,' which first appeared in 1790 in Halle and Leipzig and which, strictly speaking, is the first journal specially devoted to physics, since Rozier's ' Observations ' included material from other scientific fields. The English journals included ' The Repertory of Arts and Manufactures,' first published in London in 1794, Nicholson's ' Journal of Natural Philosophy, Chemistry and the Arts,' which first appeared in 1797 in London and continued until 1813. The most notable journal to appear in this decade was, however, ' The Philosophical Magazine,' edited by Alexander Tilloch, the first number of which was published in London in 1798. In the physical sciences it was to become second in importance only to the ' Philosophical Transactions ' of the Royal Society of London. This month of June, 1948, marks the one hundred and fiftieth anniversary of its foundation. Its distinguished services to science throughout the world and its long and eventful history are described in another article in this number.

REFERENCES.

(1) *Correspondance du P. Marin Mersenne*, ed. Tannery and de Waard, Paris, 2 vols. (1933–37).
(2) Even in the Cambridge of Newton's time it was found impossible to establish a " Philosophical Meeting," as Newton reported in a letter to Aston of Feb. 23, 1684/5, " for want of persons willing to try experiments " (C. R. Weld, 'History of the Royal Society,' etc., London, i. 305–6 (1848).
(3) See M. Ornstein, ' The Rôle of Scientific Societies in the Seventeenth Century, Chicago ' (1928), and Harcourt Brown, ' Scientific Organizations in Seventeenth Century France (1620–1680)', Baltimore (1934). Attention is drawn to a recent valuable study by Miss R. H. Syfret, ' The Origins of the Royal Society ' (Notes and Records of the Royal Society of London v. p. 75 (1948).
(4) Ornstein, *op. cit.*, pp. 198–209, and Brown, *op. cit.*, pp. 185–207.
(5) *Nouvelle Biographie Générale*, Paris, vol. 43, col. 189–91 (1864).
(6) Quoted from the Amsterdam reprint (1685) of the first volume of the *Journal* (1665). The writer has not been able to consult the original Paris issue of 1665.
(7) See a letter from Moray to Huygens, quoted by Harcourt Brown (*op. cit.*, p. 201).

(8) 'Dic. Nat. Biog.,' article on Oldenburg.
(9) *Nouvelle Biographie Générale*, Paris, vol. 34, col. 925–6 (1861).
(10) H. C. Bolton, 'A Catalogue of Scientific and Technical Periodicals (1665–1882),' etc., Washington, (1885), published in 'Smithsonian Miscellaneous Collections,' Washington (1887), vol. xxix. The number of journals listed is 5105. The second edition (Washington, 1897), carried the work to 1895 and included 8603 titles. The chronological tables given on pp. 1081ff of the second edition have been used in the present study. Bolton included in his bibliography all journals containing scientific material, but in the chronological tables he restricted the entries to purely scientific journals or seems to have done so, since he excluded the *Astronomisches Jahrbuch* (Berlin, 1774), the first successful astronomical journal and still surviving to our own time, presumably because the earlier volumes were ephemerides.
(11) The details of the title varied slightly from time to time, as may be seen by consulting Bolton (*op. cit.*, 2nd edn., p. 267, no. 2201).
(12) See Meldrum, 'The Eighteenth Century Revolution in Science—The First Phase,' Calcutta (1929), and McKie, 'Antoine Lavoisier,' London (1935).
(13) 'Observations,' etc., 1773, i. iii–vii.
(14) Many original memoirs from previous years were translated into French and given a greater currency in accordance with this policy.
(15) The influences of the *Encyclopédie* are evident in this passage.
(16) *Nouvelle Biographie Générale*, Paris, vol. 42, col. 827–30 (1863).
(17) See J. R. Partington and D. McKie, 'Historical Studies on the Phlogiston Theory,' Annals of Science, ii. 361 (1937); iii. 1 and 337 (1938), and iv, 113 (1939).
(18) See Samuel Curtis, 'William Curtis,' 1746–1799, etc., Winchester (1941). and an article by Hunkin in 'Endeavour,' v, 13 (1946).

2 ECONOMICS OF JOURNAL PUBLICATION

2. ECONOMICS OF JOURNAL PUBLICATION

I place the question of finance near the beginning, because it is obviously a fundamental factor — often *the* fundamental factor — in the publication of journals. It is also appropriate to put it at this point because the division between learned societies and commercial publishers, mentioned in the introduction to Section 1, must be stressed here more than in the later sections. The reason is that the two groups normally have a different attitude to the journals they publish. Most societies regard the production of a journal as an essential part of their activities; indeed, many have it written into their bye-laws. Commercial publishers, on the contrary, produce journals in order to make a profit: if a commercial journal consistently makes a loss, it ceases publication. In the nineteenth century, a commercial journal might be allowed to make a loss for a long time. *Nature*, for example, only started making a profit after thirty years of publication. Nowadays, few commercial publishers can allow a journal more than three to five years to make its way.

These changed circumstances are, of course, partly due to the inflation of recent years. Journals have been greatly affected by the rising costs of production (raw materials, labour, etc.) and of distribution. Commercial publishers have generally reacted faster than the learned societies to these adverse conditions, but this has not simply meant a pruning of the titles published. Rather some titles have been deleted, but new ones have been introduced in different areas. Commercial publishers have naturally also raised their subscriptions, whilst for society publishers this has been the only way of remaining viable. Hence, the purchaser has been faced by steeply rising prices, new titles still appearing, and, generally, a stand-still budget on which to operate. The most obvious response has been to cut back on foreign language material, but some of the learned societies have also found that subscriptions to their journals have been hard hit by the squeeze.

The response to inflationary pressures depends on the country concerned. The situation described in the previous paragraph applies to both the UK and the USA. In countries where much of the journal publishing is state-sponsored, the response may differ — turning, for example, to rationalisation of titles and deficit budgeting. At the same time, economic statistics are usually more easily collected in such countries (though they may not be made generally available) than in the UK or USA. Nevertheless, a considerable effort is currently being made in the United States to obtain a sound statistical picture of the economics of scientific communication. Hence, the articles selected for this section stress US data. Although there are differences in detail between the UK and USA, the overall picture presented by these statistics should apply to both countries.

The first paper sets the scene for the whole section and, at the same time, examines one of the areas where British and American experience differs — namely, the application of page charges. This is an instructive example, since the factors involved have been rather similar in the two countries, but the resultant actions have been different. This paper is followed by a concise but detailed study of the cost factors involved in communicating scientific and technical information in the United States. I include it here as a case study of this type of analysis. The third paper looks at the economic interaction between librarians and journals. It touches, in passing, on the question of photocopying — a point we will not be examining in this volume, though a number of publishers consider it to be of major economic significance.

All the extracts so far in this section derive from major US studies. The final paper is different, since, although based on the US experience, it is concerned with details of the journal distribution process. I have included it as a reminder that the commercial success of a journal depends as much on this very basic type of operation as on high-level planning. Smaller learned societies often find problems in this area; it is one reason why a number of them have formed, or are considering forming, links with commercial publishers, where there is appropriate expertise.

THE ECONOMICS OF PRIMARY PUBLICATION
GENERAL PERSPECTIVE

We shall not try to summarize all the material of the Appendix; we suggest that readers interested in a brief survey simply skim the Appendix, noting the table of contents, the underlined passages, and occasional figures. A few especially important points emerge from the data and reasoning in the Appendix that deserve the attention of all readers before they address themselves to the Recommendations section of the Report; therefore, we will discuss these points briefly before introducing the recommendations.

ROLE OF PRIMARY JOURNALS

The current problems of primary journals that we mentioned in the introduction have led some to wonder whether such journals are an anachronism and should be replaced by some entirely different mode of storage and communication of information. We reject this view. While various new modes offer exciting possibilities for the improvement of communication they will have to be used in conjunction with journals. Statistics on the rates of growth of the circulations of journals in the last decade or so (see Appendix, Section IIIB. 2) and the growth in numbers of journals (see Appendix, Section IIIB. 1) show that on the whole buyers are still very interested in them. It is noteworthy that almost no U.S. primary journals have folded in recent years (see Appendix, Sections IIIB. 1, IVA. 3). A leveling off in the funds available for science and technology may well, in the long run, even ease the problems of journals by limiting the amount of material they are required to publish.

Journals have both archival and current-awareness roles. In their archival role they have a combination of virtues that alternative systems will not be able to match for a long time: They supply the *full text* of descriptions of new knowledge that are complete enough to satisfy most of the needs of users of this knowledge; this material is under orderly *bibliographic control*; it is *quickly available* in any well-maintained collection; these characteristics are achieved in a *free-market system*, where both producers and purchasers of information have ample opportunity to exercise judgments in adapting the information system to their needs or to what they believe is the welfare of society. Alternatives to journals offer a stronger challenge in relation to the current-awareness function, that is, keeping workers in a field aware of advances made by others. But even for this role, studies show that the regular browsing of journals continues to fulfill a very important current-awareness function (see Appendix, Section IIIC. 2).

DIVERSITY OF JOURNALS: SIZES, CIRCULATIONS, PRICES

The diversity of the journal population is overwhelming. In bulk, the largest journals publish about 500 times as much per year as the smallest. In some fields (physics, chemistry, some areas of biology) the larger journals (say, above 1.5 megawords/year) publish the bulk of new knowledge, while in other fields (mathematics, psychology, many areas of biology, and engineering) the reverse is the case (see Appendix, Section IIIA. 1 and Figures 1 and 2). The average journal has been increasing in bulk by about 7 percent a year. The spread in price is also enormous, the "best buy" in 1968 having provided 90 times as many words per penny as the "worst buy" in our sample. Generally, journals published by societies are much cheaper (even for nonmember subscribers) than those issued by private publishers;

Reprinted from REPORT OF THE TASK FORCE ON THE ECONOMICS OF PRIMARY PUBLICATION, 1970, p. 6-14, with the permission of the National Academy of Sciences, Washington D.C.

journals of nonsociety, nonprofit publishers tend to be intermediate. (See Appendix, Section IIIA. 2 and Figure 3). Circulations also vary widely, though few journals of our sample were outside the range 1,500 to 15,000 (see Appendix, Section IIIA. 2 and Figure 5). The number of workers in the general field of a journal is obviously the most important factor in its circulation, but price and general quality are also significant factors, and it is not uncommon for different journals with very similar coverage to differ in circulation by a factor of 3 to 5 or more.

VALUE OF JOURNALS TO SOCIETY

The value of journals is often attested in statements such as "Journals are the life blood of research." We agree; nevertheless, it is worth noting that one can make rough quantitative estimates of certain portions of the value of journals to society, estimates that show that this value exceeds a certain lower bound already many times larger than the total cost of producing the journals. For example, one can write:

Social value of journal = Value to current subscribers, i.e., to the users they represent + Value to others, including future generations

The first term also consists of two parts: Current users receive information from journals both directly, via their own use of them, and indirectly, via contacts with others who have used journals. Thus,

Value to current subscribers = Current direct value + Current indirect value

Studies of information flow (see Appendix, Sections IIIC. 2 and IVA. 6) suggest that the latter two terms are comparable with each other. One line of reasoning to get at the current direct value (see Appendix, Section IVA. 1) is based on the roughly plausible assumption that on the average the maximum price that a potential subscriber is willing to pay for a journal represents the value of this journal to him; this price, of course, will vary enormously from one subscriber to another. Combination of this assumption with an estimated price-circulation curve (see Appendix, Section IIIA. 2 and Figure 7) gives the sums of the value estimates of all the subscribers who actually get the journal. The result is larger than the total cost of producing the journal by a factor that, though hard to estimate reliably because of uncertainties in the price-circulation curve, can hardly be much less than 5 or so for, say, a good general physics journal. Thus the total social value of such a journal is likely to be over 10 times its production cost.

Another way of getting a quantitative clue to value is to study the time people are willing to invest in reading journals (see Appendix, Section IIIC. 1). The dollar value of this time, though varying somewhat from field to field, again is typically several times the production of the journals. This fact is important not only as a clue to the net value directly received from the journals, which is not likely to be much smaller, but also as an indication of the possible economic value of improving the efficiency with which users can extract the information of value to them.

PRODUCTION COSTS

It is important to distinguish three contributions to the cost of producing a journal (see Appendix, Section IIIA. 3 and Figure 3). The first is the basic prerun cost: editorial work, copy editing, composition, proofreading, engraving, and the like, for the technical material submitted. Often this component includes "hidden costs" that do not appear on the books, for example, editor's time or office space donated by a university or other organization. The second contribution is the basic runoff cost: paper and presswork for the technical papers published, binding, wrapping, and mailing, and also monitoring the files of subscribers, and the like. The third category is what may be termed optional costs, that is, costs of operations that are not necessary to the publication of research results but that are considered desirable adjuncts. Such operations include, for example, preparation and printing of advertising and news material or production of reprints and back-number stocks (sometimes large).

Since prerun costs depend only on the bulk of material published, while runoff costs are also proportional to the number of copies printed, the relative magnitudes of these two contributions vary greatly from journal to journal. For most journals, though, the prerun costs outweigh the runoff costs (for example, see Appendix, Figure 35). Both the prerun cost per unit amount of material and the runoff cost per unit amount per copy vary moderately from journal to journal (see Appendix, Sections IIIA. 4 and IIIA. 5); these variations are in part unavoidable (e.g., due to differences in the density of mathematics), in part a result of conscious choice (e.g., a striving for speedy publication), and in part due to variations in efficiency, resulting from various specific procedures.

For journals of commercial publishers, the publisher's profit seems typically to be of the same order as the total production cost (see Appendix, Figure 35). This is understandable in terms of a simple mathematical model, if the publisher tries to approximately optimize his profit and if one accepts other evidence on the dependence of circulation on price (see Appendix, Section IVA. 1).

LIBRARY COSTS

The cost of scientific and technical journals to society includes more than the production costs just described, since those journals that go to libraries have to be cataloged, bound, and supplied to users. The increase in costs of these activities when the amount of journal material available in a library is increased is of the same order as the subscription cost of the added journals, if the latter is computed at current average rates (see Appendix, Section IIID. 4).

SOURCES OF REVENUE

Here, too, there is great diversity. Advertising can be an important source only for journals of unusually large circulation. Reprint and back-number sales, though sometimes appreciable, more commonly yield a negligible net of income over cost. The major items of income are usually subscriptions, page charges, and subsidies, both direct (usually from funds of a society) and hidden (donated editorial services, and the like). The practice of imposing page charges has spread rapidly in recent years and seems by now to have been adopted by about half of all journals published in all fields of U.S. societies or other nonprofit groups, though it is more prevalent in physics and chemistry, and somewhat less common in medicine and engineering (see Appendix, Figure 14). The page charge is much less used abroad, even among the relatively rare nonprofit journals. A sizable majority of all articles honor the page charge; the honoring percentage usually increases in the first few years after introduction of the page charge because of education of authors' institutions, but it may fluctuate erratically with fluctuations in government funding.

FOCI OF OPPOSITION TO THE PAGE-CHARGE SYSTEM

In preparing our recommendations on the sources from which the financial support of primary journals should come, we have tried to give careful consideration both to the criticisms that have been leveled against the page-charge practice and to the arguments of its defenders. We shall start by listing some of the points that have been raised most often against page charges and our evaluations of them. Four of these have to do with the basic philosophy of journal support:

1. It is sometimes argued that the financial support for journals should come from those whom the journals benefit, and that this implies that the subscribers should pay for the entire cost of production. We feel that support by those who benefit is usually a sound principle, particularly if their judgments of value received are sound and are able to influence managerial decisions (see Appendix, Section II). But two things must be borne in mind. The first is that, as we have noted in our previous discussion on the value of journals, subscribers to journals are not the only beneficiaries of their existence; authors and their institutions derive a benefit, to which there are some quantitative clues (see Appendix, Figure 10 and Section IVA. 2); the value to future users is quite important (see Appendix, Section IIIC. 2), and so is the benefit received indirectly by those who interact informally, verbally or through correspondence, with someone who has used a journal (see Appendix, Sections IIIC. 2 and IVA. 6). The second point is that it is difficult to make each subscriber pay in proportion to the benefit he receives; often there is a single price for all, and discriminatory pricing rarely extends beyond distinguishing individual from institutional subscribers. As long as the situation obtains, there will be buyers to whom the benefit exceeds the cost of supplying them with an extra copy of a journal already in existence, but is not great enough to justify their paying a price to the total production cost per subscriber. Pricing these buyers out of the market can mean a loss to society that most but not all* of us would assess as very appreciable (see Appendix, Section IVB. 1). All these considerations make the support of journals by a simple raising of subscription prices somewhat analogous to the support of schools by tuition fees alone: It can be justified only if ways can be found to charge widely different rates to subscribers of different interests and circumstances.

2. A related objection sometimes raised against the page-charge system is that by subsidizing a large part of their costs it lessens the incentive for journals to operate efficiently and relieves them from the "test of the marketplace" that otherwise could weed out uneconomic journals. We feel that the question of economic incentives is a perfectly valid one but that the question should not be so formulated as to prejudge the issue. On the theoretical side (see Appendix, Sections IVA. 3, IVA. 4, IVA. 5), it seems that subsidy of input costs can affect economic incentives in a number of ways, some of which are desirable and some not; there is a diversity of opinions among the members of the Task Group as to the appropriateness of the relative weights assigned to these in the Appendix. On the empirical side, at least two things are clear. One is that marketplace pressures are always very ineffective in eliminating uneconomic or undesirable journals (see Appendix, Sections IIIB. 1 and IVA. 3). The other is that most of the large society journals that now get page-charge

---

*Comment by J. D. Luntz: Extensive research over many years on the readership of journals clearly indicates that the mere fact that an individual or an institution pays for a subscription to a journal does not automatically mean that the journal is read or used. If the price of a journal reflects more accurately its true value to these who make use of the journal, "nonreader" subscribers to that journal may not renew their subscriptions. Loss of such "marginal" subscribers will not be a loss to society.

support are very efficiently operated when compared to journals of other types, and especially to nonprofit journals that do not have page charges (see Appendix, Section IVB. 1 and Figure 35).

3. Another complaint is that page charges are unfair to authors or other institutions if the latter are impecunious or if government support is lacking. Actually, the overwhelming majority of journals with page charges have not discriminated in any way against the publication of papers that do not pay; editorial decisions and billing are done by organizationally distinct groups and usually at different times. Thus about all that can be claimed is that sometimes the nonpaying institutions suffer embarrassment. In our Recommendations that follow (see Appendix, Section IVB. 4), we suggest that this embarrassment be mitigated by education and, sometimes, by substituting for it a real, though in practice quite small, discrimination in speed of publication.

4. An additional complaint sometimes heard is that journals with page charges confront commercial journals with unfair competition. While it is true that opportunities for commercial journals would be wider if page-charge journals did not exist, it is also true that the lower price at which page-charge journals can be marketed provides possibilities for benefit to society that are not available to subscriber-supported journals.* (see Appendix, Sections IVA. 1, IVB. 1, IVB. 4). That the competition, in practice, is not very crippling is indicated by the growth rates of the numbers and sizes of journals of different types (see Appendix, Section IIIB. 1), by the extreme rarity of financial failures (see Appendix, Sections IIIB. 1 and IVA. 3), and by the sizable profit ratios that commercial journals can achieve when they choose to charge a high price (inferrable from Figures 31 and 35 of the Appendix). We grant, however, that it would be advantageous if a practical way could be found to secure benefits for subscribers to commercial journals by providing the latter with page-charge support (see Appendix, Section IVB. 4).

Two further points have to do with the rules under which page charges are chargeable to government contracts and with the mechanics of payment:

5. The rules laid down in the 1961 statement of the Federal Council[5] stipulate, first, that the page charges "are levied impartially on all papers published by the journal, whether by non-Government or by Government authors," and second, that "payment of such charges is in no sense a condition for acceptance of manuscripts by the journal." In other words, everyone must be asked to pay, but no one required to do so. While the charge that these two stipulations are inconsistent is not quite justified, they do seem a little fuzzy: One is not to "require" payment, but is "levy" to be interpreted as "suggest", "ask", "urge", or "demand" it? Much of the ill feeling mentioned in item 3 arises from the difficulty of choosing the right operating point along this scale.

6. The general cumbersomeness of the system is cause for much criticism. It is very difficult to estimate page-charge requirements in advance, when one is preparing a budget for a research contract, especially since the occurrence and sizes of page charges vary so greatly from journal to journal. We think diversity in the journal population is a good thing but recognize that the budgetary difficulty is a real one, especially for small institutions that rely for their research funds on a very few grants or contracts. (We devote some attention to this problem in our Recommendations.)

---

*Comment by J. D. Luntz: At the same time, there may be a disadvantage to society that results from this. To be extent that there is a reduced "test of the marketplace", the quality of journals may be reduced.

CONSIDERATIONS ADVANCED IN FAVOR OF PAGE CHARGES

These can be briefly summarized as follows:

1. Page charges enable journals to have lower subscription prices, hence wider circulations. These wider circulations, in turn, may possibly result in increased utility, though one must be careful to distinguish the social value of a circulation pattern from its mere size. These facts and their approximate economic importance are discussed at length in the Appendix, Sections IIIA. 2, IIIC. 2, IVA. 1, IVA. 6, and especially IVB. 1; see also Figures 3, 7, and 35. Although we attach considerable importance to this consideration, we do not believe that there would be any danger of journals being unable to raise sufficient revenue from subscriptions to support themselves without page charges. All evidence indicates that for practically all existing journals the total revenue is an increasing function of price up to a level well above the production cost (see Attachment C to the Appendix).

2. Journals whose input costs are largely covered by page charges can adapt much more easily than otherwise to fluctuations in the amount of material submitted to them, in the market for subscriptions, and to some extent even in unit costs (see Appendix, Section IVA. 5). They are much less susceptible to economic damage from photocopying. By being freed from economic dependence on a particular pattern of subscribers to each journal, the community of journals in a given field becomes much more free to experiment with new, and possibly cooperative, user-oriented services (see Recommendations and Appendix, Section IIID.7).

TOTAL COST OF COMMUNICATING SCIENTIFIC AND TECHNICAL INFORMATION

8.1   Introduction

In this section we present estimates of the total cost of communicating scientific and technical information, the relative use of the various journal article transfer channels, the median age of cited articles, and estimates of the cost effectiveness of individual article transfer channels in terms of cost per use.

We have seen that there are six functions involved in the transfer of information from originator to user, and that each function has certain costs associated with it. We have also seen that there are several forms used in the formal transfer of scientific and technical information, chief among them being articles and books.

Table 8.1 shows the 1960-1980 trends in total cost of communication of information, subdivided by books, journals, technical reports and other media. The cost for each was calculated by determining the composition, recording, reproduction, and other costs associated with each. The highest costs are associated with journals which account for 63 and 66 percent of total communication costs in 1960 and 1980 respectively. It is pointed out that the estimated cost of producing scientific and technical journals is based on extrapolating costs of scholarly journals to the number of scientific and technical journals published in the United States that were reported by the British Library Lending Division. Scientific and technical books, on the other hand, account for a range of 28 percent to 23 percent during the 1960-1980 period. The increasing percentage of total costs accounted for by journals is a result not only of increasing numbers of journals and articles, but also the increasing costs associated with producing and distributing them.

Figure 8.1 shows the estimated and projected 1960-1980 trends in costs associated with journals and books, accompanied by constant 1967 dollar values estimated using the GNP deflator and our projection of that deflator. For both current and constant dollar values, the journal costs are increasing much faster than book costs.

Reprinted from KING, D.W., LANCASTER, F.W., McDONALD, D.D., RODERER, N.K., *and* WOOD, B.L. Statistical indicators of scientific and technical communication (1960-1980). Rockville, Md.: King Research, Inc., for National Science Foundation, Division of Science Information, May 1976. Volume II: A Research Report (PB 254 060), p. 350-70, by permission of the publisher.

Table 8.1   ESTIMATED TOTAL COSTS OF COMMUNICATING
SCIENTIFIC AND TECHNICAL INFORMATION,
BY MEDIUM: 1960-1980

(Millions of Dollars)

Year	Books	Journals	Reports	Other Literature	Total
1960	571	1,277	22	141	2,013
1961	631	1,461	26	143	2,264
1962	688	1,616	28	157	2,490
1963	752	1,788	32	165	2,737
1964	817	1,897	34	177	2,925
1965	901	2,105	57	214	3,279
1966	1,004	2,384	105	219	3,712
1967	1,116	2,724	135	235	4,212
1968	1,235	3,042	133	264	4,673
1969	1,376	3,410	175	306	5,267
1970	1,519	3,789	205	334	5,846
1971	1,660	4,145	239	360	6,402
1972	1,777	4,491	305	365	6,939
1973	1,953	5,034	364	400	7,751
1974	2,144	5,559	388	433	8,525
———————————— PROJECTIONS ————————————					
1975	2,352	6,114	471	494	9,431
1976	2,570	6,852	539	543	10,504
1977	2,807	7,572	619	597	11,595
1978	3,039	8,304	693	648	12,684
1979	3,288	9,108	781	707	13,889
1980	3,538	9,943	877	770	15,128
———————————— PERCENT CHANGE ————————————					
1960-65	58	72	159	52	63
1965-70	69	80	260	56	78
1970-75	55	72	130	48	61
1975-80	50	67	86	56	60

SOURCE: Market Facts, Inc., Center for Quantitative Sciences.

THE SCIENTIFIC JOURNAL 31

Figure 8.1   TOTAL STI COMMUNICATION RESOURCE EXPENDITURES BY MEDIUM IN CURRENT DOLLARS: 1960-1980

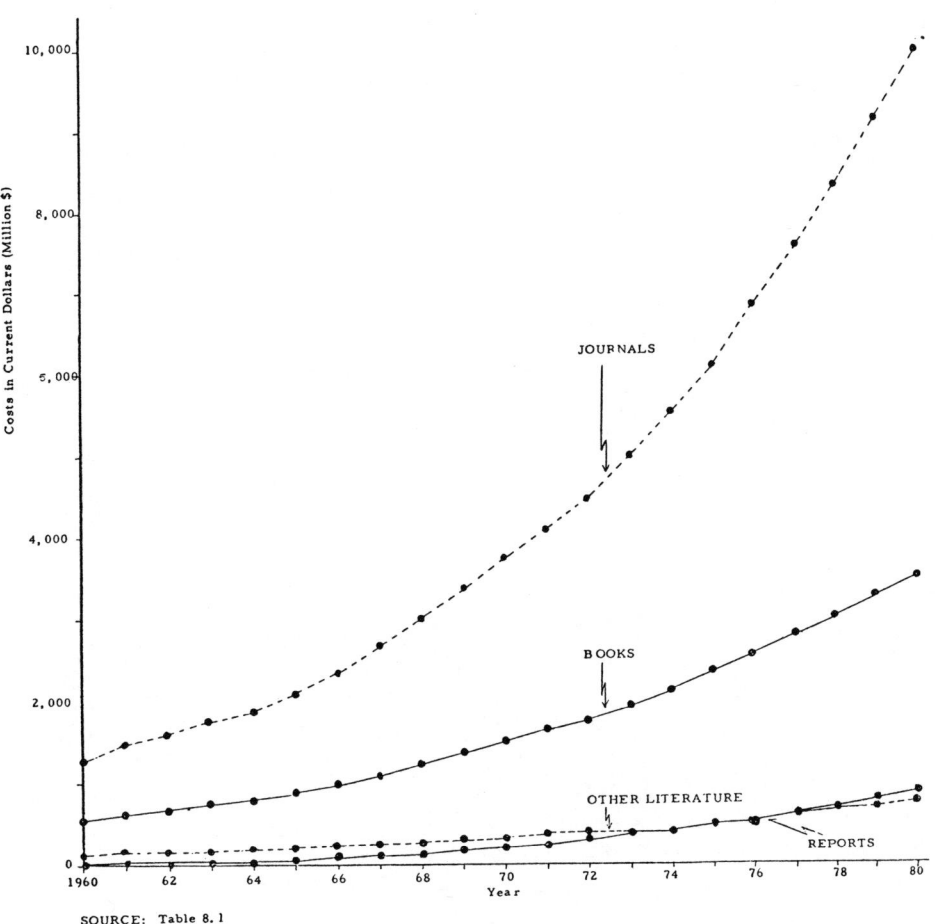

SOURCE: Table 8.1

Table 8.2 and Figure 8.2 show the estimated 1960-1980 total costs of communicating scientific and technical information, subdivided by function. The function accounting for the largest portion of total costs is assimilation, with 49 percent and 42 percent of the total in 1960 and 1980 respectively. Composition and recording ranks second over the latter years of the 1960-1980 period, and accounts for a range of 17 percent in 1960 to 23 percent in 1980. The identification and access function also represents significant costs, somewhat more than 20 percent of the total throughout the period.

These three major functions -- assimilation, composition and recording, and identification and access -- are made up primarily of scientists' labor costs. Significantly, these labor costs are rising faster than the funds expended on research and development. In current dollars, assimilation, composition and recording, and identification and access costs are projected to rise 59, 73 and 65 percent respectively while total R&D funding is expected to rise only 41 percent. These factors point to a need for reducing costs associated with the scientists' preparation and use of the literature.

As a further breakdown, the costs of communicating scientific and technical information can be shown by function for each of the four media types. This is done in Tables 8.3, 8.4, 8.5 and 8.6. Significant differences can be observed between the various media; in particular, overall growth is greatest for the technical report literature, with journals also showing substantial increases in costs based on the volume of activity. Throughout, the functions of composition and recording, identification and access, and assimilation account for the majority of the costs, with publication and distribution also playing an important role, especially for journals.

8.2   Relative Use of Journal Article Transfer Channels

As we mentioned previously, there are a variety of ways in which a user might obtain a journal article (or a copy of an article). Section 6.3 described physical access, which is one of the simplest ways of describing the path an article takes from an author to a user. Consider the following flow model where A = Author, P = Journal Publisher, L = Library, C = Colleague or office collection, and U = User:

Table 8.2 ESTIMATED TOTAL COSTS OF COMMUNICATING SCIENTIFIC AND TECHNICAL INFORMATION, BY FUNCTION: 1960-1980

(Millions of Dollars)

	Composition & Recording	Reproduction & Distribution	Acquisition & Storage	Organization & Control	Identification & Access	Assimilation	Total
1960	337	154	37	58	445	982	2,013
1961	403	183	42	67	513	1,056	2,264
1962	424	245	47	74	555	1,145	2,490
1963	482	267	52	81	607	1,248	2,737
1964	503	295	58	90	648	1,331	2,939
1965	597	320	64	101	718	1,479	3,279
1966	711	356	72	115	792	1,666	3,712
1967	834	416	83	128	883	1,868	4,212
1968	939	474	98	152	983	2,026	4,673
1969	1,065	548	110	172	1,094	2,278	5,267
1970	1,202	616	121	188	1,207	2,512	5,846
1971	1,342	684	140	218	1,311	2,709	6,402
1972	1,464	762	152	239	1,402	2,920	6,939
1973	1,670	851	164	253	1,555	3,258	7,751
1974	1,844	933	176	273	1,715	3,584	8,525
			PROJECTIONS				
1975	2,055	960	195	307	1,917	3,997	9,431
1976	2,384	1,037	205	327	2,123	4,430	10,504
1977	2,660	1,118	219	353	2,352	4,892	11,595
1978	2,941	1,201	232	378	2,590	5,343	12,684
1979	3,245	1,289	243	402	2,863	5,844	13,884
1980	3,555	1,379	256	429	3,165	6,338	15,128
			PERCENT CHANGE				
1960-65	77	108	73	74	61	52	63
1965-70	101	92	89	86	68	68	78
1970-75	71	56	61	63	59	59	61
1975-80	73	44	31	40	65	59	60

SOURCE: Market Facts, Inc., Center for Quantitative Sciences.

Figure 8.2   TOTAL STI COMMUNICATION RESOURCE EXPENDITURES BY MEDIUM IN CONSTANT DOLLARS: 1960-1980

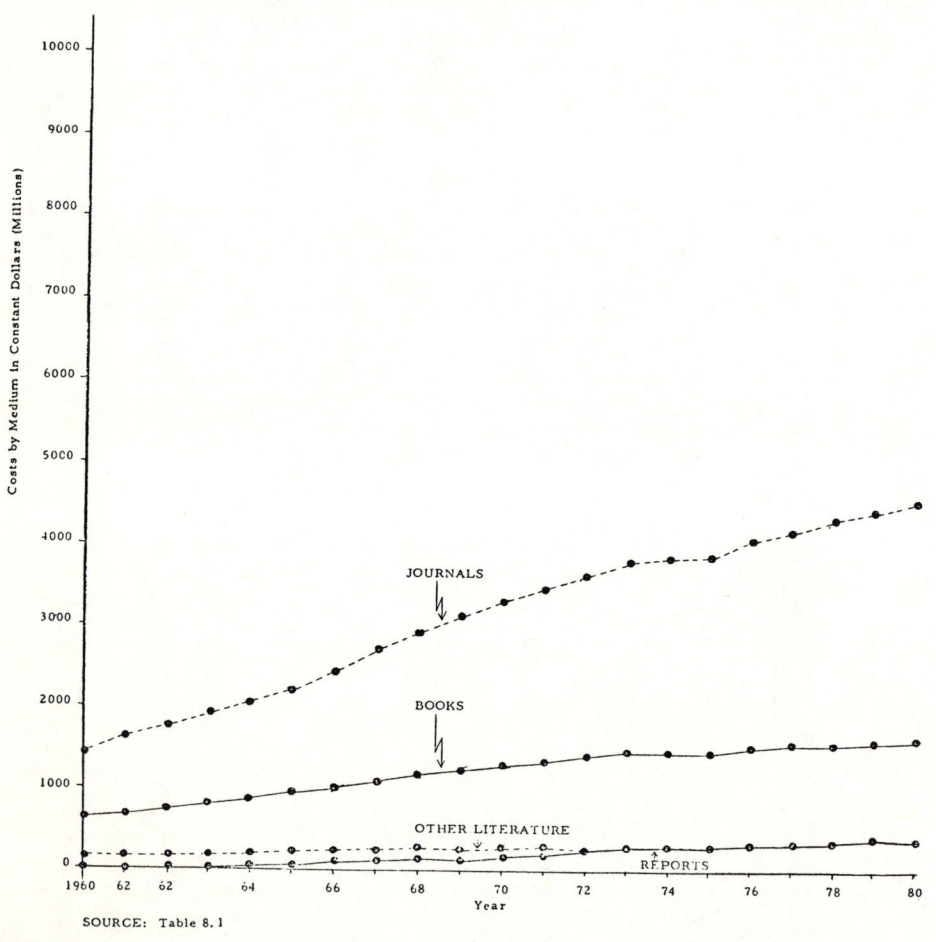

Table 8.3 ESTIMATED COSTS OF COMMUNICATION SCIENTIFIC AND TECHNICAL INFORMATION IN BOOKS, BY FUNCTION: 1960-1980

(Millions of Dollars)

Year	Composition & Recording	Reproduction & Distribution	Acquisition & Storage	Organization & Control	Identification & Access	Assimilation	Total
1960	14	66	23	23	117	328	571
1961	21	70	26	26	136	352	631
1962	26	74	29	29	148	382	688
1963	33	77	32	32	162	416	752
1964	40	86	36	36	175	444	817
1965	43	91	40	40	194	493	901
1966	50	104	45	45	215	545	1,004
1967	49	118	51	51	241	606	1,116
1968	54	128	61	61	268	663	1,235
1969	58	143	68	68	299	740	1,376
1970	74	151	75	75	330	814	1,519
1971	85	166	87	87	360	875	1,660
1972	92	180	94	94	385	932	1,777
1973	102	190	102	102	424	1,033	1,953
1974	117	200	109	109	466	1,143	2,144
PROJECTIONS							
1975	124	206	121	121	516	1,264	2,352
1976	138	216	127	127	564	1,398	2,570
1977	152	226	136	136	617	1,540	2,807
1978	166	237	144	144	669	1,679	3,039
1979	182	247	151	151	724	1,833	3,288
1980	199	257	159	159	779	1,985	3,538
PERCENT CHANGE							
1960-65	207	38	74	74	66	50	58
1965-70	72	66	88	88	70	65	69
1970-75	66	36	61	61	56	55	55
1975-80	60	25	31	31	51	57	50
1970-75	66	36	61	61	56	55	55
1975-80	60	25	31	31	51	57	50

SOURCE: Market Facts, Inc., Center for Quantitative Sciences.

Table 8.4 ESTIMATED COSTS OF COMMUNICATING SCIENTIFIC AND TECHNICAL
INFORMATION IN JOURNALS, BY FUNCTION: 1960-1980

(Millions of Dollars)

Year	Composition & Recording	Reproduction & Distribution	Acquisition & Storage	Organization & Control	Identification & Access	Assimilation	Total
1960	204	88	13	29	289	654	1,277
1961	263	113	15	34	332	704	1,461
1962	269	172	17	37	358	763	1,616
1963	316	189	19	40	392	832	1,788
1964	319	208	21	45	417	887	1,897
1965	357	227	23	51	461	986	2,105
1966	452	250	26	58	508	1,090	2,384
1967	559	294	30	64	565	1,212	2,724
1968	636	342	35	76	628	1,325	3,042
1969	707	400	40	86	697	1,480	3,410
1970	794	460	44	94	769	1,628	3,789
1971	890	512	50	109	834	1,750	4,145
1972	989	574	55	120	890	1,863	4,491
1973	1,143	651	59	126	989	2,066	5,034
1974	1,264	720	63	136	1,091	2,285	5,559
—————— PROJECTIONS ——————							
1975	1,400	741	70	154	1,221	2,528	6,114
1976	1,655	805	74	166	1,356	2,796	6,852
1977	1,855	873	79	179	1,507	3,079	7,572
1978	2,061	944	84	194	1,663	3,358	8,304
1979	2,285	1,019	87	206	1,845	3,666	9,108
1980	2,512	1,097	92	222	2,050	3,970	9,943
—————— PERCENT CHANGE ——————							
1960-65	75	158	77	76	60	51	72
1967-70	122	84	91	84	67	65	80
1970-75	76	61	59	64	59	55	61
1975-80	79	48	31	44	68	57	63

SOURCE: Market Facts, Inc., Center for Quantitative Sciences.

Table 8.5   ESTIMATED COST OF COMMUNICATION SCIENTIFIC AND TECHNICAL INFORMATION IN TECHNICAL REPORTS, BY FUNCTION: 1960-1980

(millions of Dollars)

Year	Composition & Recording	Reproduction & Distribution	Acquisition & Storage	Organization & Control	Identification & Access	Assimilation	Total
1960	–	–	–	3	19	–	22
1961	–	–	–	4	22	–	26
1962	–	–	–	4	24	–	28
1963	–	1	–	4	27	–	32
1964	–	1	–	5	28	–	34
1965	19	2	–	5	31	–	57
1966	31	2	–	6	35	31	105
1967	36	4	–	6	39	50	135
1968	38	4	1	8	44	38	133
1969	53	5	1	9	49	58	175
1970	65	5	1	10	54	70	205
1971	78	6	1	11	59	84	239
1972	95	8	2	12	63	125	305
1973	107	12	2	13	71	159	364
1974	125	12	2	14	79	156	388
PROJECTIONS							
1975	145	13	2	16	90	205	471
1976	168	16	2	17	101	235	539
1977	192	19	2	19	114	273	619
1978	216	20	2	20	129	306	693
1979	243	22	2	22	147	345	781
1980	271	25	3	25	169	384	877
PERCENT CHANGE							
1960-65	–	–	–	67	63	–	159
1965-70	242	100	–	100	74	–	260
1970-75	123	160	100	60	67	193	130
1975-80	87	92	50	56	88	87	86

SOURCE: Market Facts, Inc., Center for Quantitative Sciences.

Table 8.6 ESTIMATED COST OF COMMUNICATING SCIENTIFIC AND TECHNICAL INFORMATION IN OTHER LITERATURE, BY FUNCTION: 1960–1980

(Millions of Dollars)

Year	Composition & Recording	Acquisition & Storage	Organization & Control	Identification & Access	Total
1960	119	-	3	19	141
1961	118	-	3	22	143
1962	129	-	4	24	157
1963	134	-	4	27	165
1964	144	-	5	28	177
1965	178	-	5	31	214
1966	178	-	6	35	219
1967	190	-	6	39	235
1968	211	1	8	44	264
1969	247	1	9	49	306
1970	269	1	10	54	334
1971	289	1	11	59	360
1972	288	2	12	63	365
1973	318	2	13	67	400
1974	338	2	14	79	433
PROJECTIONS					
1975	386	2	16	90	494
1976	423	2	17	101	543
1977	462	2	19	114	597
1978	497	2	20	129	648
1979	536	2	22	147	707
1980	573	3	25	169	770
PERCENT CHANGE					
1960–65	50	-	67	63	52
1965–70	51	-	100	74	56
1970–75	43	100	60	67	48
1975–80	48	50	56	88	56

SOURCE: Market Facts, Inc., Center for Quantitative Sciences.

THE SCIENTIFIC JOURNAL

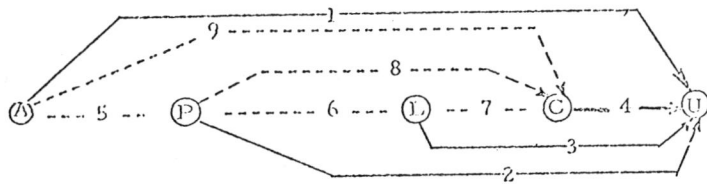

Figure 8.3   JOURNAL FLOW MODEL

In actuality, each of the channels one through nine represents a group of alternative paths leading up to use and assimilation of information contained in the journal literature. Table 8.7 describes and lists participants in these physical access channels. Each potential channels described varies according to frequency of use. This was verified by the Author Survey, which focused on the direct channels one through four.

It is possible to further subdivide the channels by method of identification. In other words, once a potential user identifies an article, there are then a variety of channels available for obtaining a copy of that article. It is reasonable to suppose, also, that there exists a relationship between how a user obtains an article and how the user identified the article. Theoretically, it should be possible to develop rough estimates of the costs associated with these various channels.

Consider the following methods of identification by which a user finds out about an article:

Table 8.8   METHODS OF IDENTIFICATION OF JOURNAL LITERATURE

1.	Discovered while reading own subscription
2.	Discovered while reading library subscription
3.	Discovered while reading colleague's or office subscription
4.	Received preprint from author
5.	Obtained preprint from colleague
6.	Received reprint from author
7.	Received reprint from colleague or co-worker
8.	Referred to article by colleague or co-worker
9.	Referred to in another article, book or report
10.	Found in search of printed indexes
11.	Found in output of computerized literature search
12.	Found in current awareness or SDI list

Table 8.7 PHYSICAL ACCESS CHANNELS FOR JOURNAL LITERATURE

Path	Participants		Alternative Descriptions
1	Author and User	(a)	User obtains reprint from author
		(b)	User obtains preprint from author
2	Publisher and User	(a)	User subscribes to journal
		(b)	User obtains reprint from publisher
3	Library and User	(a)	User reads library subscription issue
		(b)	User reads library microform edition
4	Colleague and User	(a)	User obtains reprint from colleague or office collection
		(b)	User obtains preprint from colleague or office collection
		(c)	User reads colleague or office subscription issue
5	Author and Publisher		Publisher accepts manuscript for publication
6	Publisher and Library	(a)	Library subscribes to journal
		(b)	Library purchases microform from publisher
7	Library and Colleague	(a)	Colleague obtains library subscription issue
		(b)	Colleague obtains library microform edition
8	Publisher and Colleague	(a)	Colleague or office subscribes to journal
		(b)	Colleague obtains reprint from publisher
9	Author and Colleague	(a)	Colleague obtains reprint from author
		(b)	Preprint from author

Potentially, each of these identification techniques might be combined with each of the direct paths previously described, to result in 108 potential direct channels to the user. In actuality, some of these channels might be immediately rejected as infeasible, since, for example, identification methods one through seven may occur simultaneously with physical access. Note that 108 refers to the number of direct channels to the user; information flow to the colleague may also be described in the same manner. This results in a more complicated model, however, which is not described here.

With data from our Author Survey, we estimated: (1) which channels are actually employed by users in obtaining identification and access to the articles which they cite, and (2) the frequency with which these channels are used. Note that the description is limited to channels where articles are actually used; that is, in which the final node, the user, is reached. Use is restricted to citation use. Also, data is combined across different years with the assumption made that major shifts from channel to channel are not occurring.

Table 8.9 gives the frequency (in percent) for those channels which were identified by respondents to the Author Survey. Rows one through fourteen describe the methods of identification, and columns one through fourteen describe methods of physical access.

In Table 8.10 the most frequently employed individual channels are ranked. These channels account for 64 percent of article accesses. In other words, for articles which authors cite of which they are not co-authors, 64 percent are obtained via one of these seven top-ranked channels. Forty and eight tenths percent of these identified articles are obtained through a library's own copy of a journal. Also, this table again emphasizes the importance of individual subscriptions to scientists for identification of and access to articles which they cite, with this channel as the second most frequently used.

It is clear that the channels have widely different levels of cost associated with them. Another way of comparing the various channels is mean channel length, as shown on the right side of Table 8.10. Mean channel length was calculated by subtracting year of cited article from year of citing article and computing an average. Not surprisingly, channels which involve the library

Table 8.9
RELATIVE FREQUENCY OF IDENTIFICATION AND ACCESS CHANNELS

	1. User's Own Issue	2. Library Issue	3. Library Microform	4. Colleague/Office Microform	5. Colleague/Office Copy	6. Publisher Reprint	7. Author Reprint	8. Reprint from Colleague	9. Preprint from Author	10. Preprint from Colleague	11. Colleague's Photocopy	12. No Access	13. Don't Remember	14. Other Sources, as Book	15. Total percent
1. Discovered reading own copy	15.0	-	-	-	-	-	-	-	-	-	-	-	-	1.0	16.0
2. Discovered reading library copy	-	6.8	~	-	~	-	0.7	-	1.0	-	-	-	-	-	8.5
3. Discovered reading colleague's or office copy	-	-	1.0	-	-	-	-	-	-	-	-	-	-	-	1.0
4. Received preprint from author	0.1	-	-	-	0.1	0.5	-	-	5.1	0.1	-	-	-	-	5.9
5. Obtained preprint from colleague	~	-	-	-	-	-	-	0.3	1.0	-	-	-	-	-	1.6
6. Received reprint from author	-	-	-	-	0.6	-	-	-	-	-	~	-	-	-	0.6
7. Received reprint from colleague	-	0.4	-	-	-	1.2	4.0	-	-	-	-	-	-	-	5.6
8. Referred by colleague	1.9	7.7	0.4	-	0.5	-	2.1	1.2	0.2	0.2	0.7	?	0.1	-	15.2
9. Referred by other article, book, report	1.2	22.5	1.2	?	0.8	-	1.7	-	0.2	0.9	0.9	1.0	0.4	0.1	30.5
10. Found in search of printed indexes	0.2	8.1	0.5	-	-	-	1.3	-	-	0.1	-	-	-	-	10.4
11. Computerized literature search	0.6	0.3	-	-	-	-	-	-	-	-	-	-	-	-	0.9
12. Current awareness or SDI list	-	0.3	-	-	?	-	0.2	-	•	-	-	-	0.1	-	0.6
13. Don't remember	0.3	1.3	-	-	-	-	0.1	-	0.2	-	?	0.1	-	0.6	2.5
14. Other or No Response	0.6	0.1	-	-	-	-	-	-	-	-	-	-	-	-	0.7
15. Total percent	20.1	47.6	2.0	2.5	?	0.6	9.3	5.5	5.8	1.3	2.7	1.1	1.1	0.2	100.0

SOURCE: Market Facts, Center for Quantitative Sciences, Author Survey.
Key: - = No response received in this category
~ = Less than 0.1 percent of total

Table 8.10 MOST FREQUENTLY EMPLOYED CHANNELS FOR IDENTIFICATION AND ACCESS

Rank	Frequency (%)	Identification	Source of Access	Form of Access	Mean Path Length (Years)
1.	20.0	Referred to in other article, book or report	Library	Library copy of journal	15.0
2.	13.8	Discovered while reading own copy of journal in which article appeared	Publisher	User's own copy of the journal	4.6
3.	7.5	Found in a search of printed indexes or catalogs during the course of a literature search	Library	Library copy of journal	16.8
4.	7.1	Referred to article by a colleague or co-worker	Library	Library copy of journal	12.6
5.	6.2	Discovered while reading library copy	Library	Library copy of journal	12.5
6.	4.9	Received a preprint from author	Author	Preprint	4.1
7.	4.5	Received reprint from colleague or co-worker	Colleague	Reprint	8.0
	64.0				

SOURCE: Author Survey, Market Facts, Inc., Center for Quantitative Sciences.

have the longest mean channel length, while those involving the user's own subscription or reprints or preprints have the shortest.

8.3 Median Age of Scholarly Journal Articles Used

In the Journal Tracking Survey the published data of the original article and a cited article were both noted. From this we observed the age of cited articles up to twenty years. The data were also broken out by the source used to obtain the article including individual (i.e., user or colleague subscription), library, and other (i.e., reprints, preprints and so on). The data are presented in Table 8.11 by the cumulative proportion of article citations by age of cited articles. The median age for the journal citations is often referred to as the "half-life" of the literature since one-half of the citation uses occur before and one-half after that time. The half-life is as follows: for all articles, about 10.5 years; articles obtained through individual subscriptions, 3.7 years; articles accessed through libraries, about 11.8 years; and articles found by other means such as reprints, about 7.2 years. (Note that these median values are slightly lower than the mean path length values displayed in Table 8.10, evidence of a skewed distribution). The results are as one might expect. The age of copies obtained through one's own subscription (or that of a colleague) is about one-half of the age of copies obtained through libraries. Obviously, older articles are less likely to be held by an individual because the individual is too young to have subscribed to an old issue of a journal, or because files are just not maintained for long periods by most individuals.

By comparison, Houghton (61) refers to the half-life observed for references made in articles published in leading journals in several fields during the years 1953 to 1954. These figures are displayed in Table 8.12

8.4 Cost Effectiveness of Journal Channels

We have attempted to gain some insight into the cost-effectiveness of the journal channels mentioned above. As shown, we have been able to identify in some detail the activities which are performed in the use of each channel, as well as the corresponding volume of each activity. Combining this with associated costs, we have derived a figure of cost per use for each of the major channels. This figure is a reflection, then, of the total costs which go into

Table 8.11 CUMULATIVE PROPORTION OF ARTICLE CITATIONS BY AGE OF ARTICLES FROM ISI AND JOURNAL TRACKING SURVEY

Age in Years	Total ISI[1]	Journal Tracking Survey[2]			
		Total	Individual	Library	Other
1	0.11	0.114	0.175	0.025	0.052
2	0.23	0.171	0.301	0.054	0.118
3	0.33	0.221	0.425	0.097	0.175
4	0.41	0.265	0.521	0.149	0.262
5	0.48	0.305	0.610	0.202	0.324
6	0.55	0.342	0.671	0.247	0.409
7	0.60	0.379	0.726	0.292	0.482
8	0.65	0.414	0.771	0.332	0.556
9	0.69	0.449	0.820	0.383	0.591
10	0.72	0.484	0.846	0.431	0.610
11	0.75	0.519	0.880	0.483	0.638
12	0.78	0.552	0.904	0.523	0.667
13	0.80	0.585	0.935	0.562	0.688
14	-	0.616	0.969	0.591	0.709
15	-	0.644	0.969	0.622	0.742
16	-	0.669	0.973	0.649	0.768
17	-	0.689	0.976	0.687	0.790
18	-	0.709	0.976	0.718	0.804
19	-	0.730	0.979	0.760	0.816
20	-	0.750	0.979	0.800	0.820

SOURCE:
[1] Institute for Scientific Information, Philadelphia, Pennsylvania.
[2] Journal Tracking Survey, Market Facts, Inc., Center for Quantitative Sciences.

Table 8.12 SELECTED HALF-LIFE VALUES OF THE JOURNAL
LITERATURE FOR INDIVIDUAL DISCIPLINES

(Years)

Field	Half-Life
Chemical Engineering	4.8
Mechanical Engineering	5.2
Metallurgical Engineering	3.9
Mathematics	10.5
Physics	4.6
Chemistry	8.1
Geology	11.8
Physiology	7.2
Botany	10.0

SOURCE: Houghton, Bernard, *Scientific Periodicals, Their Historical Development, Characteristics, and Control*, 1975.

the maintenance of a particular channel and the related volume of information use which occurs.

Gross estimates of figures for the cost per use are as follows:

Individual subscription	$6.80
Individual subscription (via colleague)	$9.00
Library subscription	$6.50
Reprint	$3.10
Reprint (via colleague)	$5.00

The average cost overall is about $5.95 per use.

The difference in costs are remarkably small in view of the total cost components which are included in each channel. Individual subscription costs are, of course, primarily direct and limited, whereas much more substantial figures go into the maintenance of a library journal system. This is balanced, in the cost per use figures, by the considerable use made of libraries.

The estimates above are based on cost estimates related to five channels and six sub-functions associated with these functions. These estimates are as follows:

Table 8.13 COST ESTIMATES OF COMMUNICATION BY FIVE CHANNELS AND SIX SUB-FUNCTIONS: 1974

	Channels				
Sub-Function	Individual Subscription	Colleague Subscription	Library Subscription	Reprints to Individual	Reprints to Colleague
Reproduction and Distribution	$5.56	$5.56	$2.48	$0.92	$0.92
Acquisition	1.27	1.27	0.31	0	0.09
Storage	1.27	1.27	0.33	0.09	0.09
Maintenance	0	0	2.26	0	0
Circulation	0	0	0.32	0	0
Accession	0	1.90	0.76	2.12	4.02
Total	$6.83	$9.00	$6.46	$3.13	$5.03

SOURCE: Market Facts, Inc., Center for Quantitative Sciences.

The procedure used to arrive at these average costs as described in Table 8.13 are described below.

From previous data, it has been shown that the number of scholarly journal articles published in 1974 was estimated to be 150,572 (Table 3.41). We assume that there are 690 readings per article (4) and that 24.8 percent (Table 8.9) of these go through the individual subscription channels (including colleague subscriptions). Thus, there are an estimated 25.8 million uses by this means. The total cost of individual subscriptions includes an estimated 7,144,000 subscriptions to individuals (Table 3.25) at a price of $20.08 (Table 3.26) which yields about $143.5 million estimated total cost. Thus, the estimated average cost to individual subscribers of reproduction and distribution is $5.56.

The cost of library subscriptions is computed in a similar manner. Here, about 4.57 million total library subscriptions for scholarly journals (Table 3.21) are estimated at $29.57 each (Table 3.21) for a total cost of about $135 million. About 52.4 percent (Table 8.9) of 690 readings of the 150,572 estimated articles occur in libraries. Thus, total usage in libraries is estimated to be 54.4 million and average cost of reproduction and distribution is $2.48. Reproduction and distribution cost for reprints is estimated from the cost model to be $0.036/page (Table 3.44). Since the average number of pages published per article is estimated to be 7.6, the total cost per reprint is $.274 plus $.13 for mailing to authors. This cost is divided by .51, since that is the proportion estimated to be sent to authors and not requested (Tables 3.28, 3.29). To the result ($.79), $.13 is added for mailing the request which yields a total cost of $.92 per use for reprint reproduction and distribution.

Acquisition, storage and maintenance costs in libraries are found by dividing $16.7 million (Table 4.11), $17.8 million (Table 4.13) and $123 million (Table 4.12) by 54.4 million library uses. The storage costs for individual subscriptions are found by assuming office rental at 12 journals per square foot at $5.50 or $0.46 per journal title. It is further assumed that the average life of a journal is ten years (slightly less than the average age of a citation) which yields an average total cost of about $4.60 per journal. This number is multiplied by 7.144 million individual subscriptions and divided by 25.9 million uses to yield $1.27 per use. The estimated cost of storing reprints incurred by users is 1/77th of the $1.27 since there are 77 articles per journal. Authors incur about twice this cost since they order two reprints for each one requested. The average between the two comes to about $0.09 per use. The average circulation cost in libraries is $0.32 (153).

Accession costs are based on the cost of photocopying. The photocopying cost for individuals is $0.25 times the number of pages per article (7.6). For colleague's subscriptions we assume that all copies are photocopies, thus the average cost is $.55. Reprints require typing and mailing of requests, look-up at the office of the author and so on that is estimated to take about one-half hour of secretarial time. This makes the cost 0.5 times $3.98 (Table 3.46) plus $.13 postage, plus $1.90 for photocopy if the copy comes from a colleague's reprint.

It should be emphasized that these costs reflect current patterns of provision and use of journals associated only with the citation of articles. Thus, we have assumed that the distribution of all article uses is similar to that of uses for citation. Further, in the total system each individual channel plays an important, and perhaps a unique, role. Any changes, for example, elimination of or even decreased volume through a given channel, would affect the total system. Thus, the total implications of any modification must be considered before action is taken; and conclusions drawn from the above data must be made with great caution.

Economic Interaction Between Special Libraries and Publishers of Scholarly and Research Journals
Results of an NSF Study

Herbert S. White and Bernard M. Fry

Indiana University Graduate Library School, Bloomington, Ind. 47401

■ Under NSF auspices, a study was made of the economic interaction between the publishers of 2,459 American research journals and the libraries which attempt, out of constricting budgets, to purchase them. This paper focuses on information gathered in 1969-73 about the growth and pricing trends of research journals, particularly as these are purchased by special libraries. It examines budget growth and allocation in special libraries, fiscal imbalances created, and what special libraries have done about these problems. Finally, it projects future concerns and difficulties, and touches on some alternatives.

A STUDY undertaken by the Research Center of the Indiana University Graduate Library School and funded by the National Science Foundation* sought to examine the relationship between U.S. publishers of scholarly and research journals (the for-profit sector, professional societies, university presses, not-for-profit organizations, and even individuals), and the libraries (academic, public, and special) which make up the greatest market for these publications. The need for this study was based on mounting evidence that the total economic system governing journal distribution is in difficulty. Publishers' need for revenues to support these publications is simply not sustained by the funding ability of the customer population, largely represented by libraries.

———
*NSF Grant GN-41398

The study also sought to address some assumptions which have been made by publishers and librarians about each other. In large part these assumptions turn out to be misconceptions, because of a lack of information and a lack of communication and trust between the publisher and library groups. Simply stated, the biggest concern on the part of librarians is that price increases are exorbitant, and that librarians are being made victims of publisher attempts to make unreasonable profits. Publishers, on the other hand, are concerned about the impact of networks, of expanded interlibrary loan, and of photocopying on their sales, their revenues, and their economic survival.

It was thus essential that the survey be conducted in a manner which would gain the support, understanding, participation, and trust of both the publishing and library communities. Advisory committees

Reprinted from *Special Libraries*, vol. 68, no. 3, March 1977, p. 109-14. © by Special Libraries Association.

and reactor panels including key representatives of all segments of both communities as well as the federal government, were formed, their input needed in the development of both the survey document and the analysis of results.

The survey produced a great deal of valuable information, and broke new ground in exploring the little-understood precarious economic balance which exists. It is not the intent of this paper to summarize a 401 page report containing 112 pages of tabular data. The report is available in its entirety through the National Technical Information Service *(1)*. An edited and condensed book version entitled *Publishers and Libraries: A Study of Scholarly and Research Journals,* will be published by Lexington Books in late 1976.

Methodology

It is the purpose of this presentation to extract data and conclusions specifically impacting special libraries. Nevertheless, some preliminary comments concerning the methodology, inclusiveness, and gaps are appropriate. The report surveyed both publisher and library communities for the years 1969 through 1973 and is, therefore, already in need of updating, particularly in view of the strategic changes and budgetary shifts which have occurred since 1973. Such an effort has been proposed. Further, in dealing with economic data from U.S. publishers who sell to foreign libraries and to individuals as well as to U.S. libraries, and from U.S. libraries which also purchase foreign publications and which frequently deal through the intermediary services of subscriptions agents, gaps and inconsistencies naturally develop.

Despite all of these limitations, massive and important information and conclusions emerged. The survey population of scholarly and research journals was based on 2,459 specifically identified U.S. published journals, and excluding such publications as newsletters, house organs, general, popular, free, and government publications, controlled circulation periodicals, and in general those not covered by abstracting and indexing services. The library community of academic, public, and special libraries was further subdivided by size. Special libraries, which included company, government, and not-for-profit libraries, as well as law and medical libraries where budgetary responsibility for these was separate from the academic library of the university system, were considered large if their serials budgets exceeded $50,000/year, otherwise small. It was recognized that this delineation made for a great many small and relatively few large special libraries, but a large point of cut-off was necessary to provide a basis for relating to academic library data. Library responses were not broken down by subject disciplines, although journal data from publishers was.

Survey Results

First, two general reactions are in order. There is no evidence to indicate that publishers of scholarly and research journals are utilizing price strategies designed to make unfair and unreasonable surpluses or profits. While commercial publishers do report an operating profit of close to 14%, such an operating profit, after provision for capital expenditures, debt service, extraordinary expenses, and taxes, leaves a net profit of perhaps something under 6%, a return on investment certainly not considered unreasonable, and not even treated as attractive by financial analysts. Society publishers just about break even operationally, while university presses and the small miscellaneous group of publishers show consistent and growing deficits, and are usually either subsidized by parent institutions or temporarily manage to hide their deficits because of positive cash flow. In fact, there is clear evidence that certain whole disciplines, such as the humanities, present an unviable economic posture, and that the publication of scholarly and research journals in the humanities simply could not be supported from the sales market for these journals without some form of subsidy.

Secondly, there is no evidence in this survey that interlibrary loan and photocopying adversely impact the totality of the scholarly journal/library relationship. This is not intended to suggest that individual publishers and individual journals are not adversely affected by interlibrary loan relationships in which some libraries borrow the same title repeatedly, without making any attempt to purchase it. Newly enacted copyright legislation places limits on this activity. However, even prior to this action it was doubtful that the scholarly publishing community as a whole (and as differentiated from specific individual publishers) was adversely affected by the interlibrary loan process. Funds being expended for scholarly and research journals already so stretch the library budget available for this purpose, and already so force budgetary shifts and cancellations, that the imposition of a further charge to this same budget would simply force further shifts and further entrenchments, without increasing the total dollars furnished to publishers.

Some specific publishers would undoubtedly benefit, but only at the expense of other publishers, and not because of some new, hitherto untapped source of funds for periodicals purchase. Many publishers have come to realize that these increased payments, if royalty or copying charges are to be imposed, must come from the budgets of the users of the services, and not the library budget itself. This is of small consolation to the managers of industrial special libraries, unless they decide to allocate these copying costs and royalty charges to the using departments within the organization, and there are clearly dangers in this practice as well.

Budgetary Considerations

During the years 1969–73 large special libraries increased their total budgets by an average of 13% per year, an increase rate even slightly larger than the rate at which salary costs increased at 12%. The survey did not attempt to determine the extent to which salary dollar increases were a factor of raises for constant staff, or affected by staff increases or reductions. Salary surveys, including SLA's own, can be used for the professional part of such a correlation, and the Department of Labor statistics can be employed for clerical comparisons. In any case, in increasing their total budgets at a greater rate than their salary budgets, large special libraries were unique. This in turn permitted a greater percentage growth of 14.5% in their materials budgets. Smaller special libraries, whose overall budgets increased by an average annual 10%, were nevertheless still able to cope with average salary budget increases of 8.5%, and therefore able to increase materials budgets by 12.25%.

By contrast, large academic libraries increased their budgets by 8% but their salary budgets by 10%, and were therefore forced to shift materials increase dollars to cover salaries, permitting only a 5% increase in materials expenditures. Public library overall budgets increased by about 10% or 11% per year, a figure greater than had been assumed, and this just about kept pace with the percentage increases in salary budgets. Consequently, non-salary budgets grew at the same rate in public libraries.

Special libraries, particularly large special libraries, were thus better equipped than their academic and public brethren to cope with increases in materials costs.

Spending for Periodicals

Since this survey was concerned with the relationship between scholarly and research journals and the library community, it was necessary to break library materials budgets into their component parts. While differentiation between books and serials was possible, the responding libraries were not able to distinguish in their budgets between periodicals and other serials. Dealing then, with books and serials, some startling changes appear. While at the start of the survey period in 1969 academic libraries were spending twice as much on books as on serials, they

were then forced to transfer funds from the books to the serials budget to maintain their serial collections. By 1973 the ratio had dropped from 2:1 to 1.16:1, and it is probable that by 1974 or at latest 1975 the curves had crossed, and that academic libraries are now spending more for serials than books. The transfer rate must stop at some point, or book purchase by academic libraries will simply dwindle away. Public libraries, which spend less than 2% of their total budgets on serials, and even less on research journals, are not heavily enough involved to be affected substantially by what happens to scholarly and research journals.

Special libraries, particularly large special libraries, which already spend far more on serials than on books, were able to avoid fund transfers from the book to the serials budget. During the same period special libraries reported annual price increases for renewed periodical titles of 12.4%, somewhat larger than academic libraries' 11.3% and public libraries' 8.2%. It is suspected that the greater price increase rate in academic over public, and in special over academic libraries, is caused by the increasing importance in these libraries of foreign titles. The price of foreign periodicals was affected both by double digit inflation throughout most of the rest of the world, and by the weakening of the dollar on international monetary exchanges. A specific study of price changes for non-US titles has been proposed to the National Science Foundation.

In a constant environment of publication, at least special libraries would have had enough dollars in 1969–73 to retain existing titles, something certainly not true for academic libraries. However, all libraries must make room for the addition of some new titles, even in the face of decreasing budgets, and this requires cancellation of some existing subscriptions. Here, again, differing patterns emerge.

Subscription Cancellation Policies

Academic libraries, until beset by budgetary pressures, hardly ever cancelled a subscription once placed, and still try their best to avoid it. The cancellation rate in 1969 was a trivial 0.2%, and even by 1973 it had climbed only to 0.7%. Academic libraries showed a clear preference for reducing new titles to the cancellation of existing subscriptions, and were adding only half as many titles in 1973 as in 1969. When they did cancel, reluctantly, preference was given to duplicate subscriptions, with an attempt to hang on to at least one copy of each title, in spite of the implication of Bradford's Law (2). It would appear that collection building is still a high if not the highest priority for academic libraries, and perhaps takes precedence, as Gore has suggested (3), over service responsiveness.

By contrast, special libraries, which even during happier budget days cancelled subscriptions at more than three times the academic rate (presumably because of continuing evaluation), increased this cancellation rate to 2%, in order to protect a steady 5% rate of new title acquisition, a rate which did not change substantially during the period. Clearly, special librarians are not as concerned about maintaining the continuity of the collection as academic librarians. In their cancellation patterns, special librarians were also drawn toward the elimination of duplicates, but to nowhere near the same extent. In addition, there was a heavy toll of foreign language publications. Twenty-six percent of large special libraries also reported dropping sole copies of subscriptions, including domestic titles.

While the price of the subscription is a factor in the determination of which subscription to retain and which to cancel, it cannot be considered a predominant factor. Rather, an evaluation of the entire collection seems to occur, and it is therefore possible that a periodical which did not increase its price can be dropped to make room for the price increase of an important title. Nevertheless, price appears a more important factor in special than in academic libraries. While the average price of cancelled academic subscriptions was only 13.6% greater than that of retained ones, for large special libraries the percentage was 47.3%, for small special libraries 78.9%, so that cancelled titles were almost twice as expensive as retained ones.

Borrowing and Lending Periodicals

As stated earlier, there was no evidence that increases in interlibrary loan have impacted the totality of dollars spent for research journals, at least by U.S. libraries. Nevertheless, special libraries report substantial growth in interlibrary loan activity. During the period 1969–73 borrowing by large special libraries increased by 20%, and to an even greater percentage by small special libraries. Practically all of this borrowing, as in academic libraries, is for periodicals. There is virtually no interlibrary loan activity for books among responding special libraries. By contrast, public libraries borrow and lend almost exclusively books, and have very little traffic in periodicals.

Even more startling than the growth in borrowing by special libraries is the growth of the rate at which they lend. Large special libraries report a doubling in their loans during the period 1969–73, at the same time that their borrowing increased 20%. Special libraries have long been accused of taking advantage of one-way relationships in their dealings with academic and public libraries by borrowing in large quantities, while refusing or being unable to lend. While there is no evidence that special libraries have substantially increased their lending to other types of libraries, they do appear to be lending more to one another. Special libraries may, to an increasing extent, be turning to other special libraries rather than to the major academic library collections in their geographic areas or their subject fields.

While several interpretations as to why this has happened are possible, the investigators surmise that there is more of an effort to operate within the special library community itself, perhaps in part because of improved communications, networks, and union lists. It may also be in part because many academic libraries are substantially increasing the loan transaction fee charged to commercial special libraries.

Summary and Conclusions

In summary, the survey shows, quite disturbingly, an unhealthy economic model, and one which has undoubtedly worsened since 1973. Neither librarians nor publishers demonstrate any real ability to cope with the funding imbalance through innovative or cooperative techniques. Publishers, to a greater and greater extent, pass their own cost increases along to customers in the form of price increases, and since this practice causes cancellations among individual subscribers to an even greater degree than libraries, the pressure on libraries is increased. Libraries also have come up with little in the way of innovative solutions. There is some elimination of binding and substitution of microform, but not enough to make a financial impact.

The greatest area of potential cost reduction is in cooperative technical processing, but even here, at least through 1973, verbal commitment has exceeded dollar impact. A fair amount of cost reduction is claimed in the area of automation, but, interestingly enough, about half the respondents report cost reductions through automation, while the others claim cost reduction through the elimination of automation.

It is apparent, particularly in view of what has continued to happen after 1973, that the economic model is not viable and that, unless we are willing to endure a laissez-faire environment in which entire subject area publications could disappear, the system requires subsidy by the federal government. The extent of that subsidy, steps for minimizing it, and the areas of most meaningful application (author, publisher, library, user) still require further study.

Literature Cited

1. Fry, Bernard M. and Herbert S. White / *Economics and Interaction of the Publisher-Library Relationship in the Production and Use of Scholarly and Research Journals.* Bloomington, In, Indiana University Graduate Library School, November 1975. (Available NTIS. PB 249108.) hard copy $11.00, microfiche $2.25.
2. Goffman, W. / Bradford's Law Applied to the Maintenance of Library Collections. In Saracevic, T. / *Introduction to Information Science.* New York, Bowker, 1970.
3. Gore, D. / The View from the Tower of Babel. *Library Journal* 100:1601–1604 (Sept 15, 1975).

Subscription Fulfillment

HARRY FLORENTINE

Abstract—While what constitutes fulfillment varies considerably from one publisher to another, and even from one journal to another, the key word is always service. Subscription fulfillment is defined as the processing and servicing of subscriptions from any source. This can be accomplished in a number of ways. In fact, it is not unusual to convert systems several times to find the best way of fulfilling your subscriptions. The advent of the computer has made it possible to gather statistics and demographics more easily, and an analysis of the statistics is a basic tool in new promotion. As costs increase, greater selectivity is needed in list selection, advertising, and special offers. The basic source of subscribers is renewals. As much, if not more, effort should be spent on obtaining renewals as on seeking new subscribers. When do you stop seeking a renewal order? Your response results give an indication, but a basic rule is to cease renewal efforts when the cost reaches the figure for adding a new subscriber. Credit and collection efforts follow the same pattern. Fulfillment is a cycle composed of promotion, servicing, collection, and renewal.

Subscription fulfillment, whether for a journal with a circulation of 500, or *Readers Digest* with a monthly list of 17 million, is basically the same. The mechanics of the operation, and the equipment used vary but the basic ingredients are always there. I would define subscription fulfillment as the processing and servicing of subscriptions from all sources: direct mail promotions, subscription agencies, unsolicited orders, and renewal promotion. The fulfillment manager's job is to record the subscription order in such a way that the subscriber will receive the journal as published; be invoiced properly; have the payment applied correctly; and receive renewal notices upon expiration. The subscription department must also be able to answer subscriber complaints and inquiries, prepare statistics, prepare credits and collection routines, and assist other departments such as the warehouse and accounting in aspects of their work related to journals.

Subscription fulfillment may be accomplished in a variety of ways. In fact, it is not unusual to convert systems a number of times to find the best way for an individual journal. Some of the factors to be considered in either starting up a fulfillment operation or converting an existing one are the size of the current list and its potential for growth, the frequency of mailings, and the volume of maintenance changes. A small list may be maintained on card files-or stencil plates, and a large one probably on a computer, but no matter what system exists now, or what the system being converted to will be like, there will be four basic segments of the work:

1) mail receipts and sorting;

Manuscript received April 28, 1975. This paper was presented at the 1975 IEEE Conference on Scientific Journals, Cherry Hill, N.J., April 28-30.

The author is with Cambridge University Press, New Rochelle, N.Y. 10801.

2) order editing;
3) file maintenance;
4) output.

Let us briefly look at these four divisions, keeping in mind that the specifics may vary but the basic elements will exist in every system.

MAIL RECEIPTS AND SORTING

Every day mail is received and must always be opened and sorted. If you have large amounts of mail, the post office can be used as a sorting vehicle via the use ot post office boxes. At Cambridge University Press we use a box number for all journal mail to separate it from mail for the rest of the Press, but boxes can be effectively used to segregate payments, journal titles, renewals, etc. Remember the following two important points.

1) Don't assume the post office has sorted correctly. Read each piece of mail, even though the post office box number will segregate most of it.

2) In this age of the consumer, always include your street address on all outgoing mail even though the reply envelopes are for box numbers.

Basically, the mail falls into three groups: orders, payments, and nonorder mail. This last group includes address changes, complaints, and general correspondence. The first two groups require no further breakdown and can be distributed to individuals for processing. The last group, which is a jumble of all nonorder mail should be further broken down to reflect its purpose and then distributed.

ORDER EDITING

Each new order must be edited and each renewal must be verified before processing. Do not allow a stencil typist or keypunch person to do this job. The editing must be consistent and abbreviations standardized. The first line of the name and address is the most important at Cambridge since our file is in alpha sequence. Thus it is important to edit the first line consistently or the list will be scrambled in short order. Every U.S. address must have a zip code. If the order doesn't have one it must be looked up in the directory and added to the address. Some people verify zip codes but I think it is safe to assume they are correct. If a new order, the subscriber should also be given a specific subscriber type, depending on the type of order, and an identifying number if on computer. The order is then read to determine exactly what is being ordered and the proper transaction codes used for input to the master file.

Reprinted from *IEEE Transactions on Professional Communication*, vol. PC - 18, no. 3, Sept. 1975, p. 145-7, by permission of the publisher.

FILE MAINTENANCE

File maintenance is the heart of any fulfillment system but especially in a computer operation. Simply defined, file maintenance is the processing of any transaction that affects the current status of a subscriber. Exact specifics of how these are handled depends on the particular system you employ, but in essence there are two types of maintenance. The first type is order and payment materials including adjustments to sales and amounts paid. The second type is nonorder maintenance, which is for the most part address changes, and changes in subscriber type.

OUTPUT

The end product on any fulfillment operation is the output, and although it has been said many, many times, it bears repeating: You only get out of a system what you put into it. The first three components of the system create the fourth, and if there are problems you will see the results in the output. It is essential to remember that the subscriber only sees this last part, and cares nothing at all about what you have to do to get the journal delivered. In general the output consists of four items:

1) labels;
2) invoices;
3) renewal notices;
4) reports and statistics.

The format of this output is important. I believe the individual requirements of a publisher will determine the format for invoices, renewal notices, and reports, but there is only one format for the labels: zip code sequence, with foreign labels either at the beginning or the end. If you mail second class or third class bulk, the U.S. Postal Service requires that you tie out and bag the issues in zip code order; so it is essential to produce them that way to avoid a sorting job later. I also believe the fulfillment department should maintain complete control of label selection. Do not computerize automatic label selection according to the printer's schedule. Unlike commercial magazines, where a specific schedule must be adhered to, journals often are subject to delays, and if labels are produced automatically they may be waiting weeks for the issue. When you know the delivery date for an issue, request the labels, thereby insuring an up-to-date set.

There is one other aspect of labels that must be considered. Most journal subscriptions are set up on a calendar year basis, but new and renewal orders come in all during the year. At Cambridge, our system is designed in such a way that when a late renewal is received it is processed as usual, and when the computer reads the information it also looks to the record to see how many issues have been published for that journal. The very same week labels are produced for the published issues and they are on their way to the subscriber at once. Subsequent issues are sent in the regular bulk dispatch. This eliminates a manual job of typing a label for previously published parts and insures that the subscriber will receive all the issues already published for the current year.

Timeliness is of the essence for effective fulfillment operations. There are cycles involving cutoff dates, and compressing even one day out of the fulfillment cycle can substantially improve customer service. For example, in a computer operation, if the customer file is updated once a week, missing getting maintenance into the file by one day can result in a subscriber missing the first issue by two weeks. If you batch daily and update weekly, a delay can result in a month's delay of an invoice and the receipt of payment even longer, and a subscriber who has already paid may receive a reminder. Be aware of cutoffs, because missing them will to some extent increase customer complaints that could have been avoided. To reduce processing time, it is necessary to simplify and reduce the work requirements of each operation, and to improve the operation by introducing labor saving equipment where justified. Often a simple change can result in great time savings. For example, we number our items within the daily batch, which is fairly standard practice. When we first converted to a computer system we used a revolving head stamp which did the job but was slow. We progressed to an electric numbering machine which is easy to operate and very fast. It was a small change but saved us a lot of time in one area. Labor saving equipment doesn't have to be an expensive computer; it can be a simple tool which saves processing time. It is essential to regularly look at the clerical operation and continuously ask why certain things are done. Elimination of one apparently insignificant procedure can result in hours saved.

Next to the mailing label, the output cycle produces two other items the subscriber sees: the renewal notice and the invoice. Both are straightforward forms requesting action on the part of the recipient and should be standardized with a minimum of extraneous information. If extra "punch" is desired an insert should be used, but the forms themselves should be bearers of only the essential information. The renewal notice and invoice should be "turnaround documents," meaning that when they are received back in the house they can be processed without any additional editing, with the possible exception of address changes. The essential information is

1) subscriber name and address clearly positioned to fit into a window envelope;
2) name of the journal;
3) volume numbers, subscription year, and price;
4) unique subscriber number.

A clear space should be provided for the address change information.

The renewal cycle should be timed to insure receipts in time to be processed for the dispatch of the first issue. It is less expensive to mail in the bulk dispatch than to send published parts later. We used to mail renewal notices to all subscribers, but found that on the first notice this was not productive for institutions that place their orders through subscription agencies. Most agencies have a renewal system with their clients, and by the Press contacting them directly we were generating unnecessary correspondence all around. Thus, our first notice is sent only to direct subscribers two months before expiration. At expiration a second notice is sent and three months later a final notice. This last notice is sent to all unrenewed subscribers since agency orders should be in by that time. The renewal notice encourages prepayment but does not demand it. In direct mail promotion we have experimented with credit cards and have had moderate success. Such an order is processed as a cash order with the added detail of preparing charge slips for the bank. Credit cards are guaranteed payment, and if you have a high proportion of individual subscribers, employing them can substantially reduce credit and collection expenses and bad debt writeoffs. If you require all individuals to prepay, the availability of credit cards can increase your renewal percentage. But even if prepayment is not mandatory, this additional option makes it easier to renew. The renewal should be the easiest subscription you can get since you're selling someone who is already familiar with your journal. Renewals are the hard fact of economic subscription life, and the renewal percentage represents quality of circulation.

The invoice, like the renewal notice, requires action on the part of the subscriber, action hopefully accompanied by a check. When our fulfillment operation first was computerized we mailed statements monthly. Almost at once we were flooded with duplicate payments, especially from individuals. When the publisher of a medical yearbook was converting to a computer operation, the main problem was double and even triple payments, even though statements were only sent monthly. It seems the doctor paid, the secretary paid, and the nurse paid. Well, academics and research people do the same thing. To solve the problem we send a statement every two months for six months, after which they are monthly. One month was just not enough turnaround time.

Credit and collection makes no sense unless it is related to the total picture. The collection activity has to be timed to reduce a substantial amount of correspondence. The use of insert letters in the first three statements is a positive reminder that payment is overdue. After six months a form letter from the credit department is sent requesting immediate payment. At eight months we use a letter from the fulfillment manager that is customer orientated seeking the reasons for nonpayment and advising of possible attorney action. This is followed by a letter from the credit manager threatening attorney action to individuals who still have not paid. At this point we decide on an invoice by invoice basis if we want to pursue this matter further. Usually we write off the amount due, but if it is significant we do use a collection agency. A computer system should have a built-in stop so that a renewal will not be processed for a subscriber with a balance due.

The collection activity should not solely be concerned with the effectiveness of the collection series but must consider customer relations. Prompt replies to queries about statements make for satisfied subscribers and faster payments. Once a reply is made to an inquiry, the routine collection series should cease. The account should be flagged and future follow-ups referring to the reply made. Nothing iritates a person more than receiving routine collection letters with no reference to the fact that he has replied.

The end of the fulfillment cycle is either the renewal or the cancellation. The former takes us back to square one; the latter ends a relationship. Always acknowledge cancellations and always ask "Why?" Often service problems surface when a subscription is terminated and you can take steps to correct them. And finally, end the publisher/subscriber relationship on a positive note by adding to your acknowledgement letter a sentence that regrets the individual will no longer have a personal copy of the journal but asking if he still has access to a library copy. You may get a library subscription as a result.

Journal fulfullment is the only contact you have with subscribers. It must be orientated to the customer. If it is not, it's time to go back to the drawing board.

3 SOME BASIC PROBLEMS OF JOURNAL PUBLICATION

3. SOME BASIC PROBLEMS OF JOURNAL PUBLICATION

This section brings together four papers which touch on various problems posed by journal publication. The first looks at the question — why do scientists want to publish in journals and what effect does their urge to publish have on the journals? It provides an amusingly written introduction to the whole section (something to be appreciated, since communication studies usually take themselves very seriously). The points it makes are, however, serious ones. The growth of specialisation in the pure sciences means that authors are often producing research that is of interest to only a very restricted circle of readers. Yet the author must have the research published in order for it to become an accredited contribution to science. The result is that a journal may have a circulation of thousands, although only a dozen recipients or so read any individual paper in detail. This apparently wasteful distribution will be taken up again in Section 7.

The growing number of professional scientists in the world during the present century has led to a rapid growth in the number of journal titles in existence. One of the great uncertainties is just how many journals do exist now, and how the number is changing with time. This apparently simple question proves on closer examination to be very complex; it is not only necessary to pin down what new journals are appearing, but also what existing journals are disappearing. The second paper has therefore been chosen to provide a brief analysis of this problem.

The third paper in this section draws attention to a difficulty that is as old as the scientific journal — standardisation. Lack of standardisation affects all aspects of journal production; for example, there are still journals that cling to out-of-date page sizes despite the financial penalty this involves. Most effort, however, has always been devoted to bibliographical standardisation, since this can have a major influence on the retrieval of information from journals. The problem is not simply one of agreeing to standards, though this is difficult enough; it is also one of imposing standards when they have been established. In countries where state subsidies are not a major factor in scientific publishing there are very few actions that can be taken against journals which do not follow standards.

The fourth paper is the longest in this section. It deals with the scientific journal from the point of view of both the author and the user (who may, of course, be the same person). I have included it in part to act as a reminder that the journal, as a formal communication channel, is paralleled by other, generally informal, channels. But the paper also emphasises an aspect of journal publication that should be put alongside its financial cost — namely, the time involved.

Research published in journals requires the expenditure of a good deal of various scientists' time before it is published: even so, it is usually a little out-of-date when it appears, because of the time required for processing it. The final paper in this section examines this point in detail. It presents a case study of the delay involved in publishing one particular piece of research. It is not, of course, intended as a typical example, but does suggest some of the factors connected with delays in publication. This leads us on to the material contained in the next section.

The Future of Scientific Publishing – Or, What Will Scientists Be Doing for Brownie Points?

Harold Wooster

Director of Information Sciences, Air Force Office of Scientific Research, Arlington, Virginia 22209

ABSTRACT

Several pertinent aspects of the current practices in scientific publication are discussed, and means are suggested for alleviating some of the problems. It is obvious that present-day and future economic considerations will force changes in these practices that will not readily be accepted by the scientist.

People, scientists or not, want love, sex, power, prestige, freedom, and money, in various proportions depending on the person. Scientists (and artists) typically put more emphasis on prestige and freedom than other people do. This emphasis on prestige starts early in a scientist's career. As Lawrence Kubie has written:

"The intellectually gifted child is likely to turn away from athletics and the social life which he finds difficult to more bookish activities... If success rewards his consolatory scholarly efforts during adolescence, he may in later years tend to cultivate intellectual activity exclusively... As a result, by the time adult life is reached his only triumphs and gratifications will have been won in the intellectual field, his range of skills will have become restricted, and the life of the mind will be almost the only outlet available. Because of the extra drain of the laboratory on the student's time, the young man who sets out to become a scientist spends (more of) his adolescence putting every emotional egg in the intellectual basket than is true for most other young intellectuals. By such steps as these, the sense of security and the self-esteem of the young intellectual come to stand on one leg, so that when research is begun he invests in it a lifetime of pent-up cravings... it is inevitable that scientific research will be supercharged with many irrelevant and unfulfilled emotional needs; so that the life-work of the young scientist tends to express both the conscious levels of his intellectual aspirations and his unfulfilled intellectual needs and unconscious conflicts."

Unfortunately for outsiders who try to intervene in the family quarrels, chief among the scientist's emotional outlets is his life-long love-hate affair with the scientific literature. There are, for all practical pur-

---

An address delivered to the Washington Academy of Sciences, John Wesley Powell Auditorium, Cosmos Club, Washington, D. C. on February 19, 1970.

poses, three things you can do with the scientific literature: you can write it, you can read it, you can put it in piles.

Putting it in piles is one of the few places where the value structures of the scientist and the librarian conflict, as can be attested to by anyone who has ever overheard a conversation between a librarian who wants a book back, and a scientist who wants it on permanent loan:

"I've got to have this book. Who wants it? Him! What's he going to do with it? He can't read it. I'm the only man in the place who can understand it."

Librarians (and wives) just don't seem to understand that one's books and journals must be kept within arm's reach; that the inverse-square law (the strength falls off as the square of the distance between the the source and the target) also applies to the talismanic psychic aura of well-being given off by the scientific literature or, for that matter, that this aura can diffuse through the covers of unopened books and unwrapped journals!

Keeping the literature in piles is perhaps just another example of the standard desultory warfare between the sexes. Writing the literature is where the real emotional involvement lies. The young scientist learns, as part of the formal code of behavior of the scientist, that publication of the results of his research in a standard, authorized, refereed scientific journal is not merely right and proper but a high duty and a behavior expected by his peers and employers. He learns informally that promotion comes about through visibility and that, at least up to a certain critical point in his career, visibility comes about through publication. He learns that there are "good" journals, and others not as good, but that every manuscript can eventually find a home somewhere and that, for all the platitudes about refraining from unnecessary publication, this must apply to someone else — it is better to publish something in anything, even if only a government report, than not to publish at all.

As is the way with things with which one is emotionally involved, the average scientist manages somehow to take the scientific literature for granted and think that it's wonderful. So let's look for a moment at the anatomy of the scientific literature.

World-wide, there are probably 25,000–35,000 journals in existence at any one time. We've probably reached equilibrium in this respect, with as many dying as being formed. There are some 6,200 journals of science and technology in the U.S. — 3470 in technology, 1430 in agriculture, 800 in medicine, and 500 in natural and physical sciences.

The most common publication frequency is quarterly; average circulation is 4400 copies. Average annual publication is 1,000 pages per journal, each page containing 600 words. Printing cost is about $0.075 a word or about $400 per paper, which will reach about 100 actual readers!

The American Psychological Association has been carrying out a study, sponsored by the National Science Foundation, of publication practices in psychology. They found that work on a paper published today was actually started some 36 months ago; about 26 months ago the author started talking about the work at small informal seminars. The author started writing for publication at about the same time. About 12-15 months ago the author presented his paper at a large national meeting (with no more than 100 in the audience) and more or less simultaneously sent it in to the journal.

The paper is published; about ½ of the papers in core journals will be read in detail by no more than 1% of readers; no paper will be read by more than 7%! About 90% of the authors will receive reprint requests, average number being between 11 and 15 copies.

Another depressing aspect of the journal literature shows up when you start collecting frequency-of-use statistics. Our own experience with this problem showed up when we ran a frequency curve on the 550 journals which have published 5500 articles sponsored by our headquarters, the Office of Aerospace Research. We found that the first 10 journals published 35% of the articles; the second 10 brought the total to 45%; the third 10 to 50%. The cross-over curve was at 70 journals and 70%, with perhaps 400 of the journals running from 5 to 1 articles each. We discovered the curve was shaped the same over and over — from sources of abstracts in *Chemical Abstracts* to photocopying records of libraries.

On this basis, have come up with 3 numbers applying to the journal literature — 10, 100, and 1,000:

- 10 — The maximum number of journals any average scientist can be expected to "keep up with."
- 100 — Will meet 90% of the needs of any reasonably specialized information center.
- 1,000 — Probably the number of *first class* scientific journals in the world today.

The National Science Foundation has estimated that, at $30 per page for both scientific and technological journals, the total annual cost of publishing of all U.S. journals is approximately $250 million. And yet at the same time, as the director of marketing for one of the major publishers of commercially sponsored scientific journals said in testimony before Congress, "an important and successful journal may have one thousand or fewer subscribers — where 1500 copies of a book can saturate the market."

The verb "to publish" has two different meanings depending on whether one uses it as a scientist or as a publisher.

If I as a scientist "publish" a paper, I go through the following steps: I write a paper summarizing my research to a given point, and I send this manuscript to a scientific journal where it is reviewed and eventually accepted. This article is set in type and eventually printed in a scientific journal. I receive no direct tangible remuneration for this publication. In fact, I may be asked to pay page charges on the order of $30 a page.

I eventually receive, say, 100 reprints of the article which I then mail to my friends and use to answer reprint requests. If I get more than 25 of these I feel highly flattered. When I finish I say that I have "published" an article in such and such a journal.

As explained earlier, the scientific publisher is basically quite different and makes his livelihood from processing scientific information.

A scientist's rewards from publishing are intangible, and include the approbation of his peers, being promoted, perhaps having his grant renewed. None of these is subject to income tax. The scientific publisher's rewards are highly taxable. It would be silly of me to claim that scientists aren't interested in money nor publishers in prestige, but these are not really the basic values of their societies. Nevertheless, the two communities are highly interdependent; scientists couldn't get promoted without publishers, and publishers would have nothing to publish without scientists.

The scientific publisher, whether he be with a commercial publisher or scientific journals or is the business manager of a professional society, sees two major threats to his economic survival — the computer and office copying machine.

The use of the central time-shared computer is a remote but very real threat. Any one of perhaps a hundred firms would be delighted to lease you time on their central computer. All you need in your office is a "console," which may be as simple as a touch-tone telephone; will most probably be a teletypewriter; but could, if you are willing to pay the tab, have full display-screen and light-pen capabilities. The time-shared computer offers no threat to scientific publishing when it is used for business or scientific computations. The threat comes when, as many enthusiasts of mechanized information storage retrieval systems will explain, scientific text is fed into a central computer and users call for selected portions on their consoles. After one copy of a book is bought and fed into a central computer, no one else would need buy the book but simply read it through their consoles.

Office copying machines represent yet another, but not new, threat to scientific publishing. Most of us tend to forget that, in the days when typists' salaries were much lower, the typewriter was the first feasible office copying machine. When the USDA started a mail reference service in the early 1900's, requesters got typed excerpts of pertinent articles.

This was a relatively slow and cumbersome process as was its successor, photostatting. The crisis really occurred with the advent of today's quick and inexpensive office copying machine, which can copy a page of a journal at perhaps 3-5 cents a page. It is no longer necessary for the individual user to buy a copy of an article which he wishes to have for his own permanent retention.

Coincidentally, many libraries have found that the cost of maintaining charge and loan records is high enough to make it desirable to give customers copies of journal articles rather than go to the trouble of charging out and loaning bound volumes. Publishers have nightmares of journals moving into limited editions of about 300 copies published for the convenience of copying machine owners, lessors, and the people they serve.

However moral and law abiding scientists may be in other matters, their consciences become almost non-existent when dealing with books and journal articles they want for their very own. As long as copying machines, scientists, and journal articles occur in such close and dangerous proximity, no amount of statutory labeling will deter the man who wants to copy an article. As George Bernard Shaw once said, one of the few arguments in favor of marriage is that "it combines the maximum of temptation with the maximum of opportunity."

If one is involved both emotionally and financially in an industry threatened with technological obsolescence, there are two major strategies to follow. One is to play King Canute and call for legislation outlawing, or at least making financially prohibitive, the use of these new technologies. The other alternative is to live with and even anticipate them, on the theory that as long as there are producers and consumers there is a fair profit to be made by the middle man.

Some of my wilder-eyed friends in the information trade have scared the publishers with visions of a world-wide network of optical speed computers transmitting instantaneous information in any form and in any language to many requesting users of the system. Theoretically, users will not even have to leave their homes to sit in front of a multi-channel console with input-output channels for audio video image reproduction, instantaneous language translation, and even logical filters indicating whether a given request makes sense.

Unfortunately, both now and in the foreseeable future, any material that enters a computer has to go through a keyboard. It comes out at a rate of perhaps 100 words per minute on a teletypewriter. I am not denying the possibility of either a display of this information on a video screen or a 1,000-line-per-minute printer. I merely remind you that the voice-grade telephone lines now in use have trouble at much over 100 words per minute. I also remind you that a typed page of such material may take three minutes to transmit and cost $10 in computer and transmission line time before you get it. I would rather pay $10 for a properly printed and bound book than the same amount for one page of computer print-out.

There is one class of publication, though, to which the foregoing does not apply — handbooks, encyclopedias, and dictionaries. These all go out of date as soon as printed. Revisions may and should be commissioned immediately, but these all have to be held for the next edition which may be several years away, and a new edition may contain as little as 20% new material!

If the central computer utility for libraries ever comes into being, I foresee a major market for such reference materials on tape, perhaps leased rather than sold, with a guarantee that new material will be entered immediately rather than held for the next edition. I would hate to dispense with the printed reference works in my office, but there are times when I would pay a premium to make sure that I am using the latest information.

As someone once did not say, God must love the scientific journals because he made so many of them. Scientific journals are about as clumsy, archaic, and expensive a method of distributing scientific and technical information as one could devise, yet they continue to flourish. There are so many journals that no library possibly can subscribe to all of them. It is difficult to identify any given relevant article within the 10 million that have been published since science began. Once it is identified, it is almost impossible to determine who has a copy to be borrowed.

Many plans for national information systems have been proposed. I am surprised how few of them have proposed what seems to be a necessary first step — a central warehouse for scientific journals. This need be no more complicated than any other mail-order operation. It would respond only to hard citations — those where author, volume, page, and title were correctly given. Stock clerks, not librarians, would then pull these off the shelf, photocopy the wanted articles and air-mail them to the requestors. The job of translating soft citations into hard citations would be done out in the field by reference specialists. One other aspect of this central warehouse should appeal to the journal publishers. It also would centralize photocopying and therefore make it far easier to keep track of royalty payments due, say at a flat rate of five cents per page copied.

Another alternative would be to let journal publishing find its natural economic level, for example, by requiring all page charges to be paid by the authors personally, not from grants, and if that didn't work, suggesting that they ask for royalties proportional to the cost of the research reported. I suspect that if this happened, only a few hundred of the strongest journals would survive. The rest might well become shadow journals. A "shadow journal" by my definition would have all the usual paraphernalia of editor, advisory boards, and referees. The difference would only show up when it came time to ship copy off to the printer. The printer would only get titles, abstracts, and a good gossip column, say, on who's changing jobs and what's happening to the Federal R&D budget. The actual text of the articles would go into a central store, either on microfilm, as Watson Davis proposed some 40 years ago, or into the memory banks of a computer, where it could be retrieved by any of the 10 or so people who really want to read a given article.

It turns out that the real problem is not in substituting for journal publication, which is a fairly simple technical matter, but in substituting for the prestige arising from journal publication, which is something else again.

I have occasionally proposed that this problem could be solved by authorizing the central computer to issue Brownie points which by universal academic convention would be fully substitutable for items in personal bibliographies. My tentative Brownie point scale goes something like this:

5 points .... Published doctoral dissertation — a once-in-a-lifetime event.

3 points .... Review state-of-the-art papers.

1/N points .. Joint-authored papers. Meeting papers — choice of 1 point or a paid-up travel voucher.

-1 points.... Published after-dinner speech.

-5 points.... Claiming authorship of a proposal as if it were a scientific paper.

At the end of the year the computer would add up individual scores and issue warrants entitling the recipient to wear a simple button-hole insignia:

10 points ...A bronze X
20 points ...A gold XX
50 points ...A silver L
100 points ...A diamond-studded C

Since it is difficult to enter a room waving a personal bibliography, this would give American science what it has so sorely lacked — a simple recognition of scientific stature based on true merit!

PROLIFERATION AND FRAGMENTATION OF JOURNALS

JOHN MARTYN
Aslib

We are continually being told, with varying amounts of supporting evidence, that the literature of science and technology, measured in terms of numbers of articles published, is expanding exponentially, with a doubling rate, according to Price,[1] of between ten and fifteen years. As the population of the world is increasing exponentially, it seems reasonable to assume that the population of scientists and technologists is increasing similarly (and in fact the evidence is that the number of scientists is increasing at a faster rate than that of the population); the population of authors, being a subset of the population of scientists, can therefore safely be assumed to be increasing also. Therefore an exponential increase in the amount of literature appearing annually, the phenomenon usually referred to as the 'information explosion', appears entirely credible. Because this increasing quantity of literature is published somewhere, then it seems reasonable to assume that the number of scientific journals is also increasing, probably exponentially, and Price, while showing that the number of journals founded is so increasing, suggests a doubling period of fifteen years for the population.

However, there is considerable diversity in the estimates of numbers of papers published, and a relative scarcity of estimates of numbers of current journals. At various times the number of papers published annually has been estimated at anything between a million and a half, and around 850,000, the variations arising from the different means adopted of making the estimates, and differences in the definition of a paper. If the definition be confined to that adopted by Vickery,[2] that a paper be taken as an authored contribution to a scientific or technical journal, then his estimate of approximately 850,000 (an estimate published in 1968) based on a careful sampling of current issues of journals held by the National Lending library, is most probably correct. A more common method of estimation depends on counting the numbers of abstracts produced in various services, but these estimates are confused to some extent by the continued efforts of secondary services to achieve comprehensiveness in their respective fields, and by redefinitions of their coverage, so that increase in the numbers of items they notify reflect not only increases in the literatures they cover, but increasing expertise in finding relevant items, and modifications of their definitions of relevance.

Estimating the numbers of journals published has often depended on counting entries in various bibliographies, notably the 'World List', but, as has been pointed out by Gottschalk and Desmond,[3] the World List not only contains a number of entries for journals which scarcely qualify for the title of scientific, but also carries a large number of entries for journals which are no longer current. The same is true for nationally-produced lists of periodicals. Gottschalk and Desmond report that a sample check of the third edition of the World List showed a mortality rate of 33%, and Barr[4] reports that a similar check of the fourth edition shows that only 40% of the entries represent actual current titles, 'the remaining entries being titles which have ceased publication, cross-references, and what may be termed World List ghosts.' The closest estimate of the number of actual current journals I have been able to find is that by Barr, based on the holdings and the titles on order at the

Paper presented at the Royal Society Conference of Editors, Carlton House Terrace, November 21st 1972.

National Lending Library in December 1965, which is 26,000. This estimate is well argued and well supported, and I consider it to be accurate.

These 'point-in-time' estimates are about all we have in the way of hard figures about the proliferation of journal papers and the journals in which they appear. As Gottschalk and Desmond point out, the 'phenomenal growth in serial titles from year to year assumed in most estimates cannot be supported', although they add that 'the number of articles carried in typical journal issues, the frequency of publication of journals, and the number of pages per article will reflect a considerable increase in volume.' Now, because we lack estimates made in the same way over a period of time, we do not know whether, and to what extent, the journal population is actually increasing. Nor do we have figures for the number of articles in typical journals over a period of time, for change in publication frequency, or for number of pages per article. We do not know either, the extent to which the trend towards multiple authorship tends to reduce the relative productivity of individual authors, or whether rejection rates for journals are increasing and consequently the quality of journals in increasing, or whether journal papers are tending to become shorter so that increasing numbers of publications can be catered for without a similar increase in pages of print.

As we know so little about the proliferation of journals, it will not be surprising to discover that we know even less about their fragmentation. When should a journal divide itself into sections, and how many have done so? When should journals consider amalgamation, and how many have done so? We simply do not know.

The majority of the research in this area is conducted by or on behalf of librarians or documentalists, the acquirers rather than the generators of literature. There are now a number of findings which demonstrate that, as Beaver[5] says, 75% of the literature is contained in 25% of the journals – the oldest ones, or that, as Gilchrist and Martyn[6] found, 90% of the citation of British journals is to 6% of the journals. In other words, the core of science is found in a very few journals, and the majority of journals represent, in effect, the minority of the literature. Powles[7] has commented that 'new journals, in the UK, do not make much money for editor or publisher and sometimes run for years at a loss.' As Chen[8] concludes, in a recent study of the use patterns of physics journals, 'Journal prices continue to increase, and . . . those for chemistry and physics are the highest of all. Accordingly, librarians will have to make difficult decisions on weeding, storing less needed collections, cancellation of subscriptions etc. in the near future'. I suggest that what determines mortality, fragmentation and amalgamation of journals is largely the pressures of the market, and the libraries constitute a large proportion of the market for scientific periodicals. The literature may be increasing exponentially, and the number of journals may also be increasing, although not necessarily exponentially; but the number of libraries and consequently the size of the potential market is increasing much more slowly. If, as Price suggests, the growth curve of the literature is a logistic curve, we may be approaching the levelling-off point because of the fiscal limits of the market, and I would expect, as a result, to see an increasing tendency to raise the quality of journals in order to survive: if, that is, the journal itself is to survive as the prime medium of communication among scientists.

REFERENCES

1. PRICE D. J. de S. *Little science, big science.* New York, Columbia, University Press (1963).

2. VICKERY B.C. Statistics of scientific and technical articles *J. Doc.* 24 3 (1968) pp. 192-196.

3. GOTTSCHALK C.M. and DESMOND W.F. Worldwide census of scientific and technical serials. *Am. Doc.* **14** 3 (1963) pp. 188-193.

4. BARR K.P. Estimates of the number of currently available scientific and technical periodicals. *J. Doc.* **23** 2 (1967) pp. 110-116.

5. BEAVER B. de B. *A statistical study of scientific and technical journals.* New Haven, Yale University (1964).

6. MARTYN J. and GILCHRIST A. *An evaluation of British scientific periodicals.* London, Aslib (1968).

7. POWLES J. Birth control for journals. *Nature* **218** (1968) p. 50.

8. CHEN C.C. The use patterns of physics journals in a large academic research library. *J. Am. Soc. Inf. Sci.* **4** (1972) pp. 254-265.

Standardization in Production of Journals: A Black and White Case?

MARGARET BROADBENT

Abstract—Standardization in typography, spelling, abbreviations, and citations provides a semblance of uniformity to a journal. Standardization guarantees greater flexibility in the use of copyeditors in an office that publishes several journals. However, journals in different disciplines lend themselves to different formats and styles: a large journal with many articles is more efficiently set in double-column pages of small type, while a journal containing many equations requires a single-column page with generous size type and citation of references in the text by author and date instead of by number. Such deviations from routine standardization keep copyeditors alert. Perhaps the most important area of standardization in a redactory office is in the procedures of checking galley and page proof. There can be no deviation from standard rules of proofreading. Finally, economics in publishing may dictate standardization in the future. Authors may some day be "compositors" when their typescript becomes the camera-ready copy. More standardization, not less, in the original typescript will then be required.

The Journals Office of The Rockefeller University Press is responsible for the production, distribution, and financial health of 5 monthly journals which contain original, archival articles. Karl Heumann asked me to talk about standardization of style and citation practices among the 5 journals, "and," he added, "be very specific because many in the audience will not have had experience in redactory practices!"

A good copyeditor (or redactor) is a unique breed—usually a college graduate who derives special satisfaction from turning a batch of heterogeneous typescripts and illustrations into an orderly journal whose format provides a certain uniformity. A good copyeditor is detail oriented; organized—knows how to keep manuscripts, galleys, and page proofs marching to the printing press; disciplined in checking; and diplomatic in dealing with authors and editors. The experienced copyeditor possesses, in addition, judgment—when to break style or what action in an emergency best serves the printer, author, and journal.

What about uniform practices in style and citations? Copyediting falls roughly into three areas of activity: *marking format* to achieve the correct journal typography that has been designed for the scientific content; *internal copyediting* to assure correct grammar and consistent "house" style; and finally *procedural checking* in manuscript and proof to avoid careless errors in the printed journal.

For many years the formats of the two early Rockefeller journals were identical, so identical that in the spring of 1949 the printer covered the text of the April *Journal of Experimental Medicine* with the covers of the March *Journal of General Physiology*, and vice versa! The present formats of the 5 journals differ. For example, the format of the *Biophysical Journal* is designed for a small monthly journal, averaging about 8 articles. The single-column page, with generous type size, accommodates long, involved display equations. The stock has an antique finish because there are few halftones. The *Journal of Cell Biology*, on the other hand, containing 20 to 30 articles a month, is printed on 70-pound coated paper because 200 screen reproductions of electron micrographs occupy 30 percent of the journal's pages. Specifications call for a two-column page with small type to accommodate the articles in a manageable issue averaging about 275 printed pages. Although the printer follows standard specifications adopted for a particular journal, the copyeditor must mark the manuscript for format when the typescript is ambiguous. For example, a copyeditor marks paragraphs to be set in small, setdown type; levels of text headings which serve to outline the paper; reduction of photographs to fit the page and still assure optimal readability; and any text or tabular matter whose typescript form might mislead the printer. Marking a manuscript for format is mechanical. It is a skill quickly mastered and becomes routine for the copyeditor assigned to a particular journal, who performs the function quickly, efficiently, and accurately. Owing to different formats among the journals, a copyeditor assigned to a new journal applies the skills learned, but approaches the different format like a cook with a new recipe, a step-by-step process that is slow and thorough, but at first not efficient.

Internal copyediting, on the other hand, is basically standard for all 5 journals and in general follows recommendations in the *CBE Style Manual*. Internal editing guarantees consistent house style and includes correcting grammar, using standard abbreviations for units of measure, arranging the elements of references in a standard sequence with standard periodical abbreviations, verifying unfamiliar words, and supplying manufacturers and their locale for trade names. Internal editing is not automatic, but requires concentration and careful attention to detail. Standardization in internal editing provides flexible use of staff. A good copyeditor can tackle any manuscript for any journal and use the same abbreviations, the same orderly system of reference components, the same consistent spelling of terms.

Procedural checking in typescript and proof requires the copyeditor to verify that all references, tables, and illustrations

Reprinted from *IEEE Transactions on Professional Communication*, vol. PC - 18, no. 3, Sept. 1975, p. 123-6, by permission of the publisher.

are correctly mentioned in the text. In proof, the copyeditor checks to be sure that the tables and figures appear in the correct order throughout the article, that the pagination is correct, and that the running feet (or heads) are accurate—a myriad of detail that insures the article in the printed journal is free from careless oversights. The Journals Office maintains a standard check list of these operations for manuscript and galley and page proofs. In checking various stages of publication, the copyeditor does not deviate from standard procedures. Any trained copyeditor, regardless of what journal he is customarily assigned to, can quickly and accurately handle a batch of galley or page proofs for any journal faced with a deadline.

A specific example of style among journals is references and their citation in the text. At first glance, citation practices in the 5 journals seem inconsistent because the articles in any one journal may contain any one of the following three citation systems:

1) Citation in text by number, seriatim. References are listed and numbered in order of citation. This method is inexpensive and requires less typesetting in the text.

2) Citation in text by author and date of publication. References are listed alphabetically by author. This system avoids ambiguity if many equation numbers appear in the text, it brings together authors by the same name in the bibliography, and it offers an inexpensive way of adding references in proof.

3) Combination of the two systems above. References in the bibliographies are listed alphabetically by author and then numbered; citation in the text is by number. Except for the tidy-minded reader who dislikes seeing reference (61), for example, cited in the first paragraph of the paper, the dual advantages of bringing the same authors together in the list and using the inexpensive number citation in the text outweigh the trivial disadvantage.

Although uniformity in format, house style, or procedural checking from journal to journal helps tremendously in the flexible use of staff, scientific content often dictates flexibility in format and internal editing. And an expert copyeditor knows instinctively when black and white rules should be broken.

What of the future? With increasing use of computer techniques in photocomposition and reliance on camera-ready copy, authors will be increasingly urged to submit typescript in standard form and to even prepare manuscript on a standard machine so that it in turn may be "read" by a sophisticated electronic machine. It behooves publishers to insist now on uniform standards of form and style as a future protection from the cost of recasting authors' inconsistent typescript. With the introduction of editorial processing centers and complex machinery, my crystal ball-gazing sees more, not less, standardization.

RESEARCH STUDIES IN PATTERNS OF SCIENTIFIC COMMUNICATION: III. INFORMATION-EXCHANGE PROCESSES ASSOCIATED WITH THE PRODUCTION OF JOURNAL ARTICLES*

WILLIAM D. GARVEY, NAN LIN and KAZUO TOMITA

Center for Research in Scientific Communication, The Johns Hopkins University, Baltimore, Maryland

Summary—The two studies described in this article focus on information-exchange associated with material published in journal articles. In the first study we concentrate on the prepublication information-exchange activities of article authors, from the time their work first reached a report stage until it was published. The results of the second study, related directly to the articles studied in the first one, and the results of the first study have been combined so that we could discuss how scientists assimilate and use information contained in these articles when this information is also disseminated via informal media prior to its appearance in journal articles. The findings are discussed in light of questions they raise about the function of current journal articles.

IN THE two previous articles (GARVEY et al. [1 and 2]) in this series we presented, respectively, a broad description of a program of research which we have been conducting since 1966 on the communication activities of over 12,000 scientists and engineers, and the general findings of the first of our major series of studies, the role of the national meeting in the scientific communication process. It was clear from these studies of the national meeting that the meeting presentation serves as an interim report in the total dissemination process—most of the presentation material is disseminated in written form (mainly as journal articles) in later years.

Our second two major series of studies (Study Series E,† N = 3676 and Study Series F,† N = 1935), which will be described in this article, focused on information exchange associated with material published in journal articles.

GENERAL DESCRIPTION OF TWO STUDIES DEALING WITH INFORMATION-EXCHANGE PROCESSES ASSOCIATED WITH THE PRODUCTION OF JOURNAL ARTICLES

We selected journals to be included in Study Series E in the following manner. The journals which meeting presentation authors (Study Series A) most frequently mentioned as intended outlets for their presentation-based manuscripts, as well as all journals published

---

* The research reported here was supported by a grant (NSF GN-514) from the Research and University Information Systems Program of the Office of Science Information Service of the National Science Foundation. In addition to the authors of this report, Carnot E. Nelson and Mary Buchanan contributed to the research reported here.

† These letters refer to the Study-Series identification code in the data bank, which is stored on machine-readable tapes and is available to other scholars and researchers involved in information science. For further details, see the first article (GARVEY et al. [1]) in this series.

Reprinted from *Information Storage and Retrieval*, vol. 8, no. 5, October 1972, p. 207-21, by permission of the publisher.

by the sponsoring societies,* formed the basis of citation analyses. References found in these journals, which had appeared during the previous 2 years, were analyzed. Journals which were frequently cited by this group, but not included in it, were added, and similar analyses were made of their references. This process was continued until the remaining journals were clearly out of the mainstream of a disciplines' journal literature. Those journals discovered to be central to a discipline's subject matter, plus a small selection of journals found to be closely related to this core of literature (a total of 67 journals) were selected for study.†

As soon as possible after the distribution of every issue of a journal selected for study, each (first) author of an article in that journal was sent a questionnaire pertaining to the content of his article. In this study our general concern was to determine the prepublication information-exchange activities of article authors, from the time their work first reached a report stage until it was published.

The second study (Study Series F) which we shall report in this article grew out of the one just described. Authors of the journal articles studied were asked to name persons who were conducting work in the same subject-matter areas as those covered in the articles. Persons so named by authors then served as subjects in a survey designed to determine the information flow and information exchange among different workers in the same field. Recently published articles or, more specifically, the information contained in these articles, served as the critical event in the study. Since we knew, from the study of journal article authors (Study Series E), on what occasions the authors made prepublication reports of the main content of their articles and the extent and nature of the feedback resulting from these reports, we designed this new study so we could combine the results of the two studies in relation to specific envelopes of information. One of the main purposes of this study was to determine how scientists assimilate and use the information contained in these articles when it is disseminated via informal media prior to its appearance in journal articles. A more complicated goal of this study was to determine the structure of informal networks associated with a discipline and the kinds of information which flow through these networks. The respondents in the study described above—because they were named by the authors themselves—were considered the "first generation" of workers in the areas of the authors' articles. A "second generation" was developed when the "first generation" respondents, in turn, named other persons conducting work in the same subject-matter areas. These "second generation" respondents became subjects in a survey analogous to that conducted for the "first generation" respondents, and the persons whom they, in turn, named became "third generation" respondents in this survey.

PART I: THE INFORMATION-DISSEMINATION PROCESS ASSOCIATED WITH THE PRODUCTION OF JOURNAL ARTICLES

Characteristics of authors of articles

The typical author was a young Ph.D., who was spending most of his time conducting research and teaching. Seventy per cent of the authors held doctorates and over half had received their highest degrees within 7 years of their articles' publication. Assuming that the general population of American scientists has been doubling about every 15 years,

---

* Nine professional societies representing nine disciplines partipated in the 5-year program of research.
† All articles published in the core journals were selected for study; however, for the other journals only those articles authored by members of the participating societies or which cited two or more articles published by core journals were selected.

this population of authors seems relatively young. In addition, over half of the authors who did not hold doctoral degrees were devoting some part of their time to studying for an advanced degree.

Apparently, just a few universities train most of the persons who author scientific articles within a profession; typically, 10 per cent of the institutions trained about half the authors associated with each discipline.

Basic research constituted the most time-consuming activity in which authors were involved; over half the authors designated it as one of their first two major professional activities, and about three-fourths indicated that they devoted some part of their time to this activity. Next in order of most time-consuming activities came applied research and teaching; one-third of the authors designed them as one of their two most time-consuming activities and over half of the authors indicated that they devoted some of their time to both.

The extent to which the load of administration and management is carried by active producers of scientific information is indicated by the finding that these activities were designated as the most time-consuming by one-eighth of the authors, and among the four most time-consuming activities of two-fifths of the authors of journal articles.

Prepublication schedule of work reported in articles

Authors initiated the work reported in this body of literature on the average 28 months before its publication. However, the distribution of the time when work was initiated extends over a relatively long period—10 per cent of the authors began their work more than 5 years before its publication.

Authors averaged over a year (13 months) to complete their work, which was reportable over a year (15 months) before its publication. The typical author did not waste much time ($2\frac{1}{2}$ months) between completion of work* and initiation of the journal-article manuscript. The typical manuscript required 5 months' preparation and was submitted to a journal on the average 7–8 months before its publication in a journal.

The time necessary to conduct the work (median time, 13 months) represented the main time expenditure in the total process from initiation of work to its journal publication, the actual conduct of the work consuming almost half of the total time involved. Of the remainder, half ($7\frac{1}{2}$ months) was spent in disseminating information about the work and in preparation of the manuscript and the remaining $7\frac{1}{2}$ months was consumed by publication lag. Thus, three-fourths of the time associated with this process occurred before the journal editor ever saw the manuscript.†

Prepublication reports of the main content of journal articles

Prepublication reporting of work contained in journal articles was extensive; four-fifths of the authors had made some type of prepublication report of the main content of their articles. Authors made oral reports more frequently than written reports.

Prepublication reports fell into two categories, based on when they occurred in the work schedule. (See Fig. 1.) One-fifth of the authors made preliminary reports of information contained in their articles, i.e. reports of preliminary findings (incomplete results and/or partial

---

* "Completion of work" was taken as that stage at which a detailed report of the results and their interpretation to a group of colleagues working in the same problem area was possible.

† As each stage of this process develops, from inception of work to its publication, the time distribution of a particular stage tightens increasingly so that the greatest variability in the process relates to scientists' conducting their work, the least variability to publication lags associated with the communication system in which these scientists disseminate their work.

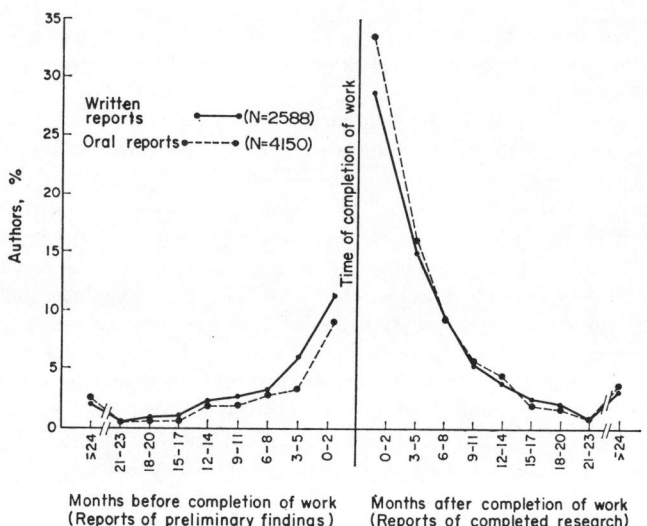

FIG. 1. Times at which authors reported their work prior to its publication in journals.

interpretation of results finally reported in an article). Most preliminary reports (two-thirds) usually took the form of oral reports to small audiences of colloquia size. Less than one-eighth of the authors had mentioned their preliminary findings in written report. Therefore, at this early stage little information about an author's findings was disseminated beyond a small group which he selected.

The major prepublication dissemination began immediately after an author had completed his work sufficiently to start writing a manuscript for submission to a journal.

TABLE 1. PREPUBLICATION REPORTS OF MAIN CONTENT OF JOURNAL ARTICLES

Type of prepublication report	Authors N=3676
Oral	
Colloquia (within author's own institution)	29·0%
Meeting of national society	24·1
Colloquia (outside author's own institution)	13·0
Thesis committee meeting	10·7
Meeting of a local, state, or regional group or society	8·3
Briefing, report to contracting agency, in-house staff meeting, etc.	8·0
Meeting of an international society	7·2
Invited conference	7·1
Scientific or technical committee meeting	3·2
Written	
Technical report (distributed outside author's institution)	21·0
Thesis or dissertation	19·4
In-house publication, bulletin, or memo	15·8
Proceedings or symposium publication	6·6
Copy of oral presentation	6·6

THE SCIENTIFIC JOURNAL

Information-Exchange Processes Associated with the Production of Journal Articles

Reports from that point until journal publication were important because they constituted dissemination of the main content of journal articles well before publication. (We address ourselves solely to these reports in the discussion that follows.)

Table 1 shows the nature of these prepublication reports and the frequency with which authors made them. Although the most frequent occasion for such reports took the form of colloquia (within and/or outside their own institutions), authors also disseminated their work frequently to relatively larger audiences, e.g. national meetings of scientific and technical associations. Articles in the body of literature studied derived relatively often from theses or dissertations—over one article in five contained work which was previously reported at a thesis committee meeting or which was written up as a thesis or dissertation.

The earliest prepublication reports typically began very shortly after the work was completed (see Fig. 1) and most of the prepublication reports occurred over a short period (4 months) from the time an author completed his work until he submitted a manuscript based upon it to a journal. After submitting their manuscripts to journals, very few authors made any further reports of the main content of their articles. Therefore, a relatively long interval (almost 8 months) apparently existed before journal publication, when most authors did not disseminate reports of their work.

Prepublication reporting of work apparently had some sequential organization. The temporal sequence of occasions wherein authors reported their work, as shown in Fig. 2, revealed a pattern of dissemination, starting with the more highly focused audiences and ending with the more general audiences. Such sequential orderliness of prepublication reports seems especially suited to help authors shape their work gradually, but effectively, for journal publication. In fact, about one-half of the authors who made prepublication reports indicated that they received feedback (comments, criticisms, etc.) because of those reports, lead-

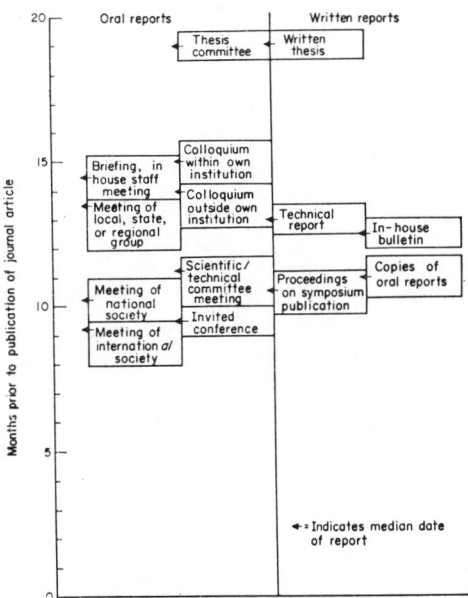

FIG. 2. Typical times of prepublication reports of main content of journal articles.

ing them to modify the main content of their work in the manuscripts later submitted to journals. Such feedback resulted slightly more often from oral reports.

Inspection of the occasions wherein authors made prepublication reports which led them later to modify their work revealed that *when* they made their prepublication reports (as long as it was before they had submitted their manuscript to a journal) was not nearly as important as *the nature of the audience* to which they made these reports. Typically the audiences which were most effective in providing authors with useful feedback were small, familiar groups such as thesis committees, colloquia within authors' institutions, in-house bulletins, and scientific/technical committee meetings. Nearly as effective was the national scientific/technical meeting, a medium upon which a large number of authors, who are not members of the subdisciplinary in-group which routinely exchanges information informally, rely for information exchange about their ongoing or recently completed work. (See GARVEY et al. [2].)

The nature of these modifications varied greatly, of course, from simple stylistic revisions to major changes which required rerunning an experiment, replication of some aspects of research, reanalysis of data, etc. While one-fourth of the authors rendering prepublication reports modified the style or organization of their manuscripts, an even larger number (about 40 per cent) reported making substantive changes; e.g. clarification or redefinition, new or further explication of theory, incorporation of other researchers' findings as well as the major changes just mentioned.

Comparison of authors who made some prepublication report of their work with those who did not, revealed that authors who made prepublication reports more frequently held doctorates, more frequently worked in academic institutions, less rapidly completed their work (from initiation of work to submission of manuscripts to a journal), more frequently distributed preprints (on the other hand, they less frequently modified their manuscripts because of feedback from preprint distribution), had less interest in speed of publication and had more involvement in new work in the same area as that treated in their articles, i.e. their new work was more likely derived from some result reported in their articles. Put differently, authors who did not make prepublication reports seemed less academically oriented, more interested in obtaining fast publication of their work, and less involved in the long-term pursuit of the specific research field reported in their articles. The data indicated that authors making no prepublication report of their work did achieve faster publication of their work, i.e. the interval from initiation of work to journal publication was shorter.

Distribution of preprints

The distribution of preprints (copies of the article manuscripts) constituted another form of authors' prepublication dissemination of the main content of their articles. Over one-half of the authors distributed at least one preprint before the publication of their articles. Authors who distributed preprints did so at various times; most (one-third) distributed them before submitting their manuscripts to journals; one-fifth waited until after they had submitted their manuscripts but distributed preprints before notification of editorial action; and one-sixth distributed preprints upon receiving such notification.* Six represented the median number of preprints distributed; however, one-sixth of the authors disseminating preprints distributed at least 25.

* Most authors distributed preprints on more than one of the aforementioned occasions.

The distribution of preprints appears highly personal and selective—three-fourths of the authors who disseminated preprints reported having distributed them to colleagues working in the same area as that of their work. Routine distribution of preprints seemed relatively minor; one-sixth of these authors used mailing lists based upon contract- or grant-obligations' distribution lists and one-sixth used their own institutions' mailing lists. Furthermore, only one-eighth distributed preprints through preprint-exchange groups, i.e. groups of persons organized to routinely exchange preprints. That almost half of the authors had distributed preprints to persons who had been familiar with their work earlier in the process and who had requested that authors send them a copy of the manuscript upon earliest availability, clearly indicates that earlier prepublication dissemination effectively alerts other workers to the progress of new research.

It is evident from this study that an author's main goal in distributing preprints is not simply to *disseminate* his work. Since authors often distributed preprints before either submitting their manuscripts to journals or receiving notification of editorial action, they had an opportunity to receive feedback potentially useful in modifying their manuscripts before journal publication. About two-fifths of the authors distributing preprints on these occasions reported having received useful feedback which caused them to modify their manuscripts. Although these authors made more stylistic than substantive modifications (two-thirds of the authors reported changes in wording, general format, etc.), they made substantive changes often, too (three-fifths reported changes in content such as different analysis of data, reformulation of concepts or theory, reinterpretation of findings, etc.).

Authors who distributed preprints, compared with those who did not, had worked in their areas of speciality longer, devoted more time to basic research, worked at academic institutions more often, conducted their work more expeditiously, and made more prepublication reports of their work (and those authors who made prepublication reports modified their work because of feedback from them more often). Additionally, authors who distributed preprints devoted more time to new work, at the time their articles were published, in the same area as that treated in their articles, and more of this work was directly derived from some result reported in their articles. In most respects, authors who did not distribute preprints resembled those who did not make prepublication reports; however, authors not distributing preprints took longer to complete their work.

Submission of manuscripts to journals

Selection of journals. The major basis on which authors selected journals to publish their work derived from the nature of that journal's audience, i.e. four-fifths of the authors reported selecting a specific journal because it reached an audience especially appropriate for their work. In addition to this general basis for selecting a particular journal, one-fifth of the authors selected journals because of their editorial policy, and one-eighth because of their speed of publication. Other reasons, cited less often, were: journal published other related articles, editor invited an author's article, prestige of journal attracted author. Only one author in 50 selected a particular journal because of its page-charge policy, i.e. the specific journal did not "charge" for publication.

Prior rejection of manuscripts. Approximately one article in eight (of the 3676 articles studied) had been submitted to another journal prior to the publishing journal. Most (7 out of 10) of these 434 manuscripts received straightforward rejections. The vast majority of the remaining manuscripts were not accepted by the journal and returned to the authors with suggestions and comments which were objectionable to the authors.

The bases for rejection of manuscripts were equally divided among general shortcomings (subject matter inappropriate) and concrete faults (statistical or methodological defects, theoretical or interpretational mistakes). Apparently a large portion of these authors routinely resubmit their manuscripts without further ado, since only about one-half made any revision at all in their manuscripts before resubmitting them to another journal. Most of these manuscripts (9 out of 10) were accepted by the second journal to which they were submitted; a few (6) manuscripts were submitted to four or more journals before achieving publication. Each "rejection" added on the average an additional three to 3–3½ months to the delay in publication of the manuscript.

A comparison of authors who experienced manuscript rejection with those who did not revealed some differences worth mentioning. Those authors experiencing rejections were slightly younger, but more of them held doctorates. They spent less time in administration and applied work but considerably more time in teaching. Although there was no difference in the frequency with which either group made prepublication reports of their work and few differences in use of various prepublication media, over one-third more of the authors experiencing rejection received feedback from these reports which led them to modify the presentation of their work in the manuscript which they submitted for journal publication. The pattern of distribution of preprints was also similar for both groups (the "rejection" group, however, tended to give more emphasis to preprint distribution, before submission of their manuscripts to journals). And again, almost one-third more of the group experiencing rejection received feedback as a result of preprint distribution which caused them to modify their manuscripts.

The two groups placed different emphasis on the determinants of their choice of journals; the authors of the rejected manuscripts selected the publishing journal almost twice as frequently because of its editorial policy and one-third less frequently because of its speed of publication.

Finally, almost one-third more of the authors experiencing rejections had abandoned the subject-matter area of their articles (within 1 year or more after publication); and those who had remained in the area tended not to have progressed as far in their new work as their counterparts who had not experienced rejection.

Keeping in mind that the rejected manuscripts which we are discussing were published in journals which were of high quality, the general picture which emerges in relation to the rejected manuscripts suggests that there were indeed some difficulties with production of these manuscripts during stages before their acceptance by the publishing journal. For example, (a) there was a longer delay between completion of work and initiation of writing for these manuscripts, (b) relatively few of these manuscripts were not at sometime revised because of feedback received during the prepublication process (reports, preprints and editorial suggestions), and (c) it took over twice as long for the *publishing* journal to process a manuscript which had been previously rejected (i.e. the time between initial receipt of one of these manuscripts *by the publishing journal* and its publication was on the average over twice as long as it was for a manuscript which had not been previously rejected). Although authors experiencing rejection were on the average slightly younger than the other authors, this difference was on the average only 1 year and does not appear to be the major reason for having difficulty in achieving publication of their manuscripts. The general characterization of these authors is some combination of less experience in, less productivity in, less prominence in, and less personal commitment to the particular subject-matter area of the rejected articles; i.e. relative to the other authors they had not worked as long in an area, had published fewer articles in the area, were less frequently named (by other authors) as workers in the area, and were less prone to continue working in the area.

PART II: INFORMATION EXCHANGE AMONG SCIENTISTS WORKING IN THE SAME SUBJECT-MATTER AREAS

We now turn to a study designed to determine how other workers assimilated and used the information contained in journal articles when it was disseminated prior to publication by informal media. In the section which follows we have combined data from our second-, third- and fourth-generation respondents. Thus, we discuss below two generations: Generation A, consisting of those other workers named by the article authors, and Generation B, consisting of those named by Generation A and all subsequently named respondents.

Some characteristics of generation respondents

A comparison of article authors (respondents in the previous study) and other workers in the field, showed authors as having less education (fewer held doctorates) and less experience in the field, i.e. the typical author had received his highest degree 4–5 years after the typical generation respondent. Basic research was more frequently a primary activity for the other workers (both generations) whereas applied work was more frequently a primary activity for the authors. Authors reported slightly less involvement in management or administration but more involvement in studying for advanced degrees. Generation A workers differed from Generation B workers in that many more held doctorates and had received their highest degrees on the average 1 year earlier.

Thus, in studying the generation subjects, we were examining the scientific communication behavior of a group of scientists who, compared with the journal article authors, were: (a) more highly educated, (b) more established in the field, (c) more involved in management or administration, (d) less involved in applied work, and (e) less involved in studying for advanced degrees.

*Involvement in same subject-matter area as that described in critical article**

Most of the persons in both generation groups had recently conducted (at least within the previous 12 months) work in the same subject-matter areas as that described in the critical articles; two-thirds of Generation A and three-fourths of Generation B reported such activities.

Both generations had actively disseminated the results of their work in the area of the critical articles; however, Generation A had more actively published articles; three-fourths had published one or more such articles before publication of the critical articles, while only one-half of Generation B had published such articles. The two groups had been equally active (three-fourths of each) in presenting work in the same subject-matter area as that of the critical articles at national meetings.

It is interesting to note that one-fourth of the generation respondents, who had been designated by authors and other workers in a subject-matter area as being involved in work in the same area, had neither published an article nor made a presentation at a national meeting

---

* Each respondent was questioned specifically in relation to the journal article which led to his being named as associated with the subject matter of the article. Thus, each respondent's communication behavior is related to only one (critical) article.

in the subject-matter area. Consequently, knowledge of their work in the area must have been acquired through informal communication media.

Respondents' contact with information in the published journal articles

This section deals with the nature and extent of other workers' contact with the same information reported in the critical articles. We shall consider first communication activities which occurred before publication of the articles and then postpublication communication activities. Figure 3 diagrams the relevant events, and the text refers to these events by letters which are also appropriately located in the diagram.

Prepublication contacts with the main content of the published articles. Most of the respondents in each generation were acquainted with the previous work of the article authors—i.e. work conducted by authors before that which they reported in the critical articles (A). Generation A, however, were more familiar with such earlier work (Generation A, eight-tenths; Generation B, seven-tenths).

As mentioned earlier, Generation A had published more frequently in the area of the critical articles; they had also more frequently cited the authors' work in their own work (B) —Generation A, three-fifths; Generation B, one-half.

Although a large percentage of persons in the Generation B group worked in the areas of the critical articles, the relationship between authors and other workers in their fields was better maintained for Generation A than for Generation B; for example, three-fifths of Generation A, compared to two-fifths of Generation B, reported that they maintained contact with the authors on a continuing basis to exchange scientific or technical information (C).

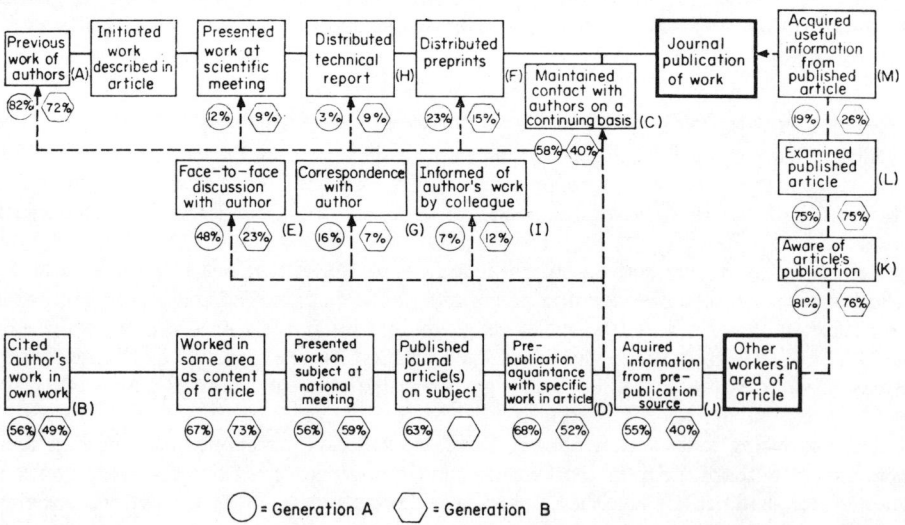

FIG. 3. Schematic diagram of pre- and postpublication dissemination of information published in journal articles. The percentages within the circles and haxagons indicate the percentage of generation respondents having participated in or having contact with the activity named in the boxes above them.

The effectiveness of this relationship is reflected in the finding that Generation A workers were more frequently acquainted with the specific work described in the critical articles before the publication of these articles (D)—Generation A, seven-tenths; Generation B, one-half. When the sources of this prepublication information were examined, the value of "personal" interaction between authors and other workers became evident. Face-to-face discussions (E), preprints (F) and correspondence with authors (G) constituted the main sources of prepublication information for Generation A. We find in the assimilation of information from these three sources the greatest discrepancy between the two generations (preprints—Generation A, one-fourth; Generation B, one-sixth; correspondence—Generation A, one-sixth; Generation B, one-fourteenth; and face-to-face discussion—Generation A, one-half; Generation B, one-fourth). For Generation B, two sources, which may be independent of any personal familiarity with authors, were more effective for them than Generation A. These were (H) technical reports (one in 10 vs less than one in 30) and (I) colleagues other than authors (one in 8 vs one in 14).

TABLE 2. EXTENT TO WHICH CRITICAL ARTICLES WERE EXAMINED

Extent of examination	Generation A N=1322	Generation B N=613
Examined content of article	74·7%	75·4%
Merely scanned content of article	15·4	17·3
Read some portion (e.g. theory, methodology, results, etc.) of article	5·7	7·3
Read entire article	53·0	49·9
Acquired information used in their work from examination of article in its published form	18·8	25·6

That Generation A workers interacted more personally with authors, while Generation B workers depended more on "formalized" sources or other colleagues, apparently constitutes the major difference in the prepublication acquaintance with critical article material.

Three-fifths of Generation A reported that they had, through one of these prepublication sources, acquired information useful in their work; two-fifths of Generation B had similarly acquired useful information (J). In other words, over three-fourths of those workers who had some prepublication acquaintance with the specific work in the critical articles, had acquired information which proved useful in their work, Generation B having had only slightly less success (77 per cent) than had Generation A (81 per cent) in this respect.

Postpublication contact with critical journal articles. Most respondents in each group (Generation A, 86 per cent; Generation B, 76 per cent) were aware at the time of the survey (8–12 months after an article was published) that the critical articles had been published (K). Two-thirds of those persons not aware that the articles had been published, had not seen the particular issues of the journals in which they were published.

Three-fourths of each generation group had examined the content of critical articles in their published form (L). Table 2 shows the extent to which the articles were examined. Half of the respondents had read the entire article in its published form. This proportion amounts to two-thirds of those respondents in each group who examined the article at all.

Compared with the prepublication sources, both groups acquired less useful information from the articles in their published form. One respondent in five of Generation A and one in four of Generation B reported that they had acquired useful information upon examination of the journal articles (or one-fourth of those Generation A and one-third of those Generation B respondents who examined the published articles had acquired useful information from them). As mentioned earlier, three-fifths of Generation A, compared to two-fifths of Generation B, had acquired useful information from some prepublication source. Thus, the extent to which scientists gained information, useful in their work, from a published article apparently is inversely related to the extent to which they had acquired useful information (eventually contained in the article) before the article was published.

DISCUSSION OF THE DISSEMINATION PROCESS ASSOCIATED WITH INFORMATION PUBLISHED IN JOURNALS

Work published in the journals studied started on the average almost $2\frac{1}{2}$ years before its publication. Shortly before the work reached a stage where its author could report his results together with an interpretation of them as reported in the journal article, the dissemination process, which grew increasingly later, began. It was not, however, until a year before its publication, when the author felt he had completed his work satisfactorily, that genuine dissemination of his work began.

The first reports were usually oral, informal and to small audiences. Generally, a pattern of increasingly wider dissemination of information about the work henceforth developed; the author apparently initiated this process with the most highly focused audiences and completed it with the most general of audiences.

This prepublication dissemination process occurred mostly over a relatively short interval of 5 months immediately after the author completed his work. This intensive prepublication dissemination served both the author and the consumer. From the author's point of view, it provided critical feedback which helped him to shape his work into a better scientific product. From the consumer's point of view, this prepublication dissemination apparently served other workers active in the same field, by acquainting them with the main content of an article, *before its publication*.

The distribution of preprints constituted another form of prepublication dissemination actively practised by authors, who apparently view such preprint distribution as a special kind of prepublication dissemination, which provides them with a final opportunity to obtain feedback from their peers before submitting their manuscripts to the journal-editorial-review process.

The interval between submission and publication of a manuscript averaged 7–8 months—i.e. the journal's publication lag consumed one-fourth of the time consumed between initiation of work and its publication in a journal.

In this period the authors typically began new work in the same subject-matter area as that treated in their articles being readied for publication. More than three-fourths of this new work evolved directly from some results of the work described in the articles.

Authors initiated this new work on the average very shortly (within 2 months) after completing the previous work; and by the time the previous work was published, over one-half of the new work had already reached a stage at which a detailed report of the results and their interpretation could be made—indeed, over one-sixth of the new work had been reported (in either oral or written form) on the average 3 months before the previous work had been published.

The finding, discussed earlier, that authors ceased reporting their previous work about 7 months before its publication (or shortly after submission of their manuscripts), is not surprising, since most of them were well into producing new information which in some respects would render the previous work obsolete. As such, they were then seeking information about the new work as it was being shaped for journal publication.

The process has been described up until journal publication (perhaps the most crucial stage in the communication process in science), where the information is transferred from the informal (prepublication) domain to the formal (archival) domain. The barriers between these domains have been established by scientists to assure the continuing efficient progress of scientific knowledge. The dimensions and distinctive functions of the two domains, the process by which information is transferred from one to the other, and the subsequent processing of information into scientific knowledge is a complicated one which has been discussed by GARVEY and GRIFFITH [3] and ZIMAN [4].

Following publication of the journal article the information in the article moves into secondary sources where "information" is processed into "knowledge". Separate items of information from separate journal articles are interrelated, and these clusters in turn become compounded into a self-consistent, meaningful body of knowledge which eventually represents the most acceptable and coherent scientific understanding of a subject-matter area at that time. Each of the secondary sources—abstracts, citations and reviews—serves a different function in this integrative process. The abstract places the article in a public secondary source, along with other contemporary works on the same subject, where it can be retrieved from a comprehensive catalogue. Next, the citation of the article by the author of another article more deeply reflects the integrative process in science, wherein the scientific information in the article is built upon, evaluated in light of, and linked to new information which has been generated since its publication. The review article which may appear next evaluates and synthesizes the content of the article, in light of recent progress in an area.

A particularly striking feature of the information-flow process, from initiation of research until integration of its results in the archival body of scientific knowledge, is that the information does not become genuinely public until its journal publication and quite often by this time journal information is out of date on the research front.* During the various stages leading to journal publication, the author of an article disseminates the main content of his article on a variety of occasions. These occasions constitute an extensive communication activity, which is not solely dissemination from the author's point of view. The author is equally, if not more, interested in inciting activity in which he might *assimilate* information, too. In other words, he uses reports of his work to gain information on other current work relevant to his own work, which he is reporting or which he has initiated since the reported work. The experienced information-consumer is sensitive to this prepublication dissemination process (he is usually, of course, an information-producer as well), and he, too, is trying to discover every means of obtaining information about ongoing or recently completed work relevant to his own work. He apparently does not want to wait to discover this information in a journal or a secondary source—he seems to use journals mainly to acquire information he may have missed during the dissemination process which occurred before the journal article's publication.

* As mentioned in the first article of this series, we can do no more in these articles than present a general description of our findings. The process being discussed has been analyzed a number of different ways. For a comparison of this process in the physical and social sciences, see GARVEY *et al.* [5].

An important feature of communication in the informal domain is that it brings about genuinely mutual information exchange. This interactive process between information-disseminator and information-consumer and the dual (often simultaneous) role of the scientist as information-disseminator/information-consumer appear characteristic of scientific communication. Much of what is currently being done to "improve" informal communication (e.g. to incorporate preprint exchange into formal retrieval systems) mainly gives certain informal media more extensive dissemination force; however, these efforts usually fail to facilitate genuine interaction among scientists. The results of our studies show that scientists spent much time and effort *interacting* or establishing mechanisms to do so, and that scientific information exchange in the informal domain was very effective for them. Any communication innovation which detracted from effective and efficient mutual exchange among scientists was not welcomed in the informal domain.

An examination of the lags in the overall information-flow process for the disciplines studied revealed a few critical points which not only confirm the need for improvement of the process, but also identify the loci where such improvement is needed.

From the time the average author of an article initiated his work, until its publication in a journal, lags in the information-flow process accumulated to a total of 28 months. It took him 2 months longer to prepare and publish a manuscript (15 months) than to conduct his work (13 months from initiation to completion). During the 2–3 month delay between completion of work and submission of the manuscript to a journal, the author actively disseminated information about his work. Once he submitted his manuscript (7–8 months before its publication), however, he usually refrained from further reporting of it. Although in the overall information-flow process $7\frac{1}{2}$ months delay may not seem too great (this delay did constitute one-fourth to one-third of the total time from initiation to journal publication of work), it was a rather critical period in the process since most of the authors had already begun new work on the same topic as that of their articles. In other words, during this 7–8 month period when his manuscript was being processed for journal publication and its main content was no longer being disseminated, the author usually had begun new work which stemmed from or built upon work reported in the manuscript.

The study of the usefulness of information published in journal articles was directed at a special class of information-consumers—workers active on the research front associated with the specific subject matter of the articles. The results of the study clearly show that most such workers had gained information useful in their work before such information was published in journals. Or, to put it another way, the scientific information in journal articles (which had been published less than 6 months) was likely to be useful only to those scientists who had *not* had earlier contact with the information through the prepublication dissemination process. (These findings are not too surprising in light of data which strongly suggest that the scientific information in most journal articles was 6 months–1 year behind the research front at the time the articles were published.)

We were concerned in our studies about the usefulness of information in current journals, which, of course, was only a portion of the potential usefulness of journals.* The studies raise some questions about the function of current journal articles: Can the journal article

---

* Some other worthwhile functions of journals are: (a) general awareness of a field, mainly for those persons who are not primarily involved in a specific subject-matter area of the field; (b) current awareness of a field, mainly for those persons who are not conducting research in the field and who have no other access to the research front; and (c) certification of the knowledge of a field, mainly for those persons who want to relate a specific piece of work suitably to other scientific work.

any longer be regarded as a vehicle which effectively conveys current scientific information? If not, can the journal article be reworked to function more efficiently in the capacity of integrating scientific information into a larger framework?

The continuity of work in science is evidenced in the finding that 7 authors in 10 had initiated new work in the same area as their articles by the time of the articles' publication. Since this scientific work was just in progress, we can expect that some of it was never completed and much was not communicated. Also, in the time process we have been following since 1966, we have come to the years 1970–1971—years of especial interest to the growth of American science. In the next article of this series we shall examine what scientific and technical information the authors of articles published in 1968–1969 produced and communicated during these ensuing 2 years.

REFERENCES

[1] W. D. GARVEY, N. LIN, C. E. NELSON and K. TOMITA: Research studies in patterns of scientific communication: I. General description of research program. *Inform. Stor. Retr.* 1972, **8**, 111–122.
[2] W. D. GARVEY, N. LIN, C. E. NELSON and K. TOMITA: Research studies in patterns of scientific communication: II. The role of the national meeting in scientific and technical communication. *Inform. Stor. Retr.* 1972, **8**, 159–169.
[3] W. D. GARVEY and B. C. GRIFFITH: Scientific communication: Its role in the conduct of research and creation of knowledge. *Am. Psychol.* 1971, **26**, 349–362.
[4] J. ZIMAN: *Public Knowledge: The Social Dimensions of Science.* Cambridge University Press, 1968.
[5] W. D. GARVEY, N. LIN and C. E. NELSON: Communication in the physical and social sciences. *Science* 1970, **170**, 1166–1173.

Some Effects of Delay in Publication of Information in Medical Journals, and Implications for the Future

DAVID A. E. SHEPHARD

Abstract—This study was designed to assess the effects of delay in publication of information in medical journals. The case study concerned the natural history of an article that appeared recently in a medical journal. The particulars of this article from the time of its conception through its consecutive submission to, and rejection by, four major medical journals, and its eventual publication, instead, in a minor medical journal have been studied. The subject of the article was a new form of treatment for Amanita verna poisoning. The period of delay between clinical treatment and publication of the article was 21 months. During this period, however, information about this clinical case received general publicity through newspapers, magazine articles, radio, and telephone. These details then were considered in the context of the medical journal's traditional role: to communicate information that sometimes may be urgent. The effects of delays and breakdowns in the information system that links medical authors with medical readers by way of medical journals and the influence of other media on medical communication also have been considered. To remain effective as channels of communication in an information-conscious society, medical journals must reassess their traditional methods of transmitting information by becoming aware of faults in this specialized communication system and by ensuring that information that is primarily of medical interest does not, by default, have to be transmitted by other channels.

CRANE has argued that "the problems of scientific communication can be understood in terms of the interaction between a complex and volatile research front and a stable and less formal communication system" [1]. As the growing edge of the biomedical sciences widens and becomes more diverse, the continuing formality of the biomedical communication system will make it ever more difficult for physicians to keep abreast of new information. One part of the formal biomedical communication system is the medical journal. This presentation examines the case history of an article published in a medical journal from the viewpoint of Crane's general argument. I shall consider (1) the case history of one particular medical article, (2) the communications aspects of the case history, and (3) the implications of the case history for the future of medical journals.

THE CASE HISTORY OF ONE MEDICAL ARTICLE

In November, 1970, a physician had to treat a man who appeared to be dying from poisoning due to the mushroom, Amanita verna [2]. The patient was one of seven persons who had picked and eaten mushrooms of this poisonous species. Two of the seven died 5 days after they had eaten the mushrooms, and the patient became so ill that on the sixth day of his illness he was transferred to a university hospital for intensive care. The problem was the specific treatment of acute liver failure and hepatic encephalopathy;[1] enquiry of various sources, including major poison centers, for a remedy was of no avail [3]. The case was publicized on the radio, however, and a Delaware chemist who was interested in mycology heard the radio report. This chemist knew that in 1963 a Czechoslovakian doctor had written a paper on a method of treatment for Amanita poisoning that was based on the use of thioctic (α-lipoic) acid [4], and he communicated this information to the patient's physician.

Although it had been first prepared in this country in 1951 [5], thioctic acid had never been used by American physicians; the drug was not available in North America. But on the eighth day of the illness, when two of the patient's friends had died after eating the same mushrooms as the patient, and when the patient was semicomatose and had signs of acute liver damage, the physician administered hastily acquired European thioctic acid. Therapy was continued for 6 days, at the end of which time the patient's condition had greatly improved, so much so that the new form of treatment was discontinued. The patient continued to recover; a liver biopsy showed evidence of repair following hepatic necrosis; he was dismissed from the hospital; and he was able to return to his job 2 months later.

The patient's physician, a clinical professor of medicine, collated the details of this interesting case and those of the other six and duly formalized the information in an article. His chief intent was to communicate information about thioctic acid and its possible usefulness in cases of mushroom poisoning so that thioctic acid might be evaluated by other physicians. The article was sent, in turn, to four major American medical journals (Journals A, B, C, and D); each, in turn, rejected the article [3]. The physician-author's hopes of communicating his unusual experience to a large medical readership were by now dashed. He turned to his state medical journal, which eventually published his paper 21 months after the episode of mushroom poisoning [2].

In the meantime, news of the survival of the patient had been transmitted across the United States and Canada through two reports in the New York Times [6], [7] and one Associated Press report [8]. As a result of these reports, many physicians communicated by letter and telephone with the Philadelphia physician to learn more about the case. These enquiries continued for many months, and, in the 21-month interval between the poisoning episode and eventual formal publication of the case in a medical journal, publicity was reinforced by magazine articles [9].

---
[1]The clinical details of this case are summarized in Appendix I.

COMMUNICATION ASPECTS OF THE CASE HISTORY

Certain aspects of this case are of great interest when considered from a communication viewpoint.

A. Inherent Energy of the Message

Simply put, the message that the physician-author attempted to transmit to his fellow physicians was this: mushroom poisoning may be fatal but Europeans have been using thioctic acid as a successful treatment for years.

In North America, although mushroom poisoning is not common, a certain number of cases occur each year. In the United States in 1969, 620 cases were reported to the Food and Drug Administration (FDA) [10]; in Canada in 1967, 183 cases were reported [11]. Sometimes mushroom poisoning is fatal; this depends on the genus eaten, and *Amanita* poisoning is particularly serious. The mortality of poisoning due to *Amanita* ranges from 30 to 60 percent [12]. On the North American continent deaths occur periodically; for example, in 1972 there were 3 deaths in California attributable to mushrooms of *Amanita* genus [13], in 1971 there was 1 death in Minnesota [14], in 1970 there were the 2 deaths in New Jersey, and in 1967 there was 1 death in Ontario, Canada [11]. Moreover, no specific antidote is known [15]. Each case must be treated according to its own individual features. In each case, both patient and physician are alone, the prognosis being uncertain until the patient either recovers or dies. Each case is literally a matter of life and death.

For these reasons, *Amanita* poisoning is always interesting. Communication of news about *Amanita* poisoning has, therefore, an inherent energy that aids communication, even when there may be obstacles to such communication. Then news spreads through different channels.

B. Obstacles to the Communication of News About Thioctic Acid

Thioctic acid appears to have been used first in the treatment of *Amanita* poisoning about 1959, the first report in a medical journal appearing in 1963 [4]; this was in a German journal. In the United States its use of thioctic acid was not described until 1972 [2]. What were the reasons for delay in publication of information about thioctic acid in this country?

(1) *Language Barrier:* The first report in a medical journal on this topic appears to have been written by the Czechoslovakian, Kubicka [4]. This report was published in a non-English journal that is seldom read, if at all, in this country. Similarly Kubicka's other papers and the many other European papers on *Amanita* poisoning were written in languages other than English and published in journals that are not read by American physicians. Indeed, all original accounts of thioctic acid in the treatment of *Amanita* poisoning have been written in Czechoslovakian, German, French, Italian, and Polish; until 1972, none were in English.

This is not surprising because *Amanita* poisoning is more common in Europe than in North America. In Germany, for example, between 1919 and 1958, 288 persons suffered life-threatening poisoning due to *A. phalloides* and *A. virosa*, and 87 (30 percent) of these persons died [12]. Other European reports have estimated the mortality to be as high as 63 percent [12]. Europeans know more about *Amanita* poisoning than we do.

The importance of one Czechoslovakian paper lay in stating that use of thioctic acid appeared to be associated with a greatly decreased mortality; 39 of 40 intoxicated persons survived [16]. Other reports have since confirmed this improvement in survival [17].

At the time of the episode of poisoning, there were no *original* case reports in English in thioctic acid for *Amanita* poisoning. Even so, the language barrier was not complete.

(2) *Limited Effectiveness of Early English-Language Reports:* In 1970 there were only three English-language references to thioctic acid, all of which were based on Kubicka's work and which were, in this sense, unoriginal. The most important of these three was a short anonymous annotation in the 1965 English publication, *Science Journal* [18]. This was neither a medical journal nor was it indexed in *Index Medicus*; but this annotation did influence the transmission of information about thioctic acid outside Europe. In a brief review, a physician in South Africa referred to it the following year in the *South African Medical Journal* [19]. This, in turn, helped to spread the news of thioctic acid because it referred to a brochure published by the Italian pharmaceutical firm that manufactured thioctic acid and because the author of the South African article regarded thioctic acid as most useful in the treatment of *Amanita* poisoning.

The third English-language reference on thioctic acid therapy for mushroom poisoning was just that, a reference [20]. This reference was a bare citation of one of Kubicka's later papers [21]; it was buried in a bibliography on the broad subject of poisoning in childhood.

Since there were, in 1970, only three references in the English language to thioctic therapy and since all three were secondary or tertiary references, it is not surprising that physicians (including journals' reviewers) on this continent were ignorant of the European methods of treatment of *Amanita* poisoning. Perhaps, therefore, it is not surprising that the *first original American* article on this topic, a topic both interesting and new, was rejected by four American medical journals before being accepted by the Philadelphia physician's peers.

(3) *Medical Journals' Rejection of the First English-Language Original Report of Thioctic Acid Therapy in AMANITA Poisoning:* The reasons for the rejection of the American physician's article were the following:

(a) Journal A, a national general medical journal: poor writing by the author; inadequate documentation of cases; misleading use of the word "new" in the title; lack of explanation of how the drug came to be used in Europe; superficial discussion of the mode of action of the drug; treatment of only one patient with thioctic acid; and the fact that in this patient one index of liver failure

(concentration of serum glutamic oxaloacetic transaminase) showed evidence of improvement on the day before thioctic acid was administered;
(b) Journal B, a journal dealing with internal medicine: simply that a negative decision had been reached;
(c) Journal C, a journal dealing with internal medicine: a backlog of patient reports, which would unduly delay publication of the manuscript;
(d) Journal D, a journal dealing with environmental medicine: unsuitable development of the paper, which might be more suited to a publication such as *GP* or *Family Physician* [3].

It is inappropriate for me to discuss these reasons at length. Brief observations, however, are in order.

First, neither the editors nor the reviewers commented on the general value of thioctic acid. I therefore sought the independent opinions of two physicians. One, the director of a poison control center, wrote [22], "I think thioctic acid is probably very useful in *Amanita* mushroom poisoning but I think more data is needed." The other, an internist with an interest in environmental medicine, wrote [23], "It would appear that thioctic acid may well have been of benefit" to the patient in question. Thioctic acid was news; the news came from a respected university; yet no interest was evinced by the editors and reviewers. Was this because they were unfamiliar with the literature?

Second, the paper was submitted to Journal A 5 months after the poisoning episode. The paper returned to the author from Journal D almost 1 year after the poisoning. The delay attributable to these four journals was 7 months; the total delay by the time the accepting journal had published the paper was 21 months [3].

Third, the circulation of the accepting journal was 13 500 in 1971. The figures for Journals A, B, C, and D in 1971 were, respectively, 212 510, 46 000, 60 695, and 8675 [24].

Fourth, the total communication process from the time of the poisoning episode to the time the paper on this subject was published was lengthy, discontinuous, and less effectual (in terms of readership) than the author had hoped.

Fifth, the relative failure of this communication process cannot be attributed solely to one party or one phase of the communication process. There were weaknesses at all points. The author, for example, submitted a paper that could be criticized for its presentation and content. The editors never made positive suggestions to assist the author in making an effective presentation appropriate to their journals, for example, a change in format to make it more acceptable (perhaps a brief "Letter to the Editor"). None of the reviewers submitted detailed comments, but this is consistent with the general ignorance about the subject in 1970.

And yet, the paper was eventually published in its original form before a relatively small readership. Ironically, while the paper was in press, an editorial on the subject of *Amanita* poisoning appeared in the widely read British medical journal, *The Lancet* [25]. This editorial did not refer to thioctic acid but it stimulated correspondence, and among the letters was one from three Hungarian doctors [17] who advocated, from their own experience, the therapy that the American physician had been trying, for 13 months, to report to his English-speaking fellow physicians.

The author's eventual success in having his article published also merits comment. The final form of his article was identical to the original form; that is, the accepting journal published this author's paper in the form in which it was rejected by Journals A, B, C, and D. Although his article was ultimately published, it is understandable why some journal editors had previously rejected it. There were three main reasons: (1) the writing and the presentation were ineffective; (2) the data presented were incomplete; and (3) the review of the literature through 1970 was fragmentary. With respect to the third point, there were at least 22 pertinent references to thioctic acid as a form of treatment for mushroom poisoning;[2] the author of the article referred to only 3. With respect to the first and second points, review of the final paper will readily demonstrate their validity.

The author, therefore, must be held largely responsible for the treatment his paper received. An author's work is as much part of a communication network as an editor's treatment of a paper and a reader's response to the paper.

C. Effects of Delayed Publication

The 16-month period of dealy in the publication of this paper had some interesting effects. These effects were of two types: (1) those modifying the communication process, and (2) those modifying the effectiveness with which the information was transmitted.

(1) *Modification of the Communication Process:* Just as the paper's author learned of thioctic acid through a medium other than the medical journal, so other physicians learned about the author's experience prior to publication through media other than the medical journal. Newspapers, letters, radio and telephone were all effective in this respect. It was as though the fundamental message was imbued with such energy that the entropy created by delays in publication was readily overcome, information naturally flowing through these other channels.

(2) *Modification of the Effectiveness of Information Transmission:* The author of the paper naturally hoped for early publication and a large readership. His opinion of thioctic acid was similar to that of the South African physician who had referred to thioctic acid in 1966 in these terms [19], "According to reports in the literature, thioctic acid is of outstanding value in the treatment of *Amanita phalloides* type of poisoning. I suggest that supplies of thioctic acid be immediately obtained...and made available to all hospitals and other institutions where cases of *Amanita phalloides* poisoning could possibly be treated." Information about thioctic acid, however, was not to be transmitted either speedily or widely, and in this sense the effectiveness of the transmission was impaired by publication delay.

[2]These references are listed in Appendix II.

IMPLICATIONS OF THE CASE HISTORY FOR THE FUTURE OF MEDICAL JOURNALS

The desire of all biomedical scientists to communicate information to their fellow scientists and physicians is a basic urge that will continue to influence the growth of the formal biomedical communication system. Within this system the medical journal retains an important role. Its general characteristics, however, have changed little over the years, and this lack of change is in sharp contrast to the dynamic and diverse change that characterizes the development of biomedical science and medical practice. It is likely, therefore, that from time to time biomedical scientist's communication of information will become impeded by the unchanging nature of the medical journal. The case that I have described appears to be an example of this situation; I believe that it also has certain implications for the future of medical journals. On the basis of these implications, I suggest certain recommendations to make medical journals effective media of communication in the future.

A. The Development of Communication Services to Assist Authors

The effective flow of information is essential to the development of medicine. Flow of information begins with the author, and to some extent the effectiveness of medical communication is the author's responsibility. But the busy physician seldom has the time or the training to make his presentation effective enough to assure himself of much wanted publication space.

To help him make his presentations effective, the physician-author should seek professional help. In the future, university or hospital departments of biomedical communication are likely to be of increasing value in this respect. Ideally an author's editor is in the best position to help an author, because the author's editor (a different species from the journal editor) can work closely with the author, for author and editor may work within the same institution. This type of help is superior to any other, whether this be copy editor's or science writer's.

Such help *before* authors submit papers to journals will provide the journals with more logical and more effective presentations at the beginning of the communication process.

B. The Changing Responsibilities of Journal Editors

As middle men linking author and reader, journal editors are in a unique position to relate authors' contributions to readers' needs. Most journal editors are aware of the specific features of this relationship and some appreciate the importance of making changes in this relationship as they become appropriate. It is likely, however, that most editors confine their horizons to the needs of their own particular journals. Editors should expand their horizons, so that they become effective participants in a wider communication network that encompasses more than one journal. A journal editor is in the unusual position of being the only one who knows what various authors submit to his journal; a group of editors would be in an even more remarkable position. Material could be matched to journals through the cooperation of journal editors, and publication delays might be shortened.

The possibilities of cooperation at this level are limitless. Editors might not only cooperate with each other; they might also assist in the formation of central pools or clearinghouses of information; they might work with specialty organizations; they might extend their cooperation to working with editors of many different countries; and they might similarly work with national and international conferences. To remain effective, journals should join international or national networks of information, and journal editors should play a greater part in helping to make information to the appropriate places. In this, the services of information specialists might well make journals more effective. Editors, too, should master information theory and practice.

C. Breaking Language Barriers

Scientific journals are published in an increasing number of languages; the average physician, however, continues to know the rudiments of one or, at the most, two languages in addition to his own. The importance of language as a barrier is nothing new; the effectiveness of the language barrier in obstructing the flow of information today is exemplified by the present case history; and language is certain to remain a barrier in the future. If medical journals are to remain effective as communication devices, the problem of foreign languages must be recognized and overcome.

The language barrier can be overcome or penetrated in a number of ways. Cooperation among journal editors is one. Participation in the UNISIST system [26] is another. Other ways are high-level international cooperation, greater use of several languages for abstracts, and use of translating machines or translating services. Unless information in foreign-language journals is communicated to English-speaking readers, information flow will remain incomplete and inadequate to the needs of the future.

D. Recognition of Changing Modes of Communication

Alternatives to the traditional journal have often been suggested. Devices such as separates, abstracts, and central storage of information are some of these, but all have the disadvantages of distance and discontinuity; and besides, they take away from readers the pleasures of browsing and serendipity. I believe that the journal can remain a journal and provide, at the same time, current information and pleasure in reading. But the journal can only do this if it is always attuned to effective methods of communication. Both form and content need attention from time to time. The introduction of the magazine format or the newspaper is one approach, but this is not always appropriate to all scientific journals. Publication of journals in conjunction with educational programs or symposia and even the stimulation by simultaneous publication of audiovisual aids such as slides or tapes might be one approach; the sponsoring of information transmission through videocassette, another.

Such experiments would be limited only by imagination and cost and might be considered outside the realm of journals. This may be so; but what I am suggesting is that journal editors and managers consider communication trends and consider how far the medical journal should be influenced by these trends. It is only through such awareness that the flow of information and the continuing education of the physician will be maintained, and this is what medical journalism is about.

APPENDIX I

SUMMARY OF CLINICAL CASE OF *AMANITA VERNA* POISONING

A 35-year-old man complained of the sudden onset of severe abdominal pain, nausea, and diarrhea 9 h after having eaten stew containing *Amanita verna* mushrooms. He was treated in his local hospital, being given fluids by intravenous infusion to correct dehydration. After 5 days, liver function tests revealed evidence of serious liver failure and he was transferred to a university hospital for further care.

The main findings were as follows: temperature, 100.6° F (rectal); pulse, 104 min; respiration, 20/min; blood pressure, 142/86 mmHg. His skin and eyes were jaundiced, the pupils being dilated and unreactive to bright light. The abdomen was diffusely tender. The serum electrolytes were normal and the blood urea nitrogen concentration was 22 mg/100 ml, but the prothrombin time was less than 10 percent of normal, the total bilirubin concentration was 7.6 mg/100 ml, the alkaline phosphatase concentration was 75 mu/ml, the serum glutamic oxaloacetic transaminase (SGOT) concentration was 2272 mu/ml, with a hematocrit of 46 vol%.

Because of hepatic encephalopathy, therapy with neomycin, hypertonic glucose, and potassium was begun. Fresh frozen plasma and concentrated blood factors 2, 7, 9, 10 were also given. Approximately 12 h later, the patient was more alert but hepatic coma remained intermittent. On the second day of hospitalization, the SGOT concentration was 2416 units, but it decreased thereafter. The bilirubin concentration was increasing, the other tests of liver function were unchanged, and liver enlargement together with ascites and peripheral edema became evident.

On the next day, thioctic acid was administered and continued for 6 days. At that time the prothombin time was 63 percent of normal, the SGOT concentration was 178 mu/ml, the bilirubin concentration was 16.2 mg/ml, ascites and peripheral edema were less marked, and the patient was able to tolerate a low-protein diet.

The patient continued to improve. The prothrombin time reached 93 percent of normal, the SGOT concentration decreased to 102 units, and the total bilirubin concentration to 3.5 mg/100 ml. A liver biopsy showed evidence of hepatic necrosis with repair, and no evidence of cirrhosis. Before he was discharged from the hospital, his diet was normal and no drugs were required.

APPENDIX II

LITERATURE THROUGH 1970 PERTINENT TO THE USE OF THIOCTIC ACID IN MUSHROOM POISONING

(1) J. Herink, *Otravy houbami (Pilzvergiftungen)*. Prague, Czechoslovakia, 1958, S46.
(2) L. Binet, M. Marquis, and D. Quivy, "Sur les troubles du metabolisme lipidique observe's chez le lapin au cours de l'intoxication phalloïdienne; influence de l'acide thioctique," *C. R. Acad. Sci.* (Paris), vol. 248, pp. 1461-1464, 1959.
(3) J. Kubicka, "Neue Möglichkeiten in der Behandlung von Vergiftungen mit dem Grünen Knollenblätterpilz-*Amanita phalloides*," *Mykol. mitt.*, vol. 7, pp. 92-94, 1963.
(4) G. von Obauer and H. Schön, "Experimentelle untersuchungen zur knollenblätterpilz-Vergiftung," *Arzeim. Forsch.*, vol. 18, pp. 1257-1259, 1964.
(5) J. Kubicka, "Prevence a léčba otrav muchomůrkou zelenou v jihočeském Kraji," *Prakt. Lek.*, vol. 44, pp. 702-704, 1964.
(6) ——"Beiträge zur Diagnostik und Therapie von Pilzvergiftungen durch Amanita phalloides (Knollenblätterschwamm)," *Z. arztl. Fortbild*, vol. 59, pp. 326-327, 1965.
(7) E. Nezbeda, "Mimoradny uspech ceskoslovenske lekarske vedy v leceni otiau muchomuzken zelenon (*Amanita phalloides*)," *Ceska Mykol.*, vol. 19, pp. 83-84, 1965.
(8) "Annotation: Treatment for poisoning from dangerous mushrooms," *Sci. J.*, vol. 1, p. 17, June 1965.
(9) D.G. Steyn, "The treatment of cases of *Amanita phalloides* and *Amanita capensis* poisoning," *S. Afr. Med. J.*, vol. 40, pp. 405-406, 1966.
(10) J. Kubicka, "Zwanzig jahre kampf gegen Pilzvergiftungen," *Schweiz. Lect. Pilzkunde*, vol. 46, p. 81, 1968.
(11) ——"La cura moderna degli avvelenamenti da Amanita phalloides," *Boll. Gruppo Micrologrio G. Bresadola*, vol. 11, p. 4, 1968.
(12) J. Kubicka and A.E. Alder, "Ueber eine neure Behandlingsmethode der Vergiftung durch den Knollenblättenpilz," *Praxis*, vol. 57, pp. 1304-1306, 1968.
(13) W. von Mittman, "Zur Klinik und Therapie der lorchelvergiftung (Gyromitra esculenta)," *Z. ärztl. Fortbild.*, vol. 62, pp. 710-713, 1968.
(14) M. Frimmer, G. Waldvogel, and G. Weil, "Schutzwirkung von Thioctsäure gegen die Kalium-freisetzende Wirkung des Phalloidins an der isoliert perfundierten Rattenleber," *Klin. Wochenschr.*, vol. 46, pp. 1288-1289, 1968.
(15) J. Kubicka, "Treatment of poisoning by Thioctic acid from *Amanita phalloides*," *Orv. Hetil.*, vol. 109, pp. 2765-2766, 1968.
(16) H. Akerblom, "Mushroom poisoning due to destroying angel [*Amanita virosa*]. A report of four cases in

children," *Ann. Paediat. Fen.*, vol. 14, no. 2, pp. 29-34, 1968.
(17) J. Kubicka, "Analysis of fatal mushroom poisoning treated with thioctic acid," *Cas. Lek. Ceska.*, vol. 108, pp. 790-793, 1968.
(18) H. von Rex and E. Schulze, "Die Hepatotoxizität verschiedener Pilzgifte," *Z. ärztl. Fortbild.*, vol. 63, pp. 851-856, 1969.
(19) T. Dyk, J. Piotrowska-Sowinska, and T. Buczkowska, "Próba oceny leczenia zatruć grzybami," *Pol. Tyg. Lek.*, vol. 24, pp. 1005-1007, 1969.
(20) "Bibliography on poisoning," *Pediatrics*, vol. 44, p. 895, 1969.
(21) H. Dabski, T. Drozd, and R. Bryc, "Leczenie zatruć muchomorem sromotnikawym tioktanowym," *Pol. Tyg. Lek.*, vol. 25, pp. 338-340, 1970.
(22) O. Zaffiri, R. Centi, A. Mastroianni, F. Francerseto, and M. Bisaini, "La terapia dell'avvelenamento acuto da amanita falloide con acido tioctico ad alte dosi," *Minerva Anestesiol.*, vol. 36, pp. 56-67, 1970.

REFERENCES

[1] D. Crane, *Invisible Colleges: Diffusion of Knowledge in Scientific Communities*. Chicago, Ill.: Univ. Chicago Press, 1972.
[2] A.J. Finestone, R. Berman, B. Widmer, et al., "Thioctic acid treatment of acute mushroom poisoning," *Penn. Med.*, vol. 75, pp. 49-51, 1972.
[3] A.J. Finestone, personal communication, 1972.
[4] J. Kubicka, "New possibilities in the treatment of poisoning by the deadly Amanita," *Mykol. Mitt.*, vol. 7, pp. 92-94, 1963.
[5] L.J. Reed, B.G. DeBusk, L.C. Gunsalus, et al., "Crystalline α-lipoic acid: A catalytic agent associated with pyruvate dehydrogenase," *Science*, vol. 114, pp. 93-94, 1951.
[6] *New York Times*, June 23, 1971.
[7] *New York Times*, June 17, 1971.
[8] *Halifax Chronicle-Herald*, June 25, 1971 (among numerous other newspapers publishing this report).
[9] *Annotation: Drug Combats Mushroom Poison*, Nature Science Annual. New York: Time-Life Books, 1971.
[10] J. Trager, *Bellybook*. New York: Grossman Publishers, 1972.
[11] J. Lough and D.G. Kinnear, "Mushroom poisoning in Canada. Report of a fatal case," *Can. Med. Assoc. J.*, vol. 102, pp. 858-860, 1970.
[12] A.E. Alder, "Erkennung und Behandlung der Pilzvergiftungen," *Deut. med. Wochenschr.*, vol. 86, pp. 1121-1127, 1961.
[13] *Newsweek*, Jan. 15, 1972.
[14] B.S. Olson, personal communication, 1973.
[15] S. Kaye, *Handbook of Emergency Toxicology*, 3rd ed. Springfield, Ill.: Charles C. Thomas, 1970.
[16] J. Kubicka, "Prevention and treatment of poisoning by Amanita phalloides," *Prakt. Lekar.*, vol. 44, pp. 702-704, 1964.
[17] R. Zulik, F. Bako, and J. Badavasi, "Death-cap poisoning," *Lancet*, vol. 2, p. 228, 1972.
[18] "Annotation: Treatment for poisoning from dangerous mushrooms," *Sci. J.*, vol. 1, p. 17, June 1965.
[19] D.G. Steyn, "The treatment of cases of *Amanita phalloides* and *Amanita capensis* poisoning," *S. Afr. Med. J.*, vol. 40, pp. 405-406, 1966.
[20] "Bibliography on poisoning," *Pediatrics*, vol. 44, p. 895, 1969.
[21] J. Kubicka, "Contribution to the diagnosis and therapy of mushroom poisoning by *Amanita phalloides* (death cap)," *Z. arztl. Fortbild*, vol. 59, pp. 326-327, 1966.
[22] J.P. Anderson, personal communication, 1972.
[23] F.T. Nobrega, personal communication, 1972.
[24] *Ulrich's International Periodicals Directory*. New York: R.R. Bowker Company, 1972.
[25] "Death-cap poisoning," *Lancet*, vol. 1, p. 1320, 1972.
[26] UNISIST: *Synopsis of the Feasibility Study on a World Science Information System*. United Nations Educational, Scientific, and Cultural Organization, Paris, France, 1971.

4 THE REFEREEING OF SCIENTIFIC JOURNALS

4. THE REFEREEING OF SCIENTIFIC JOURNALS

Some aspects of journal publication seem to generate more controversy than others. An activity that often leads to debate is the process of evaluating manuscripts for publication. As we have seen in the preceding section, many authors feel themselves under pressure to publish. Most authors have also invested considerable time and effort in the papers they submit. Hence, rejection of a paper is seen as a major personal blow. Ranged against this reaction is the typical emphasis of the scientific community as a whole on the need for thorough refereeing of submitted material, so as to prevent the publication of inferior results. Some tension is unavoidable in this situation.

I have taken the liberty of including one of my own papers in this section, and, consequently, I can cut short my comments here. There is one point, however, which the selected papers may not sufficiently emphasise. Both in principle and, usually, in practice, the fundamental role in the evaluation of manuscripts is played by the journal editors, rather than by the external referees to whom the papers may be sent. Editors normally carry out a preliminary sorting of incoming manuscripts, and may often reject a considerable proportion without invoking external assessors. Again, editors generally choose the referees for each manuscript, and all experienced editors agree that this choice can be vital. By selecting one referee, they can enhance the likelihood of a paper being accepted; by selecting another, they can enhance the probability of rejection. Above all, editors play a vital role in deciding journal policy. This must always include an assessment of how many papers they can afford to publish each year, which, in turn, must act as an ultimate limitation on what papers can be accepted.

As this suggests, the evaluation of research material submitted to a scientific journal is an activity that is not totally independent of all its other operations, although it is often treated separately. Hence, the nature of the evaluation process has changed in detail as science has developed, though the need for some kind of evaluation has always existed.

The Scientific Referee

FRANK T. MANHEIM

Abstract—In the May 1973 issue of *EOS*, I criticized tendencies in earth science periodicals to discourage referee anonymity. I stressed that exposing referees to unnecessary personal and subjective influences tended to degrade standards of quality and promoted cliques, fragmentation, superspecialization, and proliferation of scientific literature. Generally speaking, division of opinion on this question, based on letters and personal contacts since 1973, has tended (with notable exceptions) to divide along two lines: the "wise old heads" favor anonymity, whereas many young idealists favor openness. Referees can help keep literature standards high (there is no evidence that they can or do thwart new ideas, determinedly pushed), but they can do little to stop literature proliferation. If individuals do scientific work, they may as well publish or not do it at all. The only real solutions to literature proliferation are fewer scientists or a drastic paper shortage, as experienced in Bulgaria.

There are two conditions under which one can be poorly informed: when there is not enough information, and when there is too much. In general, most scientists agree with the consensus of contributors to the 1973 Conference on the Future of Scientific and Technical Journals [24] that the lines of scientific communication have become so jammed that it is often hard to discern the message from the background crackle. How to cope is a more controversial matter. Some favor more rapid and efficient transmittal of information, whereas others imply that we have reached the point of futility and ought to cut back [11] and [27]. A well-known quote of British physicist Ziman [27] expresses this view eloquently:

> Not only is there too much scientific work being published; there is much too much of it . . . the need to get recognition by publication forces each of us to shout a little longer and louder so as to be noticed at all in the gathering, swelling crowd of voices . . . . The result has been a proliferation of semi-literate, semi-scientific, half-baked and trivial material which threatens to swamp the whole system.

The referee is one of the few noise filters available, and hence one might presume that his role is and will remain an essential one. However, not all agree with the majority view; some have favored ritualizing, downgrading, or disposing of the referee's function entirely. This survey is an attempt to review briefly refereeing, its ramifications, and possible role in the future.

BACKGROUND

Few aspects of science and scientists' habits have not been put under the microscope by Merton [17, and references cited therein], and the referee system is no exception. The following section will borrow heavily from a searching inquiry into the history and function of referees by Zuckerman and Merton [28].

The practice of refereeing scientific periodicals has roots far back in the history of formal scientific publication. The *Philosophical Transactions* of the Royal Society included in its authorizing statement (1664-1665) the following: ". . . the tract . . . being first reviewed by some members of . . . the Council . . . ." However, the practice of refereeing publications is still by no means universal. Whereas a 1962 sampling showed only 2 of 49 journals published in the United States made no use of referees, 9 of 30 French journals did not do so. In the Soviet Union the use of peer review, in the Anglo-Saxon sense (as contrasted with a fixed editorial board) is relatively uncommon.

Western humanistic journals arrived much later at the widespread use of referees than did natural science periodicals. Moreover, patterns of manuscript treatment vary quite widely in different fields, as Table I shows.

TABLE I
Rates of Rejection of Manuscripts by 1967 Journals
(taken from [28])

Field	Mean Rejection Rate	Number of Journals
History	90	3
Language and literature	86	5
Philosophy	85	5
Political science	84	2
Sociology	78	14
Psychology (excluding experimental and physiological)	70	7
Economics	69	4
Experimental and physiological psychology	51	2
Mathematics and statistics	50	5
Anthropology	48	2
Chemistry	31	5
Geography	30	2
Biological sciences	29	12
Physics	24	12
Geology	22	2
Linguistics (mathematical orientation)	20	1

According to Zuckerman and Merton, many of the papers fended off by the humanistic journals are already rejected by editors as having little hope of favorable treatment by reviewers, no matter who they might be.

It has been pointed out in the current meeting that one reason for the disparity between the humanistic and the natural science rejection rates is that to pursue natural science fields frequently requires equipment and facilities. Getting these may have already put the author through a first gauntlet of grant proposal or project authorization. In contrast, articles submitted to humanistic journals may run the gamut from observations on high school classes by teachers to reports on full-scale research programs. Other differences include lesser financial support, less rigorously defined and testable problems, and a tendency toward favoring specialized approaches for the humanistic journals.

Since the report by Zuckerman and Merton, natural science rejection rates have risen in most fields.[1] A recent survey of journals in some 45 fields made by Juhasz [12] yielded a mean rejection rate of about 37 percent.

Checks on treatment by referees of manuscripts to *Physical Review*, the premier physics periodical, revealed a surprising lack of bias based on rank and age of referees and submittors. Moreover, referees were highly likely to agree in their ratings of papers. In physics, at any rate, these facts speak for a significant degree of internalization and institutionalization of scientific standards by the community as a whole. Where such self-discipline is strong, even lightly refereed or edited journals may be affected by the common standards [18].

It has been widely noted that many natural science rejections often end up published in other journals, lowering the real rejection rate. Moreover, natural scientists do not always submit quietly to critical treatment of their brainchildren: as Abelson [1] says, "I doubt that (a female grizzly bear) could match in ill temper some of the authors I have met." He subsequently implies that even an editor as tough as he must compromise else he will lose his effectiveness.

The high percentage of acceptance of manuscripts in natural science and engineering journals does not mean that the average worker is doing a lot of publishing in them. As already shown by Lotka [13] and referred to by Price [20] as "Lotka's law," an astonishingly small proportion of scientists are responsible for most of the publications. Lotka's law states that the number of people producing n papers is proportional to $1/n^2$. Thus, for every 1000 scientists who produce 3 papers in their lifetimes, there are 100 who produce 10 and there is 1 who produces 100. In practice, the curve flattens out for higher numbers of papers, and trends suggest that publishing pressure at universities has also tended to squeeze more papers out of the reluctant majority. Price's widely publicized thesis asserts that a relatively few scientists not only dominate the literature numerically, but their productivity can be equated with distinction and influence. One can understand that referees focus on members of the invisible colleges rather than the "silent majority." On the other hand, editors and publishers who are dependent on the financial contributions of readers and purchaser institutions must consider broad demand. Further, as discussed later, the practical impact of the elitists on society at large is, as contrasted with their impact on their own specialty literature, still poorly documented. Finally, the science sociologists have largely dealt with the more theoretical or basic science literature, rather than with applied science, engineering, and semitrade journals which may show different phenomena.

ROLE OF THE REFEREE

In many respects the referee's role has not changed significantly with time. His functions include the following:

1) serve as a judge of work quality and subject matter meeting the standards of publication of a given journal;
2) serve as an arbiter of priority or novelty through presumed knowledge of the pertinent literature;
3) recommend changes or specific length reductions in papers that are accepted conditionally;
4) take the heat off editors by absorbing the responsibility for unfavorable decisions;
5) lend stature or certification of professional acceptance to a publication by virtue of his distinction (collectively, with other referees) or high qualifications in the field.

Referees have been aptly called the gatekeepers of science [7]. An idealistic view of the Anglo-Saxon use of referees is given by Ziman [26]: "The referee is the lynchpin about which the whole business of Science is pivoted. His job is simply to report, as an expert, on the value of a paper submitted to a journal. He must say whether the results claimed are of scientific interest, whether they are authenticated and made credible by sound experimental methods and good logic, whether the paper is well expressed, not too cryptic nor too verbose, with adequate references, etc. He reports to the editor, and although this report may be sent to the author for action or rebuttal, he is protected by anonymity."

Blume [5] criticizes the preceding characterization as oversimplified. He points out Whitley's survey of British social science journals, in which it was found that editors exercised a very considerable degree of personal control over the content of their journals. In many cases referees' opinions are used selectively to justify the opinions of the editors. Recently the journal *Ecology* editorialized about the intellectual censorship which frequently occurs at editorial and referee levels, and gave numerous examples [25].

From a different point of view Prinz [22] has pointed out that referees do not always refrain from taking advantage of hot new information in highly competitive and rapidly developing fields. Even delaying a competitor may create personal advantage.

Some apparently constructive functions of referees may have less obvious consequences. The practice of improving manuscripts through the criticisms of referees has been criticized by the author [14] as a perversion of the role of referee from arbiter of quality to a colleague or even a school master. It has been suggested that this practice causes undesirable proliferation of the literature by raising to publishable levels manuscripts that could not have been accepted otherwise. Here one must carefully distinguish between the unquestioned benefit provided to individual papers and the

---

[1]Abelson's *Science*, which leads in circulation in the United States (circulation 154 000) among scholarly journals [except for the *Journal of the American Medical Society* (circulation 239 000)], at recent report accepts less than 20 percent of manuscripts.

overall influence of the practice in encouraging sloppiness and poor scholarship.

In recent years practices have arisen that tend to undermine the objectivity of the referee and to promote clique development. One such tendency is the move among a number of earth science journals, such as the *Bulletin of the Geological Society of America*, *Geochimica et Cosmochimica Acta*, and the *Journal of Geophysical Research*, to remove anonymity from their referees.

REFEREE ANONYMITY REVISITED

In 1973 I criticized the practice of exposing referees or putting psychological pressure on them to choose identification [14]. Though arguments in favor of such practices can be appreciated, I held that the disadvantages far outweighed the advantages. Chief among the flaws is the introduction of interpersonal relationships into the decision-making process in a way that, in my view, potentially inhibits the delivery of truly forthright opinion on papers. The practice can act directly or indirectly to increase the proliferation of schools and subdisciplines, and hence the fragmentation and unnecessary hyperspecialization of science. In this context one may consider the curious necessity of secret ballots to assure free elections in free societies, where decisions of consequence were to be made.

Since that paper appeared, correspondence and personal contacts have elicited some interesting reactions; senior researchers and scientists with a wide publication experience tend to support anonymity, whereas idealistic young scientists tend to be neutral or favor disclosure. The thought that personal factors could interfere with fair decision making appears to be particularly abhorrent. The image of the scientist as a selfless seeker after truth is clearly still cherished by some in a fashion that does not easily admit to the need for safeguards to undergird virtue.

WILL REFEREES AND JOURNALS SURVIVE?

There is a surprisingly modern and novel flavor about suggestions that journals will collapse or should be phased out in favor of centralized and user-oriented informational systems. I say surprising because the first major proposal along these lines was launched by Bernal [3] nearly 36 years ago. The detailed scheme proposed by the young British physicist included a Marxist view on redirecting science and technology to the public benefit. Bernal had little use for referees and realized that his Scientific Information Institute (SII) must fully replace competing media to be successful: "The success of S.I.I. will depend upon incorporating into it most of the existing media of scientific publications and bibliography. It will be a monopoly in the same sense that the post office department is a monopoly, operated for public benefit without profit. If it is not practically all-inclusive, it will fail."

Death knells and alarms have subsequently been sounded at regular intervals: "If we do not find some way of abstracting the abstracts, it may well happen that the printed research paper will be doomed ... " [19]. "Primary journals in their present form cannot survive because of the forthcoming overwhelming increase in technical information. Future indexing, storage, and retrieval of technical papers will have to be done through specialized multidisciplinary international organizations ... " [16].

Some cries of alarm about the survival of books and journals have been related, especially by publishers' spokesmen, to the economic threats posed by duplication by individuals and libraries [2]. In my opinion, certain publishers' practices that began in the post-World War II period have had a far more erosive influence on the health of scientific publication and the referee's function in keeping the literature lean and useful. I refer here to what Herschman [10] has called the "Maxwell principle."

In the pre-World War II period Western books and journals were to a considerable degree published and priced with the individual scientist-purchasers in mind. In the case of books, permanence and authoritativeness of content were stressed because such qualities lent themselves to larger press runs and more editions. It was apparently first realized by Pergamon Press, under Robert Maxwell, that with the upsurge of scientific activity enough institutional purchasers (e.g., libraries) were available to market a greatly expanded and more specialized published product, provided that the subject matter was "pertinent," or in the case of journals, that respectability was guaranteed by a masthead of certified authorities or society sponsorship. The pioneer was soon followed by others, notably Elsevier.

With book prices basically determined by a fixed number of institutions, individual purchasers or permanence became less important, or could be virtually ignored in the publishing equation. By no means all publishing houses followed this trend, but relatively few were needed to expand greatly the horizon of the publishable, with the net result of both price increases and proliferation of specialized literature having highly variable standards. The importance of gatekeepers declined because so many new gates were being constructed. That some hardnosed gatekeepers kept watch did not serve to slacken the onrush of the multitudes, because friendlier gatekeepers could always be found. The analogy has flaws, but is applicable from the point of view of the library or scholarly publishers, if we consider the public moving into different subarenas, rather than one large one. There are simply fewer dollars available for each gate (publisher) or for upkeep of the arena (library).

The last 10 years have seen stimulus by the National Science Foundation and several attempts at implementing computerized systems for replacing part or all of traditional journal functions, but most have had at best partial success. The American Psychological Association (APA) made a bold attempt to replace journals and preprint circulation. It set up a central clearinghouse of papers to be distributed rapidly according to need and interest of workers. However, the APA apparently misjudged the psychology of the psychologists, for the system ran into serious criticism [6]. Experiments in this line made by the American Institute of Aeronautics and Astronautics (AIAA) [8] showed member acceptance of selective dissemination of documents and miniprints for part of the literature, but opposition to complete replacement of traditional papers by the new media. Scientists are evidently willing to accept selective dissemination, microformats, etc., for the "other guy," and for subjects that are of peripheral interest, but are reluctant to give up hard-copy journal format for their publication or for topics of central interest to them. One cynic remarked that selective dissemination was perhaps less useful for retrieving information than for decently interring it. An NSF official, while predicting virtually complete electronic communication by the end of the century, admitted that one might end up transferring a mass of irrelevant information magnificently by high technology [4].

Information retrieval and dissemination systems can facilitate literature searches and provide increased efficiency in retrieval, communication, and manipulation of data, but they cannot replace prestigious outlets that stress or imply access to superior judgment and creativity or authoritativeness; and, most important, they cannot provide professional credentials to authors. Most universities now distinguish between refereed (hard-copy-high-visibility) and nonrefereed publication productivity in making their promotion, tenure, and salary increase recommendations.

Some of us harbor an exquisite ambivalence about basic science journals: we want them but would cheer if half of existing journals folded, thus simplifying our agonizing informational problems and relieving financial pressure on libraries and the top publishers. But this would also exacerbate problems in getting scientists' own papers accepted in respected media. In a choice, I suspect that the latter need may prevail.

Thus, I predict that as long as governments or other institutions fund scientists, they will find themselves directly or indirectly funding scientists' preferred information media, hard-copy journals and books. To the extent that electronic, photo, and computer techniques can provide archival and reference functions that can be made affordable to small scientific units, they may play an increasing role in complementing and supporting the prime media (not the other way around).

Whereas U.S. scholarly journals depend strongly on referees at present, other systems have shown ability to operate without them. As implied by Blume [5] the continued existence of the peer referees probably depends partly on their performance, and partly on whether the values of the sponsoring society continue to lie in furthering the presumptive goals of skepticism, disinterestedness, commonality of ownership of scientific contributions, and rationality. All gradations of attack on these latter precepts have emerged [15], [23], and we do not know where the future will lead.

ELITISM OVERRATED?

It is possible that Price [21] has overrated the influence of the invisible colleges and elitists in the natural sciences on the real affairs of society. I have made a private list of hot fields of the last 30 or so years in earth science and oceanography. Generations of distinguished academic and industry scientists have made their reputations in these areas, but significant practical developments have simply ignored most of the scientifically fashionable topics and theories, even those which have not been rendered obsolete; in some cases the cycles of acceptance and rejection of given ideas have been repeated more than once. Given the constraints of "contemporary standards," how does the referee's performance look in hindsight? It is hard to avoid the conclusion that during the "golden 60's" much of big science became more of an esthetic art form and sport for its practitioners than meaningful for the country at large.

I certainly do not intend to deprecate areas of scholarship because they may not be "useful," but it is clear that many enterprises were sold to the electorate and government on their ultimate utility, and a much more questioning attitude has been growing. In my view it would be very fruitful to study the "milestones" of science in the past, say 30-50 years, and examine both their permanence, and if possible, their critical ratings at submission. It has been intimated [9] that referees' ratings of incoming papers in some investigated areas have borne little relation to the ultimate significance of those papers as indicated by subsequent frequence of citation, via the *Science Citation Index*. Perhaps one can begin to go beyond mere frequency of citation to look at actual permanence of the contributions. Can we influence publication strategy to favor more solid and longer lived contributions via the referee system? It may be worthwhile finding out.

CAN WE BE OUR OWN "MERTONIAN SOCIOLOGISTS?"

I personally regard symposia such as this one and other pauses for reflection very healthy. For too long science has been outfitted with rational and objective external trappings while major objectives, patterns of operation, and the ramifications of our informational systems have often been guided by drift, passing inspirations and enthusiasms, and financial considerations. Some of these gaps have been noted by sociologists, who have been busy constructing a new subfield of the sociology of science ("Mertonian sociology"). Before their subdiscipline is completely walled off from those who are being described, via specialized jargon, literature, or externally incomprehensible constructs (all potentially wieldable by referees, of course) I think it would benefit all of our individual disciplines to articulate our basic philosophical objectives and communications problems. In the context of such broader awareness I feel that referees, imperfect and subjective as they are, may continue as our most powerful quality control aid.

As to the proliferation of literature, referees only man the gates; they do not really determine how many papers are to be let through. There seem to be two things we can do to reduce publication: 1) induce a paper shortage, which in Bulgaria has given rise to a remarkably succinct scientific literature, and 2) reduce the number of working scientists.

REFERENCES

[1] P.H. Abelson, "The coming evolution of scientific journals," *IEEE Trans. Prof. Commun.*, vol. PC-16, pp. 69-70, Sept. 1973.

[2] C.G. Benjamin, "Who will save the scholarly book?" *Amer. Scholar*, vol. 41, pp. 212-221, 1972.
[3] J.D. Bernal, *The Social Function of Science*. London: Routledge and Kegan, 1939; paperback ed. M.I.T. Press, Cambridge, Mass. 1967.
[4] L. Burchinal, Lecture at current meeting, 1975. "Microforms and Electronic Publication. Emerging Bases for Scientific Communication," this issue, pp. 174-176.
[5] S.S. Blume, *Toward a Political Sociology of Science*. New York: Free Press-MacMillan, 1974.
[6] P. Boffey, "Psychology: Apprehension over a new communication system," *Science*, vol. 167, p. 1228, 1970.
[7] D. Crane, "The gatekeepers of science: Some factors affecting the selections of articles for scientific journals," *Amer. Sociol.*, vol. 2, pp. 195-201, 1967.
[8] G.L. Dugger, R.F. Bryans, and W.T. Morris, Jr., "AIAA experiments and results on SSD, synoptics, miniprints, and related topics," *IEEE Trans. Prof. Commun.*, vol. PC-16, pp. 100-106, Sept. 1973.
[9] E. Garfield, personal communication, 1975.
[10] A. Herschman, In Session V, Roundup and Critique, *IEEE Trans. Prof. Commun.*, vol. PC-16, pp. 156-158, 1973.
[11] M.K. Hubbert, "Are we retrogressing in science?" *Bull. Geol. Soc. Amer.*, vol. 74, pp. 365-378, 1963.
[12] S. Juhasz, "Acceptance and rejection of manuscripts," this issue, pp. 177-185.
[13] A.J. Lotka, "The frequency distribution of scientific productivity," *J. Washington Acad. Sci.*, vol. 16, cited in Price [20, p. 43].
[14] F.T. Manheim, "Referees and the publications crisis," *EOS*, vol. 54, pp. 532-537, 1973.
[15] A.H. Maslow, *The Psychology of Science*. Chicago: Regnery, 1966.
[16] R. Maxwell, "Survival values in technical journals," *IEEE Trans. Prof. Commun.*, vol. PC-16, pp. 64-65, Sept. 1973.
[17] R.K. Merton, *The Sociology of Science*, Chicago: Univ. Chicago Press, 1973.
[18] S. Pasternack, "Is journal publication obsolescent?" *Phys. Today*, vol. 19, pp. 38-43, 1966.
[19] D.J. de Solla Price, *Science Since Bablyon*. New Haven, Conn.: Yale Univ. Press, 1961.
[20] _____, *Little Science, Big Science*. New York: Columbia Univ. Press, 1963.
[21] _____, "Some remarks on elitism in information and the invisible college phenomenon in science," *J. Amer. Soc. Inform. Sci.*, vol. 22, pp. 74-75, 1971.
[22] A.G. Prinz, cited in Zuckerman and Merton [28, p. 493].
[23] T. Roszak, *Making of a Counter-Culture*. Garden City, N.Y.: Doubleday, 1969.
[24] *IEEE Trans. Prof. Commun. (Rec., Conf. Future of Scientific and Technical Journals)*, vol. PC-16, pp. 50-182, Sept. 1973.
[25] L. Van Valen, and F.A. Pitelka, "Commentary—Intellectual censorship in ecology," *Ecology*, vol. 55, pp. 925-926, 1974.
[26] J.M. Ziman, *Public Knowledge*. New York: Cambridge Univ. Press, 1968.
[27] _____, "Ziman plays Cassandra," *New Scientists*, vol. 46, pp. 212-213, 1970.
[28] H.A. Zuckerman and R.K. Merton, "Patterns of evaluation in science: Institutionalization, structure, and functions of the referee system," *Minerva*, vol. 9, pp. 66-100, 1971.

The Problem of Refereeing

A. JACK MEADOWS
University of Leicester

I   INTRODUCTION

The refereeing of research papers prior to their publication is a long-standing practice in the academic world, though the way in which it has been implemented has varied from journal to journal, as well as at different periods in the history of individual journals. The prime reason advanced for the imposition of refereeing is, of course the need to guarantee an acceptable standard for published research work. Refereeing is therefore often seen as an essential defence against bad science; it allows scientists to accept published work on faith, without a constant rechecking of its accuracy.

An article in a reputable journal does not merely represent the opinions of its authors; it bears the *imprimatur* of scientific authenticity, as given to it by the editor and the referee whom he may have consulted. The referee is the lynchpin about which the whole business of science is pivoted[1].

Most authors would, nevertheless, agree that the refereeing system, as normally operated, has disadvantages. The most obvious of these is the additional time delay it introduces into the publishing process; but other doubts (e.g. as to the efficiency of refereeing) exist, and will be discussed below. These drawbacks are normally borne by authors with a degree of resignation, since they are described as a moderate price to pay for the advantages of quality control.

My aim in this article is to suggest that the link between refereeing and research standards is less clear-cut than is generally supposed. It is certainly necessary to provide some monitoring of the research material that is submitted to journals, but a more relaxed approach to refereeing may well be feasible in the light of available evidence. Such an approach would certainly simplify journal production; at the same time, it might remove some of the objections of authors to current refereeing practices.

II   REFEREEING AND JOURNAL PRODUCTION

Queries concerning the refereeing process fall into two categories — one relating to its cost in terms of time and money; the other to its efficiency. In this section, we examine the question of cost.

Reprinted from *Scienta*, Annus LXXI, IX - X - XI - XII 1977, vol. 112, p. 787-94, by permission of the publisher.

The direct cost to a publisher of handling refereeing (i.e. postal charges, time of office staff involved, etc.), can run into hundreds, or thousands, of pounds, depending on the number of papers submitted for consideration. Some American journals are thinking of introducing, or already have introduced, handling charges for every paper received, to cover this cost. The amount demanded is of the order of £10 per paper, and this figure probably approximates fairly well to the direct cost. However, one must also note the indirect costs of refereeing; in particular, the cost-equivalent of the time that referees devote to their work. It is hard to put a figure on this, but we can argue in the following way. Referees of scientific papers, on average, spend only a few hours over the task[2]. The cost of this time depends on the *status* of the referee. Although a greater number of junior scientists is asked to act as referees, each senior scientist tends to be used more frequently; so that junior and senior scientists are used equally. Hence, in money terms, the 'average' scientist lies somewhere in the middle of the salary scale. This implies that the hidden cost of refereeing (not allowing for various overheads) is of the same order of magnitude as the direct costs.

Although the financial aspect of the refereeing system cannot be totally ignored, it is seldom this part of the process that evokes protest from participants. Rather, their main question, as authors, concerns the interruption in the flow of publication that is introduced by refereeing. A referee may only take a short time to assess a paper; but the paper may have been resting in his in-tray for days, or weeks, beforehand, and may not be promptly returned to the editor afterwards. Most currently available information on refereeing process relates to U.S. journals[3]. For this reason, we shall be using predominantly U.S. data in this paper. We find that surveys in the U.S.A. do provide quantitative backing for the common belief amongst authors that refereeing not only appreciably delays the publication of a paper, but, moreover, that the delay varies in no very systematic way from paper to paper.

As an example of the first point, we may note that the American Institute of Physics in recent years has aimed to take three months over the reviewing process and an equal length of time for the actual process of publication. Hence, half of the time between the receipt of a manuscript and its final appearance in publication form is taken up with various aspects of refereeing. The second point — the spread of referees' reply times — can be illustrated from the experience of one social science journal in the United States that avowedly hoped to elicit replies from its referees within two weeks. In fact, only 30 per cent of the papers sent out to referees were returned within this time-limit. The actual period taken to reply varied from less than a week (for 8 per cent of the contributions) to more than six weeks (for 19 per cent of the contributions). The article that reported these data concluded: it would seem that referees who procrastinate are a major bottleneck in the editorial process[4].

Even if all referees were punctilious in their return of manuscripts, there would still be a spread in the times required for refereeing. Manuscripts that are involved in some form of controversy — for example, those rejected by one referee, but accepted by another — are almost invariably delayed, sometimes by a year or more[5]. Unfortunately, as will be noted below, more significant papers tend also to be more controversial, and so are likely to be subjected to above-average delays.

Irritation with these delays has led to various attempts to circumvent them. The most interesting approach — so far as refereeing is concerned — has hinged on the establishment of preprint exchange groups. These were intended to formalize the distribution of preprints by setting up an exchange system, perhaps run through a central office. For example, there was an ambitious scheme to set up a Physics Information Exchange for research workers in theoretical high-energy physics during the early 1960s. All such attempts have, however, been censured, especially by the editors of existing journals, as creating the equivalent of unrefereed journals. This opposition has been a significant factor in preventing the establishment of a widespread formalized system of preprint distribution. The desire to form such groups nevertheless indicates very clearly the impatience felt towards established refereeing procedures by authors in rapidly expanding fields of research.

III THE RELIABILITY OF THE REFEREEING PROCESS

If one main objection to refereeing is the delay which it introduces into publication, another, at least equally important, is the uncertain reliability of the refereeing process.

Refereeing might be considered unreliable for two reasons:
1) because referees judgements are factually incorrect;
2) because of an inherent, or even deliberate, bias on the part of a referee against (or towards) a particular kind of approach, or author. (These two possibilities are not, of course, mutually exclusive.)

The first thing to say is that biassed judgement by the referee due to the position held by the author (e.g. academic seniority, institutional affiliation) seems not to be a factor of major importance. Surveys have found some possible correlations of this type[6], but they are sufficiently small to allow, for the purpose of our present discussion, an examination of the reliability of refereeing in terms of the scientific community as a whole. It is worth beginning by pointing out that the refereeing process has, by its nature, an inbuilt bias. A person who is asked to referee a paper more often than not sees this as an invitation to criticise the paper. Consequently, referees' reports tend to overplay weak points, and to under-emphasize good points. Since, as we shall remark again below, innovative papers are more likely to be open to criticism, this 'adversary' approach may discriminate against them.

An obvious sign of unreliability in a referee's comments occurs when they contain errors of fact. Data on the incidence of erroneous criticisms by referees are naturally hard to find, but such errors may happen more frequently than is generally supposed.

For example, an author in one biomedical field has estimated that a fifth of the referees' reports contain a major factual error. He comments: «There is serious objective evidence that some referees, and even some highly respected ones in top academic positions, are at best ignorant and careless and at the worst deliberately destructive»[7]. In some instances, authors may never know of the error, since editors often do not transmit all the comments of a referee. One reason for the occurrence of such factual misstatements is the difficulty of matching author and referee. An author, almost by definition, is immersed in the subject matter of his paper, but this is not always true of the referee. Indeed, since most researchers change their fields of interest at intervals, editors' ideas of suitable referees are always slightly out of date.

There is another aspect of errors in submitted papers that reflects on the refereeing process — this is the extent to which genuine errors are detected by referees. Clearly, some incorrect material passes undetected by referees, since scrutiny of some papers in depth would require days, rather than hours, of effort on the part of the referee. So long as the error is actually contained in the paper, however, its occurrence is seldom disastrous. Anyone who subsequently attempts to make detailed use of the paper is likely to detect significant mistakes. Much more important are the errors that cannot be detected directly. These fall into two categories. Firstly, the attempt by an author in writing a paper to present results in the most favourable light can lead to a suppression, or distortion, of some of the evidence. Secondly, an author's interpretation of his, or her, results may be biassed by theoretical expectations. These factors can be very difficult for a referee to discern. For example, an analysis of the original data reported in a series of psychology papers indicated that three out of seven of the papers incorrectly interpreted the data[8]. This could not be detected by referees. Similarly, one could cite the recent instance of a series of biochemical papers, based on spurious research data, all of which were published in properly refereed journals. Refereeing has the basic limitation that it only looks at the final product, and the latter depends on the authors' skill at presentation as well as on the intrinsic value of the research results.

Assessing the reliability of refereeing judgements is by no means easy, since it may, itself, depend on value judgements by the assessor. One reasonable mode of approach, however, is to examine the incidence of disagreement between referees when the same paper is submitted to two, or more, of them. The extreme example of such disagreement — recommendation of rejection by one referee and recommendation of acceptance by another — is relatively easy to measure, and some figures are available for U.S. journals. Agreement between referees is good for physics; opposing recommendations were made for only 3 per cent of the pairs of reports investigated[9]. On the other hand, disagreement for biomedical papers is much more marked, occurring in 25 per cent of the cases studied[10]. This latter proportion is sufficiently high to raise a serious query as to the objectivity of refereeing in biomedical subjects.

Even when referees agree in their judgement of a paper, their opinions may not subsequently be endorsed by the scientific community at large. A recent U.S. study of the refereeing of chemical papers suggests that this may, indeed, sometimes be true. It compared the evaluation of papers by referees with later reader assessments, as measured especially by citation counts and informed opinion. The main conclusion is expressed as follows. «Our results are not favorable to the referees... A significant relationship is found, but one which would indicate that papers that become highly cited received generally lower referee evaluations than papers which were cited less frequently »[11]. As a generalization from this, we can say that the more original and speculative papers, if they trigger any response at all, tend to be more widely quoted. Equally, however, they are more likely to be viewed adversely by referees than, for example, papers reporting straightforward experimental results. The ultimate consequence of this is that papers later judged to be of major scientific significance, may initially run into severe refereeing problems. As one example from many, we may note that in nuclear physics in the years before the Second World War at least three major theoretical contributions are said to have been initially rejected by referees[12].

Innovatory papers also seem to be especially prone to criticism by referees on the grounds that they do not adequately acknowledge prior research. Typically a dispute develops when a referee insists that work already in the literature (often carried out by himself or his associates) should be acknowledged in a paper, whilst the author believes that this work is largely irrelevant to his own advances. We can quote again here from the investigation of U.S. chemical papers mentioned previously. «In one case, a referee went as far as to accuse the authors of plagiarism. In a few other cases, the accusations were couched in less extreme terms for example, by suggesting the authors had not acknowledged or cited the real sources of their ideas».

If the allegedly uncited work is by the referee, the latter is clearly in an advantaged position for pressing the point. The perfectly legitimate objection here can shade off sometimes in to the illegitimate. More generally, malpractice in refereeing, on the rare occasions when it occurs, consists primarily of delaying, or blocking, the publication of a paper for personal motives. Hardly surprisingly, there is little evidence in this area, but we can quote the following.

«One referee... caused a delay of over a year in the publication of this paper, requiring first prescribed revision and then a revision of the revisions prescribed by him. In the meantime he had published a paper which took some of the sting out of our paper»[13].

Such occurrences, even if infrequent, introduce an inevitable note of suspicion into the refereeing process. This is enhanced by the customary anonymity of most refereeing comment — something that has been bitterly attacked by a number of authors in recent years. As a consequence, authors are always prone to suspect that referees' comments are not entirely disinterested.

IV MODIFYING THE REFEREEING SYSTEM

We have looked at two criticisms of the refereeing system as it is currently implemented — that it is costly in terms of time and money, and that its reliability is open to question. However, it is worth noting that the employment of referees is by no means universal among research journals. Thus a survey of 156 scientific journals published in 13 different countries in the 1960s showed that only some 70 per cent of them employed referees[14]. The existence of such unrefereed journals is usually dismissed as unimportant, with the implication that they survive parasitically on the good habits induced in authors by refereed journals. This appears to be a *post hoc* rationalization, which hardly reflects the factors that are equally at work in both refereed and unrefereed journals. In the first place, incoming material is always initially monitored by an editor. An appreciable proportion of the papers rejected (perhaps as much as half) never reach a referee, because they are immediately declined by the editor. Secondly, research workers of any experience have learnt to monitor the presentation of their own work, so as not to endanger the research reputation they have gained. Thirdly, contributions, especially by recent recruits to research, are often monitored in some way (e.g. by a supervisor, or by presentation at a seminar) before submission for normal publication. Factors such as these suggest that the refereeing process might be streamlined without having a disastrous effect on the development of research.

We can begin with the point that editors habitually reject papers that are obvious non-starters. They then typically dispatch the remainder for assessment to people whom they believe to be experts in the particular topics involved. However, there is quite good evidence for supposing that opinions regarding the acceptability of a research paper do not depend very strongly on whether the assessor is an expert in the specific topic, or only in the general field[15]. Hence, the editor of a learned journal may not be able to make the same detailed comments on a paper as a suitably selected external referee, but he is likely to come to the same conclusion as regards its acceptability for publication. In terms of selecting material from the input to a journal, an editorial board with restricted membership may therefore be almost as efficient as a complex refereeing system. Use of such a board for almost all the refereeing work can unify and accelerate the process, and can also remove some of the objection to anonymous referees (since the composition of such boards is usually announced).

Clearly, the members of such a board would be worked a good deal harder than a wider circle of referees. But, so long as the prime judgement is that of acceptibility, the time required to handle each paper should be less than usual; it is the need to make detailed comments on contents that usually takes up a referee's time. Correspondingly, style of presentation and major defects would be noted, but minor defects might well pass undetected. In view of the current deficiencies of the refereeing process, it is not evident that this is too serious a problem, especially in view of the small number of people who read any published paper in real detail. (The number of readers of a research paper is a highly uncertain statistic, but probably less than ten read the average paper really thoroughly.) In any case, this drawback can be counterbalanced by the speed of evaluation possible with an editorial board, and by the greater consistency of decisions possible with a smaller group of assessors.

A more serious objection to this approach to refereeing is that it cuts down the interaction within the scientific community — authors receive less feedback on the quality of their work, young research workers have less chance of involvement in the process of assessment, and aggrieved authors have less chance of redress. None of these problems are unsolvable; for example, the work of an aggrieved author might be submitted to external referees on payment of a fee. The real objection may be that more fundamental changes will be required in the future: for the traditional journal may, itself, change, and so precipitate an unavoidable change in the refereeing process.

The introduction of synoptic publication has already raised queries concerning present refereeing systems — particularly with regard to their speed. The progression to electronic journals raises much more fundamental problems; for example, it makes it possible for the entire readership of a journal to act as the refereeing panel. It may be that in the next few decades the changing nature of publication will demand a thorough reassessment of how, and why, we carry out refereeing.

A. J. M.

BIBLIOGRAPHY AND NOTES

1 J. ZIMAN, *Public Knowledge*, Cambridge University Press, 1968, p. 111.
2 M. J. MULKAY and A. T. WILLIAMS, A sociological study of a physics department, *British Journ. Sociol.*, 22 (1971), pp. 68-82.
3 A detailed study of refereeing procedures in the United Kingdom is currently being completed by Mr. M. D. GORDON and the present author at the University of Leicester (1978).
4 H. RODMAN, The moral responsibility of journal editors and referees, *American Sociol.* 5 (1970), pp. 351-7.
5 A. J. MEADOWS, *Communication in Science*, Butterworths, London, 1974, p. 138.
6 For example, some institutional differentiation has been found in the survey, mentioned in Note 3 above. The data are presented by M. D. GORDON, Refereeing reconsidered; an evaluation of unwitting bias in scientific evaluation, in *Proceedings of the First World Conference of Scientific Editors*, Jerusalem, 1977.
7 D. F. HORROBIN, Referees and research administrators; barriers to scientific research?, *British Medical Journ.*, 2 (1974), pp. 216-8.
8 L. WOLINS, Responsibility for raw data, *American Psychol.*, 17 (1962), pp. 657-8.
9 H. ZUCKERMAN and R. K. MERTON, Patterns of evaluation in science; institutionalisation, structure and functions of the referee system, *Minerva*, 9 (1971), pp. 66-100.
10 R. H. ORR and J. KASSAB, *Peer group judgment on scientific merit; editorial refereeing*. Presented to the Congress of the International Federation for Documentation, Washington D. C., 15 October 1965.
11 H. G. SMALL, *Characteristics of frequently cited papers in chemistry*, National Science Foundation Report NSF - C795 (1973).
12 C. WEINER (ed.), *Exploring the history of nuclear physics*, American Institute of Physics, New York, 1972.
13 R. D. WRIGHT, Truth and its Keepers, *New Scientist*, 45 (1970), pp. 402-3.
14 H. ZUCKERMAN and R. K. MERTON, *Op. cit.*
15 E. O. SMIGEL and H. L. ROSS, Factors in the editorial decision, *American Sociol.*, 5 (1970), pp. 19-21.

**HARRIET ZUCKERMAN AND
ROBERT K. MERTON**

Patterns of Evaluation in Science: Institutionalisation, Structure and Functions of the Referee System

THE referee system in science involves the systematic use of judges to assess the acceptability of manuscripts submitted for publication. The referee is thus an example of status-judges who are charged with evaluating the quality of role-performance in a social system. They are found in every institutional sphere. Other kinds of status-judges include teachers assessing the quality of work by students (and, as a recent institutional change, students officially assessing the quality of performance by teachers), critics in the arts, supervisors in industry and coaches and managers in sports. Status-judges are integral to any system of social control through their evaluation of role-performance and their allocation of rewards for that performance. They influence the motivation to maintain or to raise standards of performance.

In the case of scientific and scholarly journals, the significant status-judges are the editors and referees. Like the official readers of manuscripts of books submitted to publishers, or the presumed experts who appraise proposals for research grants, the referees ordinarily make their judgements confidentially, these being available only to the editor and usually to the author. Other judges in science and learning make their judgements public, as in the case of published book reviews and the often important review articles which assess the "credibility" of recent work in a special field of knowledge.

Although the referee system has its inefficiencies, practising scientists see it even in its current form as crucial for the effective development of science. Professor J. M. Ziman puts the case emphatically:

The fact is that the publication of scientific papers is by no means unconstrained. An article in a reputable journal does not merely represent the opinions of its author; it bears the *imprimatur* of scientific authenticity, as given to it by the editor and the referees he may have consulted. The referee is the lynchpin about which the whole business of Science is pivoted.[1]

The chemist, Professor Leonard K. Nash, describes the "editors and referees of scientific journals" as "the main defenders of scientific 'good

---

[1] Ziman, J. M., *Public Knowledge: The Social Dimension of Science* (Cambridge University Press, 1966), p. 148.

Reprinted from *Minerva* vol. 9, no. 1, Jan. 1971, p.66-100, by permission of the authors and publisher.

taste ' ".[2] Professor Michael Polanyi suggests that although there are of course many cases of disparate evaluative judgements about particular works in science, the structure of scientific authority has generally operated through the years so as to exhibit a remarkable degree of concurrence. He states, for example:

Two scientists acting unknown to each other as referees for the publication of one paper usually agree about its approximate value. Two referees reporting independently on an application for a higher degree rarely diverge greatly.[3]

Observations of this sort attest to the great significance scientists ascribe to the referee system. Yet until recently, the referee system itself has not been systematically examined and assessed. Professor Gordon Tullock, an economist, has remarked that " Given the importance of these editorial decisions for science, the absence of research into them is surprising." [4]

In this paper, we undertake an inquiry into four aspects of the referee system. We deal first with the faint beginnings in the latter seventeenth century of the institutionalisation of evaluative judgements into a system of roles and procedures. We then examine and explore the implications of patterns of differences in the rates of rejecting manuscripts submitted to contemporary journals in fifteen fields of science and learning. In the greater part of the paper, we draw upon fairly recent archives of *The Physical Review* (which the editors kindly made available to us for the purpose) to identify and analyse patterns of decision by editors and referees. Finally, on the basis of these historical, comparative and quantitative analyses, we consider the significance of the referee system for individual scientists, scientific communication and the development of science.

---

[2] Nash, Leonard K., *The Nature of the Natural Sciences* (Boston: Little Brown, 1963), p. 305.

[3] Polanyi, Michael, *Science, Faith and Society* (Oxford University Press, 1946), p. 37. The evidence on the extent of agreement by referees has only begun to be assembled, but indications are that it varies appreciably among different fields of science and learning. We have found, for example, that in a sample of 172 papers evaluated by two referees for *The Physical Review* (in the period 1948-56), agreement was very high. In only five cases did the referees fully disagree, with one recommending acceptance and the other, rejection. For the rest, the recommended decision was the same, with two-thirds of these involving minor differences in the character of proposed revisions. In two biomedical journals, however, Orr and Kassab found that for 1,572 papers submitted over a five-year period and reviewed by at least two referees, " they agreed that a paper was either acceptable or unacceptable 75 per cent. of the time " (as compared with the 62 per cent. that could have occurred by chance). Orr, Richard H., and Kassab, Jane, " Peer group judgments on scientific merit: editorial refereeing ", presented to the Congress of the International Federation for Documentation, Washington, D.C., October 15, 1965. For one journal of sociology, agreement to accept or to reject occurred in 72·5 per cent. of 193 pairs of independent editorial judgments (as compared with the 53·9 per cent. that would have occurred by chance). Smigel, Erwin O., and Ross, H. Laurence, " Factors in the editorial decision ", *The American Sociologist*, V (February 1970), pp. 19–21. Systematic comparisons of variability in the extent of agreement in referee judgements would identify differences in the extent of institutionalisation of different fields of science and learning.

[4] Tullock, Gordon, *The Organization of Inquiry* (Durham: Duke University Press, 1966), p. 148.

Institutionalisation of the Referee System

The referee system did not appear all at once as an integral part of the social institution of science. It evolved in response to the concrete problems encountered in working toward the developing goals of scientific inquiry and as a by-product of the emerging social organisation of scientists.

The new scientific societies and academies of the seventeenth century were crucial for the social invention of the scientific journal [5] which began to take an enlarged place in the system of written scientific interchange which had hitherto been limited to letters, tracts, and books. These organisations provided the structure of authority which transformed the mere *printing* of scientific work into its *publication*. From the earlier practice of merely putting manuscripts into print, without competent evaluation of their content by anyone except the author himself, there slowly developed the practice of having the substance of manuscripts legitimated, principally before publication although sometimes after, through evaluation by institutionally assigned and ostensibly competent reviewers. We see the slight beginnings of this in the first two scientific journals established just 300 years ago within two months of each other: the *Journal des Sçavans* in January 1665; the *Philosophical Transactions* of the Royal Society, in March of the same year. The *Journal* was a conglomerate periodical which catalogued books, published necrologies of famous persons, and cited major decisions of civil and religious courts as well as disseminating reports of experiments and observations in physics, chemistry, anatomy and meteorology. The *Philosophical Transactions* was "a more truly scientific periodical . . . , excluding legal and theological matters, but including especially the accounts of experiments conducted before the [Royal] Society." [6]

Although not the official publication of the Royal Society until 1753, the *Transactions* was first authorised by its council on 1 March, 1664-65 in these sociologically instructive words:

Ordered, that the *Philosophical Transactions,* to be composed by Mr. [Henry] Oldenburg [one of the two Secretaries of the Society], be printed the first Monday of every month, if he have sufficient matter for it; and that the tract

---

[5] First privately printed in 1913, the classic and still useful monograph by Martha Ornstein deals with the subject in chapter VII: *The Role of Scientific Societies in the Seventeenth Century* (Chicago: University of Chicago Press, 1938), (3rd edition), see also Brown, Harcourt, *Scientific Organisations in Seventeenth Century France* (Baltimore: Williams and Wilkins, 1934).

[6] Porter, J. R., "The Scientific Journal—300th Anniversary", *Bacteriological Reviews,* XXVIII (September, 1964), pp. 211–230 at 221. In this short account of the institutionalisation of the referee system, we have drawn upon Barnes, S. B., "The Scientific Journal, 1665–1730", *Scientific Monthly,* XXXVIII (1934), pp. 257–260; Garrison, F. H., "The Medical and Scientific Periodicals of the 17th and 18th Centuries", *Bulletin, Institute for the History of Medicine,* II (1934), pp. 285–343 ; McKie, D., "The Scientific Periodical from 1665 to 1798, *Philosophical Magazine* (1948), pp. 122–132 ; Kronick, D. A., *A History of Scientific and Technical Periodicals* (New York: The Scarecrow Press, 1962).

be licensed under the charter by the Council of the Society, being first reviewed by some of the members of the same. . . .[7]

Much relevant information is packed into this summary of an organisational decision. Prime responsibility for the new kind of periodical is assigned to one person, Oldenburg, for whom there does not yet exist the designation of editor, to say nothing of specifying his obligations in the editorial role. Before long, in trying to meet the problems of maintaining the journal, Oldenburg, together with concerned colleagues in the Society, introduced various adaptive expedients which ended up by defining the role of an editor. The council also recognised the immediate problem of having " sufficient matter " for this newly-conceived periodical and institutional devices were gradually evolved to induce scientists to contribute to the journal. What is perhaps most significant here is that the council, as sponsor of the *Transactions*, was involved with its fate and wanted to have a measure of control over its contents. These adaptive decisions provided a basis for the referee system.

As with the analysis of any case of institutionalisation, we must consider how arrangements for achieving the prime goals—the improvement and diffusion of scientific knowledge—operated to induce or to reinforce motivations for contributing to the goals and to enlist those motivations for the performance of newly-developing social roles. As we have noted, the first problem was to get enough work of merit for publication. In part, this was a problem because of the comparatively small number of men seriously at work in science. But it also resulted from the circumstance that, intent upon safeguarding their intellectual property, many men of science still set a premium upon secrecy (as is evident in their correspondence with close associates). They maintained an attitude and continued a practice of (at least, temporary) secrecy which, as Elizabeth Eisenstein has impressively suggested, was more appropriate to a scribal culture.[8] With the advent of printing, however, findings could be permanently secured, errors in the transmission of precise knowledge greatly reduced and intellectual property rights registered in print. Printing thus provided a technological basis for the emergence of that component of the ethos of science which has been described as " communism ": the norm which prescribes the open communication of findings to other scientists and correlatively proscribing secrecy.[9] But it appears that this norm

---

[7] Weld, Charles R., *A History of the Royal Society*, Volume I (London, 1848), p. 177.

[8] Eisenstein, Elizabeth L., " The Advent of Printing and the Problem of the Renaissance ", *Past & Present*, Number 45 (November, 1969), pp. 19–89; esp. pp. 55, 63 and 75–76. " Many forms of knowledge had to be esoteric during the age of scribes if they were to survive at all. . . . Advanced techniques could not be passed on without being guarded against contamination and hedged in by secrecy. To be preserved intact, techniques had to be entrusted to a select group of initiates who were instructed not only in special skills but also in the ' mysteries ' associated with them."

[9] For an analysis of " communism ", universalism, organised scepticism and disinterestedness as basic institutional norms of science, see Merton, R. K., *Social Theory and Social Structure* (New York: Free Press, 1968) (enlarged edition), pp. 604–615. For extended analyses of this normative structure, see Barber, Bernard, *Science and the Social Order*

did not fully develop in response to the new technology of printing; ancillary institutional inventions served to facilitate the shift from motivated secrecy to motivated public disclosure.

Before the *Transactions* were inaugurated, the Royal Society had adopted one such institutional device to encourage men of science to disclose their new work. The Society would officially establish priority of discovery by recording the date on which communications were first received. As Oldenburg put it in reassuring terms to his friend and patron, Robert Boyle: "The Society alwayes intended, and, I think, hath practised hitherto, what you recommend concerning ye registring of ye time, when any Observation or Expt is first mentioned." And, he adds, making the function of this practice altogether manifest, the Royal Society

have declared it again, yt it should be punctually observed: in regard of wch Monsr. de Zulichem [Huyghens] hath been written to, *to communicate freely to ye Society*, whàt new discoveries he maketh, or wt new Expts he tryeth, the Soceity being very carefull of registring as well the person and time of any new matter, imparted to ym, as the matter itselfe; *whereby the honor of ye invention will be inviolably preserved to all posterity*.[10]

Soon afterward, Oldenburg writes to Boyle again and even more emphatically reiterates the function of this institutional practice:

This justice and generosity of our Society is exceedingly commendable, and doth rejoyce me, as often as I think on't, chiefly upon this account, yt I thence persuade myselfe, yt all Ingenious men will be thereby incouraged to impart their knowledge and discoveryes, as farre as they may, not doubting of ye Observance of ye Old Law, of Suum cuique tribuere [allowing to each man his own].[11]

Even before he became editor of the *Transactions*, then, Oldenburg had occasion to note that men of science might be induced to accept the new norm of free communication through a motivating exchange: open disclosure in exchange for institutionally guaranteed honorific property rights to the new knowledge given to others.

In the course of looking after Boyle's writings, the future editor of the *Transactions* came upon prompt publication as another device for preserving intellectual property rights. For, like other scientists of his time, Boyle was chronically and acutely anxious about the danger of what he described as "philosophicall robbery", what would be less picturesquely described today as plagiarism from circulated but unpublished manu-

---

(New York: Free Press, 1952), chapter IV; Storer, Norman, *The Social System of Science* (New York: Holt, Rinehart and Winston, 1966), pp. 76–136; Cournand, André and Zuckerman, Harriet, "The code of science", *Studium Generale* XXIII (1970), pp. 941–962.

[10] *The Correspondence of Henry Oldenburg*, Volume II, edited and translated by Hall, A. Rupert and Hall, Marie Boas (Madison: University of Wisconsin Press, 1966), p. 319, italics added. We have drawn extensively on the volumes of this correspondence which provide an incomparable storehouse of information on the early days of the *Transactions*.

[11] *Ibid.*, p. 329.

scripts. Boyle felt that he had often been so victimised.[12] As his agent, Oldenburg arranged for quick publication of a batch of Boyle's papers, writing him reassuringly: "They are now very safe, and will be wthin this week in print, as [the printer] Mr. Crook assureth, who will also take care of keeping ym unexposed to ye eye of a Philosophicall robber."[13] Later, as editor of the *Transactions*, Oldenburg could draw upon this motivation in having Boyle agree that he would "from time to time contribute some short Papers, to that Design you are monthly & happily prosecuting . . . ",[14] Boyle all unknowing that in this way he was helping to institute a new form for the dissemination of knowledge which would eventually become identified as the "scientific paper".

Boyle did report, however, another motive for contributing to the newly-invented journal. Almost in so many words, he saw this as a way for the scientist to have his work permanently secured in the archives of science, as he went on to say of Oldenburg's request to contribute to the *Transactions*:

I mightly justly be thought too little sensible of my own Interest, if I should altogether decline so civil an Invitation, and neglect the opportunity of having some of my Memoirs preserv'd, by being incorporated into a Collection, that is like to be as lasting as usefull.

The fugitive nature of letters as the more familiar means of communicating short reports on scientific work may have emphasised by contrast the potentially enduring character of a journal, particularly one sponsored by a scientific society. In any case, we find in Boyle's remarks an early intimation of the scientific journal as a scientific archive.

Another motive could be harnessed to the developing innovation of a scientific periodical. Property rights in discovery were sought after by scientists primarily as individuals but occasionally also as nationals.[15] As A. R. Hall and M. B. Hall, the editors of the Oldenburg correspondence, observe, by 1667, Oldenburg was eager "to demonstrate English priority [on the filar micrometer] and careful to put it in print in the *Philosophical Transactions*. Similarly he took much care to insist in the *Philosophical Transactions* that it was the English, not the French or the Germans, who had invented the idea of injecting medicines into the veins and of practising blood transfusion between animals".[16] Such interest in

---

[12] So disturbed by plagiarists of his work was Boyle that he prepared a document, later running to three folio pages of print, itemising all the ingenious devices for thievery developed by the grand larcenists of 17th-century science. See *The Works of the Honourable Robert Boyle*, Volume I, Birch, J., ed., in six volumes (London, 1772), pp. cxxv–cxxviii, ccxxii–ccxxiv and also his letter in *Correspondence of Henry Oldenburg*, Volume IV, p. 94.   [13] *Correspondence of Henry Oldenburg*, Volume II, p. 291.

[14] *Ibid.*, Volume III, p. 145.

[15] On conflicting national claims to priority, see Merton, R. K., "Priorities in scientific discovery," *American Sociological Review*, XXII (1957), pp. 635–659 and "Resistance to the systematic study of multiple discoveries in science", *European Journal of Sociology*, IV, 1963, pp. 237–282.

[16] Hall and Hall, in the introduction to *Correspondence of Henry Oldenburg*, op. cit., Volume III, p. xxv.

national priority could also be drawn upon to press reluctant scientists into contributing "sufficient matter" to the new publication. Thus, the mathematician, John Wallis, who played a large part in the early history of the *Transactions*, could argue the case for ensuring national priority in connection with the much-advertised claims of the French to having initiated blood transfusion:

Onely I wish that those of our Nation; were a little more forward than I find them generally to bee (especially the most considerable) in timely publishing their own Discoveries, & not let strangers reape ye glory of what those amongst ourselves are ye Authors.[17]

Through these and kindred institutional devices, the new scientific society and the new scientific journal persuaded men of science to replace their attachment to secrecy and limited forms of communication with a willingness to disclose their newly-found knowledge.[18] But institutionalisation is more than a matter of changing values; it also involves their incorporation into authoritatively defined roles. As the organisation sponsoring the *Transactions*, the Royal Society provided the power and authority which enabled it to institute new roles and associated rewards for acceptance of these roles. True, in its early days, the Royal Society included many members with little or no scientific competence. But, what was more consequential for the process of institutionalisation, it included all English scientists (and many foreign ones) who were producing significant scientific work. As a result, it was widely identified, both in England and on the Continent,[19] as an authoritative body of scientists.

This authority based on demonstrated competence provided mutually reinforcing consequences for scientists in their triple roles as members of the Royal Society, as contributors to the *Transactions* and as readers of it. These consequences shaped the early evolution of the scientific journal and the referee system in several ways. First, growing numbers of scientists seeking competent judgments of their work turned increasingly to the Royal Society. Thus, the distinguished astronomer Hevelius wrote of his important work *Cometographia* that "as soon as it is published I will make it my first care to submit it to the high judgment and due consideration of the Royal Society".[20] The French astronomer and engineer, Pierre Petit, paid his respects to the "celebrated Society, to which judgment I submit all my ideas".[21] Nor were these merely polite

---

[17] *Ibid.*, Volume III, p. 373.

[18] Through the process of socially induced displacement of goals, this value of open communication would eventually become transformed for appreciable numbers of scholars and scientists into an urge to publish in periodicals, all apart from the worth of what was being submitted for publication. This development would in turn reinforce a concern within the community of scholars for the sifting, sorting and accrediting of manuscripts by some version of a referee-system

[19] Hall and Hall, in the Introduction to *ibid.*, Volume II, p. xxi.

[20] *Ibid.*, Volume II, p. 1938; see also Volume IV, p. 448.

[21] *Ibid.*, Volume II, p. 595. For other cases in which the Royal Society was asked to sit as a court of scientific judges, see *ibid.*, Volume III, pp. 6, 171, 219 and 298.

phrases. As the Halls observe, it was not long before the "practice of writing for publication in the *Philosophical Transactions*" was greatly increasing among European men of science.[22] This new practice of writing *directly* for publication in a journal constituted another appreciable change in the evolving role of the scientist. With the composite institution of learned society and learned journal at hand, scientists began to seize the new opportunity of having competent appraisals of their work by other authoritative scientists,[23] a pattern of attitude and behaviour which is basic to the referee system.

The practice of having scientific communications assessed by delegated members of the Royal Society might have affected the quality of those communications. Communications intended for publication would ordinarily be more carefully prepared than private scientific papers, and all the more so, presumably, in the knowledge that they would be scrutinised by deputies of the Society.

The constituted representatives of the Royal Society, looking to its reputation, were in their turn motivated to institute and maintain arrangements for adequately assessing communications, before having them recorded or published in the *Transactions*. They repeatedly express an awareness that to retain the confidence of scientists they must arrange for the critical sifting of materials which in effect carry the *imprimatur* of the Society. Thus, the president of the Society, " before he will declare anything positively of ye figure of these Glasses, will by a gage measure ym; and if ye Invention bear his test, it will pass for currant, & be no discredit to ye Society, yt a member of theirs is ye Author thereof." [24] Or, as the editor-secretary Oldenburg later reported to Boyle, the matter could not be too carefully studied " before we give a publick testimony of it to ye world, as is desired of us ".[25] The Society was also beginning to distinguish between evaluated and unevaluated work which came to its notice. On occasion, this involved the policy of " sit penes authorem fides (let the author take responsibility for it): We only set it downe, as it was related to us, without putting any great weight upon it." [26] In the course of establishing its legitimacy as an authoritative scientific body, the Royal Society was gradually developing both norms and social arrangements for authenticating the substance of scientific work.

[22] Hall and Hall, in the introduction, *ibid.*, Volume IV, p. xxiii.
[23] In a series of papers Merton has developed the idea that this concern of scientists with having appropriate recognition of their work by peers is central to the workings of science as a social institution. See, for example, Merton, " Priorities in scientific discovery ", *op. cit*. This idea has been instructively advanced by Norman Storer as involving a concern with competent appraisal; see his *The Social System of Science, op. cit*, especially pp. 19-27 and 66-73.
[24] *Correspondence of Henry Oldenburg*, Volume IV, pp 223-224.
[25] *Ibid.*, Volume IV, p. 235. In the event, a short account of these optical instruments was soon published in the *Transactions*.
[26] *Ibid.*, Volume IV, p. 235. It is of some interest that in response to the flood of manuscripts today, with its overloading of facilities for refereeing, some journals are adopting the same policy, allowing some papers to be published though unrefereed, providing that a note appended to the article testifies to its not having been refereed.

Ingredients of the referee system were thus emerging in response to distinctive concerns of scientists taken distributively and collectively. In their capacity as producers of science, individual scientists were concerned with having their work recognised through publication in forms valued by other members in the emerging scientific community who were significant to them. In their capacity as consumers of science, they were concerned with having the work produced by others competently assessed so that they could count on its authenticity. In providing the organisational machinery to meet these concerns, the Royal Society was concerned with having its authoritative status sustained by arranging for reliable and competent assessments.

There are intimations, even in this early period, that individual scientists in their role as informed consumers would begin to affect the process making for control of the quality of publications in journals. When the editor or the Royal Society slipped up by allowing dubious materials to be published in the *Transactions*, as they not infrequently did, readers would on occasion register their protest. The French astronomer Auzout, for example, censured the editor for printing unauthenticated and doubtful accounts:

Some of our virtuosi are surprised at your speaking in your journal of parabolic lenses. Your students of dioptrics know that they are worthless and whatever fine promises are made, when these seem contrary to reason one ought not to speak of them until the results have been seen; for it is not very urgent to know what charlatans may promise.[27]

We have no evidence that such critical responses actually made for greater care in subsequent editorial decisions. The point is, however, that the newly instituted journal, unlike the printers of books at that time, provided an arrangement through which members of the scientific community could affect editorial practices. Through the emergence of the role of editor and the incipient arrangements for having manuscripts assessed by others in addition to the editor, the journal gave a more institutionalised form for the application of standards of scientific work.

Efforts to cope with immediate problems produced other adaptive changes in the learned journal. By the end of the seventeenth century, there were signs of role-differentiation, especially in journals dealing with diverse fields of knowledge, in the form of a staff or "board" of editors. The *Journal des Sçavans* for one example had by 1702 assigned responsibility for particular departments of learning to each of a staff of editors who met weekly to review copy.[28] Other aspects of the journal developed more slowly. It took a century for the format of the scientific

---

[27] *Ibid.*, Volume III, p. 111 and, in the editor's translation quoted here, p. 114.
[28] Barnes, Sherman B., "The Editing of Early Learned Journals", *Osiris*, I (1936), pp. 155–172 at pp. 157–159.

paper to become more or less established and even longer for the scholarly apparatus of footnotes and citations to be generally adopted.[29]

Almost from their beginning, then, the scientific journals were developing modes of refereeing for the express purpose of controlling the quality of what they put in print.

Patterns of evaluation in the Sciences and Humanities

Turning from those early days to the present, we find that some version of the referee system has been widely adopted. In the physical and biological sciences, for example, a recent survey of 156 journals in 13 countries found that 71 per cent. made some use of referees.[30]

What, then, are the gross outcomes of the evaluation process by editors and referees of journals in the principal fields of science and learning? Are there pronounced differences among the various disciplines? Are observed variations in outcome random or patterned? To explore these questions, we have compiled the rates of rejections in a sample of 83 journals in the humanities, the social and behavioural sciences, mathematics, and the biological, chemical and physical sciences.[31] (The results are shown in Table I, with the disciplines ranked in order of decreasing rates of rejection.)

The figures exhibit marked and determinate variation. Journals in the humanities have the highest rates of rejection. They are followed by the social and behavioural sciences with mathematics and statistics next in line. The physical, chemical and biological sciences have the lowest rates, running to no more than a third of the rates found in the humanities.

Confirming this empirical uniformity are subsidiary patterns of deviant rates within disciplines which virtually reproduce the major patterns. To begin with, consider the field of physics. The 12 journals had an average rejection rate of 24 per cent., with the figures for 11 of them varying narrowly between 17 per cent. and 25 per cent. But the twelfth journal, the *American Journal of Physics*, departs widely from this norm

---

[29] Porter, *op. cit.*, p. 225; de Solla Price, Derek J., "Communication in Science: the Ends—Philosophy and Forecast", in de Reuck, Anthony and Knight, Julie, eds., *Ciba Foundation Symposium on Communication in Science* (London: J. & A. Churchill, 1967), pp. 199–209 at p. 200.

[30] International Council of Scientific Unions, *A Tentative Study of the Publication of Original Scientific Literature* (Paris: Conseil International des Unions Scientifiques, 1962) There are marked variations by country: for example, only 2 of 49 journals published in the United States in contrast to 9 of 30 French journals made no use of referees.

[31] A first list was drawn from Bernard Berelson's compilation of leading journals in his *Graduate Education in the United States* (New York: McGraw Hill, 1960). This list was supplemented by other research journals published under the auspices of the major associations of scholars and scientists. In all, the editors of 117 journals were queried by mail; responses were received from 97 of them and usable information from 83. The *Physical Review Letters* in physics and similar journals in other sciences are excluded from this list since they are especially designed for "rapid publication". On the special problems confronted by such publications, see Goudsmit, S. A., "Editorial", *Physical Review Letters*, XXI (11 November, 1968), pp. 1425–1426.

TABLE I

Rates of Rejecting Manuscripts for Publication in Scientific and Humanistic Journals, 1967

	Mean rejection rate %	No. of journals
History	90	3
Language and literature	86	5
Philosophy	85	5
Political science	84	2
Sociology	78	14
Psychology (excluding experimental and physiological)	70	7
Economics	69	4
Experimental and physiological psychology	51	2
Mathematics and statistics	50	5
Anthropology	48	2
Chemistry	31	5
Geography	30	2
Biological sciences	29	12
Physics	24	12
Geology	22	2
Linguistics	20	1
Total		83

with a rejection rate of 40 per cent. In the light of the general pattern of rejection rates, we suggest that this seemingly deviant case only confirms the rule. For this journal, alone among the twelve assigned to physics in Table 1, is not so much a journal *in* physics as a journal *about* physics. It publishes articles dealing primarily with the humanistic, pedagogical, historical and social aspects of physics rather than articles presenting new research in physics. Accordingly, it diverges from the relatively low rate characteristic of the physical sciences in the direction of the substantially higher one characteristic of the humanities and social sciences.

We find similar patterns within other disciplines. The two journals in anthropology for example have an average rejection rate of 47·5 per cent., considerably below that for the other social sciences. But this is a composite of drastically different rates for the two journals. The *American Anthropologist*, devoted largely to social and cultural anthropology, approximates the high rejection rates of the other social sciences with a figure of 65 per cent., while the *American Journal of Physical Anthropology* with a figure of 30 per cent. approximates the low rates of the physical sciences. We find much the same difference in psychology. The journals devoted to social, abnormal, clinical and educational psychology average a rejection rate of 70 per cent. while the journals in experimental, comparative and physiological psychology diverge toward the physical sciences with an average of 51 per cent. Consider only one more case of this confirming finer pattern within the gross pattern, this time for subjects ordinarily assigned to the humanities. The journals of language and literature in the humanistic tradition have an average rejection rate of 86 per cent., whereas the journal, *Linguistics,* adopting mathematical and logical orientations in the study of language, has a rejection rate of 20 per cent., much like that of the physical sciences.

The pattern of differences between fields and within fields can be described in the same rule of thumb: the more humanistically oriented the journal, the higher the rate of rejecting manuscripts for publication; the more experimentally and observationally oriented, with an emphasis on rigour of observation and analysis, the lower the rate of rejection.[32]

These variations in the institutional behaviour of learned journals may in part reflect differences in the extent of agreement on standards of scholarship in the various disciplines. It appears to be the case that the journals with high rejection rates receive a larger proportion of manuscripts that in the judgement of the editor and his referees are not simply debatable border-line cases but fail by a wide margin to measure up even to minimum standards of scholarship. This suggests that these fields of learning are not greatly institutionalised in the reasonably precise sense that editors and referees on the one side and would-be contributors on the other almost always share norms of what constitutes adequate scholarship. In the case of one journal, for example, which rejects nine of every ten papers, about 40 per cent. are promptly turned down by the editor as hopelessly inept and unpublishable in any learned journal. The editor of a journal with a final rejection rate of about 80 per cent. perceives the standards employed by his referees as more demanding than those employed by other journals in the field. He himself rejected more than 40 per cent. of incoming manuscripts, explaining that they

> ... were manuscripts which I judged to be extremely unlikely to survive our rigorous screening no matter who reviewed them, so I carefully reviewed them myself and typically sent the authors a one- to three-page, single-spaced letter explaining why we could not accept it here and how they might revise the manuscript for submission elsewhere or how they might improve on the present study so as to do some publishable research.

And the editor of another journal with a high rejection rate of 85 per cent. reports that about 20 per cent. of incoming papers " were so clearly unacceptable that I didn't want to waste a referee's time with them. . . . We still get a flow of articles of a thoroughly amateurish quality."

---

[32] The empirical solidity of this rule of thumb is illustrated by an episode which occurred in the course of our survey of journals. The editor of a journal in chemical physics reported a rejection rate of 75 per cent., far above figures for the other journals in physics and chemistry. Taking note of this anomalous figure, we asked the editor to account for it only to have him report that it was simply a clerical error; he had reported the rate of acceptance, not the rule-like rejection rate of 25 per cent.

The influx of manuscripts judged to be beyond all hope of scholarly redemption testifies to the ambiguity and the wide range of dispersion of standards of scholarship in the discipline, all apart from the question whether the institutionally legitimated editors and referees or the would-be contributors are exercising better judgement. We do not know the comparative frequency of these reportedly unsalvageable manuscripts in different fields but the testimony of editors suggests that it is considerably higher in the humanities and the social sciences.

There are intimations in the data also that the editors and referees of journals with markedly different rates of rejection tend to adopt different decision-rules and so are subject, when errors of judgment occur, to different *kinds* of error. Editors and referees, of course want to avoid errors of judgement altogether. But recognising that they cannot be infallible, they seem to exhibit different preferences. The editorial staff of high-rejection journals evidently prefer to run the risk of rejecting manuscripts which the wider community of scholars (or posterity) would consider publishable (or even, perhaps, important)—an error of the first kind—rather than run the risk of publishing papers that will be widely judged to be sub-standard. The editorial staff of low-rejection journals, where external evidence suggests that the decisions of scientists to submit papers are based on standards widely shared in the field, apparently prefer to risk errors, if errors there must be, of the second kind: occasionally to publish papers that do not measure up rather than to overlook work that may turn out to be original and significant. Thus the editor of a journal which rejects only one paper in five acts on the assumption that a manuscript is publishable until clearly proved otherwise. As he puts it, " If the first referee recommends publication, as received or with minor revision, that is usually sufficient. If the first referee's opinion is negative, or undecided, additional referee(s) will be consulted until a consensus is reached." Editors of another journal in this class note that they " have generally published ' borderline ' papers—those on which referees' opinions differed ". Put in terms reminiscent of another institutional sphere, the decision-rule in high-rejection journals seems to be when in doubt, reject; in low-rejection journals, when in doubt, accept.

The actual distribution of these decision-rules and their consequences for the quality of scholarship in the various disciplines still remain to be determined. But even now it appears that the rules will have different consequences for scientists and scholars at different stages of their development. The Coles and Zuckerman have found that collegial recognition of the work of young scientists is important for their continued productivity.[33] This suggests that the discouragement of having papers rejected

[33] Cole, Stephen and Cole, Jonathan R., " Scientific Output and Recognition: A Study in the Operation of the Reward System in Science ", *American Sociological Review*, XXXII (1967), pp. 377–390. Zuckerman, Harriet, *Nobel Laureates in the United States*, Columbia University doctoral dissertation (1965), Chapter X provides qualitative evidence of the reinforcing effects of such recognition.

may be more significant for the novice than for the established scholar. The multiplicity of journals [34] need not entirely solve the problem for him. Since his research capabilities still require institutional certification, it can matter greatly to him whether his paper is published in a journal of higher or lower rank. Rejection of his paper by a high-ranking journal might be more acutely damaging, more often leading him to abandon his plans for publication altogether.

Whatever their consequences, the marked differences in the rejection rates of journals in the various disciplines can be tentatively ascribed only in part to differences in the extent of consensus with regard to standards of adequate science and scholarship. Beyond this are objective differences in the relative amount of space available for publication.[35] Editors of all journals must allocate the scarce resources of pages available for print, but not all fields and journals are subject to the same degree of scarcity. Journals in the sciences can apparently publish a higher proportion of manuscripts submitted to them because the available space is greater than that found in the humanities. Take the case of physics. The articles in journals of physics are ordinarily short, typically running to only a few pages of print, so that the "cost" of deciding to publish a particular article is small and the direct costs of publication are often paid by authors from research grants.[36] The increase in available journal space, moreover, has been outrunning the increase in the number of scientists. The number of pages published annually by *The Physical Review* (and *Physical Review Letters*), for example, increased 4·6 times from 3,920 pages in 1950 to 17,060 in 1965; during the same interval, the number of members of the American Physical Society increased only 2·4 times. Preliminary counts for the humanities and social sciences do not show the same disproportionate increase in journal space beyond increase in the numbers of scholars. By way of comparison, the number of pages available in the official journal of the American Sociological Association remained about the same between 1950 and 1965, while the membership of the Association increased two and a half times.

Observations of this sort deal only with the final outcomes of the

---

[34] It has often been suggested that papers which are at all competent eventually find their way into print. Tullock, *The Organisation of Inquiry, op. cit.,* p. 144; Storer, *op. cit.,* pp. 132–133; Hagstrom, Warren O., *The Scientific Community* (New York: Basic Books, 1965), pp. 18 onwards. But only now is there the beginnings of evidence on the proportion of papers published by journals of differing rank which are first, second or nth submissions for publication. See Lin, Nan and Nelson, Carnot E., " Bibliographic Reference Patterns in Core Sociological Journals ", *The American Sociologist,* IV (1969), pp. 47–50. Beyond this, nothing is known about the use made of papers which have been published only after having circulated through the editorial offices of several journals.

[35] We are indebted to Dr. Jonathan R. Cole for suggesting this line of inquiry.

[36] The effects of "page charges" to authors on patterns of publication in scientific journals constitute a complex problem in its own right which is being studied by Belver Griffith, Frances Korten and the Center for Research in Scientific Communication, at The Johns Hopkins University.

evaluative process as registered in comparative rates of rejecting manuscripts for publication. Of course this gross information tells next to nothing about the process of evaluation itself. This we can examine in some detail by turning to the scientific journal for which we have the needed archival evidence, *The Physical Review*.

Evaluative Behaviour of Editors and Referees

First, a few words about *The Physical Review*. It publishes 72 issues a year (and two index volumes) in addition to weekly publication of short research reports in the *Physical Review Letters*. It makes up six per cent. of the world's journal literature in physics (together with the *Letters*, nine per cent.). We can gauge the relative scale of this publication by noting that in 1965 *The Physical Review* itself—excluding the *PRL*—published more literature in physics than all 53 journals published in Germany, once the world centre of physics.[37]

All this quantity need not, of course, make for high quality. But it turns out that in the 1950s as now, *The Physical Review* ranked far ahead of all other journals of physics in extent to which it was used in further research. Papers published in it were far more often cited than those published in any other journal of physics and cited more often than if it were simply holding its own—that is, getting the same share of citations as its share in the physics literature. In such leading journals as the Italian *Nuovo Cimento*, the Russian *Journal of Experimental and Theoretical Physics (JETP)*, and the *Proceedings* of the Physical Society of London, the *Review* is cited far more often than these journals themselves [38]:

36 per cent. of the references in *Nuovo Cimento* are to *The Physical Review* but only 17 per cent. to all Italian journals combined;

22 per cent. of all references in *JETP* are to the *Review*, compared with 15 per cent. going to the *JETP* itself;

34 per cent. of the references in the *Proceedings* are to the *Review*, compared with 9 per cent. to the *Proceedings* itself.

This widespread use of work published in the *Review* is all the more notable since there is a general tendency for papers in each journal to cite other papers in the same journal. Kessler sums up his findings on patterns of use in the contemporary literature of physics by noting that "*The*

---

[37] Kennan, Stella and Brickwedde, F. G., *Journal literature covered by Physics Abstracts in 1965* (New York: American Institute of Physics, 1968), 68–1, Appendix II.

[38] Kessler, M. M., *Technical Information Flow Patterns* (Cambridge, Mass.: Lincoln Laboratories, (Massachusetts Institute of Technology), pp. 247–257, reporting data for the year 1957 and Kessler, M. M., "The MIT Technical Information Project", *Physics Today*, XVIII (March, 1965), pp. 28–36 at p. 30.

Physical Review is truly a definitive journal for physicists. It commands overwhelming dominance over all other journals as a carrier of information between physicists of all lands." [39]

The behaviour of physicists, both as consumers and producers of research, testifies to much the same judgement. As consumers, some 77 per cent. of the 1,300 American academic physicists queried by the Coles reported that the *Review* is among the journals they read most often (no other journal being mentioned by more than 25 per cent. of the sample).[40] As producers, the archives testify, physicists preferred to have their papers published in the *Review*, maintaining that this would give them greater visibility to their colleagues around the world. Plainly, we are dealing here with the outstanding scientific journal in its field. What, then, have been its patterns of editorial and referee evaluation?

Sampling the Archives of The Physical Review [41]

The basic data consist of the archives of the *Review* for the nine years between 1948 and 1956, containing correspondence between authors, editors and referees, records of decisions made by the editors, the allocation of manuscripts to referees, their evaluations and the final disposition of the papers. This provides a rich body of materials, both quantitative and qualitative, for analysing the infrastructure of scientific evaluation in a journal of the first class. More particularly, it enables us to find out how the workings of this structure are affected by the stratification system of science.

Consider first the population of physicists submitting manuscripts and the gross outcomes of the evaluative process. In this nine-year period, a total of 14,512 manuscripts were submitted (a little more than half of them had a single author). In this report, we deal primarily with the papers with a single author of which 80 per cent. were ultimately published. The sample we have drawn from these voluminous materials is based on a conception of the stratification system of science as a distinctive compound of egalitarian values governing access to opportunity to publish and a hierarchic structure in which power and authority are largely vested in those who have acquired rank through cumulative scientific accomplishment. It is a status-hierarchy, in Max Weber's sense, based on honour and esteem. Although rank and authority in science are *acquired* through past performance, once acquired, they then tend to be *ascribed* (for an indeterminate duration). This combination of acquired and

---

[39] Kessler, *Technical Information Flow Patterns*, p. 249.
[40] Cole, Stephen and Cole, Jonathan R., " Visibility and the Structural Bases of Awareness of Scientific Research ", *American Sociological Review*, XXXIII (June, 1968), pp. 397–413 at p. 412.
[41] We are indebted to Professor Samuel A. Goudsmit, editor-in-chief of publications for the American Physical Society, for having made these archives available to us in 1966. He has recently described the editorial and refereeing procedures currently adopted by *The Physical Review* in " What Happened to My Paper?", *Physics Today*, XXII (May, 1969), pp. 23–25.

ascribed status introduces strains in the operation of the authority-structure of science, as has been noted with great clarity by Michael Polanyi and Norman Storer.[42] These strains may be doubly involved in the processes of evaluating scientific work. In one direction, judgements *by* scientific authorities (whose status largely rests on their own past performance) may come to be assigned great or even decisive weight, and not simply because of their intellectual cogency. In the other direction, judgements *about* the work of ranking scientists may be systematically skewed by deference, by less careful appraisals involving less exacting criteria, by self-doubts of one's own sufficient competence to criticise a great man or by fear of affronting influential persons in the field. Although based on status acquired through assessed accomplishment, the hierarchy of excellence in science can militate in both ways against the unbiased, universalistic evaluation of scientific work.

With this stratification system of science in mind, we have drawn a sample of the contributors in the 1948–56 archives of *The Physical Review* which is stratified into three levels of institutionalised standing based on appraisals of past scientific work. In the first rank are *all* the physicists submitting manuscripts who, by the end of the period (1956), had received at least one of the ten most respected awards in physics (such as the Nobel prize, membership in the Royal Society and in the National Academy of Sciences).[43] These number 91 in all, with 55 of them having submitted papers of which they were the sole authors. The physicists of the second rank, although they had not been accorded any of the highest forms of recognition, had been judged important enough by the American Institute of Physics to be included in its archives of contemporary physicists. All 583 of the physicists in the American Institute of Physics list who had submitted manuscripts to the *Review* during this period make up this intermediate rank, with 343 of them having sent in manuscripts of which they were the sole authors. The remaining 8,864 contributors comprise the third rank in this hierarchy. They are not included in their entirety but are represented by two successive 10 per cent. random samples, yielding a total of 1,663 authors, with 659 of them having submitted manuscripts of which they were sole authors.[44]

---

[42] Polanyi, Michael, *Personal Knowledge* (London: Routledge & Kegan Paul, 1958), especially Chapters 6–7; Storer, *op. cit.*, pp. 103–134.

[43] See Cole and Cole, *op. cit.* (1967), p. 383 for the prestige-ranking of awards by a sample of 1,300 physicists.

[44] A first 10 per cent. random sample was selected from the physicist-authors remaining in the files after all cases of top-ranking and intermediate authors were removed. This sample of third rank authors numbered 866, with 355 of them having submitted papers which had a single author. Analysis of this first sample involving three or more variables led to results sometimes based on small numbers. To check these results, we drew a second 10 per cent. random sample of the remaining third rank authors, this yielding 797, of whom 304 had submitted papers with a single author. As it turns out, the results for the successive samples are so much the same—they vary by no more than three percentage points—that they are reported only in the aggregate.

For some special analyses, we also identified a mobile subgroup in the status-hierarchy: the 49 contributors who were in the intermediate rank during the time covered by this study but who later moved into the most eminent stratum. In effect, these physicists were observed in the course of their ascent, after having achieved a measure of distinction but before receiving the highest recognition. It will be of interest to find out how the system for evaluating manuscripts dealt with physicists whose work was later to earn them great esteem.

The 354 referees who evaluated the manuscripts with a single author submitted by our sample of authors were stratified in the same way, with 12 per cent. of them turning up in the first rank, 35 per cent. in the second, and the remaining 53 per cent. in the third.

The sample of contributors and the derivative sample of referees were designed with an eye to the general problem of the interplay between the hierarchical structure of authority and the evaluation of scientific work. More specifically, we want to examine the extent to which universalistic and particularistic standards were utilised in evaluating the papers submitted to *The Physical Review* by physicists of differing rank. Since this is our purpose, we shall limit our analysis almost entirely to papers with one author, for reasons both substantive and procedural. Substantively, it turns out that papers with more than one author, largely reporting experimental results, have so high an acceptance rate (over 95 per cent.) that they can exhibit little variability in evaluations of the kind we want to investigate. Procedurally, it is the case that the rank of the single author can be unambiguously and realistically identified. But not so in the case of papers by several hands, with their varying numbers of authors, often of differing rank.

Drawing upon the samples of authors and referees, we want to examine four main sets of questions. First, do contributors variously located in the stratification system differ in the rate at which they submit manuscripts for publication in the *Review*? Second, are there patterns of allocating manuscripts to referees variously situated in the status-hierarchy and are these allocations related to the status of authors? This leads directly to the third question: are there differences in rates of acceptance depending upon the professional identity of the physicists submitting the manuscripts? And finally, are any such differences in rates of acceptance linked to the relative status of the referees and authors?

Status-Differences in Submission of Manuscripts

It has long been known that eminent scientists tend to publish more papers and not only better ones than run-of-the-mill scientists. It comes as no surprise, then, that they also submit more manuscripts for publication. Among those physicists who submitted manuscripts, produced by themselves alone, to *The Physical Review* during the nine-year period, physicists of the highest rank averaged 4·09, the intermediates, 3·46 and the physicists of the third rank averaged 2·02.[45] These differences between the strata are presumably all the greater in the population of physicists at large than in this self-selected population of would-be contributors.

The differences in rates of submission of papers are especially marked when it comes to the most prolific physicists in the sample. The physicists of the highest rank submitted 15 or more papers to this one journal at 12 times the rate of the rank-and-file, with 18 per cent. of the highest-rank physicists, 11 per cent. of the intermediates and 1·5 per cent. of the third rank having sent that many (single- and multi-author) manuscripts.

This pattern of submission-rates also contains a striking prognostic result. The 49 mobile physicists in the sample—those who had not attained eminence by the mid-1950s but did so afterwards—were the most prolific of all, with a whopping 47 per cent. of them having submitted as many as fifteen papers to the *Review*. Plainly these were physicists at a peak period of their productivity. Six of them have since received the Nobel prize and from the look of things they will be joined by others from this group of the most prolific authors. We catch here, as with a camera, a phase in the process through which early productivity is converted into later recognition by the social system of science.

To this point, the data on submission of manuscripts merely confirm earlier findings on status differences in the number of published papers. This, it might be said, is only to be expected. In general, the more manuscripts submitted, the more find their way into print. But this does not mean, of course, that the ratio of submitted to published papers is the same for the several strata of scientists. This would assume that scientists of every stripe adopt the same standards of what constitutes a paper worth submitting for publication and that the refereeing process results in uniform rates of acceptance for scientists at all levels of the stratification system.

A first intimation that these assumptions are unfounded is provided by the rates of submission and of acceptance for papers by physicists affiliated with the seventeen foremost university departments and with less distinguished ones.[46] Among the physicists submitting any single-author manuscripts at all, those in the leading departments submitted only

---

[45] The differences in submission-rates are greatly amplified for all manuscripts (of both single and multiple authorship), as might be expected in view of the greater facilities and opportunities for collaboration enjoyed by ranking physicists. When each author of a manuscript of multiple authorship is credited with a submission, the mean rates for the nine-year period run to 9·72 for the top-ranking physicists, 7·89 for the intermediates and 1·97 for the third rank.

[46] See Keniston, Heyward, *Graduate Study and Research in the Arts and Sciences at the University of Pennsylvania* (Philadelphia: University of Pennsylvania Press, 1959) for ranks of physics departments as judged by department chairmen in 1957. To Keniston's top fifteen departments, we added California Institute of Technology and Massachusetts Institute of Technology since technological institutions were not included in his survey. There are no comparable rankings of the quality of industrial laboratories or independent research organisations.

slightly more, with an average of 2·62 compared with 2·49 for the others.[47] But when it comes to actual publication, not submission, the picture changes. Some 91 per cent. of the papers by physicists in the foremost departments were accepted as against 72 per cent. from other universities (producing average acceptances of 2·36 and 1·79 papers, respectively).

This result sets the general problem quite clearly. What patterns of evaluation intervene between the submission of papers and actual publication to produce this result? How does it happen that the physicists from the minor departments who are submitting almost as many single-author papers as their counterparts in the major departments end up by having significantly fewer of them published? The question is critical because the gross empirical finding lends itself to sharply different kinds of interpretation

One interpretation would attribute the departmental differences in acceptance rates to the operation of the stratification system. It holds that the work of scientists in the upper strata is evaluated less severely, that these authors are given the benefit of the doubt by editors and referees, because of their standing in the field or affiliation with influential departments, and that all this is reinforced by particularistic ties between authors and referees. This hypothesis suggests that the status of both author and referee significantly affects the judgement of manuscripts, so that work of the same intrinsic worth will be differently evaluated according to these considerations of status.

Another interpretation would ascribe the different outcomes of the evaluation process principally to differences in the scientific quality of the manuscripts coming from different sources. This hypothesis maintains that universalistic standards tend to be rather uniformly applied in judging manuscripts but that, on the average, the quality of papers coming from the several strata actually differs. On this view, scientists in the departments of the highest rank tend to be positively selected in terms of demonstrated capacity, have greater resources for investigation, have more demanding internal standards before manuscripts are submitted, and are more apt to have their papers exactingly appraised by competent colleagues before sending them in for publication. On this hypothesis, it is not a preferential bias toward the status of authors and their departments which makes for differing acceptance rates by referees, but intrinsic differences in the quality of manuscripts which in turn are the outcome of joint differences in the capabilities of scientists and in the quality of their immediate academic environments.

We should repeat that although the two interpretations differ in their

---

[47] It should be emphasised here that these rates of submitting manuscripts do not of course register actual differences in the " per capita productivity " of departments of different rank. Since they are confined to physicists who contributed at least one manuscript to *The Physical Review* in this period, these figures take no account of the least productive physicists who are probably present in quite different proportions in departments of differing rank.

conceptions of what goes on in the evaluative process, they are not contradictory in the sense that one necessarily excludes the other.[48] Both universalistic and particularistic standards might be *concretely* involved in the actual process of evaluation, but to varying extents and in different parts of the stratification system of science. We want to estimate the extent to which one or the other of these standards is adopted and the structural arrangements that make for use of one or the other.

It is no easy matter to disentangle these components of evaluation. The standing of physicists in their field, the Coles have found, is highly correlated with the quality of their previously published work as this is assessed by fellow-physicists on all levels of status.[49] This status, earned in part by past work, may be variously bound up with editorial judgements of the quality of their new work. If all papers submitted by Nobel laureates, for example, are accepted for publication, there remains the question whether some of these would have been rejected had they been submitted by scientists of distinctly lower standing. Correlatively, if scientists who enjoy the greatest prestige have been doing work of high quality in part because their critical associates and they themselves have demanding internal standards, then the manuscripts they decide to submit for publication are apt to be rigorously pre-selected, with consequently high rates of acceptance by referees applying similarly universalistic criteria.

These difficulties of analysis could be largely avoided if authors were altogether anonymous to referees. But arrangements designed for this purpose work imperfectly.[50] Various kinds of clues in manuscripts often provide unmistakable signatures of the authors, particularly, perhaps, the eminent ones. In any event, *The Physical Review* has not tried to provide for anonymity of manuscripts, for reasons emphatically set forth by Goudsmit:

Removing the name and affiliation of the author does not make a manuscript anonymous. A competent reviewer can tell at a glance where the work was done and by whom or under whose guidance. One must also remove all

---

[48] We note in passing that there seems to be a strong tendency to adopt one of these interpretations *to the exclusion* of the other. The first interpretation seems congenial to those who conceive of the social institution of science as dominated by influence and the exercise of power (decidedly, not intellectual power), with the evaluative system having little to do with universally applied standards for judging validity and scientific significance. The second interpretation seems congenial to those who allow no place at all for social exchange in the institution of science, with the system of evaluation involving only the exercise of universal standards, subject to some margin of socially unpatterned errors in judgement. We hazard the guess that amongst those who seize exclusively upon one or the other interpretation, the first is more often adopted by scientists in the middle and lower reaches of the stratification system and the second, by those in the upper reaches.

[49] Cole and Cole, *op cit.* (1967), pp. 384–390.

[50] In a study of social science journals, Professor Diana Crane concludes that the effort to maintain anonymity of authors does not affect differentials in rates of publication by authors from major and minor universities. As she implies, the findings are highly tentative since they are based entirely on actual patterns of publication, without taking into account patterned variations in the rates of submitting manuscripts. See Crane, Diana, " The Gatekeepers of Science: Some Factors Affecting the Selection of Articles for Scientific Journals ", *The American Sociologist,* II (1967), pp. 195–201.

references to previous work by the same author, all descriptions of special equipment and other significant parts of the paper. Nothing worth judging or publishing would be left.[51]

The archives of the *Review* nevertheless provide evidence enabling us to move a certain distance toward identifying basic patterns in the evaluation of scientific work.

Patterns of Allocation to Judges

A first phase in the evaluation process is crystal-clear. The higher the rank of authors in the prestige-hierarchy, the greater the proportion of their papers which are judged by the two editors—either singly or in tandem—without going to outside referees. Of the manuscripts submitted by the physicists of the highest rank, 87 per cent. were judged exclusively by the editors, in contrast to 73 per cent. of those coming from the intermediate rank and 58 per cent. of the rest. As we shall see, it is the more problematic papers which are sent to outside referees. All this has the immediate consequence, that the higher the rank of the physicist, the more prompt the decision taken on his manuscript (Table II), a matter of concern to many scientists, especially those wanting to safeguard their priority.

TABLE II

Duration of Editorial and Refereeing Process for Published Papers, by Rank of Author
(*Physical Review, 1948–1956*) [a]

Duration	Rank of author		
	Higher rank physicists %	Intermediate physicists %	Third rank physicists %
Less than 2 months	42	35	29
2–4 months	47	45	41
5 months +	11	20	30
Total	(202)	(1027)	(972)

[a] This table and all subsequent ones are based on a sample of manuscripts with single authors submitted to the *Review* during this period.

The referee system calls for evaluation of manuscripts by experts on their subject. It should come as no surprise, therefore, that the outside referees were drawn disproportionately from physicists of high rank. Compared with the 5 per cent. of the 1,056 authors (themselves in some

[51] Goudsmit, S. A., *Physics Today*, XX (January, 1967), p. 12.

measure a selected aggregate), almost 12 per cent. of the 354 outside referees assessing their papers were in the highest rank. Moreover, these 12 per cent. of the referees contributed one-third of all referee judgements. They refereed an average of 8·5 papers compared with 3·8 for the intermediates and 1·4 for the rank-and-file. And although some 45 per cent. of the referees were under the age of 40, thus giving major responsibility to the relatively young, it should also be noted that research physicists are a youthful aggregate, with fully 74 per cent. of the papers submitted to the *Physical Review* coming from men under 40. Much the same pattern of stratification is found when referees are classified according to the rank of the institution with which they are affiliated, rather than their individual rank. For example, about two-thirds of all referee judgements were made by physicists in the 17 major departments of physics in universities, the Bell Laboratories and the Institute for Advanced Study.

The composite portrait of referees is clear enough. Whether gauged by their own prestige, institutional affiliations or research accomplishments, they are largely drawn from the scientific elite, as would be expected from the principle of expertise.

We want now to consider patterns of allocating the referees to authors of varying rank. The possible patterns are describable in four models, which can be designated as the "oligarchical" model, the "populist" model, the "egalitarian" model and the model of expertise.

In the oligarchical model, the established elite of science alone has the power to judge the work of those beneath it in the status-hierarchy. The second model corresponds to a populistic view which assigns power of judgement to " the people ". The strictly egalitarian model, by contrast, calls for a policy in which papers are assessed only by juries of status-peers. And last, the model of expertise calls for the allocation of manuscripts to referees who, regardless of rank, are especially competent to judge them.

It is easy enough to construct the distribution of cases in our data which would correspond to an oligarchical policy for allocating referees to authors. This would require all manuscripts to be evaluated by judges ranking higher than authors with the exception of those submitted by the highest rank of scientists. Having reached the top of the status-hierarchy, they would be exempt from oligarchy and judged by peers. Put in terms of our data, this model would have physicists of the highest rank evaluating all the manuscripts by the intermediate physicists and these two ranks in turn would be charged with assessing the work of the third rank. As the lowest stratum, the third rank would do no refereeing at all. A glance at Table III is enough to indicate that the actual pattern of allocation diverges greatly from this oligarchical model. " Status-inferiors " do much more refereeing and, by the same token, " status-superiors " far less than this model requires.

The second model, expressing a populist view, would have manuscripts judged exclusively by physicists ranking lower than authors. This model is of course at odds with the traditional ethos of science which holds that the quality of scientific accomplishment is the determinant of the status ascribed to scientists. It turns out that the data on actual allocations diverge very widely from the populistic model. Relative to their numbers, lower-ranking physicists do little refereeing altogether and also referee far fewer papers by the intermediate and highest ranking physicists than would be the case under a populistic allocation.

According to the strictly egalitarian model, papers would be assessed exclusively by status-peers. The actual distribution, as Table III shows, departs very widely from this model also. As can be seen by aggregating the cases in the left-to-right diagonal, only about a third of all judgements are made by status-peers of authors, and there is a widening deviation from the model for the lesser ranks of physicists.

In short, the actual patterns of allocation of referees to authors approximate to none of these models.

TABLE III

Rank of Referees Assigned to Authors of Differing Rank

(Physical Review, 1948–1956)

Rank of authors	Rank of referees			Total judgements by referees
	Higher rank physicists %	Intermediate physicists %	Third rank physicists %	
Higher rank physicists	50	31	19	(36)
Intermediate physicists	38	41	21	(394)
Third rank physicists	27	46	26	(653)
All authors	32	44	24	(1083)

The principle of expertise requires that referees should be assigned to manuscripts on the basis of their competence. The data presented in Table III are at least consistent with the principle of expertise once it is assumed that demonstrated expertise is substantially (*i.e.,* imperfectly) correlated with rank in the hierarchy of prestige. On this assumption, the data would exhibit a preponderance but no monopoly of refereeing by physicists ranking higher than authors. Authors would occasionally outrank referees in prestige (if not in competence) and judgement by peers would be relatively more frequent for the successively higher ranks of authors. These patterns turn up in the actual data recorded in Table III as we see for the example of judgements by status-peers accounting for 50 per cent. of the papers by top-ranking physicists, 41 per cent. for the intermediates and 26 per cent. for the rank-and-file.

This suggests, although it does not demonstrate, that expertise and competence were the principal criteria adopted in matching papers and referees. That papers by distinguished scientists were assigned for review to others of like stature need not mean, therefore, that an inner circle of physicists were being asked to pass judgements upon one another's work in a closed system of mutual support. The principle of expertise would lead to such allocations just as it would to the observed pattern of referees more often outranking authors than conversely.

In any case, we now know that the more highly placed physicists had power disproportionate to their number in deciding what was to enter into the pages of *The Physical Review*. How did they act in these positions of power?

Status Differences in Rates of Acceptance

Since the anonymity of authors cannot be uniformly assured, it would require a strict experimental design to find out decisively whether papers *of the same scientific quality* are assessed differently by referees according to the status of authors. Both ethics and practicality rule out the draconian experiment in which matched samples of referees, all unknowing, would independently judge the same manuscripts variously ascribed to physicists of different rank, in order to determine the extent of status-linked evaluations. Nor can we approximate the intent of that experimental design by adopting the number of citations to published papers as measures of quality to see whether papers rejected by *The Physical Review* but published elsewhere are of the same quality as those accepted by that journal.

At best, we can bring together data which provide cumulative intimations of the extent to which judgements by editors and referees relate to the status of authors. We begin by examining the successive disposition of manuscripts as this is summarised in the abbreviated flow chart of the refereeing process (Chart I). It turns out that 90 per cent. of the manuscripts submitted by top-ranking physicists have been accepted for publication compared with 86 per cent. for the intermediates and 73 per cent. for the rank-and-file. These stratified rates are the outcome of a continuing process of evaluation (condensed into two phases in the chart). In each phase, the higher the rank of physicists, the better they fare. A larger proportion of their papers are accepted straightaway, a smaller proportion

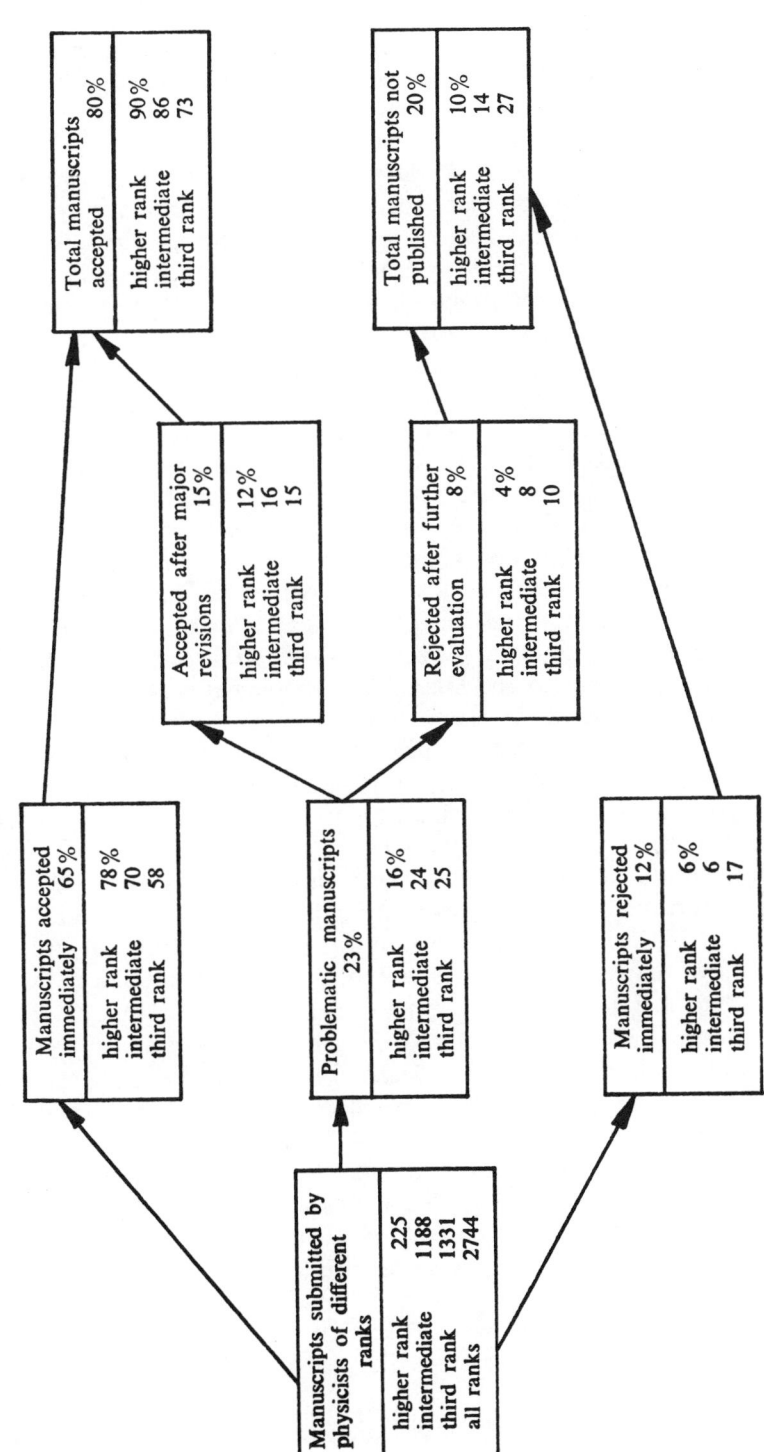

CHART 1

Evaluation of Manuscripts with Single Authors By Rank of Author (The Physical Review, 1948–1956)

rejected outright and a smaller proportion treated as problematic, requiring further assessments before final decision. Of the manuscripts judged to be problematic, moreover, a larger fraction by the high-ranking physicists ultimately get into print.

Once again, the observed patterns lend themselves to quite different interpretations. They are consistent with the opinion that physicists of the first rank submit better papers on the average and that they are also better able than the others to rehabilitate their problematic papers. But the data can also be interpreted in particularistic rather than universalistic terms. For the observed patterns would also obtain if the editors and referees were especially reluctant to reject papers submitted by the most distinguished men in their field and reluctant also to judge them as needing further evaluation and revision.

Before turning to other evidence bearing on these alternative interpretations, we should consider the patterns of stratified differences within the context of other aspects of the refereeing process which can be reconstructed from the flow chart. We noted earlier that scientific journals with high rates of acceptance seem to prefer the decision-rule: when in doubt, accept. In the case of *The Physical Review*, this preference rule found several expressions. When it came to acceptances, the ratio of immediate decisions to the later, more problematic ones was over 4 to 1 (*i.e.*, 65 per cent. to 15 per cent.) compared with a ratio of only 1·5 to 1 (*i.e.*, 12 per cent. to 8 per cent.) for rejections. Among the problematic papers undergoing further evaluation, moreover, acceptances still preponderate but at only 1·7 times the number of rejections. The decision-rule also seems reflected in the fact that *The Physical Review* mobilised more institutional machinery to reject papers than to accept them: more judges were used on the average for rejected papers than for those ultimately published. And in accord with the general pattern of stratification, the higher the rank of physicist-authors, the fewer the judges involved in accepting their manuscripts.

These patterns, we conjecture, are generally reversed in journals with low acceptance rates where the decision-rule seems to be: when in doubt, reject. In those journals the early decisions presumably exhibit higher rates of rejection than the problematic papers sent on for further refereeing. For in the case of these journals, the presumption seems to be that the manuscripts they receive are not fit to print (at least in the particular journal) since they do in fact reject most manuscripts. Thus, for the journals in the humanities and social sciences, with their typically high rejection rates, it is the potentially acceptable paper which is problematic, while for the journals in physical science, such as *The Physical Review*, with their high acceptance rates, it is the potentially unacceptable paper which is problematic.

Another piece of evidence takes us a certain distance toward gauging the possibility that assessments of manuscripts in *The Physical Review* might have been affected by the standing of their authors. For this purpose, we note again that eminence and authority in science derive largely from the assessed quality of past and not necessarily continuing scientific accomplishments. We note also that in science, as in other institutional spheres, positions of power and authority tend to be occupied by older men. (Indeed, it has sometimes been said with mixed feelings that gerontocracy may even be a good thing in science; it leaves the young productive scientists free to get on with their work and helps to occupy the time of those who are no longer creative.) From these joint patterns, it would seem that if the sheer power and eminence of authors greatly affect refereeing decisions, then the older eminent scientists should have the highest rates of acceptance.

But, at least in physics, the young man's science, this is not what we find. It is not the older scientists whose papers were most often accepted but the younger ones. And these age-graded rates of acceptance hold within each applicable rank in the hierarchy of esteem (Table IV). Both

TABLE IV

Rates of Acceptance of Manuscripts, by Age and Rank of Authors (The Physical Review, 1948–1956)

	Rank of authors			
Age of authors	Higher rank physicists % No.	Intermediate physicists % No.	Third rank physicists % No.	All ranks % No.
20–29		91 287	83 385	87 672
30–39	96 80	89 519	77 440	85 1039
40–49	95 58	83 236	73 79	83 373
50+	80 87	71 126	50 14	73 227
No information on age				61 423
All ages				80 2734

eminence and youth contribute to the probability of having manuscripts accepted; youth to such a degree that the youngest stratum of physicists in the third rank had as high an acceptance rate as the oldest stratum of eminent ones whose work, we must suppose, was no longer of the same high quality it once was. Dr. Jonathan Cole's studies of citation and reference patterns of physicists lend support to this impression.[52] He finds that older physicists are less apt than younger ones to refer to currently

---

[52] Cole, Jonathan, *The Social Structure of Science*, unpublished doctoral dissertation, Department of Sociology, Columbia University (1969), Chapter 6.

influential work in their publications, this suggesting that their own work may no longer be as much in the mainstream. Evidently there comes a time in the life-cycle of physicists, even the most distinguished ones, when they can no longer count on having their papers almost invariably accepted in a major refereed journal such as *The Physical Review*. As Max Delbrück once observed, perhaps the chief function of unrefereed *Festschriften* was to provide a decent cemetery for oft-rejected manuscripts.

Relative Status and Differences in Acceptance Rates

Perhaps it is not the status of the author as such but his status relative to that of the referee which systematically influences appraisals of his manuscripts. Such biases in judgement might take various forms, depending on the pattern of relative status.

When referees and authors are status-peers, an hypothesis of *status-solidarity* would have it that referees typically give preferential treatment to manuscripts just as a counter-hypothesis of *status-competition* would have it that under the safeguard of anonymity, referees tend to undercut their rivals by unjustifiably severe judgements.

TABLE V

Referees' Decisions to Accept, by Rank of Authors and Referees (The Physical Review, 1948–1956)

Rank of authors	Rank of Referees						Total judgements by referees	
	Higher rank physicists		Intermediate physicists		Third rank physicists			
	%	No.	%	No.	%	No.	%	No.
Higher rank physicists	*	18	*	11	*	7	50	36
Intermediate physicists	55	150	62	160	62	84	59	394
Third rank physicists	54	179	61	302	59	172	59	653
All ranks							59	1083

* The number of manuscripts by higher ranking physicists submitted to outside referees, as distinct from editorial judges, was too small for statistical analysis.

When authors outrank referees, an hypothesis of *status-deference* would hold that the referees give preferential treatment to the work of men they respect or hold in awe just as a counter-hypothesis of *status-envy* would have them be more exacting of the work of superiors.

And when referees outrank authors, an hypothesis of *status-patronage* or sponsorship would maintain that referees are unduly kind and undemanding while a counter-hypothesis of *status-subordination* would have them overly-demanding.

Differing in other respects, these six hypotheses are alike in one: they all assume that the relative status of referee and author significantly biases judgements by referees, either in favour of the author or at his expense. More concretely, all assume that the rates of acceptance for each stratum of authors will differ according to the rank of the referees making the judgements.

The data assembled in Table V run counter to all the hypotheses. Referees of each rank accept the same proportion of papers by authors from every stratum. As it happens, the highest ranking referees accept somewhat smaller proportions of papers than their fellow referees but, again, this they do uniformly for authors of every rank. There is, in short, no preferential pattern, as can be shown redundantly but emphatically by condensing the components of Table V into three categories of relative status.

Relative status	Rate of acceptance %	Total judgements by referees No.
Referees outrank authors	58	631
Referees and authors: status-peers	60	350
Authors outrank referees	59	102

All this suggests that referees were applying much the same standards to papers, whatever their source. This is confirmed further by patterns of even-handed evaluation in the case of other relative statuses of referees and authors. Referees affiliated with minor universities, for example, are no more apt to accept papers submitted by authors from universities of similar standing than were referees from the major universities. And whatever the academic rank of referees, it did not affect the rate at which they accepted papers by authors in the various academic ranks. For this journal, at least, the relative status of referee and author had no perceptible influence on patterns of evaluation.

We may conclude that the status-composition of the physicists engaged in refereeing manuscripts for *The Physical Review* during the period is one thing; what the referees did in exercising their authority is quite another.

Functions of the Referee System

As the prime journal in its field, *The Physical Review* can be assumed to apply exacting standards. All the same, the editorial and refereeing process results in as many as four of every five manuscripts being accepted for publication (a fair number of them, after greater or less revision). Does this mean that referees are largely superfluous? Like other observers of the referee system,[53] we think not. Referees, collectively engaged in sorting out good science from bad, serve diverse functions for the various members of their profession: for editors, authors, the referees themselves and the relevant community of scientists.

For the editor(s), referees serve their prime function in the case of papers difficult to assess. At the extremes, as we have noted for *The Physical Review* and a variety of other journals, papers are comparatively easy to appraise and the editor(s) can sort them out. Manuscripts which, by the core standards of the field, provide sound, new, consequential ideas and information, clearly formulated and relevant to the particular journal, can be readily distinguished from their antitheses which are mistaken, redundant, trivial, obscure and irrelevant. But not all manuscripts exhibit these neatly correlated arrays of intellectual virtues or vices. It is the often sizable number of more problematic manuscripts which particularly require examination by experts on their subjects. Apart from this manifest function of furnishing expert judgement, the corps of typically anonymous referees sometimes serves the incidental and not altogether latent function of protecting the highly visible editor from the wrath of disappointed authors.[54] But what is helpful for the editor can of course be injurious to the author. The referee system is now under severe strain on the issue of enlarging the accountability of referees by removing their cloak of anonymity.[55] Since accountability is itself so much a component of the ethos of science, it may be that the practice of maintaining anonymity of referees will increasingly go by the board.

This will surely not be misunderstood to say that the interests of referees and authors are inherently at odds. Referees who conscientiously fulfil their role of course serve major functions for authors. They can and, as we have seen in the case of *The Physical Review*, often do suggest basic revisions for improving papers. They sometimes link up the paper with other work which the author happened not to know; they protect the author from unwittingly publishing duplications of earlier work; and, of

---

[53] The operation of the authority structure in science and the social structural basis of scientific objectivity have been most fully developed by Michael Polanyi, notably in his *Personal Knowledge* (London: Routledge & Kegan Paul, 1958); the discussion of the referee system is principally in Chapter 6. See also, Ziman, *op. cit.*, pp. 111–117; Storer, *op. cit.*, pp. 112–126; Hagstrom, *op. cit.*, pp. 18–19.

[54] Based on our sample of the archives of *The Physical Review*, a qualitative analysis of the tacit rules involved in rejecting a manuscript has been set out by Raffel, Stanley, "The Acceptance of Rejection", a paper presented at the meetings of the American Sociological Association, 1968.

[55] The pros and cons of referee anonymity are being strenuously debated in various fields; for examples, see the letters by Roy, Rustum, and Henisch, H. K., in *Physics Today*, XXIII (August, 1970), p. 11; Cahnman, Werner J., in *The American Sociologist*, II (May, 1967), pp. 97–98; Steinberg, A. G., in *Science* CXLVIII (23 April, 1965), p. 444.

course, as presumable experts in the subject, they in effect certify the paper as a contribution by recommending its publication. But like other men, referees are not uniformly conscientious in performing their roles. There are, it seems, differences in this respect among fields and among referees of differing kind so that the functions of refereeing for authors and consequently for the discipline are imperfectly realised. This is scarcely the first time that an institution devoted to evaluation confronts the problem of who judges the judges? A sorting and sifting of referees would seem as much a functional requirement of the referee system as the sorting and sifting of papers for publication.

The role of referee also serves functions and creates difficulties for the referees themselves. As experts in the subject, many referees are already informed of developments at its frontier. But especially in fields without efficient networks of informal communication or in rapidly developing fields, referees occasionally get a head start in learning about significant new work. Moreover, as some referees report, the role-induced close scrutiny of manuscripts, in contrast to the often perfunctory scanning of possibly comparable articles already in print, sometimes leads them to perceive potentialities for new lines of inquiry which were neither stated by the author nor previously considered by the referee. This unplanned evocative function of the paper often puts both referee and author under stress. What the referee defines as an instance of his having legitimately and appreciatively borrowed or learned from the manuscript, the author, not surprisingly, may define as an instance of pilfering or downright plundering, as he observes the referee going on to pursue and so, perhaps, to pre-empt the new line of investigation.

The basic and, it would seem, thoroughly rational practice of selecting experts as referees makes for its own stresses in the system. Some scientists have argued that it is particularly the experts who can exploit their fiduciary role to advance their own interests and so are most subject to possible conflict of interest. Here is one among many recent expressions of this view:

The referee, or more often a member of his group or one of his graduate students, may be working on the very problem he is asked to judge. Of course we must rely upon his personal integrity not to " sit on " the submitted paper, take unfair advantage of the pre-publication information or be unduly critical of the work, thus " buying time " for his own people. He could, in fact, return the paper to the editor citing conflict of interest as his reason for no recommendation, but he cannot avoid the fact of being informed. The point becomes crucial in rapidly developing competitive fields and for publications such as *Physical Review Letters* or *Applied Physics Letters* where priority claims are important.[56]

[56] Prinz, A. G., in *Physics Today*, XXIII (August, 1970), pp. 11-12.

Plainly, the institutionalised concern with intellectual property [57] in science provides the context for these stresses on the referee system. Neither the context nor the stresses are anything new. The concern with intellectual property, which we found to play its distinctive part in the beginnings of the scientific journal, has created difficulties for the developing referee-system right along. Here, for example, is the young T. H. Huxley emphatically expressing his conviction that should "the great authority" on his subject serve as referee, he would never allow Huxley's paper to see print:

You have no idea of the intrigues that go on in this blessed world of science. Science is, I fear, no purer than any other region of human activity; though it should be. Merit alone is very little good; it must be backed by tact and knowledge of the world to do very much.

For instance, I know that the paper I have just sent in [to the Royal Society] is very original and of some importance, and I am equally sure that if it is referred to the judgement of my "particular friend" . . . that it will not be published. He won't be able to say a word against it, but he will pooh-pooh it to a dead certainty.

You will ask with some wonderment, Why? Because for the last twenty years . . . has been regarded as the great authority on these matters, and has had no one to tread on his heels, until at last, I think, he has come to look upon the Natural World as his special preserve, and "no poachers allowed". So I must manoeuvre a little to get my poor memoir kept out of his hands.[58]

With all its imperfections, old and new, the developing institution of the referee system provides for a warranted faith that what appears in the archives of science can generally be relied upon. As Professor Michael Polanyi in particular has observed,[59] the functional significance of the referee system increases with the growing differentiation of science into arrays and extensive networks of specialities. The more specialised the paper, the fewer there are who can responsibly appraise its worth. But while only a few may be fully competent to assess, many more on the periphery of the subject and in other related fields may find the paper relevant to their work. It is for them that the role of the referee as deputy takes on special importance. When a scientist is working on a problem treated in a published article, he can serve as his own referee. He may, in fact, be better qualified to assess its worth than the official referee who helped usher it into print. It is not so much the fellow-specialist as the

---

[57] On intellectual property as a significant context for the behaviour of scientists, see Merton, R. K., " Priorities in scientific discovery ", *op. cit.*, pp. 635–659; " Singletons and multiples in scientific discovery ", *Proceedings*, American Philosophical Society, CV (October, 1961), pp. 470–486; " The ambivalence of scientists ", *Bulletin of the Johns Hopkins Hospital*, CXII (1963), pp. 77–97; " Resistance to the systematic study of multiple discoveries in science ", *op. cit.*; " Behavior patterns of scientists ", published in *American Scientist*, LVII (Spring, 1969), pp. 1–23 and also in *The American Scholar*, XXXVIII (Spring, 1969), pp. 197–225.

[58] Huxley, Leonard, *Life and Letters of Thomas Henry Huxley* (London: Macmillan and Co., 1900), Volume 1, p. 97.

[59] Polanyi, *Personal Knowledge*, p. 163.

others making use of published results in fields tangential to their own who particularly depend upon the referee system.

Scientists also benefit from the refereeing of papers in their own special fields but for somewhat different reasons. They may often be equipped to test for themselves the substance of the papers on which they draw but to do so repeatedly would only subvert their motivation. The fun and excitement in doing science comes largely from working on problems not yet solved. The continuing rather than occasional need to recheck the observations, experimental results and theories advanced by others would seem an excellent means for depleting creative energies. By providing for generally warranted confidence in the research reported in accredited publications, the system of expert referees helps scientists get on with their own imaginative inquiries.

Editors of journals in many fields of learning remark, sometimes with an air of puzzlement, upon the willingness of scientists and scholars to serve in the anonymous and often exacting role of referee. In some fields, such participation is widely diffused. Almost 30 per cent. of a sample of high energy theorists in physics, for example, had engaged in refereeing and editorial work for journals.[60] A sense of reciprocation for benefits received from the referee system probably supports the motivation for serving in the role of referee as it becomes recognised that the maintenance of standards is a collective responsibility. For young scientists and scholars, there may also be the further symbolic reward of having been identified as enough of an expert to serve as a referee.

The very existence of the referee system, Dr. Simon Pasternack has suggested,[61] makes for quality control of scientific communications. In part, this control works by anticipation. Knowing that their papers will be reviewed, authors take care in preparing them before submission, all the more so, perhaps, for papers sent to high-ranking journals with a reputation for thorough refereeing. This would also make for the scientists' internalisation of high standards. Furthermore, Pasternack points out, even the " scientific journals that have little or no refereeing or editing . . . exist within a framework of the edited journals, which set the pattern and the standard ". The referee system may thus be raising standards adopted by journals ostensibly outside that system.

These observations on the functions of the referee system do not at all imply the contrary-to-fact assumption that it works with unfailing effectiveness. Errors of judgment of course occur. But the system of monitoring scientific work before it enters into the archives of science means that

[60] Libbey, Miles, A. and Zaltman, Gerald, *The Role and Distribution of Written Informal Communications in Theoretical High Energy Physics* (New York: American Institute of Physics, 25 August, 1967), p. 49.

[61] Pasternack, Simon, " Is Journal Publication Obsolescent?", *Physics Today*, XIX (May, 1966), pp. 38–43, at p. 40 and p. 42. Dr. Pasternack has been editor of *The Physical Review* since 1956 (which will be remembered as the end of the nine-year-period examined in this paper) and on its staff since 1951.

much of the time scientists can build upon the work of others with a degree of warranted confidence. It is in this sense that the structure of authority in science, in which the referee system occupies a central place, provides an institutional basis for the comparative reliability and cumulation of knowledge.[62]

---

[62] Several articles bearing on the subject of this paper have appeared since it was completed. Most directly relevant is the work of Richard Whitley on the operation of science journals. His study of an interdisciplinary journal and one in social science found that in both cases, editorial decisions on manuscripts were unrelated to the rank and institutional affiliation of contributors. (Whitley, Richard D., "The Operation of Science Journals: Two Case Studies in British Social Science", *Sociological Review*, New Series, XVIII (July, 1970), pp. 241–258.) In his study of 32 journals in social science, Whitley found that the older journals and those devoted to fundamental rather than applied science had tended, more than the others, to develop specific criteria for judging manuscripts. This is consistent with the hypothesis advanced in the present paper that differences among the disciplines in rates of rejection are associated with the extent of consensus on the criteria of adequate scholarship in the various disciplines. (Whitley, Richard D., "The Formal Communication System of Science: A Study of the Organisation of British Social Science Journals", *The Sociological Review: Monograph No. 16*, (September, 1970), pp. 163–179.) Whitley also found that the extent of control by professional associations over the communication system in social science was significantly related to the use of formal procedures for evaluating manuscripts. (*Ibid.*, p. 175).

Two studies based on surveys of journals in clinical, personality and educational psychology report substantial agreement among the editors of these journals on the criteria for judging the acceptability of manuscripts. Since these studies are not based on investigation of the archives, however, they cannot determine the possibility of socially patterned differences in the application of these criteria. (Wolff, Wirt M., "A Study of Criteria for Journal Manuscripts", *American Psychologist*, XXV (July, 1970), pp. 636–639; Frantz, T. T., "Criteria for Publishable Manuscripts", *Personnel and Guidance Journal*, XLVII (1968), pp. 384–386.)

Bearing directly upon the findings on differences in rejection rates by journals in the humanities and sciences reported in this paper is a survey of the importance assigned to various criteria for good scientific writing by members of 16 departments of social and natural science at a major university. The results indicate that "the harder natural sciences stress precise mathematical and technical criteria, whereas the softer social sciences emphasise less defined logico-theoretical standards". (Chase, Janet M., "Normative Criteria for Scientific Publication", *American Sociologist*, V (August, 1970), pp. 262–265.) We owe the information in this footnote to Mr. Aron Halberstam.

5 THE CHARACTERISTICS AND INTERRELATIONSHIPS OF JOURNALS

5. THE CHARACTERISTICS AND INTERRELATIONSHIPS OF JOURNALS

During the last couple of decades, there has been a great growth of interest in the study of journals as prime indicators of how scientists communicate with each other. Work in this area has partly had a theoretical orientation — in the sense that it has been aimed at obtaining a better picture of the scientific community and of its methods of processing information. But there has always been the additional hope that the knowledge so gained would ultimately lead to developments of practical value for the organisation and usage of journal literature. Direct spin-off of this sort has, so far, been fairly small. But the general picture of scientific communication that has been built up is clearly proving influential in the formulation of information policies. For this reason, these studies deserve attention from anyone concerned with the future of the scientific journal.

The first article reprinted in this section discusses one of the earliest regularities noted about scientific journals — the way in which research papers on a particular topic are scattered over a number of different journals. This theme has been discussed quite often in the last twenty or thirty years. The particular article selected for reprinting here differs from the majority in having been written by an expert statistician, and so benefits from his ability to fill in the statistical background.

The second paper is a classic examination of the way in which research papers in scientific journals are interrelated via their bibliographical references. Its author, Derek Price, initiated much of the work in this area. He also led the way in using the *Science Citation Index* for detailed studies of such interrelationships. Although this paper presents his early conclusions regarding the 'research front' in scientific literature and its time-dependence, the results still appear to be valid in general terms.

The third paper also relies on the *Science Citation Index*, but used here to look at the relationship between scientific journals, rather than between individual papers. I have chosen this particular item for reprinting because it indicates how this type of study can say something about the general organisation and structure of science. It has been customary, since at least the nineteenth century, to discern a hierarchy in the sciences, with mathematics at the top, followed in order by physics, chemistry and biology, with the social sciences bringing up the rear. (This same distinction is contained in the social scientists' differentiation between 'hard' and 'soft' science.) The paper by Narin *et al.* suggests a way in which this intuitive order might be substantiated by an examination of journal hierarchies.

The next paper, by Xhignesse and Osgood, although published earlier, follows logically at this point. It examines the interrelationship of journals in one specific discipline — psychology — sketching out, for example, the differences that appear between journals publishing pure and applied psychology. Besides providing a case study of a particular discipline, this article has been selected because it looks at changes in these relationships over time. There is some tendency in looking at relationships between journals (though not between individual papers) to present the situation as static. In fact, over a decade or more, one would expect changes to occur — for example, because of revisions of editorial policy.

The final paper in this section is intended as another case study, but with wide implications. It looks at the interrelationships of physics journals, with particular emphasis on the practical question of selecting journals for purchase or use. It therefore brings in some of the methodology developed in the earlier papers in this section, and examines its utility in a situation of immediate interest to librarians. At the same time, the paper provides a useful survey of the whole field of journal ranking methods.

As will be evident from reading the papers in this section, the studies reported rely ultimately on the computer handling of bibliographical data. We shall be noting in Section 7 that computer handling of information is likely to be a continuing growth area in future decades. We should therefore expect that the type of studies outlined here will become increasingly sophisticated and, perhaps, of greater applicability in the future.

The Bibliography of Operational Research

M. G. KENDALL

Research Techniques Division, London School of Economics

1. IN his book on *Documentation* (1948) the librarian, S. C. Bradford[1], discussed certain regularities in the pattern of distribution of articles on a particular subject over different journals. He gives as examples the distributions for geophysics from 1928–31 inclusive and lubrication for 1931 to June, 1933, inclusive. The typical picture is one in which, to a bibliography covering a certain short term of years, a few journals contribute a large number of articles, more journals contribute fewer and so on in a monotonic sequence ending with a large number of journals contributing one article each. Patterns of this kind have been observed by several authors, but Bradford was the first, I think, to advance an explanation of the effect in bibliographical terms.

2. Table 1 shows an analysis of the recent bibliography of operational research published by ORSA[4] in 1958. I have excluded books and unpublished or classified reports and thus include only articles actually published in available journals. For convenience of comparison the columns are arranged in the same form as those given by Bradford.

3. Without any more penetrating analysis we can at once draw some important conclusions from this table. The first five journals cover 611 out of 1763 references, about one-third. If we want a 50 per cent cover we need 18 journals.* A 75 per cent cover requires 67 journals. There is a rapidly diminishing return by way of additional articles per journal as we proceed down the table. The implications for bibliographical work in operational research are clear. Assuming that all the articles are of equal standing (in the sense that it may be necessary to consult any one to see whether it is relevant to some particular inquiry), we might expect a normal operational research library to contain the 18 journals required for a 50 per cent cover. To go much further would obviously strain its resources in money and space.

4. For a young subject like operational research the pattern may of course change; but the width of the domain which it covers suggests that the extent of the scatter of the literature will not diminish. In this connection, a similar pattern for an older subject, statistics, may be of some interest. Table 2 shows a classification of 1465 references to statistical methodology (covering the period 1925–39) given at the end of Volume 2 of my *Advanced Theory of*

* The 18 journals were as follows: *Operations Research, N.R.L.Q., Operational Research Quarterly, Management Science, Econometrica, Journal of Industrial Engineering, Journal of the Royal Statistical Society, Annals of Mathematical Statistics, Journal of the American Statistical Association, Industrial Quality Control, Applied Statistics, Proceedings of the National Academy of Sciences, Journal of Farm Economics, Journal of the Iron and Steel Institute, Operations Research Digest, Journal of the Society for Industrial and Applied Mathematics, Factory Management and Maintenance, Advanced Management.*

Reprinted from *Operational Research Quarterly*, vol. 11, nos. 1-2, March-June 1960, p. 31-6, by permission of the publisher.

Statistics.[2] This is highly selected but the characteristic pattern has survived. For some further examples see Simon (1955).[5]

5. There is an obvious resemblance between this type of distribution and that of income. If we equate journals to persons and number of references to size of income we have the characteristic pattern in which a lot of people (journals) have a low income (few references) proceeding regularly to a few millionaires (journals with a large number of references). The statistician's method of analysing Table 1, were it an income distribution, would be to

TABLE 1. 1763 REFERENCES TO OPERATIONAL RESEARCH

A No. of journals x	B No. of references $g(x)$	C Cumulative Σx	D Cumulative $\Sigma x g(x)$	E log col. C
1	242	1	242	0·000
1	114	2	356	0·301
1	102	3	458	0·477
1	95	4	553	0·602
1	58	5	611	0·699
1	49	6	660	0·778
1	34	7	694	0·845
2	22	9	738	0·954
2	21	11	780	1·041
2	20	13	820	1·114
1	18	14	838	1·146
4	16	18	902	1·255
2	15	20	932	1·301
1	14	21	946	1·322
2	12	23	970	1·362
5	11	28	1025	1·447
3	10	31	1055	1·491
4	9	35	1091	1·544
8	8	43	1155	1·634
8	7	51	1211	1·708
6	6	57	1247	1·756
10	5	67	1297	1·826
17	4	84	1365	1·924
29	3	113	1452	2·053
54	2	167	1560	2·223
203	1	370	1763	2·568

cumulate *from the bottom*, i.e. starting at the low incomes. He would then graph the sum $\Sigma x f(x)$ cumulated from the bottom as ordinate against the sum Σx cumulated from the bottom as abscissa to obtain Gini's curve of concentration or the Lorenz curve (Kendall and Stuart, 1958, **1**, p. 48).[3]

6. Bradford, however, cumulated from the other end and produced figures analogous to those of columns C and D in Tables 1 and 2. He then remarked that if we put C on a logarithmic scale, as given in column E, and graph D

as ordinate against E as abscissa, the result is nearly linear over a large part of the range.

Figure 1 shows such a graph for the data of Table 1. The linearity is remarkable and in fact is better than in Bradford's own examples.

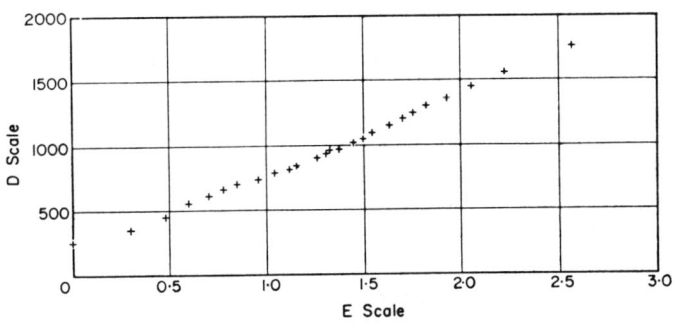

Fig. 1.

TABLE 2. 1465 REFERENCES TO STATISTICAL METHODOLOGY

A No. of journals x	B No. of references $g(x)$	C Cumulative Σx	D Cumulative $\Sigma x g(x)$	E log col. C
1	273	1	273	0·000
1	212	2	485	0·301
2	66	4	617	0·602
1	60	5	677	0·699
2	59	7	795	0·845
1	58	8	853	0·903
1	49	9	902	0·954
1	46	10	948	1·000
2	36	12	1020	1·079
1	28	13	1048	1·114
1	20	14	1068	1·146
1	18	15	1086	1·176
3	17	18	1137	1·255
1	16	19	1153	1·279
2	13	21	1179	1·322
4	10	25	1219	1·398
1	9	26	1228	1·415
1	8	27	1236	1·431
1	7	28	1243	1·447
3	6	31	1261	1·491
2	5	33	1271	1·519
5	4	38	1291	1·580
12	3	50	1327	1·699
24	2	74	1375	1·869
90	1	164	1465	2·215

7. It is therefore very tempting to seek a model which will explain the Bradford effect. Bradford advanced a hypothesis of the following kind: there are certain journals which are specifically devoted to the subject under examination, and these form a nucleus. Around this nucleus we may picture zones, each containing the same number of articles as the nucleus itself. The first zone is, so to speak, occupied by journals which are partly relevant, and contains, say, k times as many journals as the nucleus. The second zone consists of less relevant journals, standing to the first zone in much the same relation as the first zone to the nucleus; we may therefore suppose that it contains k^2 as many journals as the nucleus. And so on for further zones.

8. On the basis of this picture of periodicals as a family of successive generations of diminishing kinship Bradford thought that he had arrived at an explanation of his linear law. His demonstration, however, involved an oversight which was pointed out and corrected by Vickery (1948)[6] who showed that on Bradford's model the theoretical graph of D against E was a gentle curve.

9. There is a completely different way of looking at this topic which subsumes the Bradford-type distribution under a general class of distribution named by Simon (1955)[5] the Yule distribution. I have remarked in paragraph 5 that the more usual way of considering the data of Table 1 would be to start at the other end thus:

TABLE 3

A_1 No. of references i	B_1 No. of journals $f(i)$	C_1 No. of journals containing i or more references	D_1 Column A_1 times Col. C_1
1	203	370	370
2	54	167	334
3	29	113	339
4	17	84	332
5	10	67	335
6	6	57	342
7	8	51	357
8	8	43	344
9	4	35	318
10	3	31	310
..	..	..	..
..	..	..	..
..	..	..	..
..	..	..	..
102	1	3	306
114	1	2	224
242	1	1	242

If we multiply the number of references i (col. A_1) by the number of journals containing that number or more (col. C_1), we get the remarkably constant figures of column D_1. In short, this is almost a case of what is known as Zipf's law (Zipf, 1949).[7] Simon (1955)[5] states this in the form: for the U.S.A. and most Western countries in the present century, if $F(i)$ is the number of cities of population greater than i, then

$$F(i) = \frac{A}{i^\rho} \tag{1}$$

where ρ is very nearly unity and A is some constant.

10. This remarkable law is approximately a particular case of one which Simon derives in the form

$$f(i) = AB(i, \rho+1) \tag{2}$$

where, in our present context, $f(i)$ is the frequency of journals containing i references and B is the Beta function. Since, for large n,

$$\frac{\Gamma(i)}{\Gamma(i+n)} \sim i^{-n}, \tag{3}$$

equation (2) can be written as

$$f(i) \sim \frac{\text{constant}}{i^{\rho+1}} \tag{4}$$

and a summation gives us approximately equation (1).

11. Simon derives (2) as the steady state solution of a stochastic process. In our present terms his basic assumptions can be stated thus:

(1) If p articles have appeared, the probability that a new $(p+1)$th article will appear in a journal which already has i references is proportional to $if(i)$, that is to the total number of references in journals containing i references each. The pattern of Table 1, in fact, tends to perpetuate itself.

(2) But there is also a probability that the $(p+1)$th article may appear in a journal not hitherto included in the table. This is a constant, say equal to $1-\rho^{-1}$.

On these assumptions, equation (2) may be derived. They may, of course, be relaxed to give more general results. It appears to me that such a model is more plausible than Bradford's.

12. It remains to be examined why Bradford's way of looking at a Yule distribution with $\rho = 1$ gives an approximation to a straight line. The reason, I think, is as follows:

Column C of Table 1 is the inverted form of column C_1 and Σx of column C is thus the sum of $f(i)$ from the bottom of the table. Column D of Table 1 is the sum of $if(i)$ from the bottom in columns A_1 and B_1. Thus for Bradford's linear law to be true, we require that

$$\log \Sigma f(i) = \text{linear function of } \Sigma if(i),$$

the summation being from the bottom in Table 3.

If N is the total number of references (1763 in our case), M the number of journals, this is equivalent to

$$\log\left\{N - \sum_{j=1}^{i} f(j)\right\} = \text{l.f.}\left(M - \sum_{j=1}^{i} jf(j)\right) \tag{5}$$

or, if $f(i)$ refers to *relative* frequency,

$$\log\left\{1 - \sum_{j=1}^{i} f(j)\right\} = \text{l.f.}\left\{\sum_{1}^{i} jf(j)\right\} \tag{6}$$

Now suppose that

$$\sum_{j=1}^{i} f(j) = 1 - \frac{1}{i+1}. \tag{7}$$

This entails that the frequency of journals containing more than i references is $1/(1+i)$, not $1/i$ as in Zipf's law. The form (7), however, is of the Yule type, as discussed by Simon. Then the left-hand side of (6) becomes $-\log(1+i)$. Further,

$$f(i) = \frac{1}{i(i+1)}$$

and hence

$$\sum_{1}^{i} jf(j) = \sum_{1}^{i} \frac{1}{j+1} \simeq \log(1+i),$$

and thus the equivalence (6) is established.

13. In the present state of development it does not seem worthwhile pursuing these theoretical results much further. But when the subject has settled down it might be worthwhile reviewing the distributions to see whether a better fit is obtained with $\rho > 1$. To come back for a moment to the matter of bibliography, it must be remembered that the problem of the outliers is not completely described in terms of existing bibliographies. There is also a non-observed class of journals which have not carried a relevant article in the period examined but may do so at any moment in the future. One would like to be able to estimate the size of this potentially contributory class.

ACKNOWLEDGEMENTS

I am indebted to Mr. Geoffrey Woledge for some references and to Professor C. C. Holt for some valuable comments on an earlier draft of this paper.

REFERENCES

[1] S. C. BRADFORD, *Documentation*. Crosby Lockwood, London (1948).
[2] M. G. KENDALL, *The Advanced Theory of Statistics*, **2**. Charles Griffin and Co., London (1955).
[3] M. G. KENDALL and A. STUART, *The Advanced Theory of Statistics*, Vol. 1. Charles Griffin and Co., London (1958).
[4] O.R.S.A., *Bibliography of Operations Research* (1958).
[5] H. A. SIMON, "On a Class of Skew Distribution Functions", *Biometrika*, **42**, 425 (1955).
[6] B. C. VICKERY, "Bradford's Law of Scattering", *Journal of Documentation*, **4**, 198 (1948).
[7] G. K. ZIPF, *Human Behaviour and the Principle of Least Effort*. Addison–Wesley Press (1949).

Networks of Scientific Papers

The pattern of bibliographic references indicates
the nature of the scientific research front.

Derek J. de Solla Price

This article is an attempt to describe in the broadest outline the nature of the total world network of scientific papers. We shall try to picture the network which is obtained by linking each published paper to the other papers directly associated with it. To do this, let us consider that special relationship which is given by the citation of one paper by another in its footnotes or bibliography. I should make it clear, however, that this broad picture tells us something about the papers themselves as well as something about the practice of citation. It seems likely that many of the conclusions we shall reach about the network of papers would still be essentially true even if citation became much more or much less frequent, and even if we considered links obtained by subject indexing rather than by citation. It happens, however, that we now have available machine-handled citation studies, of large and representative portions of literature, which are much more tractable for such analysis than any topical indexing known to me. It is from such studies, by Garfield (*1, 2*), Kessler (*3*), Tukey (*4*), Osgood (*5*), and others, that I have taken the source data of this study.

Incidence of References

First, let me say something of the incidence of references in papers in serial publications. On the average, there are about 15 references per paper and, of these, about 12 are to other serial publications rather than to books, theses, reports, and unpublished work. The average, of course, gives us only part of the picture. The distribution (see Fig. 1) is such that about 10 percent of the papers contain no references at all; this notwithstanding, 50 percent of the references come from the 85 percent of the papers that are of the "normal" research type and contain 25 or fewer references apiece. The distribution here is fairly flat; indeed about 5 percent of the papers fall in each of the categories of 3, 4, 5, 6, 7, 8, 9, and 10 references each. At the other end of the scale, there are review-type papers with many references each. About 25 percent of all references come from the 5 percent (of all papers) that contain 45 or more references each and average 75 to a paper, while 12 percent of the references come from the "fattest" category—the 1 percent (of all papers) that have 84 or more references each and average about 170 to a paper. It is interesting to note that the number of papers with n references falls off in this "fattest" category as $1/n^2$, up to many hundreds per paper.

These references, of course, cover the entire previous body of literature. We can calculate roughly that, since the body of world literature has been growing exponentially for a few centuries (*6*), and probably will continue at its present rate of growth of about 7 percent per annum, there will be about 7 new papers each year for every 100 previously published papers in a given

The author is Avalon Professor of the History of Science, Yale University, New Haven, Connecticut. This article is based on a paper presented 17 March 1964 at the National Bureau of Standards, Washington, D.C., in a Symposium on Statistical Methods for Mechanized Documentation. Part of this research was supported by grant GN-299 from the National Science Foundation.

field. An average of about 15 references in each of these 7 new papers will therefore supply about 105 references back to the previous 100 papers, which will therefore be cited an average of a little more than once each during the year. Over the long run, and over the entire world literature, we should find that, on the average, *every scientific paper ever published is cited about once a year.*

Incidence of Citations

Now, although the total number of citations must exactly balance the total number of references, the distributions are very different. It seems that, in any given year, about 35 percent of all the existing papers are not cited at all, and another 49 percent are cited only once ($n = 1$) (see Fig. 2). This leaves about 16 percent of the papers to be cited an average of about 3.2 times each. About 9 percent are cited twice; 3 percent, three times; 2 percent, four times; 1 percent, five times; and a remaining 1 percent, six times or more. For large n, the number of papers cited appears to decrease as $n^{2.5}$ or $n^{3.0}$. This is rather more rapid than the decrease found for numbers of references in papers, and indeed the number of papers receiving many citations is smaller than the number carrying large bibliographies. Thus, only 1 percent of the cited papers are cited as many as six or more times each in a year (the average for this top 1 percent is 12 citations), and the maximum likely number of citations to a paper in a year is smaller by about an order of magnitude than the maximum likely number of references in the citing papers. There is, however, some parallelism in the findings that some 5 percent of all papers appear to be review papers, with many (25 or more) references, and some 4 percent of all papers appear to be "classics," cited four or more times in a year.

What has been said of references is true from year to year; the findings for individual cited papers, however, appear to vary from year to year. A paper not cited in one year may well be cited in the next, and one cited often in one year may or may not be heavily cited subsequently. Heavy citation appears to occur in rather capricious bursts, but in spite of that I suspect a strong statistical regularity. I would conjecture that results to date could be explained by the hypotheses that

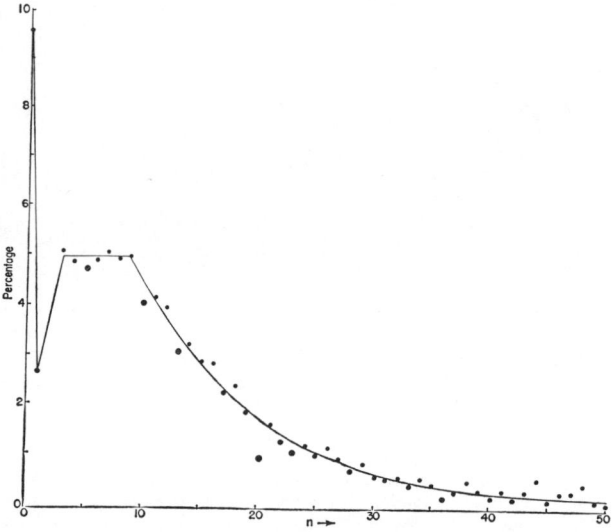

Fig. 1. Percentages (relative to total number of papers published in 1961) of papers published in 1961 which contain various numbers (n) of bibliographic references. The data, which represent a large sample, are from Garfield's 1961 *Index* (2).

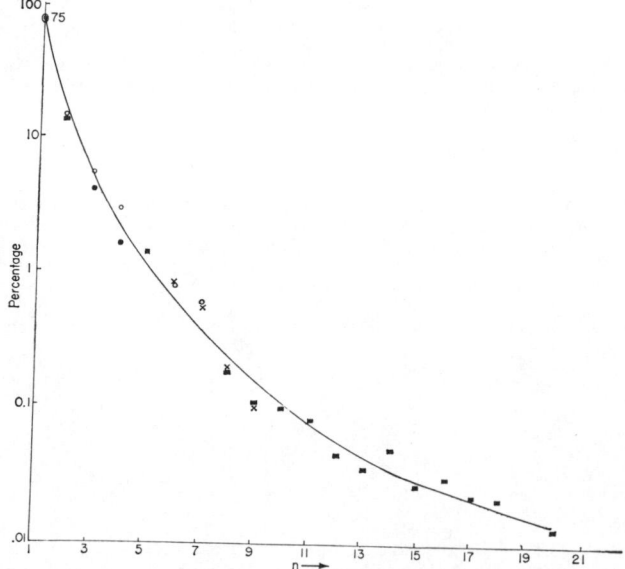

Fig. 2. Percentages (relative to total number of cited papers) of papers cited various numbers (n) of times, for a single year (1961). The data are from Garfield's 1961 *Index* (2), and the points represent four different samples conflated to show the consistency of the data. Because of the rapid decline in frequency of citation with increase in n, the percentages are plotted on a logarithmic scale.

every year about 10 percent of all papers "die," not to be cited again, and that for the "live" papers the chance of being cited at least once in any year is about 60 percent. This would mean that the major work of a paper would be finished after 10 years. The process thus reaches a steady state, in which about 10 percent of all published papers have never been cited, about 10 percent have been cited once, about 9 percent twice, and so on, the percentages slowly decreasing, so that half of all papers will be cited eventually five times or more, and a quarter of all papers, ten times or more. More work is urgently needed on the problem of determining whether there is a probability that the more a paper is cited the more likely it is to be cited thereafter. It seems to me that further work in this area might well lead to the discovery that classic papers could be rapidly identified, and that perhaps even the "superclassics" would prove so distinctive that they could be picked automatically by means of citation-index-production procedures and published as a single *U.S.* (or *World*) *Journal of Really Important Papers*.

Unfortunately, we know little about any relationship between the number of times a paper is cited and the number of bibliographic references it contains. Since rough preliminary tests indicate that, for much-cited papers, there is a fairly standard pattern of distribution of numbers of bibliographic references, I conjecture that the correlation, if one exists, is very small. Certainly, there is no strong tendency for review papers to be cited unusually often. If my conjecture is valid, it is worth noting that, since 10 percent of all papers contain no bibliographic references and another, presumably almost independent, 10 percent of all papers are never cited, it follows that there is a lower bound of 1 percent of all papers on the number of papers that are totally disconnected in a pure citation network and could be found only by topical indexing or similar methods; this is a very small class, and probably a most unimportant one.

The balance of references and citations in a single year indicates one very important attribute of the network (see Fig. 3). Although most papers produced in the year contain a near-average number of bibliographic references, half of these are references to about half of all the papers that have been published in previous years. The other half of the references tie these new papers to a quite small group of earlier ones, and generate a rather tight pattern of multiple relationships. Thus each group of new papers is "knitted" to a small, select part of the existing scientific literature but connected rather weakly and randomly to a much greater part. Since only a small part of the earlier literature is knitted together by the new year's crop of papers, we may look upon this small part as a sort of growing tip or epidermal layer, an active research front. I believe it is the existence of a research front, in this sense, that distinguishes the sciences from the rest of scholarship, and, because of it, I propose that one of the major tasks of statistical analysis is to determine the mechanism that enables science to cumulate so much faster than nonscience that it produces a literature crisis.

An analysis of the distribution of publication dates of all papers cited in a single year (Fig. 4) sheds further light on the existence of such a research front. Taking [from Garfield (2)] data for 1961, the most numerous count

Fig. 3. Idealized representation of the balance of papers and citations for a given "almost closed" field in a single year. It is assumed that the field consists of 100 papers whose numbers have been growing exponentially at the normal rate. If we assume that each of the seven new papers contains about 13 references to journal papers and that about 11 percent of these 91 cited papers (or ten papers) are outside the field, we find that 50 of the old papers are connected by one citation each to the new papers (these links are not shown) and that 40 of the old papers are not cited at all during the year. The seven new papers, then, are linked to ten of the old ones by the complex network shown here.

available, I find that papers published in 1961 cite earlier papers at a rate that falls off by a factor of 2 for every 13.5-year interval measured backward from 1961; this rate of decrease must be approximately equal to the exponential growth of numbers of papers published in that interval. Thus, the chance of being cited by a 1961 paper was almost the same for all papers published more than about 15 years before 1961, the rate of citation presumably being the previously computed average rate of one citation per paper per year. It should be noted that, as time goes on, there are more and more papers available to cite each one previously published. Therefore, the chance that any one paper will be cited by any other, later paper decreases exponentially by about a factor of 2 every 13.5 years.

For papers less than 15 years old, the rate of citation is considerably greater than this standard value of one citation per paper per year. The rate increases steadily, from less than twice this value for papers 15 years old to 4 times for those 5 years old; it reaches a maximum of about 6 times the standard value for papers 2½ years old, and of course declines again for papers so recent that they have not had time to be noticed.

Incidentally, this curve enables one to see and dissect out the effect of the wartime declines in production of papers. It provides an excellent indication, in agreement with manpower indexes and other literature indexes, that production of papers began to drop from expected levels at the beginning of World Wars I and II, declining to a trough of about half the normal production in 1918 and mid-1944, respectively, and then recovering in a manner strikingly symmetrical with the decline, attaining the normal rate again by 1926 and 1950, respectively. Because of this decline, we must not take dates in the intervals 1914–25 and 1939–50 for comparison with normal years in determining growth indexes.

The "Immediacy Factor"

The "immediacy factor"—the "bunching," or more frequent citation, of recent papers relative to earlier ones—is, of course, responsible for the well-known phenomenon of papers being considered obsolescent after a decade. A numerical measure of this factor can be derived and is particularly useful. Calculation shows that about 70 percent of all cited papers would account for the normal growth curve, which shows a doubling every 13.5 years, and that about 30 percent would account for the hump of the immediacy curve. Hence, we may say that the 70 percent represents a random distribution of citations of all the scientific papers that have ever been published, regardless of date, and that the 30 percent are highly selective references to recent literature; the distribution of citations of the recent papers is defined by the shape of the curve, half of the 30 percent being papers between 1 and 6 years old.

I am surprised at the extent of this immediacy phenomenon and want to indicate its significance. If all papers followed a standard pattern with respect to the proportions of early and recent papers they cite, then it would follow that 30 percent of all references in all papers would be to the recent research front. If, instead, the papers

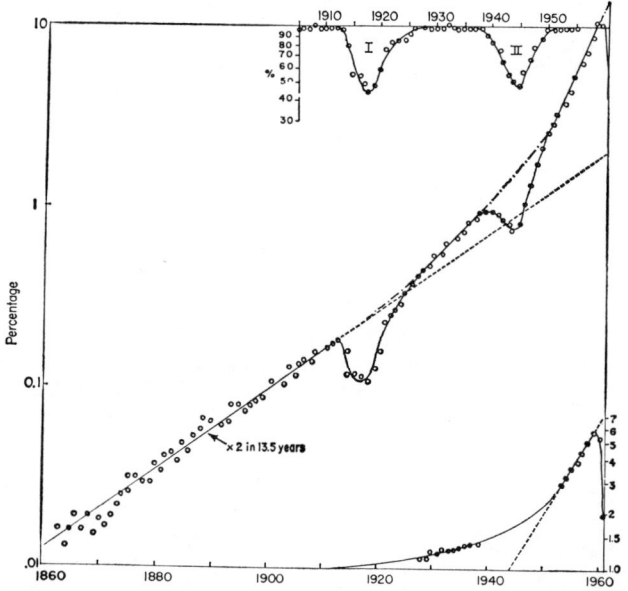

Fig. 4. Percentages (relative to total number of papers cited in 1961) of all papers cited in 1961 and published in each of the years 1862 through 1961 [data are from Garfield's 1961 *Index* (2)]. The curve for the data (solid line) shows dips during world wars I and II. These dips are analyzed separately at the top of the figure and show remarkably similar reductions to about 50 percent of normal citation in the two cases. For papers published before World War I, the curve is a straight line on this logarithmic plot, corresponding to a doubling of numbers of citations for every 13.5-year interval. If we assume that this represents the rate of growth of the entire literature over the century covered, it follows that the more recent papers have been cited disproportionately often relative to their number. The deviation of the curve from a straight line is shown at the bottom of the figure and gives some measure of the "immediacy effect." If, for old papers, we assume a unit rate of citation, then we find that the recent papers are cited at first about six times as much, this factor of 6 declining to 3 in about 7 years, and to 2 after about 10 years. Since it is probable that some of the rise of the original curve above the straight line may be due to an increase in the pace of growth of the literature since World War I, it may be that the curve of the actual "immediacy effect" would be somewhat smaller and sharper than the curve shown here. It is probable, however, that the straight dashed line on the main plot gives approximately the slope of the initial falloff, which must therefore be a halving in the number of citations for every 6 years one goes backward from the date of the citing paper.

THE SCIENTIFIC JOURNAL

161

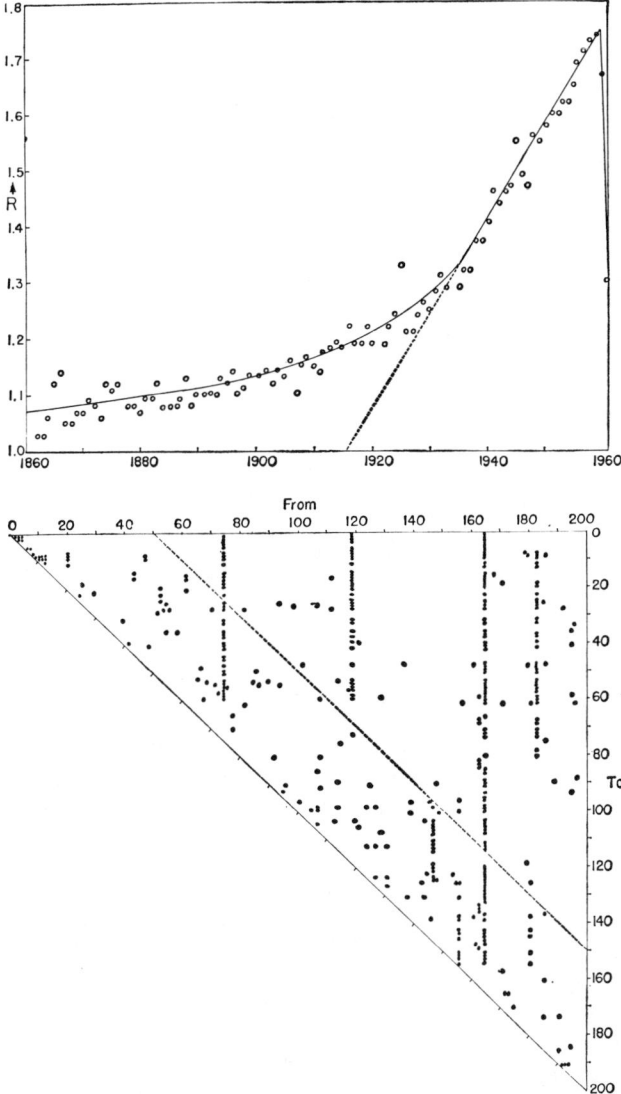

Fig. 5 (top left). Ratios of numbers of 1961 citations to numbers of individual cited papers published in each of the years 1860 through 1960 [data are from Garfield's 1961 *Index* (2)]. This ratio gives a measure of the multiplicity of citation and shows that there is a sharp falloff in this multiplicity with time. One would expect the measure of multiplicity to be also a measure of the proportion of available papers actually cited. Thus, recent papers cited must constitute a much larger fraction of the total available population than old papers cited.

Fig. 6. Matrix showing the bibliographical references to each other in 200 papers that constitute the entire field from beginning to end of a peculiarly isolated subject group. The subject investigated was the spurious phenomenon of N-rays, about 1904. The papers are arranged chronologically, and each column of dots represents the references given in the paper of the indicated number rank in the series, these references being necessarily to previous papers in the series. The strong vertical lines therefore correspond to review papers. The dashed line indicates the boundary of a "research front" extending backward in the series about 50 papers behind the citing paper. With the exception of this research front and the review papers, little background noise is indicated in the figure. The tight linkage indicated by the high density of dots for the first dozen papers is typical of the beginning of a new field.

cited by, say, half of all papers were evenly distributed through the literature with respect to publication date, then it must follow that 60 percent of the papers cited by the other half would be recent papers. I suggest, as a rough guess, that the truth lies somewhere between—that we have here an indication that about half the bibliographic references in papers represent tight links with rather recent papers, the other half representing a uniform and less tight linkage to all that has been published before.

That this is so is demonstrated by the time distribution: much-cited papers are much more recent than less-cited ones. Thus, only 7 percent of the papers listed in Garfield's 1961 *Index* (2) as having been cited four or more times in 1961 were published before 1953, as compared with 21 percent of all papers cited in 1961. This tendency for the most-cited papers to be also the most recent may also be seen in Fig. 5 (based on Garfield's data), where the number of citations per paper is shown as a function of the age of the cited paper.

It has come to my attention that R. E. Burton and R. W. Kebler (7) have already conjectured, though on somewhat tenuous evidence, that the periodical literature may be composed of two distinct types of literature with very different half-lives, the classic and the ephemeral parts. This conjecture is now confirmed by the present evidence. It is obviously desirable to explore further the other tentative finding of Burton and Kebler that the half-lives, and therefore the relative proportions of classic and ephemeral literature, vary considerably from field to field: mathematics, geology, and botany being strongly classic; chemical, mechanical, and metallurgical engineering and physics strongly ephemeral; and chemistry and physiology a much more even mixture.

Historical Examples

A striking confirmation of the proposed existence of this research front has been obtained from a series of historical examples, for which we have been able to set up a matrix (Fig. 6). The dots represent references within a set of chronologically arranged papers which constitute the entire literature in a particular field (the field happens to be very tight and closed over the interval under discussion). In such a matrix there is high probability of citation in a strip near the diagonal and extending over the 30 or 40 papers immediately preceding each paper in turn. Over the rest of the triangular matrix there is much less chance of citation; this remaining part provides, therefore, a sort of background noise. Thus, in the special circumstance of being able to isolate a "tight" subject field, we find that half the references are to a research front of recent papers and that the other half are to papers scattered uniformly through the literature. It also appears that after every 30 or 40 papers there is need of a review paper to replace those earlier papers that have been lost from sight behind the research front. Curiously enough, it appears that classical papers, distinguished by full rows rather than columns, are all cited with about the same frequency, making a rather symmetrical pattern that may have some theoretical significance.

Two Bibliographic Needs

From these two different types of connections it appears that the citation network shows the existence of two different literature practices and of two different needs on the part of the scientist. (i) The research front builds on recent work, and the network becomes very tight. To cope with this, the scientist (particularly, I presume, in physics and molecular biology) needs an alerting service that will keep him posted, probably by citation indexing, on the work of his peers and colleagues. (ii) The random scattering of Fig. 6 corresponds to a drawing upon the totality of previous work. In a sense, this is the portion of the network that treats each published item as if it were truly part of the eternal record of human knowledge. In subject fields that have been dominated by this second attitude, the traditional procedure has been to systematize the added knowledge from time to time in book form, topic by topic, or to make use of a system of classification optimistically considered more or less eternal, as in taxonomy and chemistry. If such classification holds over reasonably long periods, one may have an objective means of reducing the world total of knowledge to fairly small parcels in which the items are found to be in one-to-one correspondence with some natural order.

It seems clear that in any classification into research-front subjects and taxonomic subjects there will remain a large body of literature which is not completely the one or the other. The present discussion suggests that most papers, through citations, are knit together rather tightly. The total research front of science has never, however, been a single row of knitting. It is, instead, divided by dropped stitches into quite small segments and strips. From a study of the citations of journals by journals I come to the conclusion that most of these strips correspond to the work of, at most, a few hundred men at any one time. Such strips represent objectively defined subjects whose description may vary materially from year to year but which remain otherwise an intellectual whole. If one would work out the nature of such strips, it might lead to a method for delineating the topography of current scientific literature. With such a topography established, one could perhaps indicate the overlap and relative importance of journals and, indeed, of countries, authors, or individual papers by the place they occupied within the map, and by their degree of strategic centralness within a given strip.

Journal citations provide the most readily available data for a test of such methods. From a preliminary and very rough analysis of these data I am tempted to conclude that a very large fraction of the alleged 35,000 journals now current must be reckoned as merely a distant background noise, and as very far from central or strategic in any of the knitted strips from which the cloth of science is woven.

References and Notes

1. E. Garfield and I. H. Sher, "New factors in the evaluation of scientific literature through citation indexing," *Am. Doc.* 14, 191 (1963); ———. *Genetics Citation Index* (Institute for Scientific Information, Philadelphia, 1963). For many of the results discussed in this article I have used statistical information drawn from E. Garfield and I. H. Sher, *Science Citation Index* (Institute for Scientific Information, Philadelphia, 1963), pp. ix, xvii–xviii.
2. I wish to thank Dr. Eugene Garfield for making available to me several machine printouts of original data used in the preparation of the 1961 *Index* but not published in their entirety in the preamble to the index.
3. I am grateful to Dr. M. M. Kessler, Massachusetts Institute of Technology, for data for seven research reports of the following titles and dates: "An Experimental Study of Bibliographic Coupling between Technical Papers" (November 1961); "Bibliographic Coupling Between Scientific Papers" (July 1962); "Analysis of Bibliographic Sources in the *Physical Review* (vol. 77, 1950, to vol. 112, 1958) (July 1962); "Analysis of Bibliographic Sources in a Group of Physics-Related Journals" (August 1962); "Bibliographic Coupling Extended in Time: Ten Case Histories" (August 1962); "Concerning the Probability that a Given Paper will be Cited" (November 1962); "Comparison of the Results of Bibliographic Coupling and Analytic Subject Indexing" (January 1963).
4. J. W. Tukey, "Keeping research in contact with the literature: Citation indices and beyond," *J. Chem. Doc.* 2, 34 (1962).
5. C. E. Osgood and L. V. Xhignesse, *Characteristics of Bibliographical Coverage in Psychological Journals Published in 1950 and 1960* (Institute of Communications Research, Univ. of Illinois, Urbana, 1963).
6. D. J. de Solla Price, *Little Science, Big Science* (Columbia Univ. Press, New York, 1963).
7. R. E. Burton and R. W. Kebler, "The 'half-life' of some scientific and technical literatures," *Am. Doc.* 11, 18 (1960).

Interrelationships of Scientific Journals

A series of models of the interrelationship of scientific journals has been developed from the cross citing amongst 275 journals in mathematics, physics, chemistry, biochemistry, and biology. The data source was the Journal Citation Index (JCI), a file derived from the Science Citation Index. The JCI consists of a journal by journal tabulation of citings to and from each journal in the Index. A large amount of consistency was found between the citing characteristics of the journals in the different scientific fields, with quite clear boundaries between fields and a few well known cross disciplinary journals as cross field information links. The separate disciplines appear to relate to each other in an orderly manner, with a natural sequence: mathematics → physics → chemistry → biochemistry → biology. Within disciplines the journals form fully transitive hierarchies with very few relational conflicts.

FRANCIS NARIN
President of Computer Horizons, Inc.
53 West Jackson Blvd.
Chicago, Illinois 60604.

MARK CARPENTER
Research Associate at Computer Horizons

NANCY C. BERLT
Former staff member of the company

● **Introduction**

Most scientists would surely agree that a mosaic of the sciences exists, in which similar disciplines would be closer than dissimilar ones, and which would show an orderly progression of scientific knowledge. In a recent article in *Science*, Brooks (1) speaks of "the full interwoven fabric of science." Surely the sequence: mathematics→physics→chemistry→biochemistry→biology, is intuitively reasonable. Yet there has been little analysis of the empirical evidence for the existence of such orderly sequences among disciplines. The outer boundaries of the scientific mosaic have been sketched by de Solla Price (2), who developed a series of measures of the overall "size" of science; these measures, based on counts of scientists, or counts of publications, provide a framework within which any subsequent analysis of the component parts must be viewed.

The study reported here (3) is an attempt to use journal citing to develop empirical models and measures of scientific interrelationships, across a range of scientific disciplines. An analysis was made of the journal-to-journal cross citing for about 275 journals in the fields of physics, chemistry, biochemistry, biology and mathematics. This analysis was then used to generate models and measures of the interrelationship, importance and hierarchic dependencies among the journals.

The use of literature citations to study a scientific discipline has previously been attempted by a number of investigators. Kessler (4) in 1964 grouped together citations in 20 physics journals, and from this created a to/from matrix of the percent of cross referencing between journals. Van Cott and Zavala (5) attempted to structure the physics literature through factor analysis based on subject classification of abstracted articles. Garfield (6, 7, 8) has suggested many uses for Citation Indexes in studying science, and Margolis (9), de Solla Price (10), and Martino (11) have suggested using citing, as catalogued by citation indexing, as a measure of the value of a paper. Hagstrom (12) has studied the characteristics of the literature of different disciplines and the correlations between department prestige and publication rates. The structure and dependencies within the psychology literature were studied by Daniel and Loutlit (13) in 1953; more recently Xhignesse and Osgood

---

* The work was supported by the National Science Foundation under Contract NSF C-627. Contributions of Mr. E. Haynes, Evaluation Staff, NSF, as Project Officer and Dr. Bodo Bartocha of NSF in the initiation of the research, are gratefully acknowledged.

Reprinted from *Journal of the American Society for Information Science*, vol. 23, no. 5, Sept-Oct, 1972, p. 323-31. Copyright © 1972 John Wiley & Sons, Inc., by permission of the publisher.

(14) have studied the citation characteristics of this literature from an information theoretic viewpoint.

In this study, the Journal Citation Index (JCI), a resorted version of the Institute for Scientific Information (ISI) Science Citation Index (15) was the main source of citation data. The JCI contains, in journal by journal lists, a tabulation of all of the citings from each journal (source journal listings) and of all the citings to each journal (reference journal listings). The JCI tapes used were for the last quarter of 1969, and contain more than 750,000 citations from more than 2000 different journals.

• **Models for Individual Disciplines**

An underlying requirement for analysis of interrelationships is to devise a graphical model of the literature such that the discipline being analyzed is reasonably well defined. A series of models of citing among journals have been devised to provide this first, basic step toward a mosaic. The simplest of these is a one-step model, shown in Figure 1, for physics. This model, and the equivalent

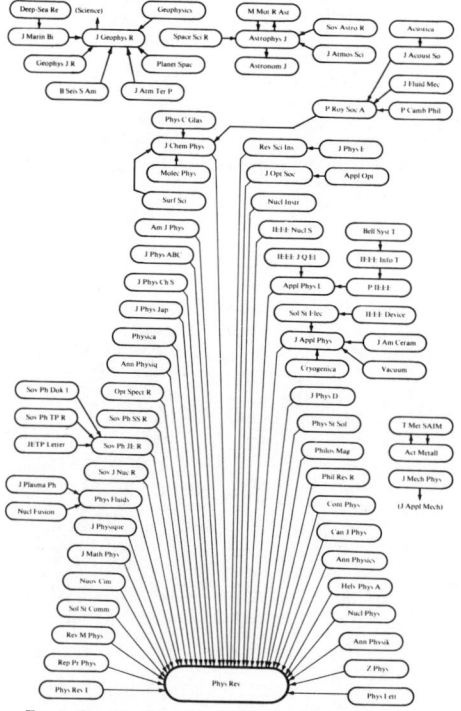

FIG. 1. One-Step Model for 79 Physics Journals in 1969

ones for other disciplines, have been highly valuable in dividing the journals by subject fields. Journal abbreviations on the models are those used by ISI.

In the one-step model an arrow from a journal points to the journal to which the given journal refers most frequently (other than for self-referencing). Note that in Figure 1, even at this elementary level, key journals are immediately apparent; it should be clear that the *Physical Review* is referred to most frequently by many physics journals, and plays a paramount role in physics, and that the *Journal of Chemical Physics*, the *Journal of Applied Physics* and the *Journal of Geophysical Research* are key journals. Also of key importance are the *Astrophysical Journal*, the *Proceedings of the Royal Society*, and *Soviet Physics JETP*. The cluster of astronomy and space sciences journals around the *Astrophysical Journal* is quite apparent, as is the cluster of geophysics journals around the *Journal of Geophysical Research*. Also clusters of journals appear near the *Journal of Applied Physics*, *Applied Physics Letters* and the *Journal of Chemical Physics*. The direction of information flow is, in a sense, opposite that of the arrows—the arrows show that the *Physical Review* is highly cited, and thus a major source of physics information.

Figure 2 shows a two-step model for physics. This is constructed in a manner similar to the one-step, except that the first and second most frequently cited journals are indicated by the arrows. At the two-step level, the important journals stand out even better than at the one-step level.

In constructing these models, an initial group of major physics journals was chosen, and journals cited frequently by those already on the model were added, so in the final model nearly all references from a journal on the model are to other journals on the model. Journals referred to first or second whose references were not analyzed, are shown in parentheses on the model. In most cases, these journals either were clearly out of the field of physics, or were not covered by the JCI, or had too few references in the last quarter 1969 JCI for analysis. For example, the journal *Science*, which appears in parentheses on the physics models, is included on the biology and cross-field models. One interesting fact is that, in creating these models such that there is a minimum of line crossing, one must group journals which are highly interactive in the same physical area of the figure. Thus the clustering revealed by journal position is natural. A cluster analysis currently under way for these journals (16), utilizing all of the journal to journal cross citings, reinforces the less formal clustering revealed by these models using only the most cited journals.

Another means of picturing the relationship between journals is to measure their referencing interdependencies. Figure 3 shows a hierarchy of physics journals, in which the journal dependency is reflected by position: journal A is placed above journal B, if A cites B a larger percent of the time than B cites A; thus highly cited journals appear at the base of the hierarchy. The hierarchy as

THE SCIENTIFIC JOURNAL

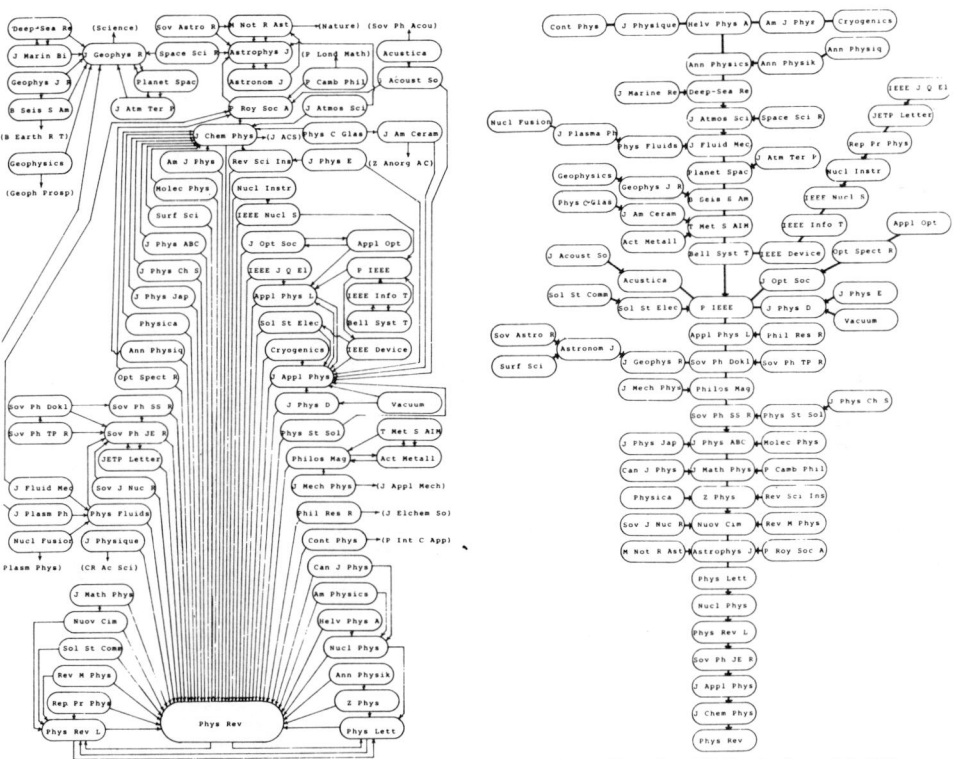

FIG. 2. Two-Step Model for 79 Physics Journals in 1969

FIG. 3. Hierarchy of 79 Physics Journals in 1969

shown is transitive—with a few exceptions every journal refers to any journal below it more than any journal below it refers to it, if there is significant referencing in either direction. For a pair of journals, if one percent of the references of one cited the other, the referencing relationship for that pair was considered significant.

For example, near the bottom of the hierarchy are, in a row, the journals *Nuclear Physics, Physical Review Letters*, and *Soviet Physics JETP*. This relationship implies that the percent of references in *Nuclear Physics* to the *Physical Review Letters* is larger than the reverse, and that the percent of references from *Physical Review Letters* to *Soviet Physics JETP* is larger than the reverse. The relationship is transitive; the percent of references from *Nuclear Physics* to *Soviet Physics JETP* is also larger than the reverse.

In this hierarchy, nearly all of the significant relationships between journals are as implied by the hierarchy. For the 79 physics journals on the hierarchy, there are

$$n(n-1)/2 = (79)(78)/2 = 3081$$

relational pairs, of which 466 are significant. A few of the 466 significant relational pairs conflict with the relation as implied by the figure; 2 (0.4%) relations conflict by more than one percent; 6 others conflict by an amount which could be more than one percent, and 2 others might conflict. Extent of conflict is defined in this manner: if Journal B is above Journal A, B cites A with X percent of its references and A cites B with Y percent of its references, then a conflict exists if $X - Y$ is negative, and the extent of the conflict is given by $|X - Y|$ percent A conflict of ≥ 1 percent is termed significant. The uncertainties are due to the grouping of references in the JCI into "other," when the level of referencing is low. Thus the rate of conflict is very low; not a single pair of journals has a relationship in conflict with the hierarchy at a level of 2 percent or higher.

The branches on the hierarchy are formed by placing a journal on the branch if its relationship to all journals above and below its connecting journal on the main stem is the same as that of the journal on the main stem; for

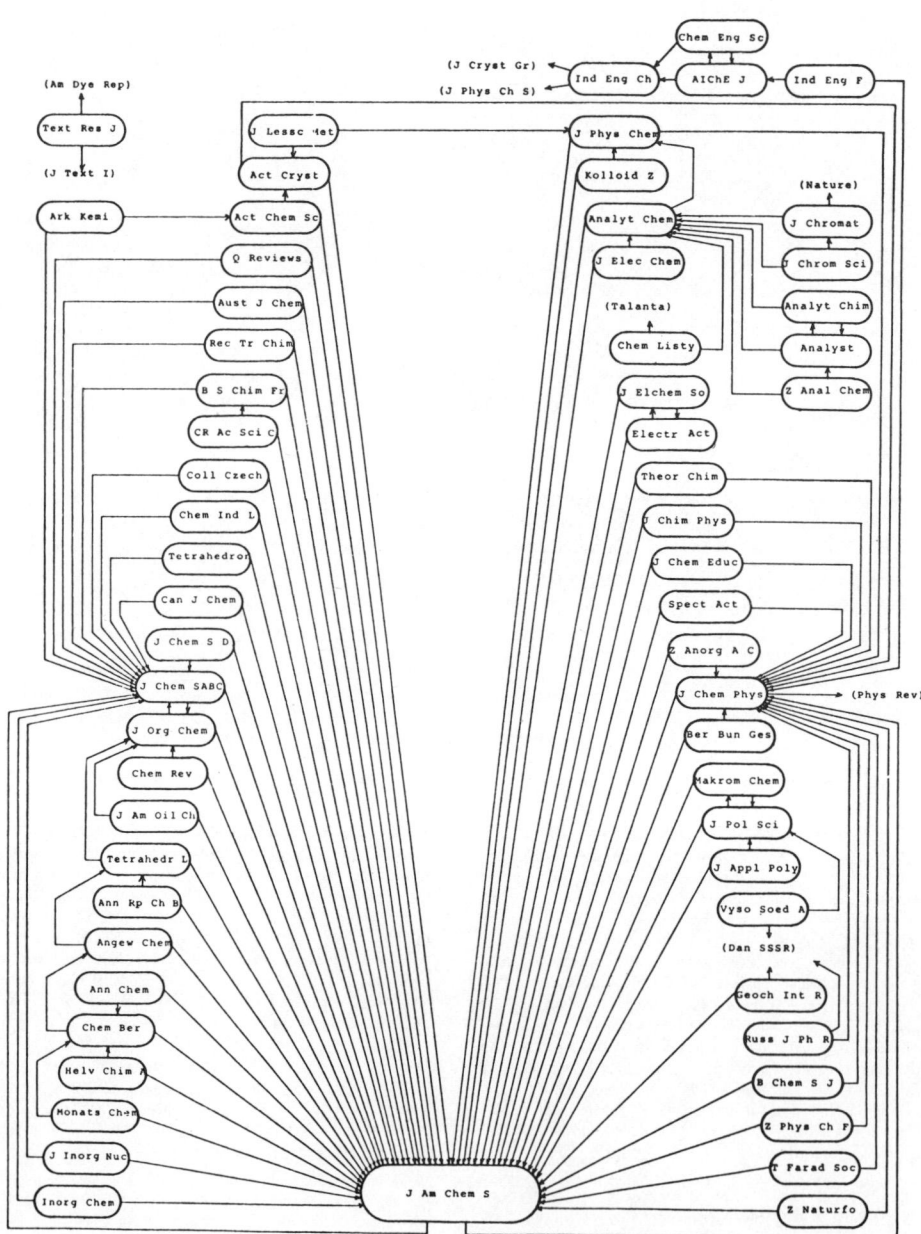

Fig. 4. Two-Step Model for 62 Chemistry Journals in 1969

example, *Nuclear Fusion*, which connects to the main stem at the *Journal of Fluid Mechanics*, has a relationship to every journal above and below the *Journal of Fluid Mechanics* which is identical to that of the *Journal of Fluid Mechanics*. Implications may also be drawn about journals in branches, those farther from the main stem being "higher."

When there is a significant relationship between two adjacent journals on the hierarchy, an arrow is used to indicate this. When there is not a significant relationship, then a line without an arrowhead is used. Thus any adjacent journals for which there is a line, rather than an arrow, could be interchanged on the hierarchy, if branching does not occur from either of them.

The structure of this hierarchy, and of all the other models, is of course influenced by the size of the journals considered, with the large journals such as the *Physical Review* and *Journal of Chemical Physics* at the base. However, size is not the major determinant of hierarchic position. For example, using the number of citations from a journal as a measure of journal size, there are more than 10 journals containing more citations than Z

Physik which are above *Z Physik*. Similarly, *Nuclear Instruments* is a relatively large journal positioned on the branch in the upper right of the hierarchy. The actual number of citations to and from each journal are given later in the paper.

Models similar to Figures 1, 2 and 3 for physics have been developed for chemistry, mathematics, biochemistry and biology. Figures 4 and 5 show the two-step and hierarchy models for chemistry; models of 49 mathematics and statistics journals, and 13 biochemistry journals exhibit the same clarity and simplicity as physics and chemistry. The models for 75 biology journals are not as regular, showing many complex interactions, without a truly central core of journals. This level of complexity seems to characterize biology far more than the other disciplines covered in this study. For example, Table 1 summarizes the conflicts in the 5 hierarchies constructed; biology, at 12 (3%) has the largest number of significant conflicts.

TABLE 1. Hierarchy Conflicts

Field	No. Journals	No. Significant Relational Pairs	Conflicts > 1%
Mathematics & Statistics	49	277	4 (1.4%)
Physics	79	466	2 (0.4%)
Chemistry	62	399	7 (1.8%)
Biochemistry	13	61	0 (0.0%)
Biology	75	402	12 (3.0%)

CROSS-FIELD MODELS

Given the one- and two-step models shown for the specific disciplines it is possible to construct cross-field models which show the flow of information from discipline to discipline in a manner analogous to the individual discipline models. Figure 6 is such a cross-field model corresponding to the two-step discipline models. Note that, as before, the direction of information flow is, in a sense, opposite that of the arrows; a heavily cited journal is a source of information. In Figure 6 all of the journals which refer first or second most frequently to journals within their own field, and are referred to first or second most frequently only by journals within their own fields, are included within the rectangular boxes. Thus the 76 physics journals within the physics box have $2 \times 76 = 152$ arrows corresponding to first and second most frequently cited journals; of these, 136 are within the rectangular physics box; of the 16 cross-field arrows shown leaving the physics rectangle, 12 are to the *Journal of Chemical Physics* and 4 are to other journals. The key role of the *Journal of Chemical Physics* as a link between physics and chemistry should be quite apparent from the figure.

FIG. 5. Hierarchy for 62 Chemistry Journals in 1969

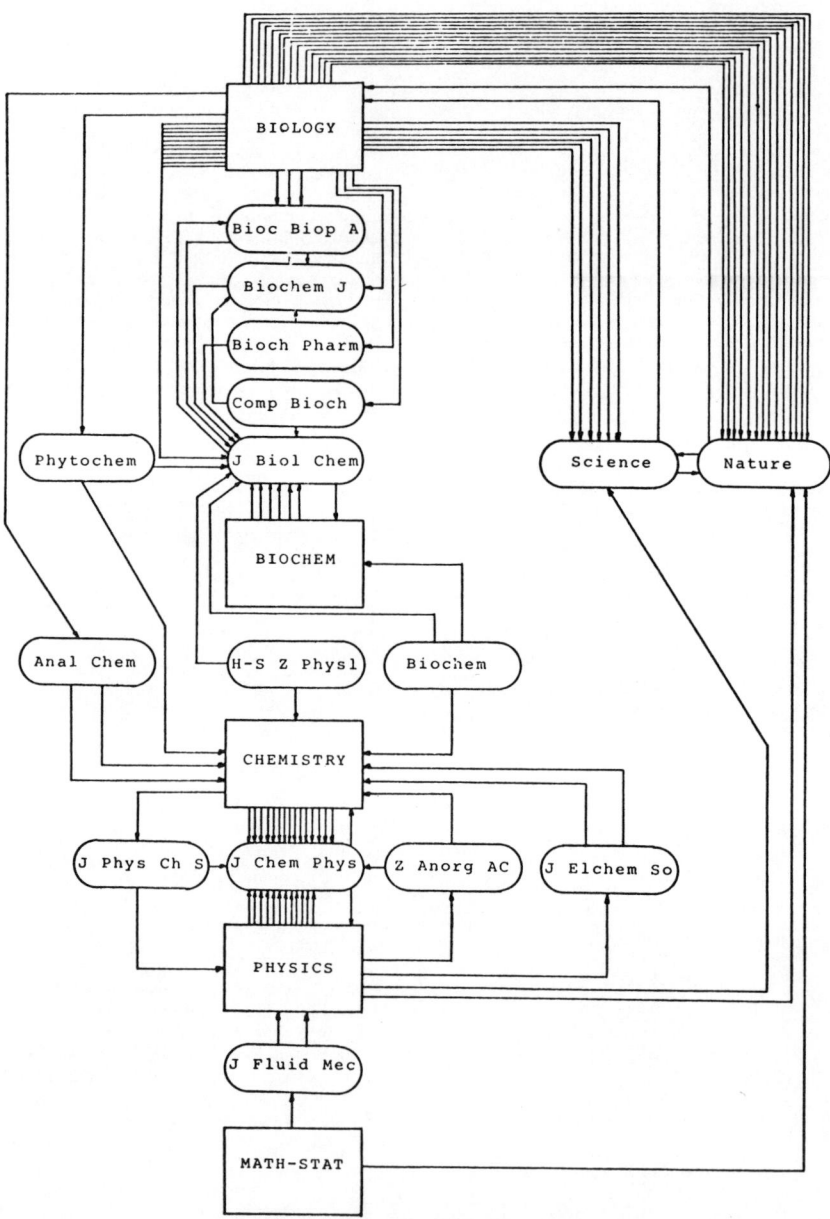

FIG. 6. Two-Step Cross Field Model—1969

Also, the roles of *Science* and *Nature* as links between physics and biology are quite clear. Furthermore, the overall relational sequence: biology→biochemistry→chemistry→physics→mathematics and statistics, is also quite clear from the model. This figure is a step toward the scientific mosaic.

A computation which has not yet been done, because of the amount of work involved, is to count the number of citations from field to field. Although in principle this would be easy, given the classifications of journals within fields from the disciplinary models, in practice it is quite difficult because of the problem of unification. On the Journal Citation Index tapes the cited journals are listed using abbreviations only partially unified from those of the citing author; therefore many variants of a single journal name may appear. For example, in the last quarter of 1969 the *Journal of the American Chemical Society* is cited 2597 times as *J Am Chem S*, 9915 times as *J Am Chem Soc* and 13,682 times as *J Amer Chem Soc*. In order to do a valid count of the individual cross-field citings, the tape would have to be unified, a process in which all the variants would be removed and each journal would be identified by a standard abbreviation. That is a tedious job, even for the 275 journals studied, and has

TABLE 2. Basic Data for 79 Physics Journals Last Quarter 1969

Journal	Cit. To	Cit. From	Cit. To/ Cit. From	Arrows To 1-Step	Arrows To 2-Step
Outstanding					
Phys Rev	20604	14354	1.44	37	43
Preferentially Cited					
Astrophys J	4438	3854	1.15	5	6
J Appl Phys	5172	5728	0.90	4	10
J Chem Phys	13687	10418	1.31	4	12
J Geophys R	3525	3567	0.95	6	9
Highly Cited					
Appl Phys L	1299	1016	1.28	2	4
Nucl Phys	3996	6929	0.58	0	3
P Roy Soc A	4768	1038	4.59	3	4
Phys Fluids	1294	1479	0.87	2	3
Phys Lett	3839	3803	1.01	0	4
Phys Rev L	6526	3223	2.02	1	6
Sov Ph JE R	4008	3170	1.26	3	6
Other					
Act Metall	1304	613	2.13	1	2
Acustica	90	306	0.29	0	0
Am J Phys	183	559	0.33	0	0
Ann Physics	1100	531	2.07	0	0
Ann Physik	390	528	0.74	0	0
Ann Physiq	43	139	0.31	0	0
Appl Optics	706	1544	0.46	0	1
Astronom J	381	705	0.54	0	1
B Seis S Am	301	533	0.56	0	1
Bell Syst T	690	497	1.39	0	1

TABLE 2. *Continued*

Journal	Cit. To	Cit. From	Cit. To/ Cit. From	Arrows To 1-Step	Arrows To 2-Step
Can J Phys	1325	1832	0.72	0	0
Cont Phys	26	217	0.12	0	0
Cryogenics	119	645	0.18	0	0
Deep-Sea Re	304	791	0.38	0	1
Geophys J R	203	740	0.27	0	0
Geophysics	140	158	0.89	0	0
Helv Phys A	354	307	1.15	0	0
IEEE Device	178	776	0.23	0	1
IEEE Info T	158	470	0.34	1	1
IEEE J Q El	299	388	0.77	0	0
IEEE Nucl S	169	646	0.26	0	1
J Acoust So	1185	1408	0.84	1	1
J Am Ceram	566	493	1.15	0	1
J Atm Ter P	363	265	1.37	0	1
J Atmos Sci	368	1291	0.29	0	0
J Fluid Mec	943	1204	0.76	0	0
J Marine Re	185	101	1.83	1	1
J Math Phys	942	1398	0.67	0	0
J Mech Phys	120	179	0.67	0	0
J Opt Soc	1607	1074	1.50	1	1
J Phys ABC	2186	2328	0.94	0	0
J Phys Ch S	1415	1003	1.41	0	0
J Phys D	450	414	1.09	0	1
J Phys E	427	536	0.80	0	0
J Phys Jap	1737	2107	0.82	0	0
J Physique	109	655	0.17	0	0
J Plasma Ph	36	329	0.11	0	0
JETP Letter	371	1070	0.35	0	1
M Not R Ast	599	1373	0.44	1	3
Molec Phys	667	763	0.87	0	0
Nucl Fusion	94	340	0.28	0	0
Nucl Instr	808	1623	0.50	0	0
Nuov Cim	2433	3793	0.64	0	1
Opt Spect R	1021	1533	0.67	0	0
P Camb Phil	367	387	0.95	0	0
Phil Res R	169	77	2.19	0	0
Philos Mag	1910	895	2.13	0	3
Phys St Sol	1296	4923	0.26	0	0
Phys C Glass	43	139	0.31	0	0
Physica	949	1036	0.92	0	0
PIEEE	1582	1663	0.95	1	3
Planet Spac	442	557	0.79	0	2
Rep Pr Phys	165	887	0.19	0	0
Rev M Phys	1349	880	1.53	0	0
Rev Sci Ins	1208	794	1.52	1	1
Sol St Comm	364	1420	0.26	0	0
Sol St Elec	345	382	0.90	1	1
Sov Astro R	504	1106	0.46	0	0
Sov J Nuc R	734	2228	0.33	0	0
Sov Ph Dokl	248	411	0.60	0	1
Sov Ph SS R	2586	3690	0.70	0	1
Sov Ph TP R	873	1032	0.85	0	0
Space Sci R	116	1125	0.10	0	0
Surf Sci	389	984	0.40	0	0
T Met S AIM	373	1688	0.20	1	1
Vacuum	64	106	0.60	0	0
Z Phys	1759	1734	1.01	0	1

not yet been accomplished. The smaller amount of unification necessary to generate the data used to this point was done by hand using a printout of the tapes.

• **Measures for Individual Disciplines**

Given the disciplinary classification of journals implicit in the models, it becomes possible to conjure a reasonably consistent importance classification for journals. To accomplish this a set of basic parameters has been extracted from the models and the raw data in the JCI. Table 2 shows these parameters for the field of physics. The first two numerical columns show respectively the number of times a journal was cited by other journals, and the number of times it cited other journals in the last quarter of 1969. These figures give a rough indication of the size of a journal. The third column is the ratio Citations To/Citations From, and is an indicator of whether the journal is a source or a sink for information. The "Arrows To," one- and two-step columns refer to the number of arrows pointing to the journal in Figures 1 and 2 respectively. The significance of the arrows has been explained in connection with these figures.

By any measure, the *Physical Review* is an outstanding journal in physics; it is very large and very heavily cited, as shown by the high ratio of citations to/citations from, by the absolute number of citations, and as shown by the extraordinary number of arrows indicating its primary rank in physics.

The next two groups, preferentially cited and highly cited, are composed of journals which seem to be significantly more important than the average journal, as measured by size, ratio of citings to/citings from, and by arrows. The division into preferentially and highly cited is largely based on the preference as reflected in the number of arrows to the journal.

Tables similar to Table 2 have been prepared for chemistry, biochemistry, biology and mathematics and statistics. In chemistry, the *Journal of the American Chemical Society* is clearly an outstanding journal as is the *Journal of Biological Chemistry* in biochemistry. The *Journal of Chemical Physics* does not seem to be quite an outstanding journal in either chemistry or physics, although its role as an interdisciplinary link makes it certainly outstanding in that sense. Biology and mathematics each lack a single outstanding journal, but do have preferentially and highly cited journals. Table 3 summarizes a tentative classification of major journals in all of these fields. While other journals not included on this table may be of special importance, particularly from the point of view of subdiscipline specialty, from an overall discipline viewpoint this appears to be a set of journals which are major in importance.

It should be stressed that the phenomena seen in this table, and in the figures, are more than sheer size; large journals tend to be cited, as shown by the ratio citations to/citations from, out of proportion to their size. This is perhaps related to some of the other links between "quality" and "size" in science. For example Cartter (*17*) found positive correlations between graduate department quality rankings and publication rates in Economics, English and Political Science; Cole and Cole (*18*) found positive correlations between citations per paper and

TABLE 3. Classification of Major Journals for 1969

Biology	Biochemistry	Chemistry	Physics	Mathematics	Cross-Field
Outstanding Journals					
	J Biol Chem	J Am Chem S	Phys Rev		J Chem Phys
Preferentially Cited Journals					
Nature	Bioc Biop A	Anal Chem	Astrophys J	Ann Math	J Biol Chem
P NAS US	Biochem J	J Chem Phys	J Appl Phys	Ann Math St	Nature
Science		J Chem SABC	J Chem Phys	Cr Ac Sci A	P NAS US
Am J Physl			J Geophys R	Math Z	Science
J Cell Biol				T Am Math S	
J Mol Biol					
J Physl Lon					
P Soc Exp M					
Highly Cited Journals					
Cancer Res	Arch Bioch	Act Cryst	Appl Phys L	B Am Math S	
Endocrinol	Bioc Biop R	Chem Ber	Nucl Phys	Biometrika	
Fed Proc	Biochem	J Org Chem	P Roy Soc A	Math Annal	
J Bact		J Phys Chem	Phys Fluids	P Am Math S	
J Exp Med		J Pol Sci	Phys Lett	Pac J Math	
J Immunol		Tetrahedr L	Phys Rev L		
J Pharm Exp			Sov Ph JE R		
Virology					

number of papers for 120 physicists; Hagstrom (19) has related departments by Cartter rank, number of citations, and number of research articles, and finds the highest correlation between number of citations and number of articles.

It is realized, of course, that each scientific field is different, and that the relative importance of archival versus letter journals may be different from field to field. Further, each scientist will have an opinion, based on knowledge of his specialty, of the relative importance of journals in his own field. Yet the overall citation data is, in effect, a vote of the scientific profession—biased by society membership and publication circulation, page charges, national origin, invisible colleges and other extraneous effects—but still a sizable statistical vote of the productive scientists.

• **Conclusions**

A series of graphic models of the cross citing between journals have revealed a rather orderly and consistent pattern of journal interrelationships within and between scientific disciplines. Rather clear delineation of disciplinary boundaries is obtained, with a few well known cross disciplinary journals as linkage points. Quite consistent hierarchic relationships characterize journals within disciplines, while cross disciplinary relations are in agreement with intuitive notions. Large, major journals seem to have importance characteristics which transcend their size.

References

1. Brooks, H., "Can Science Survive in the Modern Age?," *Science 174*, 4004, 21-29 (October 1971).
2. de Solla Price, Derek J., "Measuring the Size of Science," Israel Academy of Sciences (1969). *Science Since Babylon* (Yale University Press, 1961). *Little Science Big Science* (Columbia University Press, 1963).
3. Narin, Francis, "Exploration of the Possibility of Generating Importance and Utilization Measures by Citation Indexing of Approximately 250 Journals in the Physical Sciences," First Annual Report on Contract No. NSF-C627 for the National Science Foundation (August 1971).
4. Kessler, M. M., "Some Statistical Properties of Citations in the Literature of Physics," Symposium Proceedings, Statistical Association Methods in Mechanized Documentation, 193-198 (1964).
5. Van Cott, H. P., et al, "Extracting the Basic Structure of Scientific Literature," Report PB 175 552, U. S. Department of Commerce, National Bureau of Standards (1967).
6. Garfield, E., "'Science Citation Index'—A New Dimension in Indexing," *Science 144*, 649-654 (May 1964).
7. Garfield, E., "Citation Indexing for Studying Science," *Nature 227*, 669-671 (August 1970).
8. Garfield, E., "The Science Citation Index as a Blueprint of the Journal Literature," in publication.
9. Margolis, J., "Citation Indexing and Evaluation of Scientific Papers," *Science 155*, 3767, 1213-1219 (1967).
10. de Solla Price, Derek J., "Networks of Scientific Papers," *Science 149*, 510-515 (July 1965).
11. Martino, Joseph P., "Research Evaluation Through Citation Indexing," AFOSR Research 67-0300, AD 659 366, 266-277 (1967).
12. Hagstrom, Warren O., "Inputs, Outputs, and the Prestige of American University Science Departments," paper delivered at the Amer. Assoc. for the Advancement of Science, Chicago, Ill. (Dec. 1970). "Factors Related to the Use of Different Modes of Publishing Research in Four Scientific Fields," *Communication Among Scientists and Engineers*, Carnot E. Nelson and Donald K. Pollock, Eds. (Heath Lexington Books, 1970).
13. Daniel, Robert S. and C. M. Louttit. *Professional Problems in Psychology* (Prentice-Hall, N.Y., 1953).
14. Xhignesse, Louis V. and Charles E. Osgood, "Bibliographic Citation Characteristics of the Psychological Journal Network in 1950 and 1960," *American Psychologist 22*, 778-791 (1967).
15. The Journal Citation Index is an unpublished, resorted version of the Science Citation Index, Copyright 1970, the Institute for Scientific Information.
16. Carpenter, M. and F. Narin, "Clusters of Scientific Journals," In preparation.
17. Cartter, Allan M., "An Assessment of Quality in Graduate Education," American Council on Education (1966).
18. Cole, Stephen and Jonathan R. Cole, "Scientific Output and Recognition: A Study in the Operation of the Reward System in Science," *American Sociological Review 62*, 377-390 (1967).
19. Hagstrom, Warren O., "Inputs, Outputs, and the Prestige of American University Science Departments," paper delivered at the Amer. Assoc. for the Advancement of Science, Chicago, Ill. (Dec. 1970).

BIBLIOGRAPHICAL CITATION CHARACTERISTICS OF THE PSYCHOLOGICAL JOURNAL NETWORK IN 1950 AND IN 1960[1]

LOUIS V. XHIGNESSE AND CHARLES E. OSGOOD

Institute of Communications Research, University of Illinois

IN 1955, Osgood and Wilson completed a study on the flow of information within 21 psychological journals published in 1950. Measures derived, in the main, from information theory statistics were used to examine some of the inherent characteristics of the information network underlying the bibliographical citations found in these journals. The data used in the analysis were based upon a previous study by Boll (1952) on the bibliographical coverage of 22 psychological journals.

The aforementioned studies are related to the problem of information exchange in psychology. Journals are a part of the formal channel of scientific communication as well as storage elements for the summary accounts of research undertakings. Analysis of bibliographical citations thus can reveal certain characteristics of the pattern of information flow created by scientists in their work. The potential usefulness of this type of investigation is increased when it becomes possible to examine the trends through time of the communication network under consideration, and also when different communication networks can be compared.

The present paper deals with some of the characteristics of bibliographical citations in the same 21 psychological journals published both in 1950 and in 1960. The list of the journals used, along with the abbreviations to be used here, is given in Table 1; it includes 8 journals published by the American Psychological Association and 13 journals published by other organizations.

[1] This research was conducted as part of the American Psychological Association's Project on Scientific Exchange in Psychology with support from the National Science Foundation, Grant No. G-18494, Office of Scientific Information Service. The authors wish to express their gratitude to Sharon Wolfe for her assistance with computer analyses, and to John Darley, Arthur Brayfield, William Garvey, and Belver Griffith for their support and encouragement.

RATIONALE OF ANALYSIS

Each of the 21 journals belonging to the network under examination is treated as a communicating unit participating in the dissemination of information. The information is embodied in the articles or papers which make up the journal as well as in the bibliographical citations upon which they are based. In this framework, a journal is a *receiver* of information to the extent that the authors of the articles it contains cite articles published by other journals in the network. Reciprocally, a journal is a *source* of information to the extent that its articles are cited as bibliographical references in other journals. Although citations to materials outside the network of 21 journals have also been recorded, these permit only a one-way analysis. In other words, we cannot answer such a question as, "What references are used by a book cited by a journal in the network?" since only citations made by the 21 journals themselves were recorded.

All citations made in the 21 journals during the years 1950 and 1960 provide the raw data. Citations were coded for journal doing the citing, source (within network and outside), the year of publication of the source, and the type of source (book, article, thesis, etc.). For the 1960 sample, certain additional data on national origin, single or joint authorship, page length, and the like were also coded. Frequencies of reciprocal citation among the 21 journals are available for both years and lend themselves to matrix representation of the distribution of information throughout the network of these two periods. Treating each citation as a "message," the analytic techniques described by Osgood and Wilson (1961) can be applied.

RESULTS

Three general types of data are presented in this report: (a) Comparisons over the decade,

TABLE 1

LIST OF THE JOURNALS ANALYZED IN BOTH 1950 AND 1960 AND ABBREVIATIONS TO BE USED IN THIS REPORT

APA

Journal of Abnormal and Social Psychology (JASP)
Journal of Applied Psychology (JAP)
Journal of Comparative and Physiological Psychology (JCPhP)
Journal of Consulting Psychology (JCP)
Journal of Education Psychology (JEdP)
Journal of Experimental Psychology (JExP)
Psychological Bulletin (PB)
Psychological Review (PR)

Non-APA

American Journal of Orthopsychiatry (AJO)
American Journal of Psychology (AJP)
Education and Psychological Measurement (EPM)
Journal of Clinical Psychology (JClP)
Journal of General Psychology (JGP)
Journal of Genetic Psychology (JGtP)
Journal of Personality (JPl)
Journal of Psychology (JPs)
Journal of Social Psychology (JSP)
Psychiatric Quarterly (PQ)
Psychiatry (P)
Psychoanalytic Quarterly (PaQ)
Psychoanalytic Review (PaR)

1950–1960. These concern changes in the values of measures to be described below. (b) Comparisons among the 21 psychological journals as functioning in 1960. (c) Network structures. These involve matrices of reciprocal citations, distance measures derived therefrom, and finally an estimation of the similarity between 1950 and 1960 structures.

Decade 1950–60 Comparisons

Traffic. The traffic of any network is the total number of messages exchanged during some finite time—in this case, 1 year. Total citations within this network of journals has increased by 69% from 1950 to 1960, from 4,046 to 6,836 citations; total number of articles published increased by 50%. The eight APA journals display the greatest relative increase in traffic over this period (77% as compared with 57%). Density of citation per journal for APA journals is approximately double that for non-APA, although this is due in part to the inclusion among the latter of four psychiatric journals with relatively low densities of referencing. Looking at individual journals, we find that *JPl* (180%), *JASP* (167%), and *JClP* (178%) enjoyed the greatest increases in traffic, whereas only *PQ* (−18%) and *JAP* (−9%) showed decreased traffic over this decade. Although journals displaying the greatest increases are also generally those having the greatest absolute amount of traffic, this is not always the case; *JExP* is a clear exception to the rule, increasing by only 59% yet still carrying the heaviest absolute load.

Congruence. The congruence of any network is defined as the degree of correlation between its source and destination probabilities when these are ordered according to corresponding units. A congruent network is thus one in which journals tend to make citations in proportion to the extent that they are cited—the most active source being also the most active receivers. A negative value would characterize a network in which sending (being cited) and receiving (citing) functions were highly specialized. A zero correlation would presumably represent a highly "individualized" network in which these functions are randomly assumed with respect to particular other journals. The psychological journal network displays high congruence (.88 in 1950 and .82 in 1960), i.e., one in which level of activity is a general characteristic of journals in both citing and being cited. However, certain individual journals have shown marked transformations of function: *JEdP* (.31 to .84), *AJO* (.49 to .80), and *JCP* (.47 to .71) have increased their congruence and *JAP* (.87 to .30), *PB* (.26 to −.26), *EPM* (.74 to .04), and *JGP* (.86 to .12) have decreased. (Congruences for individual journals are based on the correlations between their individual rows and columns within the reciprocal citation matrix.)

Feeding/storing. The input/output ratio of a journal is the ratio of its probability of citing a reference to its probability of being cited as a reference. Thus journals with high ratios are "storers" of information in the network and journals with low ratios are "feeders" of information into the network. In the course of 10 years some substantial shifts have taken place. *JAP, JEdP,* and *JP* have shifted markedly from feeding to storing; *PB, JGP, JSU,* and *PaR* have merely increased their high storing functions; on the other hand, *JCP* has shifted toward the feeding function, while *JExP, JASP, P,* and *PaQ* have intensified their feeding functions over the period. Taking into account the traffic handled by individual journals, in relation to their feeding/storing functions, we may define the *network storing functions* of journals, i.e., the degree to which they operate as repositories of information (holders of citations) for the network as a whole. In these terms, *PB*, *JASP*, *JCPhP*, and *AJP*, in that order, have increased in this function; *JExP* has merely maintained its high referencing function.

Self-feeding. Self-feeding is defined as the degree to which sources of messages are their own destinations, that is, to what extent they "talk to themselves." In a network of highly specialized journals, contentwise, one would expect this index to approach unity, but this is clearly not the case with the psychological network. For 1950 the percentage of citations that were to articles in the same journal was only 30% and in 1960 it was 32%. Again, individual journals have varied in this respect over the decade, *JASP* (27% to 42%), *EPM* (24% to 42%), and *JClP* (19% to 29%) increasing in self-feeding and *JAP* (50% to 40%), *PB* (13% to 6%), and *JGP* (12% to 4%) decreasing. *JExP* (45% to 57%), *JCPhP* (47% to 52%), *P* (54% to 53%), and *PaQ* (54% to 66%) maintained or even increased their already high self-feeding characteristic.

Source and destination balances. Although the basic H (uncertainty) measures of information theory statistics are not obviously pertinent in themselves, a number of indices derivable from them are. The *relative uncertainty* of a system is the ratio of its actual uncertainty to the maximum possible; it varies from 0 to 1.00 and is comparable across systems, regardless of number of alternatives. If all journals in the network were cited and made citations with equal frequencies, both source and destination balances would be 1.00; if only one journal was ever cited, or if only one did all the citing, then source or destination balances would be 0. The former situation is approached in the psychological journal network, source balances being 92% and 88% for 1950 and 1960, respectively, and destination balances being 94% and 92%. The source balances of *JASP*, *JExP*, *EPM*, *JClP*, *JPl*, and *PaQ* have gone down during the decade—they now cite other journals less evenly; *PB* has increased its evenness of citing across the network, which is consistent with its "review" function. The destination balances of *JPs* and *JSP* have gone down—they are now being cited less evenly across the network; *JCP*, *JEdP*, *JGtP*, and *PQ*, on the other hand, have gone up in this respect.

Filter/condenser ratios. Networks and individual journals can vary in the degree to which they operate to concentrate information from many sources onto few destinations (condenser systems) or to diffuse information from few sources onto many destinations (filter systems). The filter/condenser ratio is defined as that between destination balance and source balance, large ratios indicating filter and small ratios condenser systems. The psychological network displayed almost perfect balance in this respect, in both 1950 (1.02) and 1960 (1.04), indicating that it functions neither as a filter nor a condenser system. In other words, citing and being cited functions are distributed more or less equally over journals when the network is viewed as a whole. Looking at individual journals, we find that *JExP*, *EPM*, *JPl*, *JClP*, *AJO*, *JCP*, *PQ*, and *PaQ* have increased their filtering functions during the decade, whereas *JAP*, *PB*, *JPs*, and *PaR* have increased their condensing functions (*JAP* changing from a dominantly filtering to a dominantly condensing journal, 1.13 to .94). It must be kept in mind that these ratios, as well as the source and destination balances above, reflect only the relative functioning of a journal, not its absolute level. Thus, whereas *PaQ* has a higher filtering function (1.80) than does *JExP* (1.38), it carries an insignificant traffic within the psychological network (as here defined) as compared with *JExP*.

Network organization. By definition, the organization of a network is the degree to which the destinations of messages are predictable from knowledge of their sources. The measure here is that for conditional uncertainty. Again, a relative measure is more meaningful, in this case the ratio of conditional uncertainty to its maximum (which is the uncertainty of the dependent, destination events). This index can be thought of as indicating the degree of structuring of a network. Thus, if Journal A only cited Journals B and C, and vice versa—and so forth—we would have a highly structured or organized network. If, on the other hand, an article in Journal A were equally likely to be cited in Journals B through N, and similarly for articles in other journals, we would have a completely random or unstructured network. The psychological journal network was only moderately organized in 1950 according to this index (30% of the maximum possible) and appears to have become even less so (23%) in the ensuing decade—and this despite a slight increase in overall self-feeding. The index cannot be applied to individual journals, of course.

Network citation in the time dimension. Sources cited in scientific journals during any given year are distributed over a considerable time period, and it is of interest to determine the nature of this distribution. The major proportion of all citations (60% for 1950 and 65% for 1960) are from materials published within the immediately preceding decade. The entire 40-year period from 1901 to 1940 accounts for 38% of citations in 1950, but only 12% in 1960. Citation of material prior to 1900 is infinitesimal in the psychological literature. Particularly striking is the drop in citing the entire 1901–40 literature that has occurred between 1950 and 1960 in these journals—a drop from 30% or higher to less than 10%. Another way of assessing the reduction in time perspective between 1950 and 1960 is by comparing percentages of citations that are from the immediate decade of authorship (1940–50 for the 1950 data, and 1950–60 for the 1960 data); *JExP* (57% to 72%), *PB* (44% to 60%), and *PR* (59% to 70%) in particular display this increased contemporaneousness in their citations.

Inward/outward orientation of psychological journals. All data reported so far have been based on within-network citations. What about extra-network citations? Excluding self-citations (references made to the same journal as the article is published in), we find that only 25% of total citations are within the defined network, and there has been little change over the 1950–60 decade. If we include self-citations, however, the percentage of within-network referencing rises to 37%, but again with little increase over the decade. Looking at the data for individual journals, we notice an interesting phenomenon: with self-citation *excluded*, *JASP* and *JExP* show decreasing within-network citation over the decade, but with self-citations *included*, both show increasing within-network citation—indicating that, for these journals, at least, the greater inward orientation is due entirely to self-citation. *JEdP, PB, AJP, JGP, JGtP,* and *JPl* show increases in within-network citation regardless of including or excluding self-citation whereas *PCPhP, EPM, JASP,* and all psychiatric journals show decreasing within-network dependency regardless of self-citation. There have been no significant changes in citing journals outside the network (28%) or in the proportion of journal citations to all other types of sources (65%) in the network as a whole between 1950 and 1960.

Some characteristics of authorship. The impact of foreign scholarship upon American psychologists was slight in 1960, at least as indicated by citations (only 6% of the total indicating foreign institutional affiliation), yet this was more than in 1950 (4%). The coding of the 1960 data permits analysis in terms of single or joint authorship and certain other characteristics: 59% of articles cited were by single authors, 41% by two or more; acknowledgment of help was fairly common, being noted by 31% of authors; joint domestic-foreign authorship was exceedingly rare, accounting for less than 1% of articles cited. Had such an analysis been made for an earlier period, say, the 1910–20 decade, evidence for foreign orientation would presumably have been much greater.

Journal Functioning in 1960

In this section we compare the 21 journals in the psychological network (as we have defined it) in terms of their contemporary functioning (1960) as indexed by the various measures described above. Table 2 summarizes the pertinent data: *activity,* as indicated by numbers of articles, numbers of citations, and density of citation per article (Columns 1, 2, and 3); *orientation,* as indicated by percentage of citations within network, percentage of self-citation, and degree of network self-feeding (Columns 4, 5, and 6); *network role,* as indicated by traffic within the network, congruence between citing and being cited, and input/output ratio, or storer/feeder ratio (Columns 7, 8, and 9); *characteristic function,* as indicated by source balance, destination balance, and filter/condenser ratio (Columns 10, 11, and 12); and *time perspective,* as indicated by percentage of citations prior to 1940 versus percentage of citations in the 1950–60 decade (Columns 13 and 14).

Number of articles published by year (Column 1) is perhaps the best single index of a journal's contribution to scientific information exchange—in quantity if not necessarily in quality. Density of citation (Column 3) is perhaps the best single index of a journal's scholarliness—in the sense that

TABLE 2
Some Quantitative Characteristics of Individual Journals in 1960

Journal	N articles	N citations	Citations/article	% citations in newtork	% self-citations	Network self-feeding	Network traffic	Congruence	Input/output ratio	Source balance	Destination balance	Filter/condenser ratio	% citations prior 1940	% citations 1950-1960
JASP	154	1,754	11	.41	.17	.42	1,371	.81	0.76	.72	.76	1.06	.09	.63
JAP	87	624	7	.32	.13	.40	295	.30	1.15	.66	.62	.94	.07	.69
JCPhP	123	1,280	10	.45	.24	.52	882	.84	0.97	.51	.56	1.11	.14	.68
JCP	114	1,224	11	.40	.15	.39	935	.71	0.77	.71	.72	1.01	.07	.69
JEdP	58	495	9	.32	.07	.21	230	.84	1.51	.81	.75	.92	.13	.70
JExP	123	1,152	9	.61	.35	.57	1,532	.89	0.58	.51	.71	1.38	.12	.75
PB	29	1,892	66	.47	.03	.06	1,274	−.26	2.08	.83	.88	1.07	.11	.59
PR	28	855	31	.45	.12	.28	779	.35	0.76	.68	.80	1.18	.14	.72
AJO	88	836	10	.19	.06	.35	237	.80	1.16	.72	.68	.96	.09	.70
AJP	85	772	9	.50	.16	.33	686	.87	0.91	.56	.74	1.33	.24	.59
EPM	81	639	8	.33	.14	.42	294	.04	1.23	.64	.58	.91	.11	.69
JClP	144	834	6	.38	.11	.29	475	.70	1.30	.66	.65	.99	.07	.73
JGP	64	858	13	.41	.02	.04	495	.12	2.27	.84	.83	.99	.14	.59
JGtP	64	778	12	.37	.08	.21	470	.41	1.20	.80	.75	.94	.19	.52
JPl	40	625	15	.45	.08	.18	443	.89	1.34	.64	.74	1.16	.06	.77
JPs	75	795	12	.31	.06	.20	394	−.02	1.22	.82	.81	.99	.15	.67
JSP	71	729	10	.27	.06	.21	285	.61	1.55	.72	.67	.92	.11	.66
PQ	46	575	24	.12	.04	.30	102	.58	1.28	.67	.63	.94	.16	.60
P	41	550	13	.13	.07	.53	140	.74	0.70	.54	.68	1.26	.09	.70
PaQ	24	392	17	.10	.07	.66	100	.72	0.47	.35	.62	1.80	.33	.44
PaR	41	675	16	.10	.03	.29	96	.62	1.52	.70	.57	.81	.32	.40
	(1)	(2)	(3)	(4)	(5)	(6)	(7)	(8)	(9)	(10)	(11)	(12)	(13)	(14)

its authors depend more or less heavily upon their knowledge of the work of others. The degree to which journal articles cite literature within the psychological network, cite other articles in the same journal and are self-feeders (including citing other articles by the author)—Columns 4, 5, and 6—indicates progressively orientation toward the profession, toward a specialty and toward oneself and his ingroup scientifically. The network traffic of journals (Column 7) indicates where their authors "do business"—within the psychological network or outside it—and the congruence measure (Column 8) indicates the degree to which a journal's recognition of others is reciprocated by their recognition of it. Journals with high input-output ratios (Column 9) cite more often than they are cited, and vice versa for journals with low input-outuput ratios. The evenness with which other journals are cited by a given journal (Column 10), the evenness with which other journals cite it (Column 11 and the ratio of the latter to the former (filter/condenser ratio, Column 12) are indicators of selectivity—in usage of sources, in being used, and in the balance of these, reflecting "distributing" or "gathering" functions. And finally, percentage of citations prior to 1940 versus percentage within the 1950–60 decade indicates the depth of a journal's orientation in time.

Journal of Abnormal and Social Psychology. JASP produced the largest number of articles in 1960 and nearly the largest total number of citations of any journal, with much of its heavy traffic being in the form of self-citations; it displayed a high degree of congruence, citing journals in proportion to their citing of it, and a relatively short perspective in time.

Journal of Applied Psychology. JAP authors gave few citations per articles; a relatively small proportion of these citations were to other journals in the network, and of these many (40%) were to itself. Its network traffic was slight and this had low congruence in terms of reciprocal citing by other journals; JAP was both selectively cited by other journals and cited others more often than it was cited. It had a short perspective in time.

Journal of Comparative and Physiological Psy-

chology. *JCPhP* published a large number of articles with a correspondingly large number of citations to the literature; a large proportion of these citations were to journals in the network (45%), many of which (52%) were to itself. It displayed high congruence with other journals in terms of reciprocal citing, but it was very selective in both citing and being cited. *JCPhP* was a filterer of information through the network, with a moderate depth of citation in time.

Journal of Consulting Psychology. *JCP* produced many articles in 1960 with a correspondingly large number of citations being made; within the network it tended to be a self-feeder and was cited considerably more than it cited. It had a short time perspective.

Journal of Educational Psychology. *JEdP* produced a relatively small number of articles and made a correspondingly small number of citations; a relatively small proportion (32%) of its citations were to other journals in the network and it contributed little to the network's total traffic. However, it displayed a high degree of congruence with other journals by tending to cite those journals which cite it, but it cited twice as much as it was cited; it thus maintained a relatively good balance among sources (more so than among destinations) and functioned more as a condenser of information than as a filterer.

Journal of Experimental Psychology. *JExP* was another large producer of articles and citations, but the number of references (9) per article was rather small; it was both professionally oriented (61% of its citations being to other network journals) and the heaviest self-feeder (57%) within the psychological network. *JExP* cited other journals in proportion to their citing it, but it was cited almost twice as often as it cited, and it was highly selective in citing others. It functioned as a filterer of information into the network and displayed a relatively short time perspective.

Psychological Bulletin. *PB* packed the largest number of citations into nearly the smallest number of articles in 1960, averaging 66 references per article. It was professionally oriented (47% within-network citations), but had the lowest self-citing tendency—only 6% of its large (1,274 messages) traffic. It displayed negative congruence, being cited inversely to its citing of others. *PB* cited other journals more than twice as often as it was cited, but maintained high degrees of balance in both citing other journals and being cited by them. It had a relatively deep perspective in time.

Psychological Review. *PR* published very few articles in 1960, but they contained a relatively large number of literature citations (31 per article); it was professionally oriented (45% citations within network). Although it had relatively low congruence with other journals in terms of reciprocal citing, it maintained a high degree of balance across the network in being cited; furthermore, it was somewhat more a filterer than a condenser of information to the network. *PR*'s time perspective was relatively broad.

American Journal of Orthopsychiatry. Although *AJO* published an average number of articles and made corresponding numbers of citations, comparatively few of these were from the psychological network (19%), its network traffic being small, and few of its citations were to itself (6%). Nevertheless, it displayed relatively high congruence in reciprocal citing with other journals in the network, and it is clearly the closest of the psychiatric journals to the psychological core. It was relatively contemporary in its time perspective.

American Journal of Psychology. *AJP* was perhaps the closest to the psychological core in its functional characteristics. It was oriented toward the psychological profession, with 50% of its citations being within the network, and it displayed very high congruence with other journals in the network—but being cited more than it cited. It was selective rather than balanced in citing other journals in the network, and it functioned more as a filterer of scientific information than a condenser. It had the deepest time perspective of any psychological journal (excepting the psychoanalytic ones), 25% of its citations being to sources published prior to 1940.

Educational and Psychological Measurement. In 1960 *EPM* had a relatively low density of citations (8 per article), was somewhat remote from the psychological network (33% within-network citations), and was not a self-feeder. It had low congruence with other journals in reciprocal citing ($r = .04$) and was a collector rather than a distributor of scientific information, with a low balance in the destinations of its messages.

Journal of Clinical Psychology. *JClP* produced a large number of articles in 1960, but with the lowest citation density (6 per article). It was selectively cited by other journals and had a very short (contemporary) time perspective. It was average in other characteristics.

Journal of General Psychology. JGP produced an average number of articles with an average number of citations (13 per article). It had an extremely low self-citing level along with a low congruence—i.e., its citing of other journals was unrelated to their citing of it. Nevertheless, it maintained balance in both citing and being cited across the network (suggesting that its articles were highly diversified in content). It had one of the deepest time perspectives in the network.

Journal of Genetic Psychology. JGtP produced an average number of articles with an average number of citations (12 per article). It was peripherally involved in the network (37% of its citations) and minimally self-feeding. It had a higher source than destination balance, and hence was tending toward condensing scientific information. But it had a relatively long time span, in terms of the references it cited.

Journal of Personality. JPl produced a relatively small number of articles in 1960 (40), but they had a fairly high citation density (15 per article). JPl was oriented toward the professional core (45% citations within network) and maintained very high congruence with other journals in the network, in terms of citing in proportion to being cited. It was a filterer of information through the psychological network, but had a very contemporary time span.

Journal of Psychology. JPs was oriented extraprofessionally (31% within-network citations) and did not cite itself with high frequency. It had low congruence with other journals, in the sense of being cited in proportion to citing them, but yet it maintained a high degree of balance in both its network sources and its network destinations. It had a moderate time perspective (15% references published prior to 1940).

Journal of Social Psychology. Publishing an average number of articles with an average density of citation (10 per article), JSP was relatively extranetwork oriented (27% within-network citations) and was not given to self-citation. It tended to be a condenser of information and it cited much more than it was cited. Its time perspective was average.

Psychiatric Quarterly, Psychiatry, Psychoanalytic Quarterly, and Psychoanalytic Review. These journals were sufficiently similar—in their functioning within the *psychological* network, at least—to justify common description. They were all extranetwork oriented (about 11% within-network citation) and they tended (with the exception of *Psychiatry*) to have a deep time perspective, relative to most psychological journals. They were self-citers (within this network, by virtue of their noninvolvement with it), but not when the base was their own self-citations. Within the network, again with the exception of *Psychiatry*, they were all cited unevenly. P and PaQ tended toward filtering information while PQ and PaR tended toward condensing information.

Network Structures: 1950 and 1960

To the extent that the network of scientific journals servicing a profession is organized, in the sense of nonchance predictability of who cites whom, we would expect this fact to appear as unevennesses in the density of flow of citations within the network. We have already seen that the psychological network is *organized* to about 25% of the maximum possible. Tables 3 and 4 give the basic frequency data for reciprocal citations in 1950 and 1960, respectively, the rows defining "being cited" frequencies and the columns defining "citing" frequencies. Unevenness in the flow of citing ("messages") is clearly indicated, and, further, the high density paths are precisely those one would expect from knowledge of the contents of the journals involved. For example, *JASP* (1960) is cited with relatively high frequency by *JCP, PB, JClP, JPl,* and *JSP,* whereas *JExP* is cited by *JCPhP, PB, PR, AJP, JGP,* and *JPs* with relatively high frequency.

In order to represent the citation structure of the psychological network in a systematic, quantitative way, we have applied the interpoint distance procedure recently developed by Roger Shepard (1962). Starting with the minimal assumption of no structure, and hence equal distances between all journal points, the method makes iterative adjustments in distances designed to match the actual rank orders of citation frequencies for each journal in relation to every other journal, in as small a number of dimensions as possible. Since each "message" or citation in the network was coded as to both source and destination journal, and since there appeared to be no reason for assuming that A citing B is a better indicator of closeness than B citing A, we summed both types of relations be-

TABLE 3
Raw Data Matrix for the Network of 21 Psychological Journals Published in 1950

Input of citations (being cited)	JASP	JAP	JCPhP	JCP	JEdP	JExP	PB	PR	AJO	AJP	EPM	JCIP	JGP	JGiP	JP	JPs	JSP	PQ	P	PaQ	PaR	Row totals
APA journals																						
JASP	79	1	4	29	1	9	38	17	2	3	7	24	14	7	29	12	15	3		2		304
JAP	9	97		30	10	2	3		4		23	10	7	9	1	4	16	1	11			229
JCPhP	4		130		1	69	64	46		13			15	21	1	11	17					375
JCP	21	18		97	2		2	1	3		6	43	6	5	1	6	2	2				230
JEdP	7	12		1	18		6			6	17	3	5	43	1	2	2					123
JExP	10	2	62	2	11	253	100	48	1	44	3	3	63	24	8	13	1	1	5	3		648
PB	16	2	10	16	3	30	54	12	7	7	12	14	27	19	3	19	6	2	1	1	1	265
PR	38	8	29	4	1	73	37	87	7	14	11	2	36	13	15	26	10					405
Non-APA journals																						
AJO	11	2		17	2			2	42		2	2		2	3	2	1	5	5	3	4	103
AJP	8	4	8	4	1	45	28	22	2	58	5	1	15	17	2	15	1	3	1	1		242
EPM	7	16		2	1		1	1	1		36	4	3		2	4		3				79
JCIP	10	5		20	1		2		1		5	30	5		1	2	2	1				89
JGP	10		9	13	3	43	29	12	1	5	7		30	12	3	3	1	1				189
JGiP	1	1	16		3	18	10	4	2	3	1	2	7	47		5	1		1			124
JPl	10			2	1		1	9	1			4	8	4	20	5						63
JPs	23	17	6	24	2	22	12	9	6	6	9	6	12	12	14	25	3	2	2		1	237
JSP	20	9		1	8	1	14	1	5		3	2	2		6	9	22		1		6	109
PQ	1	1		3	1				10				3		1	2	26	32	2	1	1	62
P	3			2				1	3			1	2		3	1	1	13	38	7	3	80
PaQ									7				3		1			16	3	22	8	62
PaR			1			1			2			1	1					9	2	5	6	28
Column totals	288	193	275	267	69	567	401	272	107	159	147	159	259	235	115	167	127	94	71	41	33	

Note.—Total number of citations within the 1950 data matrix: 4,046. All entries are frequency counts.

tween journals—which amounts to folding each of the Tables 3 and 4 over on itself along the diagonal. Table 5 gives the interpoint distances for the 1960 data. Logic requires that each journal be closer to itself than to any other journal, and hence that self-citation always be more frequent than any other-citation; this situation is only approximated. For example, in 1960 we find that *PB* makes many fewer self-citations than are involved in its reciprocal relations with *JExP, JASP,* and some others. The trends in lack of reciprocality, as might be expected, are from smaller journals to larger, in terms of numbers of articles, and from non-APA to APA journals in the same content areas.

The Shepard procedure was carried out for eight dimensions, accounting for approximately 75% of the total variance. However, since the interjournal distances based on three dimensions correlated highly with those based on eight, and since only three dimensions could be represented visually in any case, distances in three dimensions were used for constructing the solid model displayed as Figure 1. This represents the citation pattern for 1960; however the correlation across corresponding cells of the 1950 and 1960 distance matrices was .84, indicating very little shift in pattern. In constructing the visual model, three reference journals, *JExP, JSP,* and *JClP,* were assumed to lie on the same plane in the third dimension (hence given equal sized circles)—as an arbitrary reference framework—and all other journals were located in terms of their distances simultaneously from these three.

The general accuracy of the model (Figure 1) can be estimated by checking its reproduction of the distance values for 1960: *JCPhP,* for example, is closest to *JExP* (.29), quite close to *JGtP* (.39) and to *PR* (.41), and then to *AJP* (.46); it is farther away from *JEdP* (.59), but in the third dimension primarily; it is relatively remote from *EPM* (.92), *JSP* (.83), and *JClP* (.89), and maximally distant from all of the psychiatric and psychoanalytic journals in terms of reciprocal citations. *JPl* and *JASP* were so close (.18) that they had to be superimposed in the model. *PaQ* is almost equally remote from every journal, and therefore its location is only suggested.

By using a conveniently small criterion distance of .55, it is possible to define clusters of interacting journals. *JCPhP, JExP, AJP,* and *PR* form one such cluster, with *JGtP, JGP, JPs,* and *JCP* on the periphery; *JASP, JSP, JPl,* and *JCP* form another cluster; *EPM* and *JAP* participate in no clusters, although they are within hailing distance of each other; *JClP* and *JCP* form another nucleus, which would include *JASP* as well by our criterion; the psychiatric and psychoanalytic journals form no clusters with the psychological journals or with each other (but it must be kept in mind that the "universe" here is only a set of 21 "psychological" journals, arbitrarily defined). Appropriately, *PB* overlaps all of these clusters, being .45 from *JExP,* .24 from *JASP,* and .19 from *JCP;* PR displays the same tendency.

Comparing the 1950 and 1960 distance matrices —which as noted above are quite similar—we may report the following differences: Both *JCP* and *JClP* have shifted toward *PB* (.73 to .53 and .86 to .39); *JGtP* has moved toward both *JSP* and *JPl* (1.10 to .57 and .99 to .51); *PQ* and *PaQ* have moved away from the psychological journals gen-

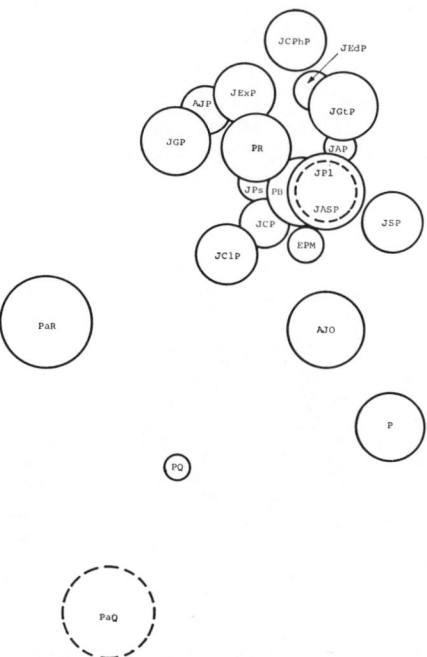

Fig. 1. Distances between journals in terms of reciprocal citations.

TABLE 4
Raw Data Matrix for the Network of 21 Psychological Journals Published in 1960

Input of citations (being cited)	Output of citations (citing)																					Row totals
	JASP	JAP	JCPhP	JCP	JEdP	JExP	PB	PR	AJO	AJP	EPM	JCIP	JGP	JGiP	JPI	JPs	JSP	PQ	P	PaQ	PaR	
APA journals																						
JASP	305	29	10	91	12	20	108	40	12	4	19	47	32	27	111	12	64	2	4		2	951
JAP	9	79		10	11	3	15	2	5		18	6	11	1	1	5	3					174
JCPhP	11	2	303	1	1	35	80	29	15	26			42	41		26						602
JCP	49	12		*189*	7	3	130	8		4	23	97	32	15	14	14	16	2	1		5	636
JEdP	4	5		8	*34*	3	15	1		2	9		6	7	3	2	1				1	105
JExP	55	14	96	8	23	*403*	194	97	3	138	4	4	82	29	30	40	6					1,228
PB	50	23	22	30	16	50	52	39	5	17	22	6	26	14	24	10	8		1			430
PR	47	8	61	10	7	67	37	*106*	2	40	1	21	32	31	22	21	5				3	504
Non-APA journals																						
AJO	6	1		18			11		*54*		2	4	3	3	9	5	3	7	8	6	8	135
AJP	22		36	6	6	72	47	23		*127*		2	22	12	5	26	6	4		1	3	426
EPM	7	14	1	20	13	2	4	2			*90*	5	3	1	1	1	3	1	1			172
JCIP	7	1		32	7		52	2	12		5	*93*	11	5	2	6	8	1	4			247
JGP	15	2	8	14	8	26	11	7		11		6	15	19	3	10	1	1				156
JGiP	12		39	4	6	14	52	4	6	10	6	8	6	*60*	3	4	3				4	241
JPI	59	3	2	18	3	1	18	12	3	4	1	5	7	3	*51*	4	11	1	5			211
JPs	28	2	5	10	4	7	24	6		4	7	4	9	17	4	*48*	15	3	2			199
JSP	18	3		9	1		28	2			5	8	2	4	1	4	*41*					128
PQ	4			5			6		7			1	5			2		*21*	1	2	2	54
P	9	2		3			5	1	21			2	1		2	3	4	5	*39*	27	6	105
PaQ	6			2			3		8				2					16	8	*27*	14	86
PaR	2					1	4		3				5					6		5	*20*	46
Column totals	725	200	583	488	159	707	896	381	156	387	212	321	354	289	283	243	198	69	74	41	70	

Note.—Total number of citations within the 1960 data matrix: 6,836. All entries are frequency counts.

TABLE 5
Interjournal Distances in Reciprocal Citing (Shepard Method): 1960

	JCPhP	JExP	AJP	PR	PB	JGiP	EPM	JEdP	JAP	JASP	JSP	JPI	JCP	JCIP	P	PaR	JGP	JPs	AJO	PQ	PaQ
JCPhP	.00	.29	.46	.41	.61	.39	.92	.59	.67	.69	.83	.71	.74	.89	1.60	1.52	.60	.66	1.22	1.86	2.33
JExP	.29	.00	.23	.32	.45	.45	.76	.60	.66	.58	.77	.61	.52	.64	1.48	1.54	.35	.48	1.05	1.59	2.25
AJP	.46	.23	.00	.53	.57	.65	.75	.62	.73	.75	.92	.80	.60	.65	1.59	1.74	.40	.51	1.16	1.56	2.31
PR	.41	.32	.53	.00	.47	.42	.91	.83	.77	.44	.73	.38	.53	.67	1.36	1.24	.34	.39	.91	1.54	2.09
PB	.61	.45	.57	.47	.00	.50	.49	.64	.49	.24	.39	.38	.19	.39	1.05	1.46	.53	.49	.67	1.52	2.24
JGiP	.39	.45	.65	.42	.50	.00	.91	.59	.72	.51	.57	.51	.66	.81	1.41	1.30	.69	.51	1.05	1.76	2.48
EPM	.92	.76	.75	.91	.49	.91	.00	.67	.44	.69	.64	.86	.49	.55	1.09	1.92	.86	.76	1.28	1.69	2.40
JEdP	.59	.60	.62	.83	.49	.59	.67	.00	.55	.83	.72	.94	.78	.88	1.56	1.88	.91	.61	.91	1.96	2.74
JAP	.67	.66	.73	.77	.64	.72	.44	.55	.00	.65	.59	.79	.60	.78	1.21	1.79	.86	.84	1.28	1.96	2.34
JASP	.69	.58	.75	.44	.24	.51	.69	.83	.65	.00	.38	.18	.30	.49	.95	1.23	.59	.61	.99	1.50	2.16
JSP	.83	.77	.92	.73	.39	.57	.64	.72	.59	.38	.00	.51	.52	.67	.92	1.41	.90	.67	.55	1.73	2.48
JPI	.71	.61	.80	.38	.39	.51	.86	.94	.79	.18	.51	.00	.43	.59	1.03	1.07	.57	.65	.70	1.47	2.11
JCP	.74	.52	.60	.53	.19	.66	.49	.78	.60	.30	.52	.43	.00	.23	.99	1.49	.49	.54	.60	1.37	2.14
JCIP	.89	.64	.65	.67	.39	.81	.55	.88	.78	.49	.67	.59	.23	.00	1.04	1.58	.54	.53	.57	1.19	2.21
P	1.60	1.48	1.59	1.36	1.05	1.41	1.09	1.56	1.21	.95	.92	1.03	.99	1.04	.00	1.62	1.41	1.41	.52	1.74	2.22
PaR	1.52	1.54	1.74	1.24	1.46	1.30	1.92	1.88	1.79	1.23	1.41	1.07	1.49	1.58	1.62	.00	1.45	1.54	1.34	1.88	2.29
JGP	.60	.35	.40	.34	.53	.69	.86	.91	.86	.59	.90	.57	.49	.54	1.41	1.45	.00	.59	.92	1.31	2.00
JPs	.66	.48	.51	.39	.49	.51	.76	.61	.84	.61	.67	.65	.54	.53	1.41	1.54	.59	.00	1.00	1.40	2.56
AJO	1.22	1.05	1.16	.91	.67	1.05	.87	1.28	.99	.55	.70	.60	.57	.61	.52	1.34	.92	1.00	.00	1.35	2.37
PQ	1.86	1.59	1.56	1.54	1.52	1.76	1.69	1.96	1.96	1.50	1.73	1.47	1.37	1.19	1.74	1.88	1.31	1.40	1.35	.00	2.01
PaQ	2.34	2.25	2.31	2.09	2.24	2.48	2.40	2.74	2.34	2.16	2.48	2.11	2.14	2.21	2.22	2.29	2.00	2.56	2.01	2.37	.00

erally; *P* has moved away from *JCPhP* and *AJP*, but toward *EPM* (changing orientation of *Psychiatry* toward measurement and away from physiology?); *PaR* has shifted away from *AJP* and toward *JGtP* (1.15 to 1.74 vs. 1.79 to 1.30). Another way to gain insight into changes that have occurred in citation patterns over the 1950–60 decade is to see what journals have moved toward or away from the "psychological core"—which, on the basis of its central and overlapping position with all identifiable clusters here, as well as its centrality affectively (cf. Jakobovits & Osgood, 1967), we identify as *PB*. *AJP, EPM, JAP, JASP, JSP, JPl, JCP,* and *JClP*, along with *P* and *AJO*, have moved closer to *PB* in terms of reciprocal citation; *JCPhP* and *JExP*, along with *PQ* and *PaQ*, have moved away from *PB*.

Interpretive Summary

In order to have a closed network, within which patterns of reciprocal citation could be determined, it was necessary to specify some particular set of journals as "the psychological network." Instead of defining inclusion within this network in terms of a journal being published by the American Psychological Association—which would have been simple, but which would have eliminated such obviously psychological journals as *AJP, JClP,* and all of the Murchison journals—we widened the definition to include these, along with a number in the educational and psychiatric fields. Had the study not been limited for comparison purposes to the 21 journals originally used by Boll (1952) for the 1950 analysis, we would now have included others, such as the *American Psychologist, Psychometrika,* and *Behavioral Science.* Thus, it is clear that our definition of the psychological journal network is arbitrary.

The reciprocal citation data, particularly the distance measures, provide a functional criterion for inclusion within the psychological network. Using *PB* and *PR* to represent the "psychological core" (justified by the fact that they are simultaneously close in reciprocal citing to all three major clusters of journals, experimental, personality-social, and clinical), four psychiatric journals, *P, PQ, PaR,* and *PaQ*, stand out as being remote, hardly participating in the network. *AJO* (the *American Journal of Orthopsychiatry*), on the other hand, appears to be moving in toward the psychological core, as indicated by its reciprocal citing with *PB* and its distances from other psychological journals. Although the distance matrices for 1950 and 1960 were quite highly correlated (.84), the shifts that have occurred seem to involve movement of journals representing newer and more applied fields inward toward the "core" and movement of journals representing the traditional experimental fields away; thus *EPM, JAP, JASP, JSP, JCP, JPl,* and *JClP* have moved inward while *JExP* and *JCPhP* have moved outward. However, *AJP* shifts inward, contrary to the trend.

Whether the extraordinary increase in sheer mass of information exchange, judged either in terms of network traffic or numbers of articles published, is peculiar to psychology or parallels increases in all fields cannot be told from our data alone. However, it seems likely that equivalent analyses in other fields would have shown the same trend. Increases in the activity of specific psychological journals parallel increases in membership in APA rather neatly, as reported by Robert C. Tryon (1963). According to his data, total division membership has gone up from 5,344 to 12,309 between 1948 and 1960, or 130%. Of particular interest is the fact that those journals servicing the divisions of APA which Tryon records as increasing most in membership (Personality and Social and Clinical) are those we record as increasing most in citation traffic—*JPl, JASP,* and *JClP*. The more people working in an area the greater the density of messages exchanged, which is not surprising, of course. Two of the journals which have increased most in both articles and citations, *JASP* and *JCPhP*, have doubled the number of volumes per year within the decade; *PB*, which has more than doubled its citations but without increasing numbers of articles, did the same thing in 1964. The notable increase in density of citation per article, particularly for APA journals, could represent either changing habits of scholarship or merely "packing" of articles in an increasingly competitive acceptance situation.

High congruence indices for the psychological network as a whole indicate that journal "activity" tends to express itself in both citing and being cited. The high congruence values for most individual journals indicate that journals tend to cite others in proportion to the extent that others cite them. This is what one would expect in a network composed of relatively specialized units, subject-matter-wise. In the distance matrices based upon reciprocal citation frequencies, this situation reveals itself as several identifiable clusters of journals: a "Division 3 cluster" (*JExP, JCPhP, AJP*, and *PR*, along with *JGtP, JGP* and *JPs* more peripherally); a "Division 8 cluster" (*JASP, JSP, JPl*, and *JCP* peripherally); a "Division 12 cluster" (focusing on *JClP* and *JCP*, but including *JASP*). Given the functions of *PB* and *PR*, the former as a review journal and the latter as a theoretical journal, one would expect them to be centrally located in the space defined by reciprocal citing, and this is the case.

The psychological network as a whole is balanced, in the sense that journals replicate each others' functions rather than being sharply divided into producers and receivers of scientific information. It also tends neither to filter information out from few sources to many destinations nor to condense information from many sources onto a few destinations. It is about one-fourth as organized as it might be theoretically, in the sense of being able to predict the source of a citation from knowing the destination. These are not necessarily "good" characteristics for a communication network, of course. However, networks that were extreme in any of these characteristics would be pretty strange: Some journals would never make citations and others would only cite; *JASP* would speak only to *PR*, *PR* would speak only to *JExP*, and *JExP* would speak only . . . to God! If any trend can be discerned over time, however, it is toward a somewhat less balanced and more functionally differentiated system, with certain journals like *PB, JEdP, JGP*, and *JPs* coming to record and "store" information being produced by increasingly specialized research, "feeder" journals like *JASP, JExP, JCPhP, EPM*, and *JClP*. In terms of sheer bulk of referencing, *JASP, JCPhP, JExP*, and *PB* are the major information storers in the psychological network (*Psychological Abstracts* excluded, of course).

The self-feeding characteristic presumably indicates the degree of self-sufficiency or specialization of a network or particular journal. How the roughly constant 30% self-feeding by psychological journals and the 37% of within-network citations to all citations are to be interpreted—as indicating relatively high or low self-sufficiency— would depend upon comparisons with other professional networks. Among psychological journals, *JExP, JASP, EPM*, and *JClP* are the heaviest self-feeders, and increasingly so over the 1950–60 decade. High self-feeding within a network may be symptomatic of the development of potentially independent disciplines, and we note that each of the greatest self-feeders above represents a different area of specialization. In general, APA journals display more inward (professional) orientation, as indexed by within-network citations, than do non-APA journals; *JExP, AJP, PB, JCPhP, JPl, PR, JASP*, and *JGP*, in that order, are the most psychologically oriented and (excluding the psychiatric journals, which, on our evidence, are not really part of the network at all) *JSP, JPs, JAP, JEdP*, and *EPM*, in that order, are the least psychologically oriented.

The citations made in any given year have a distribution over the time dimension. One would expect the time perspective of different disciplines to vary considerably—from great time depth of citation in philosophy, say, to shallow time depth in home economics, perhaps. Without having comparative data from other scientific networks, it is difficult to interpret the situation in psychology. However, the fact that in both 1950 and 1960 over 60% of all citations were within the most recent decade, the fact that only about 1% of citations were to sources published prior to 1900, and the fact that citation of the entire 1901–40 period dropped off abruptly between 1950 and 1960—together suggest that the time perspective of psychology is short and getting shorter. If this is true, then it would seem that psychology as a science is in danger of "forgetting where it has been," of repeatedly rediscovering facts and theories that have been well worked in the past. Within this network, psychological journals dealing with theory and traditional experimental topics (e.g., *PB, PR, AJP, JGP*, and *JGtP*), along with the psychoanalytic (*PaQ* and *PaR*) but not the psychiatric journals, have relatively deep time perspectives; the more applied journals (e.g., *JAP, JCP, JClP, JPl*, and *JSP*, but not *JEdP* or *EPM*) seem to have the shallowest time perspective—which could be simply a reflection of the available literature from the past in the older versus the newer fields.

Finally, this paper contains "thumbnail sketches" of the journals within the network as they appeared to be functioning circa 1960. These sketches include data relating to activity levels, inward versus outward orientation, role within the network as congruent or incongruent with other journals and as feeder or storer of information, characteristic functioning in terms of balance among its sources and destinations, and time perspective. These "function profiles" for individual journals, along with their affective connotations to members of the profession (reported in Jakobovits & Osgood, 1967), may provide food for some thought by their readers, writers and, indeed, editors.

REFERENCES

BOLL, J. J. The input and output of 22 psychological periodicals; a study of bibliographical coverage. Unpublished manuscript, University of Illinois, Urbana, 1952.

JAKOBOVITS, L. A., & OSGOOD, C. E. Connotations of twenty psychological journals to their professional readers. *American Psychologist*, 1967, **22**, 792–800.

OSGOOD, C. E., & WILSON, K. V. Some terms and associated measures for talking about human communication. University of Illinois, Institute of Communications Research, Urbana, 1961.

SHEPARD, R. N. The analysis of proximities: Multidimensional scaling with an unknown distance function. I & II. *Psychometrika*, 1962, **27**, 125–140, 219–246.

TRYON, R. C. Psychology in flux: The academic-professional bipolarity. *American Psychologist*, 1963, **18**, 134–143.

JOURNAL RANKING AND SELECTION: A REVIEW IN PHYSICS

ALAN SINGLETON
Institute of Physics, Bristol

Over several decades many ranking techniques have been proposed as aids to journal selection by libraries. We review those closely related to physics and others with novel features. There are three main methods of ranking: citation analysis, use or user judgement, and size or 'productivity'. Citations offer an 'unobtrusive' quantitative measure, but not only is the absolute value of a citation in question, but also there is no consensus on a 'correct' way to choose the *citing* journals, nor of the ranking parameter. Citations can, however, point out anomalies and show the *changing* status of journals over the years. Use and user judgement also employ several alternative methods. These are in the main of limited applicability outside the specific user group in question. There is greater 'parochialism' in 'use' ranking than in 'judged value' lists, with citation lists the most international. In some cases, the attempted 'quantification' of subjective judgement will be misleading. Size and productivity rankings are normally concerned with one or other formulation of the Bradford distribution. Since the distribution is not universally valid, for library use the librarian must satisfy him/herself that the collection conforms to the distribution, or that his users would be well served by one that did. This may require considerable effort, and statistics gained will then render the Bradford distribution redundant.

Rank correlations are calculated on many of the lists. Correlations between methods are generally low, although there may be a case for a study of various techniques on one journal/article collection and user group.

The lack of an agreed quantitative measure should ensure continued reliance on subjective judgement of librarian and user. The appropriate role for more apparently sophisticated techniques should be a minor, auxiliary one.

"CONDITIONS ARE becoming financially acute for the large research libraries which are attempting to satisfy the bibliographical needs of their patrons.... Present conditions would seem to demand that professional organizations give all the assistance possible to perplexed librarians to enable them to reach wise decisions in the selection of the serials most valuable for their libraries and also in the discarding or transferring to other libraries of little used publications. Greater attention to cooperative agreements in regard to the acquisition of scientific serials would seem to be a necessity if scientists are to obtain copies of research papers necessary for their projects".[1]

Charles Harvey Brown wrote that 20 years ago in the introduction to his book giving lists of most cited publications in various fields. We can find quotations 20 years earlier or later expressing similar sentiments. It may be that current financial stringency is making life particularly difficult for libraries, but certainly the debate on journal prices, library budgets, photocopying and interlibrary loan has returned with renewed vigour. It is fashionable to regard current difficulties for libraries as arising after a period in the sixties and early seventies when they had 'grown fat'. Whether or not this is so, certainly many libraries are and will be considering how to prune, rather than expand, their journal collections. This makes it an appropriate time to review the techniques suggested by and for librarians in journal ranking and selection.

There is a great deal of advice in the library and documentation literature on how to decide which periodicals to buy. Techniques suggested often involve ranking the 'potential' journals in some way, e.g. by citation analysis, usage, time spent reading, user preference etc., with the implication that the ones coming out on top are the most likely best buys. A typical article will contain a couple of references to early work by Gross and Gross[2] and Brown[1] and some caveats that the results of any statistical analysis must be tempered by awareness of the 'real' world. Vickery's paper[3] is an early example dealing with purchasing sets of periodicals.

Of course, most librarians do not have the problem of starting from scratch. There is usually already a periodicals section, and some of the titles will have long back-runs, and to some extent, the longer they 'stretch' back in time the greater 'momentum' they have in the present. In this case the statistical techniques are presented as an additional tool to help decide which titles to discard. Since very few of these papers indicate whether and where such techniques are in fact *used*, even by the authors themselves, it is not too sceptical to suggest that when they *are* used, it is probably mainly in a subsidiary way, e.g. put in as back-up statistics to management when they support decisions arrived at in other ways.

Although there are now one or two small studies looking into it, we do not have any broad-based surveys of decision making in purchasing for libraries. We do not really know who in fact has the 'power' in most cases. This is, of course, not a trivial point for publishers who, in difficult days, may adopt more of the marketing techniques from other areas. In books for example, publishers in America at least may have some misconceptions:[4] "Publishers believe that faculty members make most of the selections for academic libraries. Not so, say librarians . . . 'while it is true that in all of the academic institutions faculty requests play an important part in stimulating selection procedures, it is a member of the professional staff who has the final authority for selection decisions.'"

Physics has a large share of papers on ranking techniques for journals and in this article we look at these together with more general methods, attempt to compare them and assess their usefulness.

I. CITATION ANALYSIS

As is well known, citation analysis has been proposed or used for a wide variety of applications (see e.g.[5,6,7]). For journals, there are at least two well known studies using them to form groups related by inter-citation or bibliographic coupling, those of Kessler[8] and Narin and Carpenter[9]. These remain interesting techniques for mapping certain subject fields or showing other strongly connected (e.g. national) groups but have not been proposed as practical techniques for journal selection. There are always limitations in the data, and a large variety of techniques for obtaining different sets of clusters.

It is not surprising that so much work has been done on citations, since at first sight they provide a quantitative and 'computer-manipulable' measure of something or other. The debate is joined on what that 'something or other' is. It is quite clear that a citation can be made for one or more of a number of different purposes, but what is not clear is the extent to which citations relate to each particular purpose (e.g. Moravcsik[10], for studies on 5 years of Physical Review). There has been a continuing (and continual) debate on citation over the years with people asking whether citations are in general for 'dazzling bystanders with a display of erudition or corroboration'[11] or suggesting that they are 'in large part a social device for coping with problems of property rights and priority claims', and that viewed as an 'acknowledgement of indebtedness' are 'an institutionalised form of modesty'[12] or, as here, to indicate that the author has read the relevant literature. Even back in 1962, there was enough debate for it to be worth Pauline Atherton's while[13] to make a six-page collection of remarks on citation indexes. At least now most scientists know of the existence of the Science Citation Index.

Citation analysis for *journal* evaluation, has most often taken the form of analysing the references in the papers in a standard journal to other journals, and thereby producing a list of journals ranked according to the number of citations received. These rankings are then sometimes adjusted to take into account the size of the cited journal etc. The 'sampling technique', if one can call the arbitrary selection of a journal that, has been severely criticised by Raisig[14] who not unreasonably points out that a statistical analysis 'must satisfy basic statistical requirements' and that taking a standard journal denies the validity (or necessity) of the concept of the random sample. He analyses a number of previous studies and criticizes them on statistical grounds.

The existence of a whole mass of citation data, from 2,000 or so journals, through the production of the Science Citation Index (SCI) gives a potential way round these statistics objections. Garfield[15] has fairly thoroughly outlined its use, particularly for a large scale study in 1971, from which came the development below.

About the end of 1973, ISI produced Journal Citation Reports (JCR).[16] When first produced, JCR was a computer print-out and available in 3 separate packages. Total price was $540 (+ shipping). It is not therefore surprising that there were very few UK subscribers. A new JCR has recently been issued,[17] as a separate volume in the SCI 1975 annual. This was based on source data from the SCI using references in items published in the last quarter of 1969. This gave 926,928 citations. Then: 'through an assortment of computer manipulations, the number of citations *received* by a specific journal was counted and the journals giving the citations were identified. The number of citations *given* by a specific journal was also counted and the journals receiving the citations identified. Finally, citations received and given were distributed according to the year of publication of the journal issue to which the citations were made. With these counts and distributions serving as the base, various indicator values were calculated and a number of different rankings of the journals involved were established.'[16]

Inhaber[18] has used the JCR data to do an analysis for physics journals. There are other citation ranking lists of journals and we now discuss in more detail these and other lists.

Table 1 reproduces Garfields's figures for all journals many of which, as we can see, are clearly relevant to physics. Inhaber has taken a slightly narrower

TABLE I.

Item No. (1)	Cited Journal (2)	1969 Times Cited Last Quarter 1969 (3)	Citations to 1967 and 1968 Articles (4)	Articles Published in 1967 and 1968 (5)	Impact Factor (6)	Item No. (1)	Cited Journal (2)	1969 Times Cited Last Quarter 1969 (3)	Citations to 1967 and 1968 Articles (4)	Articles Published in 1967 and 1968 (5)	Impact Factor (6)
1	J AM CHEM SOC	26323	22156	3946	5.614	77	AM J OBSTET GYNECOL	1657	1440	1193	1.207
2	PHYS REV	20674	20740	5767	3.596	78	PLANT PHYSIOL	1646	1808	1149	1.573
3	J BIOL CHEM	17112	10768	1777	6.059	79	IND ENG CHEM	1644	928	856	1.084
4	NATURE LONDON	15325	15956	6811	2.342	80	ANN SURG	1641	1036	642	1.613
5	J CHEM SOC	14028	17764	5827	3.048	81	B CHEM SOC JAP	1639	2004	1567	1.278
6	CHEM PHYS	13690	11696	3738	3.128	82	EUR J BIOCHEM	1635	1992	501	3.976
7	SCIENCE	9753	11880	3968	2.993	83	GENETICS	1618	1340	738	1.815
8	BIOCHIM BIOPHYS ACTA	9550	10956	3531	3.102	84	BLOOD	1514	1256	566	2.219
9	J NAT ACAD SCI USA	8260	11548	1348	8.566	85	J IEEE	1510	1856	756	2.455
10	BIOCHEM J	7638	6348	2074	3.060	86	J OPT SOC AM	1587	1196	1322	0.904
11	LANCET	7617	8164	5496	1.485	87	ANALYT BIOCHEM	1519	1672	502	3.330
12	PHYS REV LETT	6581	11380	2317	4.911	88	J GEN PHYSIOL	1507	1208	407	2.968
13	CR ACAD SCI	5789	6576	8345	0.788	89	ARCH INTERN MED	1501	860	486	1.769
14	AM J PHYSIOL	5420	3156	1013	3.115	90	AM HEART J	1453	1036	539	1.922
15	ORG CHEM	5401	5756	2475	2.325	91	J EXP PSYCHOL	1449	1152	644	1.788
16	J APPL PHYS	5190	5072	2880	1.761	92	J GEN MICROBIOL	1445	1136	534	2.127
17	SOC EXP BIOL MED	5079	3468	1920	1.806	93	J COMP PHYSIOL PSYCH	1444	888	476	1.865
18	MOL BIOL	4982	7340	833	8.811	94	J PHYS CHEM SOLIDS	1430	1572	801	1.962
19	J PHYSIOL LOND	4966	3036	1248	2.432	95	CANCER	1416	1224	593	2.064
20	J ROY SOC LOND	4864	1916	621	3.085	96	AM J PATHOL	1401	960	529	1.814
21	J CELL BIOL	4813	4596	1357	3.386	97	RUSS J PHYS CHEM	1400	1116	1545	0.722
22	J CLIN INVEST	4785	3652	1086	3.362	98	METHODS ENZYMOL	1391	1456	482	3.020
23	J CHEM PHYS	4703	4516	1939	2.329	99	J INORG NUCL CHEM	1391	1356	908	1.493
24	CHEM BER	4541	2128	1037	2.052	100	PEDIATRICS	1382	1060	709	1.495
25	NEW ENGL J MED	4512	5252	2226	2.359	101	SURG GYNECOL OBSTET	1374	868	535	1.622
26	AM MED ASS	4492	3980	3787	1.050	102	ANAT REC	1365	555	408	1.493
27	BRIT MED J	4304	4224	6238	0.677	103	REV MOD PHYS	1364	816	189	4.317
28	SOV PHYS JETP	4295	3400	754	4.509	104	J MET SOC AIME	1359	1196	901	1.327
29	ASTROPHYS J	4271	5440	1167	4.661	105	CAN J PHYS	1356	2156	1019	1.115
30	ANALYT CHEM	4259	2424	1510	1.605	106	BRIT J PHARMACOL	1348	1348	507	2.658
31	J BACTERIOL	4147	4712	1410	3.341	107	APPL PHYS LETT	1337	2556	721	3.545
32	BIOCHEMISTRY	4076	6344	1114	5.694	108	PHYS STAT SOLIDI	1327	2192	1485	1.476
33	NUCL PHYS	4034	6716	2345	2.863	109	J ELECTROCHEM SOC	1308	1208	1538	0.785
34	PHYS LETT	3943	7160	3034	2.359	110	ACTA METALLURG	1304	1908	452	2.132
35	TETRAHEDRON LETT	3937	2902	2902	2.843	111	PHYS FLUIDS	1304	1548	1050	1.474
36	J EXP MED	3871	2700	325	8.307	112	EXPERIENTIA	1297	1592	1565	1.017
37	ANN NY ACAD SCI	3787	2344	1216	1.927	113	GASTROENTEROLOGY	1286	1428	1244	1.147
38	ARCH BIOCHEM BIOPHYS	3689	3776	1169	3.230	114	Z ZELLF MIKR ANAT	1286	1800	653	2.756
39	J GEOPHYS RES	3537	5312	1569	3.385	115	SURGERY	1274	968	700	1.260
40	J POLYM SCI	3458	2888	2069	1.395	116	REV SCI INSTR	1272	1148	860	0.843
41	BIOCHEM BIOPHYS RES	3395	5108	1190	4.292	117	AM J ROENTGENOL	1272	1044	860	1.213
42	FED P	3372	4036	7374	0.547	118	AIAA J	1246	1456	1231	1.182
43	J PHYS	3308	3256	2379	1.368	119	T ASME	1240	800	332	2.600
44	FARADAY SOC	2922	1808	879	2.056	120	AM J CARDIOL	1238	1600	737	2.170
45	ACTA CRYSTALLOGR	2917	2164	1803	1.200	121	J HISTOCHEM CYTOCHEM	1229	1076	362	2.287
46	DOKL AKAD NAUK SSSR	2869	2456	5385	0.456	122	J PEDIAT	1229	2196	783	3.374
47	PHARMACOL EXP THER	2781	2020	566	3.568	123	J ACOUST SOC AM	1219	1016	1091	0.462
48	ANGEW CHEM	2728	3660	1251	2.925	124	NATURWISSENSCHAFTEN	1218	1484	1091	0.865
49	J IMMUNOL	2627	2992	726	4.121	125	J NUTR	1209	952	488	1.946
50	INORG CHEM	2620	3976	1247	3.188	126	SPECTROCHIM ACTA	1201	1248	679	1.837
51	SOV PHYS SOLID STATE	2620	2984	1561	1.941	127	Z ANORG ALLG CHEM	1188	580	549	1.056
52	CIRCULATION	2601	2624	2160	1.214	128	J PERSON SOC PSYCHOL	1186	676	581	1.163
53	ENDOCRINOLOGY	2548	2276	783	2.906	129	RADIOLOGY	1175	1244	835	1.488
54	ACTA CHEM SCAND	2444	1984	943	2.103	130	AM J BOT	1171	644	726	0.887
55	NUOVO CIMENTO	2431	3436	1938	1.772	131	Z PHYS CHEM LEIPZIG	1170	332	252	1.271
56	J ORG CHIM FRANCE	2416	2664	2704	0.985	132	J CHROMATOGR	1161	1708	1043	1.636
57	VIROLOGY	2376	2020	584	4.489	133	HOPPE SEYLERS Z	1145	1412	863	1.636
58	CANCER RES	2349	2344	814	2.879	134	J UROL	1142	656	712	0.921
59	CAN J CHEM	2280	2392	1182	2.023	135	ARCH PATHOL	1138	420	400	1.359
60	HELV CHIM ACTA	2200	1648	1650	0.827	136	AM J DIS CHILD	1134	748	867	0.862
61	Z NATURFORSCHUNG	2200	2172	1316	1.316	137	AM J DIS CHILD	1127	748	610	1.226
62	AM J MED	2191	1784	395	4.516	138	ACTA MED SCAND	1112	680	472	1.440
63	J LAB CLIN MED	2120	1284	754	1.702	139	ANN PHYSICS	1105	692	224	3.089
64	TETRAHEDRON	2071	3220	1313	2.452	140	COLD SPR HARB SYMP	1091	1456	196	5.495
65	EXP CELL RES	1958	1464	655	2.075	141	J ORGANOMET CHEM	1089	2784	796	3.497
66	J LIEBIGS ANN CHEM	1952	768	492	1.550	142	PFLUGERS ARCH	1076	896	732	1.224
67	ANN INT MED	1946	1844	1098	2.157	143	OPT SPECTROSC USSR	1070	1100	814	1.351
68	PHIL MAG	1943	1168	547	2.157	144	KLIN WSCHR	1070	800	1198	0.667
69	J CLIN ENDOCR METAB	1903	1888	488	3.858	145	CHEM IND LOND	1049	648	1703	0.380
70	J APPL PHYSIOL	1836	1460	1024	2.270	146	BER BUNSEN PHYS CHEM	1044	688	771	0.892
71	ACTA PHYSIOL SCAND	1816	1600	413	2.479	147	BIOCHEM PHARMACOL	1030	1292	688	1.888
72	J PHYS SOC JAP	1786	1768	2074	0.852	148	PHYSIOL REV	1022	572	407	1.733
73	J PHYS	1764	1228	1454	1.454	149	J BONE JOINT SURG	1021	500	745	0.671
74	CIRC RES	1750	1820	584	4.212	150	J NEUROPHYSIOL	1015	692	156	4.435
75	PHYTOPATHOLOGY	1713	1632	1597	1.021	151	CR SOC BIOL	1010	596	1316	0.452
76	J NAT CANCER I	1668	1672	417	4.009	152	REC TRAV CHIM	1010	728	337	2.160

The 152 most frequently cited journals ranked by frequency of citation in journals covered by the SCI. Column 1 gives rank, and column 2 gives abbreviations of the titles of cited journals. Column 3 shows the total number of times each journal was cited during the last quarter of 1969. Column 4 gives an estimate of the total number of citations in 1969 of items published in 1967 and 1968 (the estimate was made by quadrupling the 1969 citations of 1967 and 1968 items in the 3-month sample). Column 5 shows the total number of items processed from each journal by the SCI during 1967 and 1968. Column 6 indicates the impact factor (average citations per published item) derived by dividing the numbers in column 4 by those in column 5.

(Reproduced with permission—E. Garfield: Citation analysis as a tool in journal evaluation, *Science*, 178, pp. 471–79, Fig. 4, 3 November 1972. Copyright 1972 by the American Association for the Advancement of Science.)

---

definition of physics journals and presents the same information graphically, (reproduced as fig. 1).

There are some minor differences in order between Fig. 1 and Table 1. More significant, however, and worth illustration, is the fact that Inhaber's decision to decide that physics journals were those listed as such by SCI, leaves out many strongly physics-related journals. It is very striking that, from Table 1, we have 40 (36%) physics-related journals in the first 111 journals covering all fields. (Fig. 1 has only 24 journals). [Even more striking is that 24 of these come with the top 46 placings], several of these are inter or multi-disciplinary journals, and performing the same calculations for chemistry-related journals gives us 44 journals (40%), many of which are the same as the physics-related ones. Inhaber was aware of these problems: "Although another list of physics journals could have been used instead" (i.e. instead of SCI list) "for example those journals included in Physics Abstracts, this would have made little difference as far as the list of

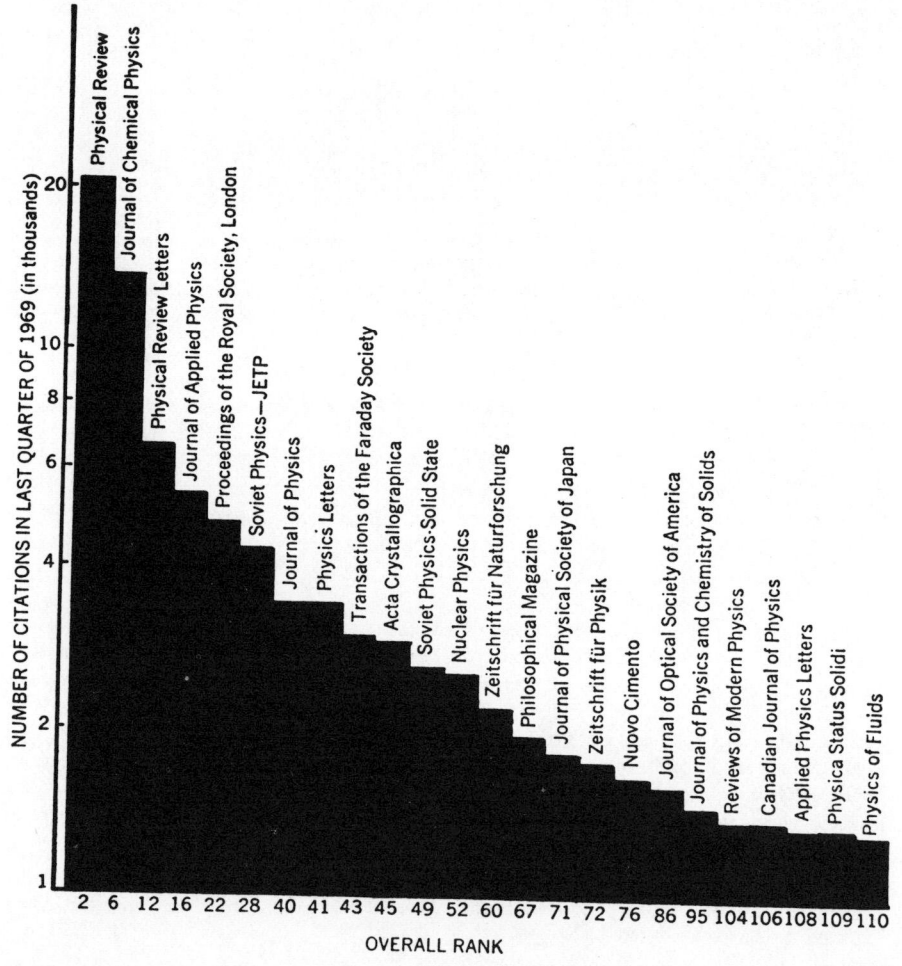

FIG. 1 (*from Inhaber*[17])

(Reproduced with permission—H. Inhaber: Is there a pecking order in physics journals, *Physics Today*, May 1974, p. 40, Fig. 1. ©American Institute of Physics.)

Notes: One or two major points to note on what the information refers to:
(i) the citations refer to *all* citations over the journals life, and therefore there will be some bias to older journals.
(ii) Journals produced in sections (e.g. Phys. Rev. or Journal of Physics) are considered as one journal.
(iii) No account is taken of the size of the journal.

most-cited journals was concerned." In fact there is no separate list of all journals included in Physics Abstracts, since INSPEC scans its journals for selection for any of its 3 sections. The coverage, in fact, covers 41 (37%) of the top 111 journals (by this criterion) of *all science*.

The I o P's Journal of Physics, which presumably not only includes all its sections extant in 1969, but also the old Proceedings of the Physical Society and Brit. J. Appl. Phys, Journal of Scientific Instruments etc., ranks 43 on this 'World List' of all sciences, 21st on the physics-related list from Table 1, and 7th on the strictly physics journals list of Inhaber (Fig. 1).

As we said in the earlier notes these placings take no account of the size or number of articles published. It would be an enormous undertaking to do this for all the journals for all of their history. What Garfield did was to consider all citations in the 1967 and 1968 issues of journals and divide these tables by the total no. of articles appearing in those journals over that period. For some reason, he has called the resulting figure the impact factor. This certainly changes the order. It reduces any historical bias, and gives much more weight to small journals which may have highly cited papers e.g. Review journals. Here 11 out of the top 16 journals are review serials. One might want to make a case out for another ranking by citations/page (since review articles are on the whole much longer than primary papers) but certainly this table (not shown) shows the high value accorded reviews by the primary (+ review) literature.

There are now fewer physics-related journals, (41 compared to 49), particularly at the top end (only 11 out of the top 49), only 24 common to both lists, 15 of these from the top 18 from Table 1. Quite a few major journals, e.g. Journal of Physics and Nuovo Cimento, drop out altogether. Again Inhaber also lists his top physics journals.

Another fairly thorough study, carried out in the early seventies, is that by Dierks.[19] Apart from the study itself, it also gives a good bibliography. It analyses citation data from several viewpoints—e.g. age, country citing and cited etc. Unfortunately, it is fairly long and not well known here. [It is, however, included in Meadow's book,[20] where he also summarizes some of these citation studies.] Again 1969 is taken as the year for study. Dierks takes nine physics journals from six countries as his citing sources, to construct an international list for comparison with others formed in different ways.

He took 1,000 citations from each journal, sampling each journal at intervals to achieve this (e.g. for Z. Phys) which contained 5,800 citations, he took every 5·8th (!) citation, and so on, giving 9,000 citations in all. He then constructs his ranking list, and analyses for self-citation, citation within and outside the group of nine journals. He also compares the ranking of journals derived from one source country with the overall list.

In his overall list he includes all journals receiving more than five citations (173 in all). The top twenty-one are given in Table 2, together with no. of citations, and % and cumulated %.

We will attempt a comparison of various lists later, but features to note about Table 2 are:

(i) The top four journals are from the US followed by two Dutch journals.
(ii) There is the usual strong core effect, with the top six journals just mentioned having 36% of all the citations, 50% of all citations being taken up by just fourteen journals.

(iii) The I o P's publications are split into three, i.e. J. Phys A–C+Proc. Phys. Soc., J. Phys. D., and J. Phys. E. The first group comes ninth in the overall list. If the groups had been combined, the overall Journal of Physics Series would have been seventh with 250 citations.

Dierks himself compared his studies with those done in previous decades by Brown[1] and Hooker[21] and concluded: "a comparison of the rank list with earlier investigation showed that this kind of analysis dates rapidly."

TABLE 2. *Physics journal ranking* (Dierks[19])

Journal	No. of citations	%	Cumulated %	Rank
Phys. Rev. (USA)	1,401	15·6%	15·6%	1
Phys. Rev. Letters (USA)	483	5·4%	21·0%	2
J. Appl. Phys. (USA)	412	4·6%	25·6%	3
J. Chem. Phys. (USA)	361	4·0%	29·6%	4
Nuclear Phys. (Neth.)	294	3·3%	32·9%	5
Phys. Letters (Neth.)	281	3·1%	36·0%	6
Z. Eksp. Teor. Phys. (USSR) (JETP)	202	2·2%	38·2%	7
Z. Phys. (Ger.)	194	2·2%	40·4%	8
J. Phys. A–C Proc. Phys. Soc. (UK)	180	2·0%	42·4%	9
Proc. Roy. Soc. (UK)	169	1·9%	44·3%	10
Rev. Mod. Phys. (USA)	155	1·7%	46·0%	11
C. R. Acad. Sci. (B) (France)	154	1·7%	47·7%	12
Nuovo Cimento (Italian)	130	1·4%	49·1%	13
J. Phys. Soc. (Japan)	114	1·3%	50·4%	14
Phys. Stat. Solid (E. Ger.)	111	1·2%	51·6%	15
Phil. Mag. (UK)	110	1·2%	52·8%	16
Z. Eksp. Teor. Fiz. (Letters) (USSR) (JETP Letters)	95	1·1%	53·9%	17
Z. Natur. F. (Ger)	94	1·0%	54·9%	18
J. Opt. Soc. Amer. (USA)	83	0·9%	55·8%	19
J. Phys. Chem. Solids (UK)	83	0·9%	56·7%	19
Dokl. Akad. Nauk. (USSR)	83	0·9%	57·6%	19

Brown in fact produces two sets of lists, some from an earlier study in 1942–4, and some from ten years later. The fact that he has carried out separate studies for eight subject fields makes possible some interesting comparisons e.g. no. of citations/100 pages, different ageing rates etc. but these are now all so out of date that it is not useful to present any of this information without having an up to date, similarly derived, set of data for comparison. For his overall list, Brown also took nine journals, but he checked citations for the period 1952–4 (in most cases). Therefore large self-citing journals will be given more weight than in Dierks study.

A study trying to evaluate British journals,[22] and discussed in,[23] published in 1968, shows us yet more variations in the way one can rank journals by the citations to them. They used data from the 1965 SCI. Their main list is simply the numbers of citations received. Anthony et al.[23] extracted the purely physics titles, but if we follow our usual practice and consider the top physics-related titles we get the list of Table 3, which also gives their rank in the overall list. Altogether twenty physics related-journals are included in the top sixty overall.

Martyn[22] then relates these citations to the internal characteristics of the journals. Firstly, they produce a ranking by 'ratio of items cited to items published' i.e. as a measure of the *proportion* of each journal that is cited. One has to select certain time periods to make this a practicable study, and their ranking is based on 1964 items cited in 1965. Not surprisingly, this gives a very different order, with a preference to journals having a limited number of long but 'citeworthy' articles e.g. review journals. Nature now ranks sixty-fourth with a ratio of 55%. The first five items are:

Overall citation ranking		1964 items cited	Items published	Ratio
49	Q. Rev.	15	15	100%
26	Immunology	63	63	100%
99	Adv. Phys.	7	7	100%
127	Rep. Prog. Phys.	10	10	100%
141	Prog. Mater. Sci.	1	1	100%

This ranking of course takes no account of the *no. of times* any article is cited.

Their last ranking is by 'number of citations per cited item' i.e. a measure of the value of journals when not considering the articles *not* cited in that journal, thereby differing from the 'impact factor' in Garfield's list, which has the average number of citations per item *published*. Physics-related journals and review journals rank highly on this list. e.g. the top six journals of all types are:

1. Physics
2. Adv. Physics
3. Q. Rev.
4. Proc. Roy. Soc. A.
5. Proc. Chem. Soc.
6. Mol. Phys.

We have not yet exhausted the citation ranking methods. Sengupta,[24] in an analysis of biochemical literature, not only gives the straight citation list, but for the top ten journals also gives the number of citations per 10,000 words, which he boldly describes as 'the scientific value of the papers in relation to compactness of presentation'. He is also less tentative than other authors in suggesting that such measures are useful for journal selection, and the last one mentioned 'is a good index of value to the research biochemist and may prove to be a better guide to selection of journals than position in the ranking list.'

In taking Sengupta to task on this point, Line[25] suggests yet another measure: 'These measures are interesting, but the most valid guide to selection is surely references per unit cost per journal', where cost should include 'not only subscription but processing, accounting, binding and storage.' He then does some calculations on the ten journals of Sengupta and produces two more ranking lists, with and without storage costs, which are very similar to each other, but fairly different from Sengupta's.

Line concludes: "Any library that wants to optimize its expenditure would be

TABLE 3. *Citation rank of British Physics-related journals** [22]

Journal	No. of citations	Rank	Rank in overall British list
Nature	10,244	1	1
Proc. Roy. Soc. A	1,108	2	10
Phil. Mag.	1,023	3	12
Trans. Faraday Soc.	951	4	13
Proc. Phys. Soc.	910	5	14
Spectrochim. Acta	762	6	16
J. Phys. Chem. Solids	718	7	17
Mol. Phys.	635	8	20
J. Inorg. Nucl. Chem.	597	9	22
Dis. Faraday Soc.	369	10	27
Planet-Space Sci.	366	11	29
Br. J. Appl. Phys.	339	12	34
Proc. IEE	332	13	36
Solid State Electron.	302	14	41
Electrochim. Acta	237	15	51
J. Fluid Med.	233	16	52
J. Sci. Instrum.	223	17	54
J. Inst. Metals	218	18	56
J. Atmos. Terr. Phys.	200	19	59
Talanta	199	20	60
Solid State Commun.	198	21	61

* This data refers to cited journals for 1963 and 1964 only.

ill advised to use rank lists based either on the total number of citations received ... or on the number of citations per paper, or per words published."

It is not necessarily valid to include either binding *or* storage costs in this calculation, since these may both be optional as far as the library is concerned. For long term storage, for example, one might have a policy of trying to sell these to back-number agents in which case this would be a sum to *remove* from the subscription price. However, this is the first time we have seen value *for money* entering as a consideration.

One might also note, as does Line, that the study by Sengupta uses a different type of source, i.e. a 'review journal'. There may be an argument that citations from critical review articles have extra value as measures of quality, but sometimes, e.g. Martyn and Gilchrist's study,[22] review articles, along with bibliographies were *excluded* as sources 'on the ground that these citations represented notifications of the existence of an item, not actual uses of that item', (presumably because of the difficulty in differentiating between types of review articles i.e. the annotated bibliography from the critical review).

Though this review has been lengthy nevertheless we have not mentioned studies into the subfields of physics. We have picked those dealing with all science or physics to show both the results and the large variety of methods.

Subfields that have been studied include plasma physics[26] and astronomy and astrophysics.[27] As far as journal *ranking* is concerned, the methods are fairly standard—with the slight differences that East[26] takes as source 1,026 articles whose abstracts were in the relevant section of Physics Abstracts, and Meadows[20] analyses the citations for ranking by type of citing institution (e.g. university, government), by authors from various countries (UK, France, Germany, USSR, USA), and by a finer subject breakdown within astronomy and astrophysics. Hockings[28] used as a source the technical reports written by the staff at RCA whose library holdings he was investigating.

TABLE 4. *Citation Ranking of Journals*

TABLE 4. *Source Journals*

A. Physical Review, various issues from July 1897 to 1899
B. Physical Review, 1919 + US NBS Sci. Papers Vol. XV.
C. Physical Review, Proc. Roy. Soc., Z. Phys., J. Phys. (Fr), Phys. Z. Sowj.
D. Physical Review, J. Appl. Phys., J. Opt. Soc. Amer., Rev. Mod. Phys.
E. Physical Review, Rev. Sci. Instrum., J. Phys. (Fr), J. Appl. Phys., Z. Phys., Phil. Mag., Helv. Phys. Acta, Nuovo Cimento.
F. Physical Review (500 refs taken)
G. Physical Review, all issues 1950–58
H. Physical Review, Zh. Eksp. Teor Fiz (JETP), Proc. Roy. Soc., Zeit. Phys., J. Phys. (Fr), Can. J. Phys., Rev. Sci. Instrum., Zh. Tek. Fiz, Z. für Angewandte Phys.
I. All journals covered by SCI in 1969 (i.e. 2,200)
J. All journals covered by SCI in 1974 (i.e. 2,400).

Citation Analysis for journal ranking—a summary

At first sight citation ranking may seem to be an unambiguous, quantitative way of measuring journal use and value, the only substantive argument centring on what exactly a *citation* expresses. The detail and variety of the above methods should indicate that this is not so. In this section we bring together the above results so that they may be more easily compared, and we discuss the methods and objectives of such analysis.

Notwithstanding the diversity of possible methods and rankings, we have seen that several studies have used a common method i.e. checking the citations in a few major physics journals and presenting a ranking list on bare number of citations received. To these we can add the study of Fussler[29] which covered the period 1899–1946 and used mainly the Physical Review as source. As we stress later the use of these ranking lists for library subscription practice is not recommended, but a historical picture is interesting for the study of physics, the changes in national prestige in physics, and the journals themselves. We collected the (roughly) comparable data of the studies by Fussler,[29] Hooker,[21] Brown,[1] Kessler,[30] Dierks,[19] Garfield,[16,17] and Inhaber[18] and present it in Table 4. [For the top twenty journals].

Here we have citation counts from 1899 to 1974. The number of citations accorded each journal in each study is given alongside the journal so that the size of each study can be roughly compared. The most noticeable feature is of course that whereas the USA has only one journal in the top five in 1899, (Physical Review at position four), it has four out of the top five by 1974. We notice, however, that for the list as a whole, the US has not dramatically increased its share, but rather the list has become more international. (See country breakdown at the foot of each column). The marked decline of German journals over the 2nd World War period shows only slightly in the decrease in numerical representation but strongly in the reduced stature of some of the old major journals. French journals have also suffered a decline, having only one representative by 1969, now in thirteenth place, compared with four in 1899, in positions 3, 10, 11. The two major UK journals from the last century, Proc. Roy. Soc. and Phil. Mag. show a certain decline, but the two last columns indicates that this decline *for physics* may be compensated by an increasing use or interest by other fields (i.e. the last two columns derive from citation characteristics from journals in all fields.)

We see also that three of the top five in 1899 are still in the top twenty in 1974. Citation studies on any other measure (e.g. 'immediacy', citations/paper etc.), have not been done in sufficient number to warrant comparison.

TABLE 5. *Choices of sources and methods for citation ranking and their implications*

Sources	
Choices	Some implications of the choice
1. 1 major journal in the discipline (e.g. Gross[2])	1. Bias, sample possibly not statistically sound, distortion possible through self- (either author or country) citing bias.
2. Review journal/s. (e.g. Sengupta[24])	2. As *1*, plus added problem of different nature of citation, i.e. not necessarily representing a *use* for subsequent research work.
3. Several 'major' journals in a discipline (e.g. Hooker,[21] Brown,[1] etc.)	
4. As 3, but sampled according to size of journal (e.g. Dierks[19]).	3. As *1* & *2*, plus possible bias through various citing *weights* (i.e. related to size) of journals.
5. Citations from papers grouped by subject (e.g. 1,000 abstracts on plasma physics—East[26]).	4. Removes last objection of 3, but questionable whether this is desirable.
6. Citations from works by defined author population e.g. electronics laboratory, Hockings.[28]	5. Difficulty in defining subject area?
7. Citations from very large numbers of journals and many disciplines (e.g. Martyn & Gilchrist,[22] Inhaber,[18] and Garfield.[15]	6. Limits realm of interest—i.e. reflection of current in-house use.
	7. Includes citations from all other disciplines not representative of particular user groups.

Ranking methods	
Choices	Some implications of the choice
A. By total number of citations.	A. Bias to larger, older journals.
B. By citations per paper published—usually restricted to particular time period (e.g. Inhaber).	B. Nearer to measure of quality, but not overall use or value?
C. *Citations per chosen year*—including B above and investigation of possible obsolescence factors and variations e.g. immediacy (Inhaber).	C. Not a measure of whole back-runs. Use may change over time-dependent on source (i.e. citing) journals' time lag.
D. Citations per cited item (e.g. Martyn & Gilchrist).	D. No account of non-cited items + B.
E. Proportion of items cited (e.g. Martyn & Gilchrist).	E. No account of *amount* of citations of each item—difficult to compute for long time period.
F. Citations per x words (e.g. 10^4) (e.g. Sengupta).	F. As *B.* and assumes 10^4 words as a constant *unit of information* as does B for a *paper*.
G. Citations per unit of cost (e.g. subscription cost, or subscription + binding, storage, or per unit of shelf space etc.) (e.g. Line[45]).	G. As B, does not give gross value. Adding binding, storage costs only applicable in specific libraries and (i) where no option for binding/not binding, storage/not storage or (ii) to determine titles for binding/storage, rather than acquisition.

To get an overall view of citation ranking for journals we group together the different types of sources used and ranking methods in Table 5. Also given are what seem to me the major implications of each choice. This can be compared with Line and Brittain's analysis.[7] This list is not exhaustive e.g. the 'age' of citations is a factor affecting each method of ranking. Each source choice (i.e. 1-7) will affect the interpretation of each ranking 'output' (i.e. A-G), giving us at least fifty combinations.

Use of citation rankings for libraries or physics?

Citation ranking of journals has now been carried out for fifty years, but as we said at the start of this section there is little evidence that rank lists have in fact been used for journal acquisition policies [though Brown[1] (p. 12) certainly suggests that his large 1944 lists were used by librarians]. I imagine that a brief look at Table 5 would help dissuade any librarian from rushing off to cut subscriptions according to some general SCI or other list. There are two main questions:

(i) Are citations a valid measure?
(ii) What is the most useful way of study and presentation of results?

Most authors pay at least lip service to the problems encountered in (i). Unfortunately, a typical article will mention the various objections to or dangers of taking a citation as a measure of use or value, and then suggest possible uses which in fact would be vitiated if any of the previous objections were upheld. Hockings[29] used citations because they have the advantage of 'unobtrusively providing numerical data that can be analysed'.

Martyn and Gilchrist's study[22] is a good example of the 'citations may well not be a valid indicator of use or value, but if they were, look at the marvellous possibilities for citation ranking' type.

They wisely say 'We must remember that the authors of scientific papers are not typical of the whole class of users of scientific information, and it must constantly be borne in mind that the criterion of value used here represents the value of British journals to the (relatively) small elite group of research scientists who actively contribute to the growth of science'.

Having obtained the usual 'core' effect for journals, they tentatively express some possible uses e.g. that they represent the 'core' journals of British Science, which would form the basis for any 'British Science Index' if one were wanted. That 'core' journals might be given some sort of Royal Society imprimatur— (given various minimal agreed editorial and refereeing standards) to which other periodicals could be added when they acquired the proper status—that these would be the journals for rapid and wide secondary service treatment e.g. photo-offsets of contents pages (a bit like 'Current Contents' of ISI)—that regular reviews of the articles in these core journals could be commissioned as means of becoming informed of 'current trends in British Science'.

I think the authors were aware that any application of these ideas was not remotely likely in 1968 (the year of publication) and are hardly any more likely now.

However, one other suggestion does seem attractive and brings out a general point about 'core' journals. Martyn and Gilchrist made out a 'check list' of 1,842 British journals. Only 590 (32%) of 1963/4 issues were cited in the 1965 SCI. However, it is the type of non-cited journal that is significant here. In the main, they appear not to be journals for the primary communication of research results, but trade and technical journals, professional magazines etc. Some (perhaps extreme) examples of the non-cited journals are:

Aluminium Courier
Anti-Locust Bulletin
Bee Craft
Bee World
Bottling
British Caver
Brompton Hospital Reports
Fireman
Kent Field Club Bulletin
Machinery
Modern Tramway

We have seen before (e.g. in our look at library holdings[31]) how the study of journal literature is complicated by the grading of types from 'Physical Review' to 'Bee World'. The distinction is not always easy to make. Martyn and Gilchrist's suggestion is that, having identified the 'core' journals, these should be scanned and information disseminated to the non-core (and assumed 'non-primary') journals as a more efficient way of promoting communication of research results by helping the technical magazines etc. to keep abreast of what is happening. This would seem a useful systematization of what I imagine already happens in some editorial offices of technical magazines.

For libraries, there is the obvious implication that citation analysis will simply not apply to many of their journal holdings. Dierks[19], by comparing his citation lists with other national and international lists produced in other ways, was persuaded that this method identified the core journals, and more particularly, that citation analysis *can give a list of non-physics journals which have proved to be of use and which are not easily obtained by other methods.*

I think that the above may be one of the more valuable uses of citation analysis for journal ranking, and we should note that it *depends* on taking, as source citing journals, recognized *physics* journals. The type of grand analysis obtained from SCI data *cannot* give this type of information. On the other hand, it *is* the type of analysis which, when compared with a *physics* analysis (e.g. à la Dierks) can show the relative usefulness of physics journals to other fields. This, however is much less relevant to the librarian. (In fairness, we should point out that the latest and more sophisticated version of JCR[17] contains enough detail for the interested researcher to be able to isolate and identify at least the major journals *citing* any journal under study.)

What is the general conclusion on citation analysis as an aid for libraries? Garfield says[15] 'The results of this type of citation analysis would appear to be of great potential value in the management of library journal collections.' [He also mentions value for money correlations] I think we must disagree. His own type of broad-based Science Citation Index analysis is relevant to studies of journals in general and studies of the scientific literature, not to subject collections, for the reason given in the last paragraph.

On to the basic problem of the relevance of 'a citation' we see superimposed all the choices and implications of Table 5. Each implication represents a point for argument on the value and objective of any citation ranking list.

Citation ranking is an attractive concept. For librarians, its use and value are severely limited. It would appear that its best use would be for a library operating in a well-defined subject area. In this case, the best source choice would appear to be no. 5 of Table 5, i.e. using the citations from papers *on the subject* (as opposed to papers from *subject journals*) where these can be found through e.g. abstracts journals. Then, ideally, most of the rankings A-G of Table 4 should be carried out and the implications of each discussed. The use of this type of analysis would then be to identify journals not previously appreciated, and to see whether there are any glaring anomalies in terms of 'value for money' in the ranked lists. It might also help to identify journals still taken through 'inertia' (e.g. a journal once requested by a now-retired researcher) which are in fact of little value or use. The effort in preparing such an analysis would be considerable, could only rarely be done in a form applicable to other libraries or libraries in general, and its cost unlikely to be justifiable.

Citation analysis is, however, a useful technique for examining journals in general, mapping trends in those journals or literature as a whole or of a particular country. Partly because of its many possible interpretations, it remains interesting.

2. JOURNAL RANKING BY LIBRARY 'USE' AND 'USER' JUDGEMENT

Ranking journals by the use made of them by a group of library users has been a popular method for libraries. Again there are several ways of doing it, e.g. asking users how often they use a journal, watching them, examining the journals left on desks, putting 'unobtrusive seals' on volumes and then checking whether they have been broken subsequently, inter-library loans, photocopy requests. On the other hand, the ranked lists themselves have not been quite as varied as with citation rankings—normally a simple ranked list, sometimes with an analysis by date of journal, to provide some so-called 'obsolescence' data. It is only recently that this type of ranking has been subjected to modification by considering the changing *size* of journals over time, to demonstrate the 'absence of obsolescence' (Sandison,[32] 1974). Lists are rarely presented by 'uses' per page or paper etc. Neither have I seen any suggestion that any subjective value judgements by users should be subdivided in this way. Nevertheless there are still several ways to achieve a rank order.

Rankings have generally been made for particular libraries and it is obviously questionable whether their results have any wider applicability. The National Libraries do, on occasion, prepare general lists of items requested more than a certain number of times (e.g. [33,34]).

There have been some studies devoted particularly to groups of physicists, or use of physics journals. We will not go into any great detail in describing these separately, but present the general data in Table 6 (pp. 274-5). The notes to the table are particularly important since they indicate the different nature of each study.

There are a few points to note, especially when comparing one column with the other or with the citation rankings.

(i) The lists have much greater variation than the citation ranked lists.
(ii) (i) is no doubt caused by the different bias in subjects of study—see e.g. column five where Aviation Week is top (this study obviously looked at a very mixed bunch)—and this often by whatever the library holdings happen to be.

(iii) There is greater 'parochialism' in these use or value lists than in the citation listings. The country breakdown given at the foot of each column indicates an enormous dominance of USA in surveys carried out there, with a swing to UK in studies performed here.
(iv) A relative 'parochialism' is present within the lists of Table 6 between those lists indicating actual *use* (i.e. 1, 2, 4, 5, 6) and those over judgement of value (i.e. 3, 7), the latter being more international.
(v) Nature appears surprisingly low on the US lists, not appearing *at all* on lists 1, 4, 5, 8.
(vi) I o P journals only appear on two lists, both from UK studies.
(vii) Not a *single* journal publishing predominantly in a foreign language is mentioned on any list.

The cost element of journal ranking by use has not been entirely neglected. The Case Institute study,[36] made a rather curious ranking of journals by estimated publication cost per journal 'reading', but admitted that there were a great many pitfalls in trying to draw conclusions from their results. [In fact they were so worried that the ranking list would be used in a 'misleading' way that they produced their ranking list without giving the names of the journals.]

Chen[40] produces the interesting graph on use and subscription cost which we reproduce here as Fig. 2.

This shows that, if her fairly limited data are correct, then for the oft-mentioned '90% library', we need 22·3% of the total number of titles (35·5% of the *used* titles) and that these will cost 51·5% of the total *used* title cost (i.e. they are on average, the more expensive titles). Again, this method would mainly be useful for identifying any very little or not-used expensive titles which could then e.g. not be stored, not put on open shelves or not even subscribed to (e.g. or taken only in microfilm). As a result of Langlois' survey[41] they cut 9·6% of the surveyed collection, resulting in a 6% cost saving. [However, in this case there was also a lot of consultation with staff etc. to see whether cancellations would be acceptable.]

Gore[43] shows that general use studies like those of the BLL can be used to justify cutting subscription lists (which is what he did) thus neatly reversing Line's argument[44] i.e. Gore would say that low use of a journal at the NLL or BLL means 'we don't need to take it either'.

There is then, a little more evidence that journal usage studies carry more weight and actually sometimes result in action. This seems only natural since they are basically simpler and easier to interpret. They cannot, however, start you off on a journal collection, or suggest what titles you *should* have but don't have.

We have seen that Line[25,45] (although he was not the first) has said that we ought to take account of the number of uses 'per monetary unit' where the costs will include the ordering, acquisition, subscription, storage and binding costs—we have already said why this total may be unrealistic in general, and needs to be considered as a cumulative total where any specific cost is optional (e.g. Binding).

Kraft's Method
Let us look at this problem in a different way. Let us assume that the crude number of uses (over a particular time) of a journal (published in a particular

TABLE 6. *Physics journal ranking by 'use' and 'user' judgement*

Rank	1 Case Institute 1960 (USA)	RP* Physicist Reading time	2 Martyn 1964 (UK)	RP % Reading	3 Malley 1971 (U.K.)	RP Users 'use' Judgement (points system)	4 Chen 1971 (USA)	RP use frequency measure (observation)	5 Langlois & Schultz 1972 USA
1	Physical Review (USA)	11.9%	Phys Rev	62%	Nature (UK)	286	Phys Rev	597	Aviation Week & Space Tech.
2	J. Amer Chem Soc (USA)	7.8%	Proc Phys Soc	52%	Scientific American	236	J. Chem Phys	560	Science
3	Rev. Sci. Instrum. (USA)	6.6%	Proc. Roy. Soc. A.	42%	Phys. Rev. Lett.	230	J. Appl. Phys.	227	Amer. Med. Ass. J. (USA)
4	Physics Today (USA)	6.1%	Nature	35%	New Scientist (UK)	222	J. Acoust. Soc. Amer. (USA)	192	J. Geophys. Res.
5	J. Phys. Chem Solids (UK)	4.1%	Phys. Rev. Lett.	34%	Phil. Mag. (UK)	208	Phys Rev Lett.	155	J. Chem. Phys.
6	Phys. Rev. Lett (USA)	3.8%	Phil. Mag. (UK)	28%	Proc. Roy. Soc. A	208	Phil. Mag. (UK)	101	Phys. Rev.
7	Proc. Inst. Rad. Engineers (USA)	3.5%	Rev. Sci. Instrum.	27%	Nature Phys. Sci.	200	Phys of Fluid (USA)	97	New Scientist
8	Chem & Engr. News (USA)	3.0%	Phys. Lett.	22%	Am. J. Phys (USA)	198	J. Opt. Soc Amer.	92	Scientific American
9	Scientific American	3.0%	Rev. Mod. Phys	22%	J. Phys C	192	Phys Lett. (Neth)	86	J. Acoust. Soc. Amer.
10					Phil. Trans Roy Soc A	186	J.Fluid Mech. (UK)	81	Applied Optics
11					Rev. Mod Phys	182	Nuovo Cimento (Ital)	81	National Geographic (USA)
12					Phys. Bulletin	176	J. Mol. Spectrosc. (USA)	80	Railway Age
13					J. Appl. Phys. (USA)	174	Trans. Faraday Soc. (UK)	78	Audio
14					Phys. Rev. B	168	Canadian J. Phys.	75	Natural History
15					Physics Today	168	Rev. Mod. Phys.	66	Phys of Fluids
16					J. Phys. E.	162	Sov. Phys. JETP (USSR) U.S. trans.	65	Smithsonian
17					Advances in Physics (UK)	158	Rev. Sci. Instrum.	63	Sky and Telescope (USA)
18					Phys. Rev. A.	158	Appl. Phys. Lett. (USA)	63	Astrophys. Jnl.
19					Phys. Education (UK)	158	Nuclear Phys (Neth)	63	Radio Electronics
20					Rev. Sci. Instrum.	156	J. Phys. Chem Solids. (UK)	62	Appl. Phys. Letters
Country Breakdown	9 U.S.A. 1 U.K.		4 U.S.A. 4 U.K.		9 U.S.A. 11 U.K.		2 Neth. 12 U.S.A. 4 U.K.		18 U.S.A. 1 U.K.

*RP = Ranking Parameter

Notes to Table 6

1. [35,36]—refer to 1960 Case Institute Study which included the reading times of 404 physicists in 71 institutions (USA) (Random Alarm Techniques).

2. Study by Martyn of research scientists in several types of institutions (i.e. academic,

RP Use Frequency (+ Citation)	6 Chen 1973 (USA)	RP Journals Scanned Weekly No. of Physicists	7 Chen 1973 (USA)	RP User 'Value' Judgement (points)	8 Chen 1973 (USA)	RP No of Physicist Subscribers	9 BLLD SINFDOK 1975	RP No. of Loan/Photo-Copy Requests
252	Phys. Rev. Letters	73	Phys Rev.	321	Phys. Rev. Letters	55	Science	184
146	Phys. Rev.	66	Phys. Rev. Letters	321	Phys. Rev.	41	Biochim & Biophys Acta	154
106	Phys. Letters	30	Phys Letters	150	Physics Today	7	Nature	122
102	Nuovo Cimento	12	Nuclear Phys	79	Rev. Mod. Phys.	7	J. Amer. Chem. Soc.	114
97	Science	12	Nuovo Cimento	44	Astrophys. J.	6	Proc. Nat. Acad. Sci. (USA)	97
89	J. Chem. Phys.	10	Astrophys. J.	33	Science	6	Scientific American	90
87	Nuclear Phys.	10	J. Chem Phys.	30	Am J. Phys.	5	J. Acoust. Soc. Amer.	78
82	Phys. Today	9	J. Math. Phys.	26	J. Chem. Phys	5	J. Opt. Soc. Amer.	71
60	Rev. Mod Phys.	9	Science	26	Appl. Phys. Letters	3	J. Chem. Phys.	67
55	Nucl. Instr. Methods (Neth)	8	Nucl. Instr. Methods (Neth)	25	American Scientist	2	J. Appl. Phys.	65
51	J. Phys.	7	Rev. Mod. Phys.	23	Ann. Phys. (USA)	2	Proc. Roy. Soc. A.	61
51	Nature	6	Amer J. Phys.	22	Astrophys J.	2	Biochem & Biophys Res. Comm.	59
50	Solid State Comm.	6	Solid State Comm.	21	J. Amer. Chem Soc.	2	J. Phys. Chem.	54
50	Astrophys. J.	5	Astronomy Astrophys (Ger)	20	J. Amer Stat. Assoc.	2	J. Electrochem Soc.	50
48	J. Appl. Phys.	5	Nature	16	J. Geophys. Res.	2	J. Colloid & Interface Science	44
45	Amer. J. Phys.	4	Phys. Today	16	J. Math. Phys	2	J. Geophys Res.	43
44	J. Phys. Chem Solids	4	J. Amer. Chem Soc.	15	Phys Fluid	2	Phys. Stat. Solidi	40
40	IEEE Proc.	3	J. Geophys. Res.	15	Scientific American	2	J. Sound & Vib. (UK)	36
40	J. Amer. Chem. Soc.	3	J. Appl. Phys	14			Trans. Amer. Geophys. Union	36
	J. Geophys Res.	3						
	J. Phys. Chem.	3						
38	Nuovo Cimento Lett.	3	J. Low Temp. Phys.	12			Proc. IEEE (UK)	35
	Scientific American	3						
	14 U.S.A		12 U.S.A.		All U.S.A.		12 U.S.A	
	3 U.K.		3 U.K.				4 U.K.	
	2 Ital.		3 Neth.					
			1 Ital					

industrial and 'official') Number of physicists = 85. Note on journals read,[37] full description of methodology.[38]

3. Unpublished study by Ian Malley, Librarian of Maria Mercer Physics Library, Bristol[39] 227 currently taken (in 1971) journals were ranked by 34 members of the staff of the

physics department. Alternatives were given weights 0, 2, 4, 10 points for their value as judged by respondents. Note that this list splits Phys. Rev. and J. Phys. series into their respective parts. It would, of course, in this case be invalid to add the points to get a joint 'score'.

4. Study of material not re-shelved and in photocopying area at MIT library. Surveyed 3 times a day for 3 months, only 'physics' journals according to the MIT classifications were considered—220 titles. General titles e.g. Science, Nature, Comptes Rendu, Proc. Roy Soc. etc. are therefore not included.[40]

5. 1973 US study at the R. E. Gibson Library (Applied Physics Laboratory of John Hopkins University) and 500 titles were considered. Total usage figures were a curious mixture of frequency with which a journal was consulted over a $2\frac{1}{2}$ month period + citations of the journal by currently produced (i.e. in a 3 year period) laboratory reports. As a result of the study, apparently, several cancellations were made and storage etc. policies modified.[41]

6. 1973 US study of 179 responding academic physicists at 6 institutions in the Boston area, including MIT and Harvard. Rank tables are based on questionnaire responses. In this column the titles scanned weekly are given, ranked by the number of physicists who claimed to scan them. One should note that most of these journals do not in fact *appear* weekly, which gives some cause for doubting this list. [Unless they consult a bit at a time.][42]

7. Same study as 6, ranking by value judgements similar to 2, but with a weighting of 1–5 on a scale of 'importance'—note the relatively low position of Nature.

8. Same study as 6, but ranked by number of physicists individually *subscribing* to a journal (some complications with journals received on a membership subscription e.g. Phys. Today).

9. Analysis by title of requests in all disciplines for loans/photocopies from the British Library Lending Division in c. the first quarter, 1975[33] I have selected from the list the top 20 physics-related titles. Requests can come from UK or overseas. The 20th journal on this ranks 152nd on the overall list. Note: No Phys. Rev. or I o P journals.

---

time period) is a measure of the worth of that journal. We then make the rather large assumption that the worth of *not* having the journal is a negative fraction of this measure. Let us assume that the cost of acquisition, maintenance, storage, binding etc. for each journal can be worked out, and that we can find a formula for this. We have a limited budget, and this with its spread over the items just mentioned represents the major constraint.

We then are left with the problem of maximizing this 'worth' within this constraint. This is then a linear programming problem, and this is how it has been viewed by Kraft.[46,47] I cannot imagine that many librarians could or would read this, but it rests on the fairly simple basis outlined above [in order to get something manageable he in fact assumes that the 'negative fraction' is <1 i.e. the worth of acquiring an item is greater than the worth of not acquiring it.] A description of his method is given in Appendix A.

The idea is quite simple, but the working out very complex and cannot be easily handled on a computer without breaking it down into smaller groups—('Knapsacks'). However, it's basic assumptions are similar to those in all those 'use' rankings we have mentioned where a points system is used to ascertain the use of a journal (e.g. one point for each 'use') i.e. that the value of the journal is quantitatively measured in this way.

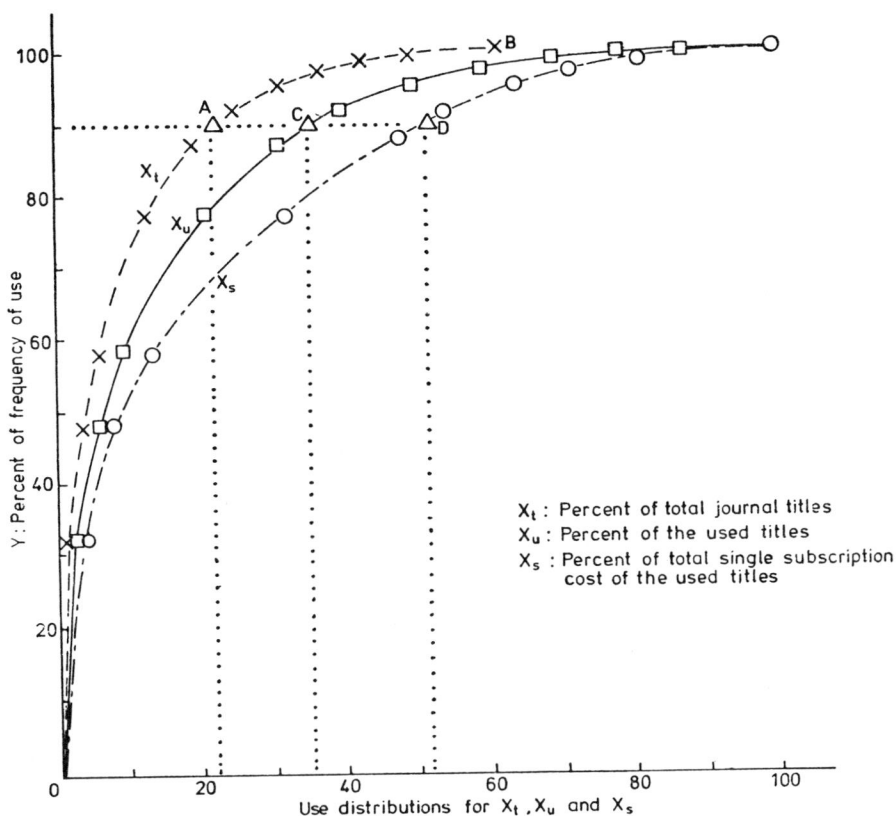

A e.g. 22·3% of the total physics journals accounted for 90% of use.
B 62·7% of the total physics journals accounted for 100% of use.
C 35·5% of total used journals accounted for 90% of use.
D 90% of users' needs could be met by spending an amount equal to 51·5% of the total single subscription cost the used titles.

FIG. 2.

(Reprinted with and by permission of *Journal of the American Society for Information Science*, Vol. 23, No. 4, 1972, pp. 254–70. Copyright 1972 by the American Society for Information Science, 1155 16th Street, N.W. Washington, D.C. 20036, USA.)

Once you accept this as a reasonable idea, the linear programming technique in fact brings *more*, not less, reality into the calculation by considering many of the other budgetary factors, especially time periods, and storage and acquisition costs etc. The arguments come in the expression for obsolescence, and the actual costs for storage, acquisition etc.

There are two arguments why any detailed use of use measurements may be unreasonable.

(i) Use measurements assume that each 'use' is equivalent 'value' and that a total use gives a total value i.e. no account is taken of the *extent* of each use, the value of the use, which may be connected with the quality of the work published, which in turn may be connected with the prestige of the journal, and on to its refereeing procedures and even rejection rates, which in turn may be reflected in its price. Use measurements are in fact suggestive, but are hardly 'hard' data.

(ii) Even if use measures *were* accurate and quantitative measures, such that they could be cumulated to give a total 'value', this does not mean that this use can be subdivided to give a valid use per page, paper, foot of shelf-space, £, etc. The overall value judgements arrived at in this way may denote an absolute ranking, i.e. if the overall value of Journal A, is greater than that of Journal B, then we have Journal A rather than Journal B, and that is an end to it. If Journal A is three times as expensive as Journal B, this may give us a budget problem, but this in no way suggests that Journal B is a viable *alternative* to Journal A. It is in this area that librarians will be aware of the dangers of becoming divorced from the real world of scientific research and publishing.

The conclusion on Kraft's work must be that it illustrates the logical extension of attempting to find quantitative value judgements on journals into the realm of operational research. It in fact results in highly technical (his Ph.D. Thesis runs to 286 pages[47]) and (presumably) costly operations on somewhat shaky foundations.

[The impracticability of this approach is indicated by the one example of application by Kraft[47] (p. 184-201). Here the problem is whether to add all or any of an extra four journals to an on-going collection. Parameters a, b, c, c_1, c_2, c_3, b_q have to be established, as well as λ, K etc. Kraft then presents some sixteen possible solutions. The one maximizing the 'objective function' is to buy all four journals but this is 'infeasible'. The best feasible solution in fact means loss of continuity i.e. to buy journals 1, 2, 4, during the first part of the time period, journals 1, 2, 3, for the second part—and this is for a simple case.]

Journal ranking by size or productivity—(+Bradford)
There is one last method of ranking we shall briefly consider. This is according to the size or productivity of the journals.

'Size' is simple—we think of some measure e.g. no. of papers, no. of pages, words, thickness, and rank the journals accordingly.

'Productivity' is rather different—this again refers to some measure of quantity (usually number of articles) but this quantity has to be *relevant* to the subject field of interest. i.e. Some journals will contain a wider range of subject interests (as we saw in section 1). [When dealing with physics-only journals, the size and productivity are equivalent (assuming no value judgements)]. Here we are back in the realms of the Bradford distribution.

Although this has been a major concern of information science over the last couple of decades, I do not propose to review it in great detail, since not only is the validity of the distribution in doubt, but there are varying formulations of Bradford's 'Law' which are apparently inconsistent or at least not equivalent. For the purposes of library selection it can at best be indicative, and the 'Law' itself cannot tell you which journals to pick.

For his linear programming method Kraft[47] considered using 'productivity' as his 'worth' measure, but rejected it because of the difficulty of predicting *future* literature growth—an interesting point which should be added to the comments of Line and Sandison.[45]

An obvious way of producing a productivity list is to let Physics Abstracts define the subject area and see which journals contribute the most abstracts. This was done for many of the physics literature studies in the early sixties. Table 7 gives one of these lists, taken from Anthony's[23] Appendix 2 for Physics Abstracts in 1964.

TABLE 7. *Journals ranked by no. of abstracts in Physics Abstracts 1964*

Rank	Journal	No. of abstracts	Rank	Journal	No. of abstracts
1	Phys. Rev. (USA)	1,770	11	Phys. Rev. Lett. (USA)	469
2	J. Chem. Phys. (USA)	1,541	12	Fiz. Tver. Tel. (USSR)	435
3	Phys. Lett. (Neth.)	940	13	J. Phys. Soc. Japan (Jap)	431
4	C. R. Acad. Sci. (Fr.)	863	14	Zh. Tekh. Fiz. (USSR)	421
5	Zh. Eks. Teor. Fiz. (USSR)	863	15	J. Phys. le Radium (France)	420
			16	Nature (UK)	407
6	J. Appl. Phys. (USA)	830	17	Prib. Tekh. Eksp. (USSR)	388
7	Nouvo Cimento (Italy)	632	18	Dokl. Akad Nauk. (USSR)	359
8	Nuclear Phys. (Neth.)	587	19	Phys. Fluid (USA)	343
9	Rev. Sci. Instrum. (USA)	522	20	Opt. i Spekt. (USSR)	342
10	Fiz. Metall. Metal. (USSR)	522			

Country breakdown: USA = 6, USSR = 7, France = 2, Neth. = 2

The striking difference between this and the lists ranked by other methods is the number of Russian journals now included (seven), and that only one UK journal, Nature, figures in the top twenty.

Although Bradford's ideas of scattering were concerned with the type of productivity mentioned above, we can see that, if valid, there, they might also have been applied to citations, and journal usage and value. Hockings[28] used his citations to define what he called a 'Bradford set' of periodicals, and O'Neill[50]

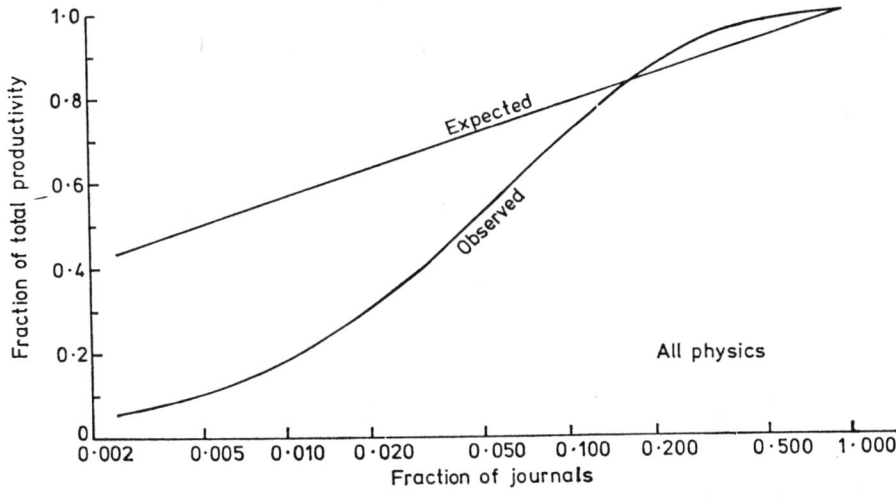

FIG. 3. *Bradford distribution fitted to the Keenan-Atherton physics data*

spends a lot of time comparing thesis citation scattering with Bradford expectations.

O'Neill, for one of his studies, takes an early (1964) American Institute of Physics study of the physics literature,[51] which looked in a fairly comprehensive way at the 1961 issues of Physics Abstracts, giving counts of abstracts by journal in each of the sub-fields of the classification. O'Neill takes a computer to this data and produces plots of expected (according to the Bradford distribution) and 'observed' values of 'Productivity'. His overall graph (i.e. all physics) is reproduced here as Fig. 3.

This overall graph suggests a wide deviation from Bradford's law, although as O'Neill says 'It should be noted, however, that the semi-log plot greatly exaggerates the difference between the actual and expected values since it enlarges the lower portion of the graph where the maximum difference usually occurs.' The amount to agreement between sub-fields varied greatly. Some appear quite close (e.g. Fig. 4. for Optics)

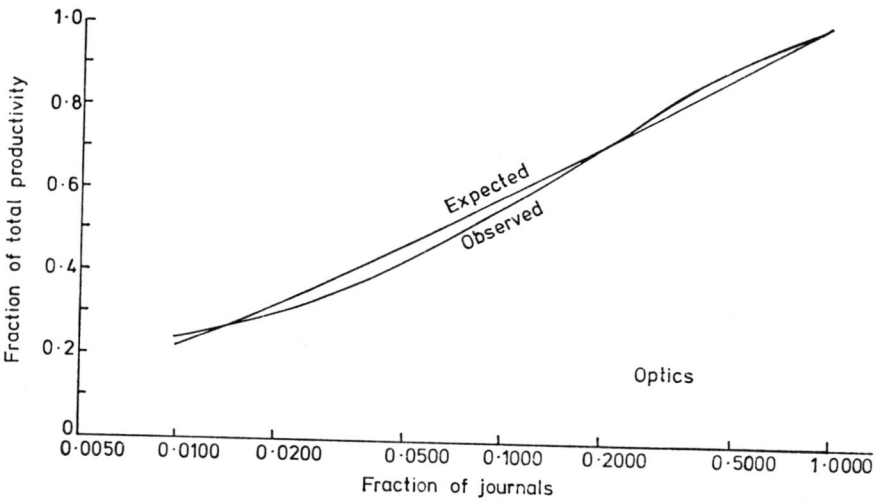

FIG. 4. *Bradford distribution fitted to the Keenan–Atherton physics data for optics.*

O'Neill says 'Only for half (eleven) of the subject fields was it impossible to reject the hypothesis that the scattering followed the Bradford distribution'.

It should be said that in some of the other areas, he studied, often where a smaller total no. of journals is involved, the Bradford distribution fits well. i.e. when we get a large number of journals, a very large 'tail' seems to distort the distribution. All these data depend on a definition of subject area and judgement of relevance of articles to that subject area. O'Neil (in his 400 page Ph.D. Thesis) has some interesting points to make on the relationship between, and 'breadth' of disciplines, but we don't end up with any practical way of sorting the problem out, or defining limits where the Bradford distribution could be used with safety. Again, though the whole thesis is directed toward library activity, we do not find any practical method for journal selection.

One of the main UK proponents of the Bradford (or Bradford-Zipf) distribution has been B. C. Brookes and he has recommended its use in libraries (e.g.[52]).

Using his formulation of the Bradford-Zipf distribution (see e.g.[53]) he suggests[56] as a way of estimating the likely savings if a library changes over to getting photocopies from say, BLL, when the number of relevant papers, photocopy charge/average paper, is less than the subscription and other library costs of obtaining the periodical. Really, his basic suggestion here lies mainly in the last sentence, not the application of Bradford-Zipf. Not only does it require the librarian to estimate the number of relevant papers in at least the most productive journals, but also assumes a maximum situation of one photocopy per relevant article—and *averages* subscription/photocopy costs etc. One would have thought that this would have rendered this suggestion impracticable, but in fact, Houghton and Prosser, did look at this. In fact there is not a mention of Bradford-Zipf in the journal report on their work[54] although they refer to the idea of photocopying versus buying costs as 'Brookes' Model'.

Houghton and Prosser did consider it 'impractical to count the number of relevant papers' and used journal usage figures instead. A lot of the effort went into finding the average journal cost. Their first result indicated an economic 'cut-off' at 41 titles out of a total of 316 (which, in fact, meant that 50% of the photocopying would be done through BLL). They felt this unrealistic—we note that there appears not to have been an attempt to verify whether the journal collections fitted a Bradford distribution. Suffice to sum up that the method proved 'unrealistic' if they kept strictly to Brookes' 'method', [e.g. a cost/use criterion, which took into account varying subscription prices, seemed more suitable.]

One of the problems for using Bradford's law in libraries was that, as stated (i.e. 'zones' of periodicals each contributing an equivalent number of relevant articles, the number of periodicals in the zones rising as $1:n:n^2$ . . .) is that the size of the first zone is entirely arbitrary (Bradford himself thought that his law satisfied a 'mathematical' criterion of being useless in application). Goffman et al.[55,56] have attempted to show that a 'minimal' nucleus can be established, and recommended analysing a library collection into Bradford zones of various time intervals and basing acquisition policy on the observed performance of journals (by usage) over these periods.

In his formulation of Bradford-Zipf,[56] Brookes is able to estimate the total number of contributing sources to a journal collection, once data on the 'nucleus' is established, and therefore could be used by a library.

Another possible use would be if the Bradford distribution/ranking approximated to a cost-effective ranking (e.g. cost/use) where there would then be a saving in effort since computing the actual cost of a journal, as we have seen, is no simple matter. Robertson and Hensman[57] examined the assumptions and implications of transferring the Bradford distribution to use statistics, and to a relevance *ranking* (i.e. proportion of relevant items in a journal, rather than just the number) and a full cost per relevant item ranking for a set of articles selected by the Biodeterioration Information Centre, Birmingham.

In answer to the question—how can we acquire 90% of the items at minimum cost? They found, not surprisingly, that the cost-effectiveness approach was most efficient and the relevant journal size-ranking gave a better estimate than Bradford order (at this level, but not at other levels—therefore not reliable). However, the 90% level was achieved by dropping just one journal which contributed 10%. This was a high cost large journal which ranged over wider areas therefore cutting down on its cost-effectiveness—they say "the importance of a single journal suggests that we should be very wary of generalizing from this one experiment."

For libraries, the Bradford distribution *could* be useful. However, the librarian would either have to show in the first place that his present collection satisfies such a distribution, or, that his users would be satisfactorily served by one that did. To make paper productivity and relevance assessments for all journals would seem out of the question, and he/she would probably have to use other means e.g. abstract coverage, use or citation statistics. Whatever the case, quite a lot of work is involved. Then, when you have the statistics, *you have the statistics*; i.e. the Bradford distribution becomes irrelevant except as some convenient grouping device. [The extrapolation technique advanced by Brookes only saves time if the data collection can be limited to those journals which you have, in advance, identified as the minimal nucleus.]

This does not, of course, suggest that a librarian should not examine his library holdings in some systematic way to aid decision-making.

Rank Correlation

We have so far seen three basic ways of ranking journals.

1. By citations
2. By use and value judgements
3. By journal size or 'productivity',

although 3 turned out to be, quite often, related to 1 and 2.

This has produced many lists of journals. We have mentioned some of the differences between rankings. Is there a way of getting a better indication of the relationship between the rankings? Some of the lists will not be 'comparable' i.e. produced for specific subject user groups etc., but there are several with similar objectives.

There is a fairly simple statistical technique for rank correlation involving the use of Spearman's coefficient[58] (Ch. XIV). Dierks[19] used this to compare his rankings with those of Brown[1] and recently Scales[59] in an interesting article, used it to compare lists of the JCR[17] and an NLL survey. She found little correlation and concluded that citation rankings are not good indicators of actual use, and thus do not constitute valid guides for journal selection. Can we generalize further with the larger number of lists for consideration?

Spearman's coefficient is given by

$$R = 1 - \frac{6\Sigma d^2}{n(n^2-1)} \quad (1)$$

where d is the difference in rank order for a journal, and n is the number of items ranked.

The derivation of rank correlation coefficients assumes that the objects to be ranked are identical, i.e. in two ranked lists, there should not be some objects in one which do not appear in the other. Therefore, to apply Spearman's coefficient rigorously we can only consider the items in common between two lists. This leads to some unavoidable distortion.

One can imagine an extreme case where, say, two lists of twenty items have only two titles in common. Imagine that on one list they are ranked 1 and 20 and on the other 8 and 14. Then we have in fact 'perfect' correlation although we can see that in fact the lists have little relation to each other. Therefore, we need to remember here that Spearman's coefficient refers to the *journals listed, and not the lists themselves*. As the number of common titles increases, the coefficient more nearly gives a measure of the relatedness of the ranking methods. We thus end up with two measures, (i) Spearman's coefficient, R, and (ii) fraction number of titles in common in first twenty, C. The nearer each of these two is to 1, the greater is the link between the lists. If either is very low, there is little link. Where the correlation is positive, the product of these two numbers gives a measure of the inter-relationship.

As an example, if we look at columns 1 and 2 in Table 6 we see there two nine-title lists of physics journals ranked by some form of reading measure, one study performed in the UK and one in the USA, about four years apart. In fact, they have only three titles in common. C is thus 0·33, R is 0·67. This fairly high value of R would not be significant. The product RC is also low at 0·22.

From Tables 5 and 6 we select some lists and calculate their rank correlation and overlap.

It is perhaps also worth pointing out that this correlation is of methods of ranking (i.e. the ranking 'variable') and while it is useful to compare 'ranking by 1919 citations' to 'ranking by 1954 citations', or 'ranking by 1969 citations' with 'ranking by 1971 use', it is less useful to compare, e.g., '1899 citations' to '1973 use'.

Fig. 5 shows the 'correlation matrix' for all the straight citation rankings of Table 4. This gives, for each pair of lists, the number of titles in common, the fraction of overlap, C Spearman's coefficient of correlation, R, and where R is positive, the product RC. Also indicated is where the correlation coefficient equals or exceeds the value for a given level of *significance*, as derived from probability tables for rank correlation.[60] As we would expect, the high values, both of correlation and overlap, are mainly close to the diagonal, indicating the large change over time of the relative positions of the journals (R) as well as the death of old and introduction of new journals (C).

We take a more limited look at the lists of Table 6 (i.e. use + 'value judgement' ranking). Most show only a slight correlation, if at all. It would certainly appear that 'use' statistics are not 'transferable' to other locations.

If we take the Chen listings (columns 4, 6, 7 of Table 6) we get the following:

Column 4
Measured use 'groupings' 1971

Vs

Column 7
Use 'value judgement' 1973

R (Correlation) = 0·21   C (overlap) = 0·4
RC = 0·08

Column 4

Vs

Column 6
Jnls scanned weekly 1973

R = 0·58   C = 0·45
RC = 0·26

Column 6
Jnls scanned weekly 1973

Vs

Column 7
User 'value judgement' 1973

R = 0·89*   C = 0·85
RC = 0·76

* significant at 0·001 level.

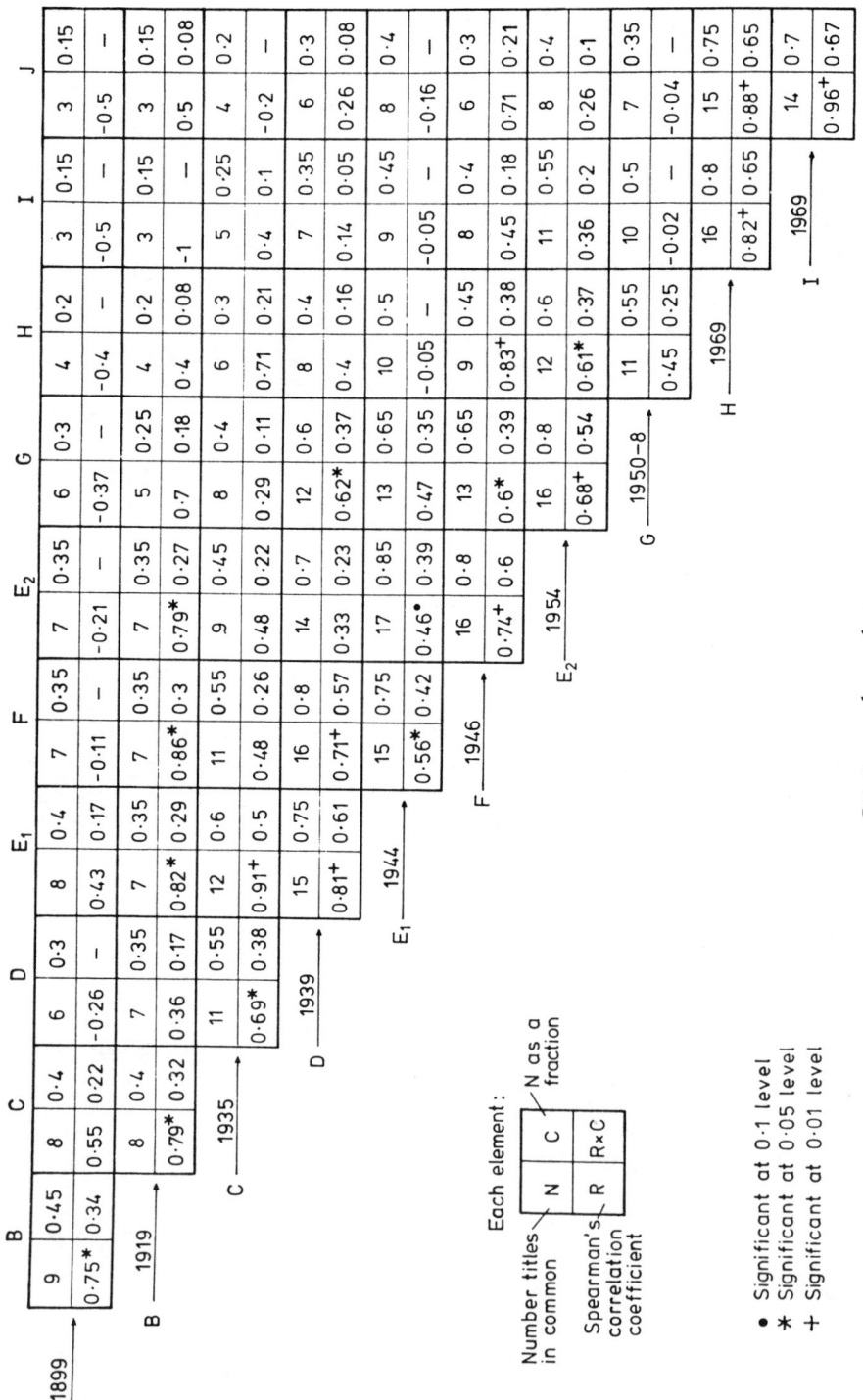

FIG. 5. *Citation rank correlations*

Only the last one is significant, where the same group of users are in fact questioned at the same time. More work could be attempted to show correlations between different methods *at the same place*, so that, if correlations were high, the easiest method would be the one to use for practical purposes.

There is almost no correlation between the 'use' and the photocopy/loan figures (column 9), e.g.

Column 4   *Column 9*
Measured use   *Vs*   BLLD photocopying $R = -0.6$ $C = 0.2$
frequency

Column 5   *Column 9*
Use frequency   *Vs* $R = 0.1$ $C = 0.25$
+ citation $RC = 0.025$

The correlation between columns 4 and 5, which has R high at 0.9, is in fact only just significant at the 0.1 level, because of the small amount of overlap (five titles in common).

Use-citation correlation
If we compare Chen's 1971 use figures (column 4 of Table 6) with the citation data of Dierks (column H of Table 5) and Inhaber (column I), we get fairly good correlations, i.e.

A *Columns 4 and H*
   Overlap = 12 titles, i.e. $C = 0.6$
   Correlation coefficient, $R = 0.63$ — significant at 0.5 level $RC = 0.38$

B *Columns 4 and I*
   Overlap = 13 titles, i.e. $C = 0.65$
   Correlation coefficient, $R = 0.72$ — significant at 0.2 level $RC = 0.47$

There is, however, little correlation between the 'judgements' of physicists (e.g. column 7) and citation data.

It is tempting to link the higher correlation of B above with the fact that each of these lists refers to a multidisciplinary use or citing of physics journals, whereas Dierks' list (A) referred to the citing *by* physics journals only.

Conclusions on rank correlation
Citation rankings tend to date fairly rapidly (see Fig. 5). Results from use studies, as one would expect, cannot be transferred from one user group to another. It seems likely (e.g. A & B last section) that measurements of *actual* use will correlate better with citation studies than user's subjective judgement. Where one is studying a set of physics journals (e.g. column 4 of Table 6, compared with column 5 which is more interdisciplinary), the fairly high correlation between the citation and use might be useful. For example, as we have said, the citation ranking tends to be more 'international' than a user ranking, and this might be useful in pointing out a possible parochialism in the users.

CONCLUSIONS

Several techniques have been proposed, and to a lesser extent used, for ranking as an aid to selection of physics journals. On the whole, correlation between methods is low, although there is scope for further work involving a number of different techniques on a particular user group and journal holdings. Within any major technique, there is an enormous variety of sample selection procedures, and of ways of presenting the output, each leading to a different ordering in the lists. It is doubtful whether a consensus could be achieved on the technique suited to a particular overall purpose.

The debate on an appropriate quantitative measure will ensure continued reliance on subjective judgement, of librarian and user, and thus on simple techniques of asking the user group. The appropriate role for more apparently sophisticated techniques would appear to be a minor, auxiliary one. They might point out, for example, (i) large anomalies in price per page, number of uses or citations compared with costs, or (ii) a citation analysis might indicate a journal which had proved useful for other research workers in a field, but had been relatively ignored by a library's own user group. In each case there would be points for further *subjective* consideration. Whether the effort expended on such a task would be worth while would itself be a subjective matter. Certainly, blinding the users with our own 'science', without exposing its shaky foundations, will not do them or ourselves any service.

APPENDIX A

KRAFT'S METHOD FOR JOURNAL SELECTION

In his PhD Thesis, Kraft initially considers the 'worth' measure as either size of journal (productivity) or usage, before plumping for usage. His cost 'contraint' is based on models by Leimkuhler[48] and Williams,[49] which themselves contain a 'use' measure but not a 'worth' indicator. To indicate how complicated this can get, the cost model constraint thus used by Kraft is

(A) $$\sum_{j=1}^{s} \sum_{l=0}^{q} Y_{j,\,q-l,\,1} (C_1 + C_2 + C_3\, \lambda_{j,\,q-l,\,1} + K_{j,\,q-l,\,1})$$
$$- \sum_{j=1}^{s} \sum_{l=0}^{q-1} Y_{j,\,q-l,\,1} (C_1 + K_{j,\,q-l,\,1}) \leqslant b_q$$

where
b_q = budget for period q for use in acquisition of new journals and maintenance of collection
C_1 = cost of acquisition, *excluding* subscription cost
C_2 = periodic storage and recurring costs
C_3 = cost per expected use of an item for circulation
$K_{j,\,q-l,\,1}$ = the subscription cost to acquire the issues of journal j published in period l if acquired in period q
$\lambda_{j,\,q-l,\,1}$ = the expected *usage* in period q of the issues of journal j published in period l
$Y_{j,\,q-l,\,1}$ is the so-called 'decision variable' which is one if the library has acquired the issues of journal j published in period l, and zero if not.

For journals, a total period q $(l \leqslant q)$, he shows that the problem reduces (given the previous assumption of the worth of *not* having the journal) to maximising 'worth', i.e.:

(B) $$Z = \sum_{j=1}^{s} \sum_{q=0}^{r} \sum_{l=0}^{q} Y_{j,\,q-l,\,1}\, G_{j,\,q-l,\,1}$$

(where $G_{j,\ q-1,\ 1}$ is the worth of acquiring the issues of journal j published in period l as of period q).

Kraft puts G equal to λ, i.e. worth equal to expected usage. He then has a fairly complicated expression for $\lambda_{j,\ q-1,\ 1}$ to represent its variation with time, using a 'Markovian' approach, based on a 'probabilistic obsolescence'.

This may appear complicated, but the basic idea is fairly simple, i.e. the maximisation of (B), which in fact means a maximisation of total λ over the set of journals s over a defined period (where λ itself is modified by time) subject to the budget constraint (A).

The parameters modifying λ, call them a, b, c, must be determined by experiment (obsolescence), as are C_1, C_2 and C_3 of (A). a, b, c, C_1, C_2, C_3 are calculated as average values per journal, and therefore are not different for different journals, and would therefore not meet Line's criteria for change of size of journals. It seems λ (usage) could be easily adjusted to take account of this, but I imagine this is more difficult for C_1, C_2, C_3 (perhaps these and the subscription cost could be defined for, say, the 1,000-page journal, if we wished to meet this criterion).

Thus the expression as given will pick these journals of maximum usage, subject to a financial constraint which includes their subscription price and factor times the usage, which will be different for each journal, together with other constraints, which will overall give different weights for the journal (i.e. the journal with greater use is not automatically included).

REFERENCES

1. Scientific serials: characteristics and lists of most cited publications in mathematics, physics, chemistry, geology, physiology, botany, zoology, and entomology. C. H. BROWN. Association of College and Reference Libraries (ACRL Monograph No. 16) Chicago. 1959.
2. College libraries and chemical education. P. L. K. GROSS and E. M. GROSS. Science, 66, 1927, p. 385–9.
3. Periodical sets: what should you buy? B. C. VICKERY. Aslib Proceedings, 5 (2), May 1953, p. 69–74.
4. Book marketing and selection: selected findings from the current AAP/ALA study. S. K. PAUL and C. A. NEMEYER. Publishers Weekly, 207 (24), June 16th 1975, p. 42–5.
5. The use and value of citations: a state-of-the-art report by ANGELA M. HALL. INSPEC report no. R70/4 November 1970. 32 pp.
6. Progress in documentation: citation analysis. JOHN MARTYN. J. Doc., December 1975, 31, p. 290–7.
7. Sources of citations and references for analysis purposes: a comparative assessment. J. M. BRITTAIN and M. B. LINE. J. Doc., 29 (1), March 1973, p. 72–80.
8. Analysis of bibliographic sources in a group of physics-related journals. M. M. KESSLER. Massachusetts Institute of Technology. Report R-4. 1962.
9. Clustering of scientific journals. M. P. CARPENTER and F. NARIN. J.A.S.I.S. 24, Nov.–Dec. 1973, p. 425–36.
10. Studies of the nature of citation measures. 1: Some results on the function and quality of citations. M. J. MORAVCSIK and P. MURUGESAN. (University of Oregon, USA, 1973/4) Preprint 8 pp.
11. Citation Indexing. J. MARTYN. The Indexer, 5 (1), 1966, p. 5–15.
12. The norms of citation behaviour—prolegomena to the footnote. N. KAPLAN. American Documentation, 16 (3), 1965, p. 179–84.
13. A collection of remarks about citation indexes. P. ATHERTON. New York, A.I.P. 1962. 6 pp.
14. Mathematical evaluation of the scientific serial. L. M. RAISIG. Science, 131 (3411), 1960, p. 1417–19.

15. Citation analysis as a tool in journal evaluation. E. GARFIELD. Science, *178* (4060), 1972, p. 471–9.
16. Users guide to the ISI Journal Citation Reports. Institute for Scientific Information. Philadelphia. 1974? 14 pp.
17. Journal Citation Reports. A bibliometric analysis of references processed for the 1974 SCI. Compiled and edited by E. GARFIELD. SCI. 1975 Annual Volume 9. 1,340 pp. 1976.
18. Is there a pecking order in physics journals? H. INHABER. Physics Today, *27* (5), May 1974, p. 39–43.
19. Uber die Zitierfahigkeit von Zeitschriften auf dem Gebiet der Physik. H. DIERKS. Arbeiten aus dem Bibliothekar-Lehrinstitut des Landes Nordrhein-Westfalen. Heft 41. Koln, Greven Verlag, 1972. (ISBN 3 7743 0541 2) 115 pp.
20. Communication in Science. A. J. MEADOWS. London, Butterworths, 1974.
21. A study of scientific periodicals. R. H. HOOKER. Rev. Sci. Instrum., *6*, 1935, p. 333–8.
22. An evaluation of British scientific journals. J. MARTYN *and* A. GILCHRIST. London, Aslib, 1968. 51 pp. (Occasional publications no. 1.)
23. The growth of the literature of physics. L. J. ANTHONY, H. EAST, *and* M. J. SLATER. Reports on Progress in Physics, *32* (6), Dec. 1969, p. 709–67.
24. Recent growth of the literature of biochemistry and changes in ranking of periodicals. I. N. SENGUPTA. J. Doc., *29*, 1973, p. 192–211.
25. Optimization of library expenditure of biochemical journals. M. B. LINE. J. Doc., *31* (1), March 1975, p. 36–7.
26. A study in the source literature of plasma physics. H. EAST *and* A. WEYMAN. Aslib Proceedings, *21* (4), 1969, p. 160–71.
27. A survey in depth of a selected information field (astronomy and astrophysics) Final Report: An Analysis of selected journals. A. J. MEADOWS *and* J. G. O'CONNOR. Report No. SI/18/21B. Leicester University, 1971.
28. Selection of scientific periodicals in an industrial research library. E. F. HOCKINGS. J.A.S.I.S., *25* (2), March/April 1974, p. 131–2.
29. Characteristics of the research literature used by chemists and physicists in the United States. H. H. FUSSLER. Library Quarterly, *19*, 1949, p. 19–35, p. 119–43.
30. Analysis of bibliographic sources in the 'Physical Review' (Vol. 77–112) M. M. KESSLER *and* F. E. HEART. Massachusetts Institute of Technology, Cambridge, Mass. Report R-3. 1962. 35 pp.
31. Where does the money go? A. SINGLETON (Note submitted to Aslib Proc. 1976).
32. Densities of use, and absence of obsolescence in physics journals at M.I.T. A. SANDISON. J.A.S.I.S., *25*, May–June 1974, p. 172–82.
33. BLLD/SINFDOK survey 1975. Table 1 rank list of titles—requests by date of publication. British Library. 1975. 61 pp.
34. Uses of scientific periodicals. D. J. URQUHART. Proc. Int. Conference on scientific information. Washington, 1958. p. 287–300.
35. From primary journals to technical business magazines. R. L. KENYON *and* R. N. HADER. Jnl. of Chemical Documentation, *5* (3), August 1965, p. 135–9.
36. Operations research study of the dissemination and use of recorded scientific information. Operations Research Group, Engineering Administration Department. Case Institute of Technology. Dec. 1960.
37. Further minor by-products of research B. Serials read by research scientists. J. MARTYN. Aslib Proceedings, *16* (3), March 1964, p. 117–18.
38. Report of an investigation of literature searching by research scientists. J. MARTYN. London, Aslib, 1964.
39. Notes on the questionnaire of journal usage. I. MALLEY. (Maria Mercer Physics Library, University of Bristol) Unpublished. Jan. 1972. 7 pp.
40. The use patterns of physics journals in a large academic research library. CHING-CHIH CHEN. J.A.S.I.S., *23*, July/Aug. 1972, p. 254–70.
41. Journal usage survey: method and application. D. C. LANGLOIS *and* J. V. VON SCHULZ. Special Libraries, *64*, May/June 1973, p. 239–44.
42. How do scientists meet their information needs? CHING-CHIH CHEN. Special Libraries, *65* (7), July 1974, p. 272–80.
43. Sawing off the horns of a dilemma, or how to cut subscription lists and expand access to journal literature. D. GORE in: Management problems in serials work. Proceedings of a conference held at Florida Atlantic University, March 26–7 1973. P. SPYERS-DURAN *and* D. GORE (Eds.). Greenwood Press. Connecticut and London. 1974. p. 104–14.

44. The effect of a large-scale photocopying service on journal sales. M. B. LINE and D. N. WOOD. J. Doc., *31* (4), Dec. 1975, p. 234–45.
45. Practical interpretation of citation and library use studies. M. B. LINE and A. SANDISON. College and Research Libraries, *36* (5), Sept. 1975, p. 393–6.
46. The journal selection problem in a university library system. D. H. KRAFT and T. W. HILL. Management Science, *19* (6), Feb. 1973, p. 613–26.
47. The journal selection problem in a university library system. D. H. KRAFT. PhD Thesis. Purdue University, Indiana. 1971. (PB 71–20, 488). 286 pp.
48. Storage policies for information systems. F. F. LEIMKUHLER. Research Memorandum Series 69–8, School of Industrial Engineering. Purdue University, Lafayette, Indiana, USA. June 1969.
49. Library cost models: owning versus borrowing serial publications. G. WILLIAMS, E. C. BRYANT, R. WEIDERKEHR and V. E. PALMOUR. Center for research Libraries. Chicago. 1968.
50. Journal usage patterns and their implications in the planning of library systems. E. T. O'NEILL. PhD Thesis. Purdue University, Indiana, USA (PB 70–18, 704). 1970. 393 pp.
51. The journal literature of physics. A comprehensive study based on Physics Abstracts 1961 issues. S. KEENAN and P. ATHERTON. (PB 166 388). AIP DRP-PA-1904. American Institute of Physics 1964. 163 pp.
52. Photocopies versus periodicals: cost-effectiveness in the special library. B. C. BROOKES. J. Doc., *26* (1), 1970, p. 22–9.
53. The derivation and application of the Bradford-Zipf distribution. B. C. BROOKES. J. Doc., *24* (4), Dec. 1968, p. 247–65.
54. Rationalisation of serial holdings in special libraries. B. HOUGHTON and C. PROSSER. Aslib Proceedings, *26* (6), June 1974, p. 226–35.
55. Dispersion of papers among journals based on a mathematical analysis of two diverse medical literatures. W. GOFFMAN and K. S. WARREN. Nature, *221*, 1969, p. 1205–7.
56. The complete Bradford-Zipf bibliograph. B. C. BROOKES. J. Doc., *25* (1), March 1969, p. 58–60.
57. Journal acquisition by libraries: scatter and cost-effectiveness. S. E. ROBERTSON and S. HENSMAN. J. Doc., *31* (4), Dec. 1975, p. 273–82.
58. Statistics in theory and practice. 5th Edition. L. R. CONNOR and A. J. H. MORRELL. London, Pitman, 1964.
59. Citation analyses as indicators of the use of serials: A comparison of ranked title lists produced by citation counting and from use data. PAULINE A. SCALES. J. Doc., *32* (1), March 1976, p. 17–25.
60. Elements of statistics. E. B. MODE. 3rd Edition. Prentice-Hall. USA. 1961. 319 pp.

This work is supported by a grant from the British Library R & D Department.

6 AN ALTERNATIVE VIEWPOINT

6. AN ALTERNATIVE VIEWPOINT

I have concentrated throughout this volume on papers published in the UK and USA, with the intention of producing a reasonably coherent picture of the scientific journal in these countries. Although many of the conclusions clearly have a world-wide validity, there remain some distinguishable differences between countries. By way of emphasising this point, I insert here a section devoted to papers from the USSR. The Soviet Union presents a contrast to the UK and the USA in the degree of state involvement in information transfer. Moreover, owing in part to the language problem, the Soviet research literature is by no means widely read in the West. These Soviet papers are therefore also worth including for the different style and approach they reveal. My own assessment of Soviet research papers is that they tend to be more diffuse in style, yet at the same time more summary in their treatment of research results than equivalent British or American papers. Consequently, it is sometimes difficult to pin down exactly how the reported research was carried out.

The first paper reprinted in this section follows from the material contained in the previous section. It provides a Soviet view of the world-wide provision of research results by scientific journals, and examines in a quantitative manner how Soviet journals are used at home and abroad. The emphasis changes in the second paper reprinted here, to the structure of the research publications themselves. I have chosen this particular paper because it illustrates a topic, and an approach, which has, so far, been stressed more in the USSR than elsewhere. More especially, the tendency to mix different avenues of research – psychology, information theory, etc. – in discussing information problems is characteristic; it also appears in the Soviet enthusiasm for applying cybernetics to communication studies.

The final paper in this section describes an attempt to streamline the communication of research. The implementation of this system in the USSR illustrates one way in which change can sometimes be more readily introduced under a state-controlled system. At the same time, this paper leads on to the questions which will be considered in our concluding section.

INVESTIGATION OF SCIENTIFIC JOURNALS AS COMMUNICATION CHANNELS. APPRAISING THE CONTRIBUTION OF INDIVIDUAL COUNTRIES TO THE WORLD SCIENTIFIC INFORMATION FLOW.

Z. B. Barinova, R. F. Vasil 'yev, Yu. V. Granovsky, V. M. Mul 'chenko, V. V. Nalimov, Ye. V. Napastnikov, I. M. Oriyent, G. B. Preobrazhenskaya, A. B. Strakhov, A. T. Terekhin, T. L. Farberova, Yu. A. Shcherbakov

Summary

    A statistical analysis of publications cited in scientific journals covering mathematical statistics, physical chemistry, spectroscopy, analytical chemistry, physical metallurgy and philosophy and published in the USSR, USA, Great Britain, Federal Republic of Germany, France, and in some cases, Japan and India. It was established that the USA and Great Britain, on the one hand, and the USSR, on the other, form two rarely intersecting information flows based primarily on previous publications of the authors of their countries. About 55% of the publications fall into the first of these flows and about 20% in the second. The journals of other countries do not form such closed national information flows. The citing index of authors writing in the English language in the journals of the majority of other countries is about 55%, but in journals of the Soviet Union the contribution of Anglo-American papers sometimes drops to 25-30%. The citing index of Soviet authors in the journals of other countries is about 3-4% and never exceeds 5%. Here there is a sharply expressed lack of correspondence between the efforts expended on scientific development and the effectiveness achieved. It is demonstrated that the low influence of Soviet works on world information flows is because the USSR has a poorly organized information service.

Reprinted from PB 178 666T, English translation of *Nauchno-Tekhnicheskaia Informatsia*, Series 2, no. 12, 1967, p. 3-11, by permission of both publishers.

Introduction

An information model of the process of scientific development was investigated in reference [1]. Within the framework of this model journals may be considered as communication channels, and the bibliographic reference system, as a special scientific information language. In compact form this language characterizes the intellectual atmosphere in which the work was created. To evaluate the contributions made by individual countries to the world scientific information flow, it was proposed that two categories be investigated: 1) the efforts expended by the country on scientific development and 2) the effectiveness of these efforts. The relative number of publications passing through the filter of the abstract journals may be taken as the measure of the effort. The measure of effectiveness may be the relative number of bibliographic references to the authors of various countries. It is postulated here that if references to a work exist, this means that it has influenced the development of world information flows.

The purpose of the present article is to set forth the results of statistical analysis of the language of scientific references in the scientific journals of various countries and to evaluate the effectiveness of the efforts made by these countries in the development of world science as an information system.

§ 1. Distribution of References to Authors of Various Countries in the Journals of the Exact and Technical Sciences

Journals in the following fields of knowledge were selected for the investigation: physical chemistry, molecular spectroscopy, physical metallurgy, analytical chemistry, mathematical statistics and philosophy[1].

The investigation was carried out primarily with complete sets of journals for 1965. We tried to keep the volume of examined bibliographic references on the order of 1000 (that is, within the limits of 500-1500). If the complete set of journals for the year turned out to be too large, a sample was taken from it; if it turned out to be too small, complete sets of the journal for several years were examined. Only bibliographic references to basic publications in scientific periodicals were subjected to statistical analysis; references to short communiques, reports, letters to the editors and book reviews were excluded.

---

[1] The selection of the fields of knowledge was arbitrary to a great extent -- it was made by the same group of specialists as engaged in this project.

The analysis techniques were developed during the course of the project; therefore, there are slight variations in the processing techniques and presentation of material with respect to different sections. Self-citing (citing of ones own works) was not, as a rule, excluded. A supplementary analysis revealed that this does not introduce any noticeable shifts in the evaluation. To evaluate the efforts made by various countries in the development of science, as a rule, domestic or foreign abstract journals were used. In one case (physical metallurgy) a reference work on phase diagrams published in the US was also used. In another case (analytical chemistry) Fisher's [2] data were used.

At first it was proposed that the country in which the work had been performed would be established for each bibliographic reference. Later it turned out that this identification was excessively labor-consuming. In a number of cases, countries were combined by language.

The results of the statistical analysis are presented in tables 1-7.

If we read these tables by columns (from top to bottom), it becomes clear how the bibliographic references in a journal of one country are distributed by countries. If the tables are read by rows, we get an idea of the contribution each of the countries is making to the bibliographic system of the investigated journals. The diagonal elements of the square submatrix indicates how authors are cited in their own countries (or languages).

In the abstract journal Matematika [Mathematics], a total of 583 articles were published on probability theory, 627 on mathematical statistics and 433 on the application of probability theoretical and statistical methods.

In Mathematical Review, publications in the section on mathematical statistics for 1966 were distributed in the following way (%): USA (39.0), India (17.0), USSR (7.4), Japan (6.0), Great Britian (5.7), German language (5.3), Australia (3.5), Polish Peoples Republic (2.5), Scandinavian countries (2.3), Italy (1.8), France (1.6), the Rumanian Peoples Republic (1.6), and the total number of articles for the year was 564.

The distribution of publications by countries appears in the first column of tables 1-5. The distribution by countries of publications on mathematical statistics is indicated in table 6, and the distribution by countries of the bibliographic references for this field of knowledge is indicated in table 7.

The data from tables 1-7 indicate that:

1. The effort made by the leading countries of the world to develop world scientific flows are characterized by the following figures (in percentages):

        USSR approximately   20
        USA and Great Britain   25-60, more frequently about 50
        GDR and Fed. Rep. Germany 5-10
        France about   5

2. The percentage of bibliographic references to authors of their own countries varies within the following limits:

Journals of the USA and Great Britain	68-91
Journals of the USSR	42-65
Journals of the Federal Republic of Germany	24-46
Journals of France	33-35

3. The citing index of Soviet authors in journals of other countries varies within the limits of about 3-5% and never exceeds 5%. It was stated above that the efforts made by our country in the development of the information flows are estimated at about 20%. There is a sharply expressed lack of correspondence between the efforts made and the effectiveness achieved in this case.

4. The citing index of authors writing in English in the journals of the majority of other countries is about 55%. Here the effectiveness corresponds to the level of effort. Soviet journals alone are an exception -- the contribution of Anglo-American works sometimes drops to 25-30% in them.

5. Papers written in German are cited from 5 to 10% which corresponds quite well to the level of publishability of these works. Only one field of knowledge -- mathematical statistics -- constitutes an exception. Here the Anglo-American school occupies a very special position. The statistical works of the German school do not fall in with this trend which has now received world recognition.

6. Papers written in French are cited less than 5% -- here the effectiveness is almost always below the level of publishability, but this difference is not so great as are papers written in Russian.

Thus, in the investigated fields of science it may be stated that there are two basic, almost nonintersecting information flows -- one of them is in the English language and the other in Russian. About 55% of the publications fall in the first flow, and about 20% in the second. The first flow is cited in the journals of other countries, as a rule, on the level of publishability; the second, on a level of 3-4%.

§ 2. Development with Time

The variation with time in the level of citability of authors of various countries appears to be significant. This analysis was made for only one journal, the <u>Journal of the American Chemical Society</u>, in which papers are published on basic divisions of chemistry including organic and physical chemistry. The complete annual sets were subjected to

Table 1. Distribution by countries of articles on physical chemistry and bibliographic references to publications taken from the journals: Zhurnal fizicheskoy khimii [Journal of Physical Chemistry] (USSR), Zeitschrift für physikalische chemie, N. F. (Federal Republic of Germany), (Journal of Physical Chemistry (USA), Journal de chemie physique (France)

	Percentage of articles in Chemical Abstracts	Percentage of references in the journals of			
		USSR	FRG	USA	France
USSR	28	44	3.6	2.7	4.8
GDR and FRG[1]	5	11	29	5.6	7.6
English Language countries	38	38	58	88	64
France	4.3	2.3	2.3	0.3	13
Japan	3.9	1.3	1.2	0.8	4.1
Holland	0.9	0.9	1.5	1.1	1.1
Scandinavian countries	1	0.5	1.4	0.7	1.5
Number of articles or references included in the statistics	933	1542	841	1512	727
Average number of references to an article		13	16.4	21	

Note. Selfciting was excluded in compiling this table.

[1] German Democratic Republic and Federal Republic of Germany

Table 2. Distribution by countries of articles on molecular spectroscopy and bibliographic references to publications taken from the journals: <u>Optika i spektroskopiya</u> [Optics and Spectroscopy] (USSR), <u>Berichte der Bunsengesellschaft für physikalische Chemie</u> (Federal Republic of Germany), <u>Journal of Molecular Spectroscopy</u> (USA, Great Britain), <u>Canadian Spectroscopy</u> (Canada), <u>Comptes Rendus des Seances de l'Academie des Sciences</u>, <u>Bulletin Societe Chimique de France</u> (France)

	Percentage of articles in Chemical Abstracts	Percentage of articles in the Abstract journal Khimiya [Chemistry]	Percentage of references in the journals of			
			USSR	USA, Great Britain and Canada	FRG	France
USSR	21.6	18.5	51	4.2	2.6	4.7
English language countries	50	59	30	68	54	45
GBR and FRG	7.5	7	7	7.2	38	20
France	8	5.8	7.5	5.5	1.7	23
Japan	4.9	5	3.1	5.3	1.7	3
Italy	1.2	2.5	0.9	0.7	0.9	2.5
Number of articles and references included in the statistics	1538	1286	1300	850	680	730
Average number of references to an article			13	14	16	17

Table 3. Distribution by countries of bibliographic references to publications on molecular spectroscopy in the international journal Spectrachimica Acta

	Percentage of references in publications represented by the countries of					
	USSR	Great Britain and USA	GDR, FRG	France	Japan	Italy
USSR	0	2.8	4.5	5.4	0.5	3
English Speaking Countries	0	79	47	67	54	45
GDR and FRG	0	6.6	44	4.3	10	8
French language	0	3.6	2	16	3.5	2.5
Japan	0	4.2	0.8	0.6	23	7
Italy	0	3	1.2	2	1.5	30
Number of references included in the statistics		1524	265	185	202	135
Average number of references		15	14	17	18	21

statistical analysis for 65 years using 10 year intervals. The results are presented in Table 8. It is interesting to note the following:

1) the citability of American works increases noticeable with time, and the citability of papers written in German and French drop sharply;

2) the citability of English works remains suprisingly constant;

3) for Russian and Soviet works the level of citability remains constant beginning with 1910;

4) in recent times an increase in the contribution made by Japanese works is noted.

The data presented in Table 8 indicate how the adjustment takes place in the contribution made by individual countries to the information flow running through one of the well-known chemical journals.

Table 4. Distribution by countries of articles on analytical chemistry and bibliographic references to publications in the journals: Zhurnal analiticheskoy khimii [Journal of Analytical Chemistry] (USSR), Analytical Chemistry (USA)

	Percentage of articles by Fisher [2] data	Percentage of references in the journals of the	
		USSR	USA
USSR	21.5	42	3.8
USA	20.5	18	61.4
GDR and FRG	10.0	10	5.9
Japan	6.8	2.5	2.7
Poland	5.1	0.3	0.8
Great Britain	4.3	6.6	9.7
France	4.2	3.1	2.9
Czechoslovakia	3.6	5.5	1.3
Number of references included in the statistics		500	1536
Average number of references to an article		16	13

Table 5. Distribution by countries of articles on physical metallurgy and bibliographic references to publications in the journals: Metally [Metals] (USSR), Zeitschrift für Metallkunde (Federal Republic of Germany), Trans. AIME (USA), Journal of the Institute of Metals (Great Britain), Revue de Metallurgie (France)

	Percentage of articles in		Percentage of references in the journals of				
	Reference work on phase diagrams (USA)	Abstract journal Metallurgiya [Metallurgy]	USSR	FRG	USA	Great Britain	France
USSR	29	24	64.8	4.6	3.1	3.0	4.1
FRG	5.2	12	8.9	46.4	7.2	11	17
USA	48	36	16.5	34.6	72	42	28.5
Great Britain	7.5	14	8.6	11.2	14.8	37	13
France	3.9	3.5	0.8	0.4	1.0	4.0	35
Number of references included in the statistics			595	867	526	638	270
Average number of references to an article			9.6	18.9	16.4	11.2	9.8

Table 6. Distribution of abstracts (in %) by countries in the abstract journal Matematika (Mathematics), for 1965

Probability theory		Mathematical statistics		Application of probability theoretical and statistical methods	
USA	44	USA	47	USA, Great Britain	60
USSR	20	Great Britain	20	USSR	23
GDR and FRG	9	USSR	10.6	GDR and FRG	10
France	8	Japan	7	France	5
Great Britain	6	Scandinavian countries	7		
India	6				

Table 7. Distribution by countries of the authors of bibliographic references to publications on mathematical statistics in the journals: Technometrics (USA), Revue de Statistique Applique (France), Calcutta Statistical Association Bulletin (India), Annals of the Institute of Statistical Mathematics (Japan) [1], Journal of the Royal Statistical Society, Series B [2], Biometrika [Biometrics] (Great Britain)

	Percentage of references in the journals of					
	USA	France	India	Japan	Great Britain	
USA	79	53	53	70	44[1]	46[2]
France	0	6	0	0	0	0.5
India	2.5	0	31	7.7	0	3
Japan	0	0	0	6.9	0	0.7
Great Britain	12	6	5	5.2	33.5	38.5
USSR	0	1.2	0	2	0	0.6
Australia	1.7	0	2	0	4.4	4
Average number of references to an article	5.4	4.0	5.8	8.4	5.0	6.7
Number of references included in the statistics	277	82	81	285	167	512

§ 3. **Detailed Investigation of the Citability of Domestic Papers on Analytical Chemistry**

In order to understand the principle of relatively low citability of domestic works it was necessary to perform a series of additional investigations. One of them was a detailed study of citability in individual, comparatively narrow fields of knowledge. It was possible for us to undertake this investigation in only one field of knowledge -- analytical chemistry.

A group of productive authors was selected -- specialists in analytical chemistry who had published no less than two works in the last three years in the Zhurnal analiticheskoy khimii [Journal of Analytical Chemistry] or in the analytical section of the journal Zavodskaya laboratoriya [The Plant Laboratory]. The citability of these authors was investigated with respect to the SCI (Scientific Citation Index)[1] for 1965; the results are presented below:

The total number of authors selected for the investigation	119
Number of authors cited in 1965	90
not cited	29
Total number of references in print	
domestic	508
foreign	590

The total average citability of one author is 12.2; the average citability in the foreign press is 5.6, in domestic journals, 6.6. These data indicate the comparatively high citability of the selected group of authors -- specialists on analytical chemistry, especially if we consider the fact that the average citability of an author getting into the SCI is only 5.5 according to the data of E. Garfield.

Out of the group of productive authors a subgroup of leading scientists was isolated, who were cited in the SCI (for 1965) more than 25 times and for whom the citing level in foreign print was more than 40%. This group turned out to be quite numerous -- it included 15 scientists. The level of citability is high in this case -- for three scientists the total citability varies around 100 in which the citing drops more than 50% in foreign periodicals. The data presented in Table 9 acquire special significance if we remember [4] that the Nobel Prize

---

[1] A bibliographic reference index published in Philadelphia (USA) and edited by U. Garfield. A detailed description of this index in the Russian language may be found in reference [3].

Table 8. Distribution by countries of the articles cited in the *Journal of the American Chemical Society*

	Year						
	1900	1910	1920	1930	1940	1950	1965
USA	27.5	26.8	45.4	41.0	48.1	56.2	66.6
GDR and FRG	59.7	42.7	32.0	36.4	26.0	18.8	7.1
England	3.5	7.7	13.1	11.5	12.4	12.9	13.3
France	9.5	8.5	7.3	3.8	5.0	3.6	2.1
Russian and Soviet works	0.2	1.5	0.8	1.5	2.0	1.2	1.9
Italy	0	0	0.2	2.0	0.9	0.8	1.0
Japan	0	0	0	0.3	1.4	1.0	1.9
Holland	0	1.0	0.4	1.2	1.2	1.1	0
Belgium	0.2	0.1	0.1	0.7	0.7	0.6	0
Switzerland	0	0.2	0.1	1.0	1.0	1.2	0.5
Number of references included in the statistics	454	826	904	1030	1016	1602	730
Average number of references to an article	5.1	19	10	7	12.4	9	18

Table 9. Citing of 30 leading Soviet scientists in the field of analytical chemistry in 1965 (according to the SCI)

Number of references (for each scientist)			
total	in domestic print	in foreign print	% references in foreign print
74	23	51	(69)
110	50	60	(55)
45	18	27	(60)
33	15	18	(54)
28	8	20	(71)
46	24	22	(47)
40	15	25	(62)
31	16	15	(46)
39	6	33	(85)
35	20	15	(43)
26	15	11	(42)
27	13	14	(52)
75	27	48	(64

Note. The number of references in parentheses is given in percentages of the total number of references in domestic and foreign print.

Table 10. Comparison of the number of publications in the journals Zavodskaya ladoratoriya [Plant Laboratory] and Zhurnal analiticheskoy khimii [Journal of Analytical Chemistry] and the citing levels with respect to areas of analytical chemistry

Area	Number of publications per year	Total number of references to authors of works in these areas	Specific citing	
			total	in foreign print
Organic reagents	86	223	2.6	1.4
Polarography	67	197	3	0.8
Coulometry, potentiometry, anhydrous nitration	49	46	1	0.4
Technical Analysis	46	110	2.4	0.2
Extraction	38	87	2.2	1.4
Gas chromatography	33	58	1.6	1
v-v basic purity analysis	30	102	3.4	2.4
Amperometry	21	66	3.1	1.2
Fluorescent techniques	14	30	2.2	0.8
Kinetic techniques	9	43	4.9	2.3

Laureates for 1962 and 1963 were cited in SCI in 1961 an average of 169 times; the leading authors of complex works on an important new problem such as decoding genetic codes were cited only 112 times in 1961, and the co-authors of these complex works were cited only an average of 48 times.

The next stage of this investigation was evaluation of the specific citing of works[1] according to the SCI for 1965 for individual narrow areas of analytical chemistry. The results of this analysis are presented in Table 10. Here we see that the specific citability of our works in Russian print varies by almost 10 times. Papers in such divisions of analytical chemistry as coulometry, technical analysis, fluorscent techniques, potentiometry and anhydrous titration were cited very little. The explanation for this will be given in § 6.

Thus, whereas it was demonstrated in § 1 that, on the average, domestic works are cited very little, here, on the other hand, we see that many scientists are cited on a very high level. Then it is noteworthy that the citability in individual, quite narrow fields of knowledge varies sharply. A detailed interpretation of these phenomena will be presented below.

§ 4. Delays in the Information Flow Running Through Soviet Journals

The information flow delay time is essentially different for different countries. This situation is subjected to careful analysis.

First of all the delay time in publishing articles was taken into consideration. In Figures 1, 2 and 3 histograms are presented which reveal the distribution of articles by the time they are held by the editors of journals publishing articles on molecular spectroscopy, physical chemistry and science of metals. We see that our journals occupy a "record" position with respect to length of time the articles are held by the editors. In practice, our publications are held up by the editors twice as long as abroad. On being published they turn out to be approximately a year older than the foreign papers appearing simultaneously. The data presented above on the time the articles are held by the editors of our journals are not the worst. In the Zhurnal analiticheskoy khimii [Journal of Analytical Chemistry], the average publishing delay of an article is 13 months, the minimum is six months, and the maximum is 34 months. The most striking data on publishing delays in biological journals are presented by L. L. Balashev [5]. It turns out that the greatest publishing delay for Izvestiya ANSSSR, serya biologicheskaya

---

[1] Here specific citings is the number of references to a work published in the investigated journal.

THE SCIENTIFIC JOURNAL 237

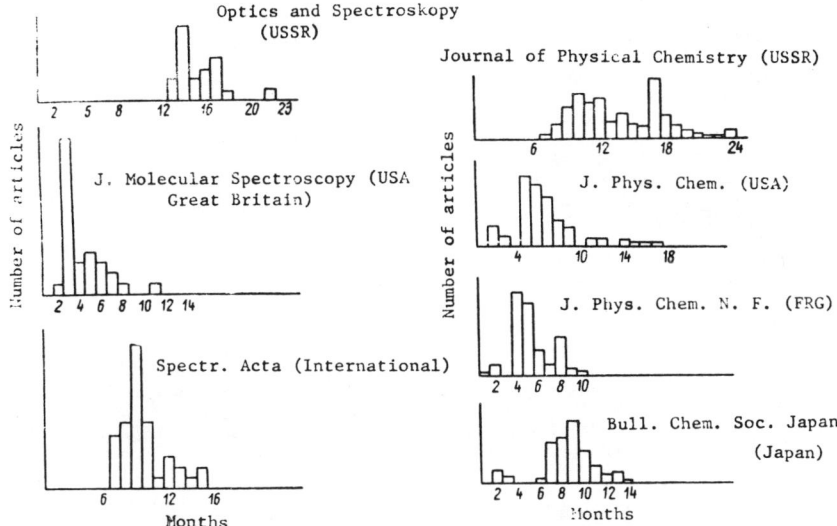

Figure 1. Delay in publication of articles on molecular spectroscopy

Figure 3. Delay in publishing articles on physical chemistry

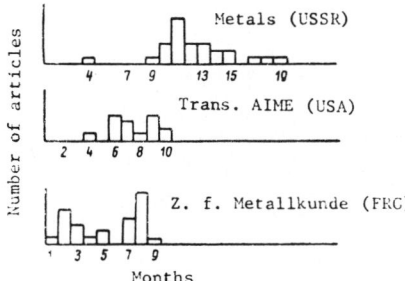

Figure 2. Delay in publishing articles on the science of metals

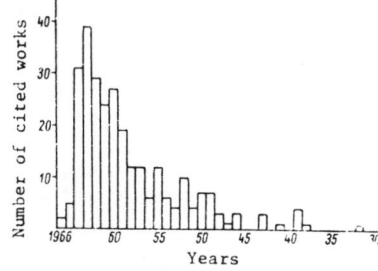

Figure 4. Histogram of distribution by years of publication of works cited in the journal Technometrics for 1966.

[News of the Academy of Sciences USSR, Biological Series], is 63.8 months; for Botanicheskiy zhurnal [Botanical Journal], it is 54.2 months; for Pochvovedeniye [Soil Science] it is 40 months. In analogous foreign journals the maximum delay usually varies from 10 to 20 months and for only one of the journals investigated by L. L. Balashev did it reach 22.2 months. It is still a question what sense there is in publishing a paper if it has been held five or six years by the editors.

The second characteristic of the time shift of information flows is the citing delay. Figure 4 contains a histogram which represents the distribution by years of publication of works cited in the journal Technometrics for 1966. This histogram may be approximated by a logarithmically normal distribution law. The displacement of the mode or medians with respect to the reference point[1] may be used as a measure of the citing delay. Table 11 contains values of the mode and medians for a number of journals. We can see that in such Soviet journals as Metally [Metals], Optika i spektroskopiya [Optics and Spectroscopy] and Zhurnal analiticheskoy khimii [Journal of Analytical Chemistry], foreign literature is cited with a delay of several years. G. M. Dobrov [6] noted the same phenomenon earlier in literature on electrical engineering (in analysis of references in the journal Elektrichestvo [Electricity] for 1966). Apparently this delay is caused by lack of proficiency in foreign languages and the necessity of using abstract journals and other secondary sources of information.

In some cases it may be of interest to study the irregularity of the histogram. In Figure 5 the distribution by years of publication of works written in the German language is illustrated. There is a trough corresponding to the collapse of German science during the years of Nazism.

Figure 6 illustrates the distribution by years of publication of Soviet works cited in the journal Voprosy filosofii [Problems in Philosophy] for 1966. Here two flows of works are clearly apparent. One flow contains rapidly aging works of a short-lived nature reflecting topical questions; the second flow contains slowly aging classical works written in 1925-1930. To evaluate the aging rate of the works on which the information flows are based, it was proposed that the concept of half-life be introduced analogous to the term used in nuclear physics [7].

We shall construct curves for the integral distribution functions with the publication date of the cited works on the x-axis and the total number of cited works on the y-axis. These curves may be approximated by one exponent or the sum of two exponents as shown in figure 7 where the integral distribution curve is presented with respect to years of publication of domestic works cited in the journal Metally [Metals]. Knowing

---

[1] The middle of the year in which the set of analyzed journals was published is always taken as the reference point.

THE SCIENTIFIC JOURNAL

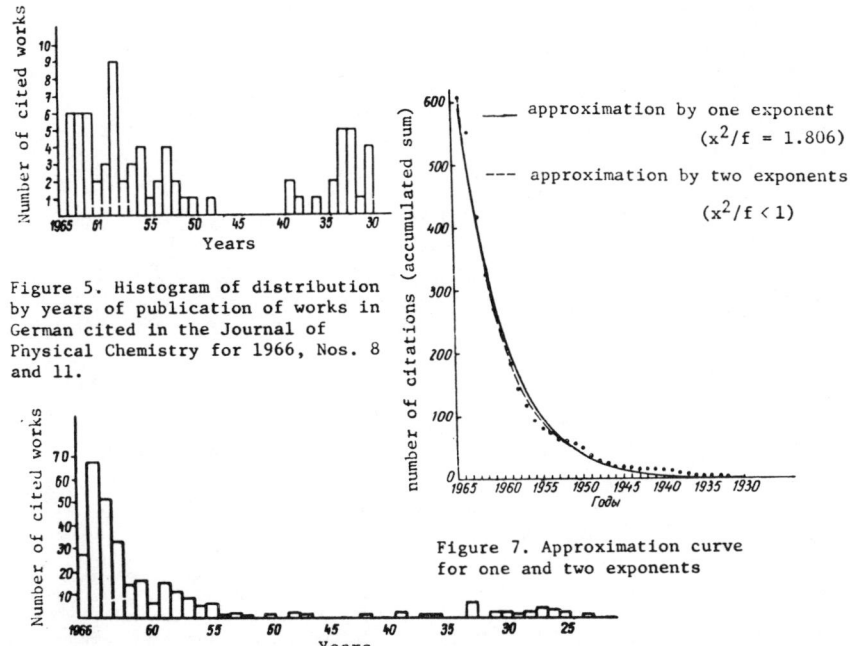

Figure 5. Histogram of distribution by years of publication of works in German cited in the Journal of Physical Chemistry for 1966, Nos. 8 and 11.

Figure 6. Histogram of distribution by years of publication of domestic publications cited in the journal Voprosy filosofii [Problems in Philosophy] for 1966

Figure 7. Approximation curve for one and two exponents

—— approximation by one exponent ($x^2/f = 1.806$)

--- approximation by two exponents ($x^2/f < 1$)

the approximating function, it is easy to calculate the half-life (the time during which half the cited works were published). This quantity varies in a reasonable manner on going from one field of knowledge to another -- this question has already been discussed in reference [7].

Within the limits of one field of knowledge it is interesting to evaluate the half-lives for citing domestic and foreign works separately. The results of this analysis are presented in Table 12. We see that the foreign works, as a rule, age more slowly than domestic works. This phenomenon may be explained in two ways. The first hypothesis is the effect of the language barrier. Our scientific workers, as a rule, become acquainted with foreign works later than with domestic works. Therefore, the foreign publications age more slowly. The second hypothesis is that foreign scientists deal with more important topics and their works are executed on a higher level. The first hypothesis agrees well with the data presented above on displacements in mode and median for domestic and foreign publications. Here it might be noted that evaluation of the displacement with respect to modes and half-lives represents two different approaches to evaluation of the same factor.

Thus, the easily observed delay in the motion of domestic information flows is caused on the one hand by a publication delay at the journal editors, and on the other by a delay in becoming acquainted with foreign works.

§ 5. Article Size

The average article size in a journal determines the thoroughness of discussion of the material read. Many of us know from personal experience that often an article must be shortened so much that it practically loses its meaning, being converted from a scientific publication to a brief announcement of what has been done. The conceptual content of the article is extremely impoverished and sometimes completely lost. Published works, according to the descriptive statement by Derek Price frequently are "wrung out" -- all the most interesting, but frequently controversial, insufficiently clearly crystallized ideas are removed from them. It is well-known that many boards of editors of our journals have tried to decrease the publication delay time by cutting the size of articles. For example, in the journal Zavodskaya laboratoriya [Plant Laboratory], in recent years the article size has been reduced by more than half but in spite of this the delay time is still very large.

It was interesting to compare the average size of a Soviet scientific paper with the average size of publications in other countries. The results of this analysis are presented in Table 13. We see that the average size of our article is always essentially less than the size of foreign articles. There is reason to assume that in a number of cases this makes them difficult to understand. In particular, we have heard this many times with respect to articles published in the mathematical section of the journal Zavodskaya laboratoriya [Plant Laboratory].

Table 11. Values of mode and median (in years) for histograms indicating the distribution of works with respect to citing years

Title of journals	Median		Mode	
	References to domestic works	Reference to foreign works	Reference to domestic works	Reference to foreign works
Metally [Metals] (1965)	4.7±0.3	8.3-0.6 +0.7	2.6-0.2 +0.3	5.0-0.5 +0.6
Optika i spektroskopiya [Optics and Spectroscopy] (1965)	4.8±0.6	8.9±0.3	3.3±0.3	7.8±0.3
Fizicheskaya khimiya [Physical Chemistry] (1966)	6.8±0.4	8.7±0.6	3.7-0.3 +0.4	4.2±0.5
Zhurnal analiticheskoy khimii [Journal of Analytical Chemistry] (1965)	6.3-0.5 +0.6	7.6±0.6	3.2-0.4 +0.4	3.5-0.4 +0.5

§ 6. Discussion of the Results

It is now possible to discuss the basic problem which came up during this project: what is the reason for the low influence of Soviet works on world information flows? It is hardly possible to accept the hypothesis that our works are below the world scientific level. If this can be said at all, then it must be said only in individual special cases, for example, with respect to certain divisions of analytical chemistry.(see § 3) where the experiment has not been performed with modern equipment.

As a rule, this work is done on homemade instruments and therefore it is natural that foreign specialists do not attach sufficient significance to them. At the same time, such divisions of analytical chemistry as the development of new organic reagents and kinetic techniques do not require especially complex apparatus, and at the same time they have great significance for the development of analytical chemistry. Techniques for analysis of substances of special purity are basically on a high level. The world scientific press quickly reacts to our new ideas in this field. As a result the level of citing Soviet works in these areas is quite high.

A second example is the science of metals. During statistical analysis of journals on the science of metals attention was given to the following fact: in frequently cited works written in German, there are many bibliographic references to journals in which problems in the science of metals are investigated from the point of view of the physics of metals

Table 12. Half-life of publications. (The observation results are approximated by one exponent $N_T = N_0 e^{-\lambda t}$; the degree of the approximation was estimated by calculating the ratio of x^2/f where f is the number of degrees of freedom; the half-life was calculated by the formula $T = \ln 2/\lambda$)

No.	Title of journal	λ	$\sigma(\lambda)$	x^2/f	T
1	Metally [Metals] (1965) References to domestic works	0.181	0.003	1.806	3.829
2	Metally (1965) References to foreign works	0.113	0.003	3.943	6.133
3	Fizicheskaya khimiya [Physical Chemistry] (1966) References to domestic works	0.122	0.002	< 1	5.680
4	Fizicheskaya khimiya (1966) References to foreign works	0.082	0.001	1.437	8.451
5	Optika i spektroskopiya [Optics and Spectroscopy] (1966) References to domestic works	0.244	0.009	< 1	3.094
6	Optika i spektroskopiya (1966) References to foreign works	0.107	0.004	< 1	3.094
7	Analiticheskaya khimiya [Analytical Chemistry] (1965) References to domestic works	0.143	0.002	4.366	4.846
8	Analiticheskaya khimiya (1965) References to foreign works	0.113	0.002	4.208	6.133

Note: During the calculations weights were introduced which are inversely proportional to the square root of the number of observations. It is postulated that the distribution law is close to Poisson. Approximation of the results of the observations by an exponent turned out to be bad for the data presented in the rows of the Table Nos. 1, 2, 7 and 8. The approximation by two exponents in certain cases gives a noticeable improvement, but this has little influence on the calculation of the half-life.

and solid state physics. Among these journals are Acta Metallurgica, Journal of Applied Physics, British Journal of Applied Physics, Philosophical Magazine, Physical Review, etc. In rarely cited French works there are no references at all to these journals -- their works in the science of metals bear an outmoded, classical nature; there are not even any references to the physics journals of our country. In the works on the science of metals written in Russian (the journal Metally [Metals]), there are only references to domestic physics journals. This is evidence of the narrowness of the theoretical base and cannot be considered as a negative reflection on the value of the projects described in the article.

Both the above investigated examples are only two special cases in no way characterizing the position of our science as a whole. It has already been reported earlier [1] that the citability of the academicians of the Academy of Sciences USSR has been investigated in the fields of chemistry, physics and mathematics. It was demonstrated that they, as a rule, are cited on the same level as the Noble Prize Laureates and leading scientists in the field of genetics. It was also demonstrated that a large group of scientists working in the field of analytical chemistry are cited on a high level. All of this indicates that our leading scientists earn high recognition abroad. Why then does the average level of citability of works turn out to be low?

It seems to us that it is possible to give this question a quite simple answer. It is apparent that the whole thing is that in our country we do not have a sufficiently well-organized information service -- there is an intolerably long delay in the movement of new ideas through the communication channels. A preliminary calculation indicates that this delay may be five years and more. If our new ideas get into the world scientific flow with such a large delay, then naturally they are of significantly less value. Only exceptionally great works with respect to their significance will continue to draw a response after this much of a delay. Let us remember that the half-life of publications in many fields of knowledge is five-eight years.

What are the barriers creating the delays in the movement of ideas?

The first barrier is the absence of regular direct communications with foreign scientists. It is well-known that the information crisis has led to new forms of scientific organization -- "invisible collectives" [8]. Scientists of different countries have begun to create unofficial collectives in order to regularly exchange information by frequent personal contact, participation in small international seminars, constant exchange of industrial trainees and professors, and also by personal correspondence and broad exchange of preprints usually published without any editing and reviewing. Our scientific workers, as a rule, do not enter into these invisible international collectives. The foreign scientist who participates in such a collective becomes acquainted with new ideas during the process of their formation long before they will be published. He gains no less than a year of time by comparison with our scientists. Some publications turn out to be difficult to understand because we are not acquainted with all the long discussions which preceded them. Sometimes it is necessary to form special groups to decode these difficult to understand publications. These publications must be decoded, discussed in the form of a review accessible to the reader and published in our press. Several years may be required for all of this. Finally, the fact that foreign scientists are not acquainted personally with many of our scientific workers often leads to their paying insufficient attention to our publications and not reacting to them opportunely.

The second barrier is the delay in obtaining foreign journals. They arrive at our libraries with some delay, and it is especially bad that many of the most important journals come in reproduced form on which no less than a half-year is wasted. The situation is quite bad with respect to various types of collections and works of conferences. Our experience shows that in some fields of knowledge more than 10% of the publications which appear in foreign bibliographies are entirely impossible to obtain within the borders of our country.

The third barrier is insufficient proficiency in foreign languages on the part of our scientists. For various groups of scientists this barrier is of different magnitude -- in individual cases it may fall to nothing. Often insufficient knowledge of languages appears to have a selective form. For example, in works on the science of metals foreign works on traditional science of metals are cited quite broadly, but when we get to the new and difficult fields of knowledge for the physical metallurgist -- solid state physics -- only domestic works are cited.

The fourth barrier is preparation of articles for printing. Some amount of time, often a significant amount, is spent on preparing accompanying documents. Then the article is held up for a long time in editing. Losses of one to one and a half years have become quite common here. In record cases the losses may even reach five years. Meanwhile, abroad less than a year or sometimes even a half year is lost on this process.

The fifth barrier is lack of proficiency in Russian on the part of foreign scientists. Our journals are sent to England and the USA and are translated into English there. A half year is spent on this. In contrast, let us say, to Japan and a number of other countries we are not concerned that our works be translated into the language which is most accessible to the majority of world scientists although this could be done quite effectively. We practically never appear on the pages of international journals. Let us remember, by the way, that at one time journals were published in foreign languages in the Soviet Union, but then for some reason this practice was curtailed.

Table 13. Standard average size of an article[1]

	USSR	USA	Great Britain	FRG
Molecular spectroscopy	1	1.6	1.3	
Physical chemistry	1	1.8		1.4
Science of metals	1	2.6	1.7	2.1
Analytical chemistry	1	1.7		

[1]With respect to the average size of an article in Soviet journals; a correction was made for the journal format. The count was made in printed symbols

We again repeat that all these barriers have different magnitudes for the scientific workers of various rank and position.

Thus, we advance the following hypothesis: the response to our scientific works is significantly lower than our scientific potential -- this is explained by the delay in movement of scientific ideas through the communication channels.

§ 7. Feedback in Science and Its Use to Control the Process of Scientific Development

Much has been said about the control of science, planning and coordination of scientific research. However, until recently no logical model of the process of scientific development had been proposed which was convenient for the development of a control system, and no planning and coordination algorithms had been created.

It seems to us that science may be considered as a self-organizing system controlled by information flows running through the scientific journals. Feedback plays a large role in this process.

Quite recently each scientific collective still could see to the editing of its own works by ordinary means. Now it has become necessary to create a special feedback system based on statistical analysis of the scientific journals as communication channels. If each scientific collective systematically received detailed data on statistical analysis of the process of scientific development, this would permit the collective to approach the organization of its work with more caution and more critically.

It is clear that self-organization of every field of knowledge is possible only within the limits of the resources released for this by the state. The data from statistical analysis of journals may be used when discussing the problem of detailed distribution of appropriations for scientific development. In particular, from the data we have obtained it follows that in our country we expend great efforts on scientific development, but we economize severely on resources for organization of the information service. This economy is obviously very small by comparison with the great expense of scientific development and leads to unfavorable consequences: our great efforts turn out to be an order below their effectiveness when evaluating the contribution of Soviet science to the world information flow.

Conclusions

This work was conceived as methodological. We wanted to develop the methodology of statistical analysis of journals as communication channels and demonstrate that as a result of such analysis material could be obtained of interest for further discussion. It appears to us that we should continue work in this area, expanding the range of investigated fields of knowledge and stating the goals more profoundly. It is clear that we must again state the problem of creating a permanently active information center to systematically trace the development of science based on statistical analysis of the information flows. This center organized on the basis of computer techniques and equipment could execute the following functions: 1) trace the contribution made by individual countries to world science; 2) follow the development of individual scientific areas; evaluate the effectiveness of efforts expended on the development of these areas; 3) trace the penetration of new research methods into other areas. It is hardly possible to seriously discuss the development of optimal forms of control of the process of scientific development in this or any other country without having data of this type available. It is obviously necessary to strive in every way toward international cooperation in the organization of such a system for tracing the development of science.

BIBLIOGRAPHY

1. V. V. Nalimov, V. M. Mul'chenko, "Studying Science as an Information Process" (Statement of the Problem and Review), in the collection: Informatsionmiye materialy (Information Materials), No. 6, Moscow, 1967 (Scientific Council on Cybernetics).
2. R. Fisher, Analytical Chemistry, No. 12, 1965.
3. R. S. Gilyarevskiy, Z. M. Mul'chenko, A. T. Terekhin, A. P. Chernyy, "Study and Experience of Working With the Scientific Citation Index," in the collection: Prikladnaya dokumentalistika (Applied Documentalistics), Moscow, Nauk Publishing House, 1967.

BIBLIOGRAPHY
(cont.)

4. E. Garfield, J. Sher, R. Torpie, The Use of Citation Data in Writing the History of Science," Philadelphia, I. S. I., 1964.
5. L. L. Balashev, "Scientific Information Problems in the Field of Biology," NTI [Scientific and Technical Information], series 2, No. 2, 1967, page 9.
6. G. M. Dobrov, "The Information Principle of the History of Scientific and Engineering Development," in the collection: Prikladnaya dokumentalistika (Applied Documentalistics), Moscow, Nauk Publishing House, 1967.
7. R. Burton, R. Kebber, Amer. Docum., Vol. 11, No. 1, 1960, pages 18-22.
8. V. V. Nalimov, "Quantitative Methods of Investigating the Process of Scientific Development," Vopr. filosofii (Problems of Philosophy), No. 12, 1966, page 38.

Received 30 August 1967

OPTIMIZING THE STRUCTURE OF SCIENTIFIC PUBLICATIONS
Yu. A. Novikov

Nauchno-Tekhnicheskaya Informatsiya, Series 1, No. 9, pp. 12-17, 1975

The increase in published and unpublished information materials has brought out the problem of improving the forms and methods in which scientific and technical information is conveyed to its users. The problem is to provide specialists with information in a form convenient to use [1, p. 102].

One way to make this improvement is to optimize the structure of scientific publications and the way in which the content of the material is conveyed so as to allow the information user to rapidly, completely, and accurately perceive, interpret, and assimilate—and consequently, use—the content. "We must work out a typology of scientific documents and the optimum form of each type. We can resolve these problems only by making extensive use of the various methods of modern psychology" [2, p. 67].

To study how the structure of articles (one of the most important types of scientific publication*) affects the quality of the user's perception and utilization of the material they contain we ran information psychological experiments and did some theoretical research. These experiments and research led us to conclude that we should understand structure of a scientific publication as a specific interaction or mutual arrangement of these properties of it: the meaningful significance of aspects described, the forms of the linguistic presentation of the content; the symbolic information (for example, graphs, diagrams, charts), and break down of the content into parts. The experiments also showed that the content of scientific articles with a structure close to the optimum one is more rapidly, fully, and accurately perceived, assimilated, and used by the information user in solving creative problems.

A number of Soviet and foreign studies (for example [3,4,5,6]) have intuitively solved, to some extent, the problem of finding ways to affect the reader's perception of scientific publications on the basis of editorial work. However, practical scientific information work of recent years and the rapid increase in the total amount of scientific and technical information and the need to overcome this growth through intensifying the study of consolidating (synthesizing) information and development of automated information systems are evidence that the problem of finding methods and ways of improving the structure (composition) of scientific publications in order to raise the effectiveness of the perception of their content not only still remains but has become a more pressing problem than it used to be, say, in the sixties. And, as Shekhurin has pointed out, "problems of the composition of the scientific work have not been worked out theoretically" [3, p. 218]. Likhtenshtein notes almost the same thing, "Problems of the composition of various types of literature are poorly developed in editorial theory" [5, p. 48]. And, which is particularly important, to raise the effectiveness of information perception we must answer not only the question of what we should do but also the more complex question of how we should do it. We must therefore thoroughly investigate the *psychological* patterns of how scientific publication structure affects the quality (speed, completeness, and accuracy) of the perception, interpretation, remembering, and creative use—i.e., how it affects how the person uses the content.

Psychological studies of the optimum structure of articles are also needed because "development of a method for analyzing a text for content is now one of the most vital

---

*By scientific publications we mean primary documents—scientific articles, reviews, reports, etc. In this article we are analyzing the structure of the scientific article, and if we use the term "scientific publication," it means that we are referring to all primary documents of the type scientific article, review, or report.

problems of the psychology of perception. Its solution is important not only to the field of psychology itself but also to the psychology of perception, memory, and language teaching, which are no less in need of criteria for the understanding of a text. This problem has also come to the fore in connection with the development of scientific fields such as information science and machine translation, whose object is also the text" [7, p. 115].

This article uses the findings of information and psychological experiments involving 88 persons as the basis for studying the psychological patterns of how the structure of scientific articles affects the quality of their perception and the utilization of their content in the solution of creative problems. We used questionnaires to identify a number of parameters in these experiments.

THE INTERCONNECTION OF MEANINGFUL PARTS OF THE MATERIAL AND THEIR EFFECT ON THE ASSIMILATION OF INFORMATION

For the experiment we especially selected one scientific article and one popularized scientific article so we could compare the results of the perception of the content of scientific articles of different levels; these articles were "Attention: liquid aluminum!" in *Znanie—sila* [Knowledge is Power] no. 11, 1972 and "An automatic shop for mass-produced bearings" from the 1957 Annual Supplement to the *Great Soviet Encyclopedia*. We shall say that articles with a structure modified by us for the experiments are variant O, and articles with unmodified structures are variant N.

Let us first analyze the changes in the structure of experimental scientific articles that we made to create the O variants—in the sequence of presentation of more significant and less significant facts and in the content of informational interaction and grouping of these facts. In making these changes we took into consideration mainly the findings of theoretical and experimental research into the psychology of human perception of scientific information and the experience of editorial work and recommendations for preparing materials for publication [3,5].

For the article "Attention: liquid aluminum!" we used the content, the peculiarities of its parts, and style of presentation, etc. as a basis for grouping all the material into three parts, which we called "The old method of casting aluminum," "The new equipment for casting the metal," and "Creators of the equipment." The material of the largest section ("The new equipment for casting the metal") is presented in this sequence: first the equipment is described, then casting of metal into molds using the equipment, and last its positive properties accompanied by a summarizing conclusion, *this equipment opens up vast possibilities for automating the founding industry*. In support of this conclusion and the just-described positive properties, one final typical and psychologically convincing fact is noted: *this equipment has been patented in four of the highly developed nations (USA, West Germany, France, Belgium); many foreign firms are acquiring licenses*.

This grouping of facts and the sequence in which they are presented are in line with psychology and the logic of thinking when a person studies a new subject of objective reality: first its general structure is recognized by comparison against known structures (what is it?), and then its main subjective property is defined (why is it necessary?), then its constructional peculiarities are identified, for example, by analogy with previously studied ones (how is it constructed?), and finally, the specific, secondary properties, positive and negative aspects are studied (what is typical of it?). Shekhurin notes that "Most scientific and technical articles describing the findings of research and design projects are constructed on the principle of going from the general to the particular; clearly it is easier for a writer and more comprehensible for a reader to describe an instrument by starting with a rough diagram that presents an over-all view of the operational peculiarities of the instrument or mechanism" [3, p. 221].

In variant N of this article the description of the old method of casting aluminum is interwoven with an analysis of the merits of the new equipment for casting, a presentation of its constructional features, with a story about the technology of metal production, etc.; despite the individual clear comparisons, it is hard for the reader to mentally grasp the entire description of the new equipment for casting metal with its complex construction, original technology, and many advantages, whose description is scattered throughout the article. "The lack of logic in organization and the semantic and stylistic discontinuity of the individual parts impair perception of the material" [4, p. 20]. Shekhurin correctly states. It is therefore "very important that the reader be prepared to perceive every new idea, that an idea be a logical continuation or development of something said previously" [3, p. 219].

Let us consider the order of presenting an important aspect like the process of casting metal into molds using the new hydrodynamic equipment. It would obviously be more useful to describe this process in a strict temporal sequence and isolate the naturally delimited stages, which was done in variant O. The entire process was split into three stages: the first is a description of how a batch of melted metal is fed to the reservoir of the equipment; the second is a description of how voltage is applied to electromagnet coils and the metal forced out of the reservoir by the magnetic field thus created; the third is a description of how the required amount of metal is poured into the ingot mold and the pump is stopped.

This natural and strictly technological presentation of the process, describing in sequence its general, characteristic, and specific aspects (properties) with a specific organization of certain psychological accents in order to activate the user's attention, allowed significant improvement of the quality of the perception and utilization of the content of this aspect of the article. Experimental findings indicate that every fact in this section was reproduced between 70% and 450% better by students who studied variant O. On the whole, for variant O the total number of facts recalled from this part of the article was 2.8 times greater than the facts from variant N. Answers obtained from variant O were much more complete than answers from variant N.

Our psychological experiments thus show that the advantage of presenting material following the principle of going from the general to the particular is not only that "even at the beginning of an article the reader can familiarize himself, without going into the details, with the main thought of the writer and decide whether he needs to study the article in all its details" [3, p. 221]; it is mainly that this approach greatly improves the quality (completeness and accuracy) of the reader's perception of the content of the publication.

In variant O of the article "An automatic shop for mass-produced bearings" we used approximately the same sequence of presentation as in the first article: first the construction and structure of the shop is described, then the technological process and positive aspects (advantages) of the automatic shop. The section "Construction" is divided into four consecutive parts: machining department, heat-treatment department, grinding department, and the assembly department. The content of the section "Positive aspects (advantages) of an automatic shop" is subdivided into: constructional features, labor productivity, accuracy in manufacture, and quality control.

Within these subsections we have attempted to present the material in line with the psychology of human perception of information. For example, the constructional features of the shop as positive aspects are presented in this sequence: first the most general aspects, covering the object being described in general: the over-all advantages of the shop—*all technological processes including inspection, washing, and packaging of bearings are automated*; then the more specific, but still covering the object as a whole—*management of the shop is centralized at the dispatcher post*. With a text organized in this way, when the last communication or fact is received, the image of the whole automatic shop is brought to consciousness, an image that has already been formed in the human brain, but now we receive new additional information that more specifically describes the object on which our attention is focussed. This image is then made even more specific through the perception of new facts describing more specific aspects of the object and is thus made fuller and richer - *a pre-planned tool replacement system is provided in the automatic shop*. Finally, a specific feature of the object is described—*the bearings are assembled in a separate closed room equipped with air conditioning*. The image of the object being described has acquired a characteristic, identifying "special feature" and has firmly taken its place in the human brain in the arsenal of similarly clear and fruitful images, which are the bases of creative thinking.

Our experimental findings also confirm our conclusion that an image of an object being described is formed and registered in the human brain in this manner. The constructional features of an automatic shop were more fully described by experimental subjects who studied variant O of the article, since they formed a mental image of these features because of the sequence of presentation described above: the completeness of the answers here was 18% higher than the completeness of answers for variant N. It was also remarkable that not one participant who studied variant N reproduced the last fact of this part of the article (*the bearings are assembled in a separate closed room equipped with air conditioning*), whereas 15% of the participants who studied variant O reproduced this fact; second, 28% more participants who studied variant O reproduced the main advantage of the automatic shop (*all technological processes, including inspection, washing, and packaging of bearings are automated*).

The order and interconnection of the aspects of a description as meaningful parts of a scientific publication actively influence the quality of the perception, interpretation, remembering, and creative utilization of the content of the publication. Shekhurin believes (and we agree) that improvement of the perception of text requires following "the principle of presenting the material from the simple to the complex, from the known to the unknown" [3, p. 219]. He then explains the sense of this principle: "In presenting the findings of complicated theoretical research, experienced authors very often begin an article with an examination of the simplest case, thereby creating a clear although usually primitive picture of the general principles of the process or phenomenon. Later, as various additional principles are disclosed, this picture becomes more real. By thus gradually disclosing various principles in succession an author leads the reader toward assimilating otherwise difficult ideas" [3, p. 219]. This, however, is insufficient for the present level of development of review and analytical work, primarily work in synthesizing information and creating factographic information for data banks.

Our experimental findings indicate that the completeness and accuracy of the perception and recall of factographic information presented in synthesized material can best be improved by first presenting general information about the object, since this allows the information user to imagine the object as a whole and thus recognize it in general, or learn what it is in comparison with material objects already known to him.

When the object has been perceived in general and its outlines consciously grasped, the person expects information about the major functional qualities of the object or its main property, so he can compare the entire object's image with known objects of the material world and thereby more fully grasp the substance of the studied object. And only then is the user's consciousness ready to fully perceive the characteristic features, the positive and negative aspects, and other properties of the object so that its outlines can be converted into a picture of the image, making the image clearer. If the structure of a scientific publication takes these characteristics of the psychology of human perception of information into account, its contents will be more fully and accurately perceived and remembered.

COMBINED MEANINGFUL ELEMENTS IN THE STRUCTURE OF A SCIENTIFIC PUBLICATION

When we designed variant 0 for articles used in the experiments, we had in mind this feature of the psychology of perception: if information is offered in larger meaningful portions, the volume of information that a person is capable of perceiving and interpreting in a given unit of time is actually increased. Miller [8,9] has drawn attention to this. In explaining why combining information into large units helps overcome the limited capabilities of our brain to store it, Miller presents this curious analogy. Imagine, he says, that we could put all our money into a purse that could hold only seven coins no matter what they are—pennies or silver dollars. It is obvious then that it would be better to put coins with a higher value into the purse so as to increase the total amount of money in the purse. "There is some limit to the number of units of information," stresses Shekhter, "that can be processed in a unit of time. It is therefore useful to receive information in the form of 'large units,' thereby increasing the total amount of received and processed information" [10, p. 83].

But for a scientific text the concepts of "large unit of text" and "small unit of text" are quite diffuse and it is very complicated to determine what these terms mean. And it is not because the text (say, of an article or review) cannot be objectively broken down into some elements that are meaningful units of information different from sentences or paragraphs, but because this problem has not yet been studied very well.

Some writers have attempted to solve this problem but unfortunately only from one point of view: by dividing the text into parts. "In many articles," writes Shekhurin, for example, "it is not difficult to identify the parts of a text that can be formed into sections, subsections, paragraphs, and sometimes even chapters" [3, p. 223]. Problems of combining parts of text as an effective psychology means of raising the quality of perception of the content of a scientific publication are largely ignored by writers dealing with problems of editing scientific text. Therefore the theoretically true statement that "a well-thought-out system of headings lends order and clarity to a presentation and improves the accessibility of the material" [3, p. 223] offers nothing to the reader (or editor or author of a future article or book), because the formula "well-thought-out system of headings" is unclear: what does "system" mean, or "thought-out," not to mention "well-thought-out system"?

Our experiments led us to approach this problem to some extent from objective positions and offer incomplete but reassuring answers for these and similar questions of the division and rubrication of a scientific text. Whereas the variant N publications were divided into meaningful units such as sentences and paragraphs, in the O variants the parts of these texts were combined into new meaningful units by grouping the material in terms of its major aspects by assigning headings to these groups.

The experimental subjects unanimously noted that the larger grouping of information and facts permitted more rapid and fuller perception of all of the content of an article. Findings also indicate that the grouping of meaningful units of text is desirable. For example, the technological information presented in variant N of the article "An automatic shop mass-produced bearings" in small text units of separate sentences and paragraphs were concentrated in variant O into a single meaningful complex (section), "The technological process," a total of nine facts. Subjects who used variant O cited in their responses almost three times as many of these facts than those who used variant N: a variant O subject reproduced on the average 2.1 facts, and a variant N subject, 0.7. An even more meaningful advantage of variant O can be seen in the completeness in the description of these facts. Thus, the over-all completeness of variant O subjects' responses was 11.5, and of variant N subjects' responses, only 2.4, i.e., variant O is almost five times better.

The problem of grouping the meaningful units of a scientific publication using the psychology of perception is connected with the problem of consolidating (synthesizing) information. Information synthesis is the generalization or compression of some initial information, the compilation of new (derivative) information, and the combining of informational elements that all together help speed the transmission of information to the user by reducing its volume but not its content, extracting from all the initial information what is main and essential and obtaining information in a new, more convenient form. In variant O of the experimental articles we tried to meet only the two last requirements of information synthesis—to extract the main thing and to present it in a more easily perceived form. Let us now consider these transformations of the structure of articles and their effect on the perception and recall of content.

IDENTIFICATION OF THE MOST INFORMATIVE PARTS OF TEXT

We know that the clarity of presentation of material and the completeness with which its content is apperceived is greatly affected by the "correct separation of a text into paragraphs and skillful utilization of separational devices" [3, p. 223]. But what is this "correct separation of a text," "skillful utilization of separational devices," and what are the "separational devices"?

To further study these problems and the nature of the psychological effect of the most meaningful parts of articles on the quality of the perception and utilization of their content, we used a number of devices for separating out or accenting the indicated parts of text in the experimental O variants of texts: printing a meaningful part of text indented marking such a part by a thick vertical line on the right or left; delimiting a meaningful part of the material with a horizontal line or ordered symbols (numbers, letters); underlining the characteristic, most informative (key) words and phrases; printing a part of the text in a different typeface (for example, boldface) or letterspaced, etc.

Unfortunately, typewriters are relatively limited in the available ways to accent the most meaningful elements of the structure of an article. We did not make use of the capabilities of typewriters to print colors (black, red, and blue), since the materials were duplicated by xerography.

Several of these methods were used for variant O of the second article in the section "Positive aspects (advantages) of an automated shop." Thus, words denoting the names of four factors by which the advantages were grouped were written letterspaced; the beginning of the description of every advantage started with an indent and was marked off by a horizontal line (dash); a bold line was used to emphasize the most informative or typical ("kernel") words in a given description (for example, *management of the shop is centralized, increases grinding productivity two to three times*). One sentence conveying very important information (*the output per worker was doubled*) was printed in capitals and underlined.

This accenting of the most informative parts of the structures of the experimental articles increased the effectiveness of perception and creative utilization of the content of this material when experimental problems were solved.

The first two questions in the questionnaire given the experimental subjects dealt entirely with the section "Positive aspects (advantages) of an automatic shop," which was most typical of an article in the use of methods to emphasize the meaningful informative parts. Analysis of the responses to these questions ("what are the positive aspects (advantages) of the shop?" and "How have the positive aspects (advantages) of the shop been achieved?") indicates that many more facts were remembered and reproduced by the subjects who read variant O. Of the 17 facts in this section, variant O subjects reproduced all but two (i.e., about 12%), but variant N subjects did not reproduce seven (i.e., more than 41%). Variant O subjects reproduced 52 facts altogether, and variant N subjects reproduced 41, which is 21% fewer.

The results of reproducing facts, for example, numbers 23 and 25, which dealt with the description of the grinding lines, are very indicative. In variant O these facts were emphasized using three devices simultaneously: the text was indented, facts were delimited by letters followed by a close parenthesis, e.g., a) and b), and the most informative words in the description of the facts were underlined, e.g., *over 3-4 hours..., completion of the assignment per shift, grinding productivity is increased 2-3 times.* As a result, there were three times as many variant O subjects who remembered and reproduced these facts in their responses.

We obtained similar results with the article "Attention: liquid aluminum!" For example, the description of the major reason behind the slow mechanization of operations connected with the transportation of liquid aluminum were emphasized in three ways in variant O: indenting, marking the text with vertical and horizontal lines (an angle), and printing especially important keywords of this description (*its [aluminum's] high corrosivity*) in Capitals. Four times as many facts as presented in variant N were reproduced.
When the sentence *extensive introduction of the equipment in production will help change the idea held for decades that foundries are sectors of industry with the most arduous working conditions* was indented and underlined, completeness of perception and reproduction was doubled.

Thus the experimental findings indicate that:

1. A correct division of a text is a division that concentrates the presentation of one aspect of an object being described, arranges the aspects presented in a text in accordance with the psychology of the perception of an object being studied, and delimits single aspects, separating them from other similar parts of text through the paragraph, the section with a subheading, etc.

2. The skillful utilization of separational devices is the application of the above-described methods for stressing parts of text where first, a psychological effect on the reader is required, on his perception of the particular material or on his apperception (assimilation) of the material, or on his thinking; second, the user's attention must be activated for more rapid, precise, and complete utilization of the information offered. Emphasis through the visual methods used in our experiments raised the quality (completeness and accuracy) with which the user perceived, assimilated, remembered, and reproduced the content of scientific publications [11].

HOW THE PRESENTATION OF INFORMATION AFFECTS ITS PERCEPTION

The emphasis on the most meaningful parts of a text is closely connected with the transformation of information into a form that is the most convenient to perceive. Approximately the same methods are used to prepare information in a form that permits more rapid and complete transmission of its semantic and pragmatic value to the user; and at times it is difficult to distinguish emphasis of the meaningful aspects of the description of an object from improvement of the representation of this description. And putting information into the best form is connected with the arrangement or organization in a strictly defined sequence of the most meaningful and the less meaningful parts of text and with consolidating meaningful elements in its structure, because all these transformations of the structure of a publication have the same aim - to present information to the user in a form that permits him to more rapidly, completely, and accurately assimilate, remember, and later use it in his creative activities.

We can therefore treat the concept "the type of information most conveniently perceived" in two ways. In the broad sense the structure of a scientific publication is transformed by the methods described—by arranging it into a necessary sequence of more and less meaningful and informational parts, by grouping the meaningful units of text, and by emphasizing the most informational elements of the text. In the narrow sense separate parts of the structure of an article are transformed by visual methods so as to lend them greater external expressiveness. In this section we shall analyze the most conveniently perceived form of information in the narrow sense and do this apart from other aspects of the perception of a text, so we can more comprehensively describe its capabilities and characteristics. The well-known Soviet bookman E. S. Likhtenshtein remarked, "Any work other than a short essay or article should be divided into parts that are closely interrelated. We can even state that breaking a work down into small parts makes it easier to understand" [5, p. 50].

To find the most convenient form of representing the content of an article, we divided the material in variant O of "An automatic shop for mass-produced bearings" into three independent sections, each identified by subheadings that were underlined with a bold line and centered on the page. Other devices were also used to transform the information into the best form. However, we were unsuccessful in changing the individual parts of the structure of the text in such a way as to only create a more convenient form for the perception of information (in the narrow sense) for this article. Such changes are interconnected with other transformations of the structure—the creation of the necessary sequence of elements, the consolidation of meaningful units, etc., and it was therefore impossible to obtain experimental results for this article that would characterize the perception of its content with respect to this and only this aspect of the transformation of the structure of the scientific publication.

We were able to achieve this kind of "pure" transformation to some extent in the article "Attention: liquid aluminum!"

Let us consider the experimental data on the reproduction of facts relating to the design of the magnetodynamic equipment. In variant N the description of the installation was scattered throughout the text, and in variant O this description was concentrated in a single place and organized as a table - one of the most effective and convenient forms for presenting synthesized information. Because of the tabular organization of the material (and the content allowed this) as a visual attention-getter, the user's attention was drawn to a number of meaningful informational parts of text: the main aspects of the installation of the equipment: the name of an assembly, its purpose, constructional features; important characteristics: properties of materials of assemblies, their forms and arrangements; differences between these assemblies, etc. Experiments showed that the tabular form of presenting information about the design of the equipment almost doubled the total number of facts reproduced by the experimental subjects.

In variant O of this article the description of a very important positive property of the installation (it greatly improves casting quality) was presented in a special manner: as a separate small section with a large indent and short lines (35-40 characters long). In the questionnaires, 10 of the 14 variant O subjects reproduced this fact, i.e., 72%, and 7 of the 13 variant N subjects did so, i.e., 54%. Subjects who read variant O also were better able to provide a complete description of this fact; this advantage was about 27% per fact and 70% per experimental subject. And one final example. The representation of, for example, the names of four nations that held patents for the installation, in a column instead of in a line also increased the accuracy and completeness of the responses about this fact; this was a 33% increase per experimental subject.

Thus, optimizing the structure of a scientific publication by presenting its individual parts in a more conveniently perceived form increases users' grasp of technical and scientific information.

CONCLUSION

The experimental and theoretical analysis of journal articles with different structures showed that the content of materials with a structure close to the optimal is more rapidly, completely, and accurately perceived, assimilated, and used by information users in solving creative problems. Analysis showed and allowed us to formulate some additional effective methods and devices for optimizing scientific publication structure using human psychology.

This conclusion is also confirmed by research done by Zholkova and Teplov [12]. Their experiments on studying the abstracting processes showed that human psychological activity has "a more or less fixed internal algorithm for processing information" [12, p. 78].

This assumption that human informational and psychological activity follows this kind of information processing algorithm (or specific rules, using our terminology) underlay our first investigations of the psychological problems of information science [11], and we believe that this algorithm will be one of the factors in optimizing scientific publication structure. Another and perhaps more important factor is the capacity of the human brain to transform received information into a heuristic system [13].

Further research should show which principles (rules, patterns, algorithms) of activity of the human brain should be the basis for optimizing the structure of scientific publications to raise the effectiveness of the utilization of scientific, technical, economic, etc. information used in social practice.

REFERENCES

1. A. I. Mikhailov, "Scientific and technical information and effectiveness of science," Kommunist, no. 16, pp. 98-107, 1971.
2. A. I. Mikhailov, A. I. Chernyi, and R. S. Gilyarevskii, Fundamentals of Information Science [in Russian], Nauka, Moscow, 1968.
3. D. E. Shekhurin, "Clarity and accessibility of presentation (a study of scientific and technical articles)," in collection: The Editor and the Book [in Russian], no. 3, Iskusstvo, Moscow, pp. 204-251, 1962.
4. D. E. Shekhurin, Efficient Forms of Publishing Scientific and Technological Achievements [in Russian], LDNTP, Leningrad, 1968.
5. E. S. Likhtenshtein, "Editing the Scientific Book; Some Problems in Editorial Sophistication [in Russian], Iskusstvo, Moscow, 1957.
6. E. S. Likhtenshtein, "How can we raise the effectiveness of scientific publications?", Nauka i zhizn, no. 11, pp. 147-151, 1971.
7. G. D. Chistyakova, "A psychological study of the meaningful structure of a text in connection with the problem of understanding," Voprosy psikhologii, no. 4, pp. 115-127, 1974.
8. G. A. Miller, "Human memory and the storage of information." IRE trans. on information theory, IT 2, no. 3, 1956.
9. G. A. Miller, The magical number seven, plus or minus two: some limits on our capacity for processing information,: in collection: Readings in Perception, 1958.
10. M. S. Shekhter, Psychological Problems of Cognition [in Russian], Prosveshchenie, Moscow, 1967.
11. Yu. A. Novikov, "Psychological problems in information science," NTI, ser. 2, no. 1, pp. 6-9, 1969.
12. A. I. Zholkova and Yu. D. Teplov, "Some psychological features of the abstracting process," Vopr. psikhologii, no. 1, pp. 72-79, 1974.
13. Yu. A. Novikov, "Psychological aspects of optimizing documentary systems," in collection: Documentation 69; Materials of the First All-Union Symposium on Documentation [in Russian], RINTIP, Vilnius, pp. 59-66, 1970.

THE DEPOSITING OF SCIENTIFIC PAPERS (FROM THE EXPERIENCE OF VINITI)*

I.M. Basova and I.F. Kuznetsova

The intensive growth of information in all branches of science and technology has made it impossible to publish all material of scientific value. At the same time, even papers that are accepted for publication may have to wait their turn for a long time. This applies even to publication in journals, which do not always maintain their role as the effective source of information on the latest achievements in science and technology, although the network of journals in this country is constantly being widened and increased in volume, frequency, and circulation. At present, rather a long time is spent on the publication of an article.

In this country and abroad, with the object of speeding up the delivery of scientific information to the user, new methods of publishing primary documents have been used, which consist of cutting down the volume of primary publications, so that, instead of long articles in journals, letters to the Editor or short communications are published; moreover, the method of depositing scientific papers has been introduced. "Depositing scientific papers is one general way of solving the problem of disseminating the increasing flow of scientific research papers ... The resolutions of the 24th Congress of the Communist Party of the Soviet Union turned all branches of our national economy to the intensification of production and to increasing the effectiveness of Soviet science. Increasing the network of journals and their volume represents an extensive method. Surveys, letters to the editor, short communications, abstracts, together with depositing, certainly form an intensive method. This is an important advantage and there is therefore an urgent need to introduce it widely in practice" (1).

The deposition method consists of the following. Papers that have a narrow theme, and are of interest to a comparatively small number of readers, are taken for depositing by some organ of information, which publicises the paper, as mentioned in the Instructions (2), through the Abstracting Journal (*R. Zh.*)*. It catalogues, indexes, and stores the paper, and, at the request of a user, will also issue a copy.

At present, information on a deposited manuscript is located in the Catalogue of Deposited Manuscripts, published by the All-Union Institute of Scientific and Technical Information and State Committee of the Council of Ministers of the USSR on Science and Technology and the USSR Academy of Sciences (VINITI), and in the indexes of the All-Union Scientific Research Institute of Medical Information (VNIIMI), the Centre for Scientific Information on Power and Electrical Engineering of the USSR Ministry of Power and Electrification (INFORMENERGO), a Department of the Scientific Researcch Institute for Economic Research (ONIITEKHim, in Cherkassy), the Central Scientific Research Institute of Information and Economic Research in the Oil-refining and Petrochemical Industry (TSNIITENeftekhim), and so on, which issue the accumulated material as fas as possible. The editorial boards of journals that send manuscripts for depositing in most cases also place information on these manuscripts in the pages of their journals. They may send to be deposited manuscripts of articles, surveys, monographs, proceedings of conferences, congresses and symposia of a specialist character which are inappropriate for publication by the usual means.

*Russian acronyms have been retained in the translation (Translator).

Translated from *Nauchno-Tekhnicheskaia Informatsia*, Series 1, no. 8, 1975, by permission of the publisher.

The depositing of scientific papers, in spite of its comparative youth, already has its own history. In the 1930's the question of depositing scientific papers arose in the pages of the press, but the practical realization of the idea has occurred only in our own day. The starting date of depostiting scientific papers in our country must be reckoned as October 1961, when VINITI was entrusted with the task of depositing manuscripts of those completed scientific papers produced by the institutions of the USSR Academy of Sciences which were inappropriate for publication in a large edition. VINITI had to accept for deposition manuscripts on the exact, natural and technical sciences, whilst the Fundamental Library for Social Sciences of the USSR Academy of Sciences accepted manuscripts on the social sciences.

In the first period (1961-1966), depositing could be regarded as a means of providing information on scientific papers intended for a restricted circle of readers, but not as a method of publishing such papers, since at that period a deposited manuscript was not regarded as a published paper. This probably partially explains the small influx of manuscripts at this time. Up to 1967 VINITI accepted 552 manuscripts for depositing from the Institutes of the Academy of Sciences of the USSR and the Union republics.

The second phase of development of depositing began at the end of 1966 and lasted until May 1971. In this period there appeared three very important directives on depositing: one was the Instruction "On the procedure for awarding academic degrees and conferring academic titles", sanctioned by the Higher Attestation Commission (VAK) on 28 September 1966, according to which manuscripts of papers and papers annotated in scientific or abstracting journals and deposited in VINITI were equivalent to published papers.

No less important for the future development of the deposition of scientific papers were the resolutions of the Praesidium of the USSR Academy of Sciences on 25 February 1966 and 22 March 1968, which established the right of editorial boards of journals of the Academy of Sciences of the USSR and of the Union republics to send manuscripts of articles to be deposited, with compulsory advertisement of these articles by annotations, abstracts or short communications in the journal. The Praesidium of the USSR Academy of Sciences began to regard depositing as a means of speeding up primary scientific publication and decided to consider the depositing of articles from the journals of the Academy of Sciences of the USSR and of the Union republics as a main objective for the immediate future.

In this period, the growth in the number of submitting organizations, (that is, organizations that send manuscripts for depositing and bear the responsibility for the maintenance and registration of manuscripts) led to an increase to 4,500 in the number of manuscripts accepted for depositing; that is, compared with 1961-1966, their number had increased by more than eightfold — at the expense of the academic journals.

By the middle of 1971, depositing had become quite widespread among academic institutions and editorial boards of journals, as a new method of publishing scientific papers. By this time VINITI had accumulated great experience in this field. Permanent submitting organizations were formed (approximately 110), among which editorial boards of academic journals took an important place. We should note that in 1965 a special resolution of the State committee for the coordination of scientific research papers in the USSR by central departmental organs of information authorized the depositing of manuscripts in these. But papers accepted by such information centres were not equated with published papers, since VAK up to May 1971 apparently regarded as printed only those papers accepted for depositing at VINITI.

In terms of the variety of manuscripts accepted for deposition, and their volume and experience of handling them, VINITI was clearly the main organization. The work of depositing manuscripts was taken on by a depositing group of the Department of Scientific Resources.

In May 1971, by a joint resolution of the State Committee of the Council of Ministers for Science and Technology, the Praesidium of the Academy of Sciences and the Ministry of Higher and Middle Special Education, an "Instruction on the procedure for depositing manuscript papers on the natural, technical and social sciences" was issued. The third period of the development of depositing began at this point. The resolution of 1971 marked the beginning of the all-union depositing network.

According to the new Instruction (1971), besides VINITI, 48 organs of scientific and technical information are able to act as depositories. These are all-union, central departmental and republic organs of information. Only five of them have the right to carry out the whole process of depositing: receiving, storing and copying manuscripts, and also providing information about them through their abstracting journals. These are VINITI, the Institute of Scientific Information on the Scocial Sciences (INION), the Central Institute of Scientific Information on Building and Architecture (TSINIS), the All-Union Scientific Research Institute of Information and Technical-Economic Research on Rural Economy (VNIITEISKH) and VNIIMI. Deposited manuscripts, abstracts of which are placed in the abstracting journals issued by these organizations, are regarded as published scientific papers. The remaining 44 centres also have the right to receive, store and copy manuscripts and to advertise information on deposited manuscripts in their informaiton publications, but these manuscripts, abstracts of which are advertised only in the publications of these information centres, are not equivalent to published papers. In order that manuscripts should be regarded as published, these centres need to send abstracts of papers deposited with them to one of the five centres mentioned above.

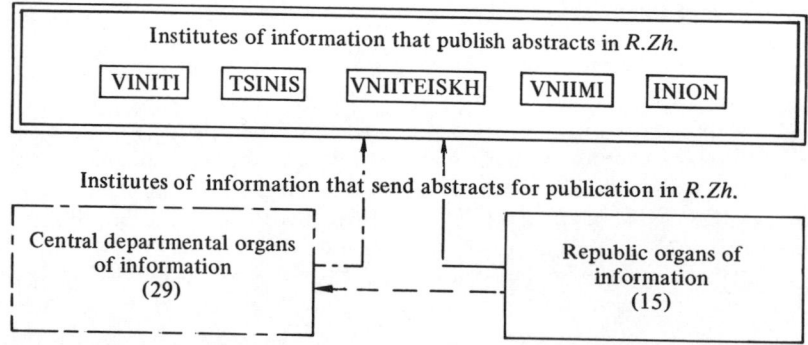

Fig. 1. Network of institutes of information that accept manuscripts of scientific papers for depositing, send abstracts for publication in *R.Zh.*, and send copies of abstracts to the corresponding central departmental organs of information.

Fig. 1 shows the interaction of the organs of information in the depositing network. The Instruction of 1971 gave the right to take a decision on sending manuscripts of scientific papers for deposition not only to academic institutions and editorial boards of academic journals, but also to editorial boards of scientific and technical journals of other departments and to the scientific, technical and editorial councils of the main scientific research, design and construction institutes and higher educational institutions which, in accordance with established procedure, enjoy the right to publishing activity.

A manuscript is sent for depositing only with the agreement of the authors who, together with the submitting organization, take responsibility for its contents and registration. However, depositories (organs of information that carry out the reception and storage of manuscripts and distribute copies at the request of users) have the right to reject manuscripts on reasonable grounds.

The author of a manuscript accepted for depositing, after the publication of an abstract of it in *R.Zh*, is sent information on depositing with a reference to the name of the author, the title of the manuscript, and the name and number of the publication in which the abstract is published.

Certain journals that send manuscripts to the depositories advertise in their pages abstracts or annotations of these manuscripts with references to the depositories and the registration numbers under which the manuscripts are stored. The editorial offices of these journals send reprints of abstracts or annotations to the authors of deposited manuscripts. In this case, in our view, it is inadvisable to distribute to authors further information on the location of an abstract in an abstracting journal. This saves depositories and editorial offices of journals unnecessary work — the preparation and distribution of thousands of documents a year.

According to the "Instruction on the procedure for awarding academic degrees and conferring academic titles", approved by the Higher Attestation Commission on 23 June 1972, manuscripts of papers annotated in scientific or abstracting journals and deposited in the research institutes of the state system of scientific and technical information were equated to published papers. Authors of deposited manuscripts have the rights that follow from the legislation on authors' rights, but cannot claim a royalty payment.

In 1971, VINITI was entrusted with the deposition of manuscripts on the natural and exact sciences. However, with the agreement of the State Committee of the Council of Ministers of the USSR on science and technology, VINITI also takes manuscripts on the technical sciences from academic institutions. Manuscripts on the social sciences are deposited by the Institute for Scientific Information on the Social Sciences; those on technical and practical economic sciences by the central departmental scientific research institutes of information and economic research corresponding to the topics of information activity associated with them; those on specialist questions of the development of science and technology, of interest only to a given union republic, by the republic institutes of information. It is advisable to grant to the republic institutes of information the right to take for deposition manuscripts of scientific papers of a specialist character on various subjects, for example, papers on various questions of economics which at present are not allocated to one central departmental institute of information that accepts deposited manuscripts. Thus at VINITI, in the sphere of depositing, there arose new important considerations:

- to continue to accept for deposition papers from academic institutions and journals on the natural, exact and technical sciences;
- to extend depositing in the natural and exact sciences, by taking manuscripts from non-academic institutions and editorial boards of journals;
- to advertise in its *R.Zh.* abstracts, the existence of manuscript paper in the technical and practical economic sciences, accepted for depositing by the central departmental and republic organs of information.

In the state system of scientific and technical information, VINITI played an important role in the sphere of depositing, not only because its position as a main institute obliged it to, but also because, among institutes of information, it had great experience of work in this field (more than 10 years) and the right to accept manuscripts over a very wide range. In fact, in its *R.Zh.*, the Institute gave information about deposited manuscripts in all sciences except the social sciences.

In connection with the new problems of the operational organization of work in the field of depositing, a special unit was set up — the Section for the Theory and Practice of Depositing Scientific Papers. From the beginning of its existence, the Section had to give systematic help to the submitting organizations and the depositories. The general system of depositing in VINITI was reorganized.

The technology of processing manuscripts accepted for depositing, and abstracts of them, was not restricted by the bounds of activity of the Section, but was a rather complicated system (Fig. 2), which was constantly improved. A manuscript

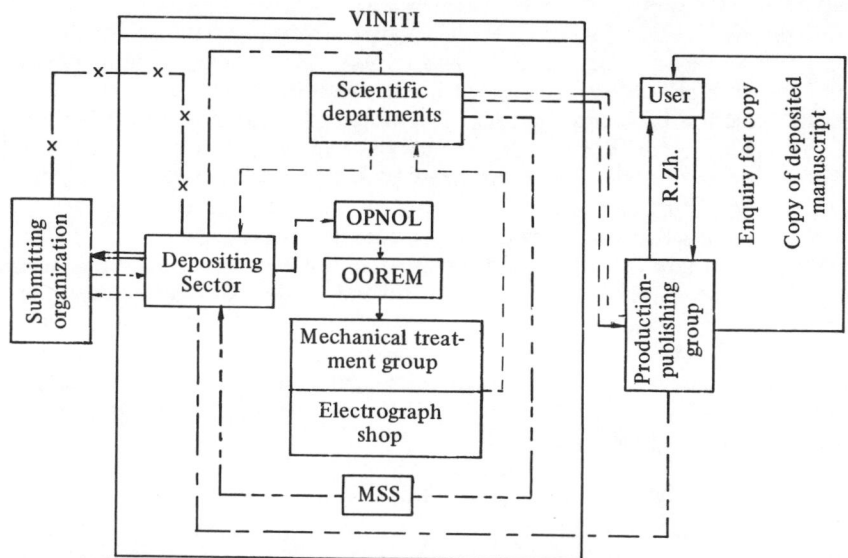

Fig. 2 System of depositing in VINITI (Key to diagram on P.268).

received for depositing at VINITI, once given the office stamp, which shows the date of receipt at the Institute, is directed to a reception group of the Section. This group verifies the presence and correctness of registration of all the documents accompanying the manuscript, which give instructions on depositing (3), an extract from the decision of the academic council of the corresponding scientific, research or educational institution (or editorial board of a journal, if appropriate), a review and so on. Then both copeis of the manuscript are looked over page by page with the object of determining its conformity with printing requirements, and the identity of both copies. When it has been read through, the manuscript is sent from the Section to the corresponding scientific department of the Institute, for a preparatory examination, where scientific editors determine the correspondence of the manuscript with the objectives of the abstracting journal. Manuscripts whose initial value causes the editor doubt are sent for a second review. A refereed manuscript is sent back to the Section where a decision is taken on depositing it or sending it back to the submitting organization for reworking. Manuscripts are also sent back to the submitting organization when their contents do not conform with the VINITI *R.Zh.* In this case, the Section recommends the submitting organization to send the manuscript for depositing to a suitable organ of information.

A manuscript accepted for depositing is given a number by the Section, which is reported in a letter to the submitting organization, and then the manuscript enters a processing group. This finally verifies the correctness of all the accompanying documents, title pages and bibliographical descriptions of abstracts, carries out a little printing work, and prepares the manuscript for its transfer to microfilm. In this group, work is carried out using card indexes. The Section began transferring manuscripts to microfilm in 1973 with the object of creating a convenient form of deposited manuscripts for storage, which also allows the future possibility of going over to automatized document searching. After the transfer to microfilm, the first copy of the manuscript is sent for storage and copying at the request of users to the production and publishing group of VINITI. An abstract of a paper accepted for depositing follows, by a different technological chain, an independent path: depositing Section to abstracting journal.

A manuscript accepted for depositing is regarded as published only after an abstract of it, or, in rare cases, a bibliographic reference is placed in the Abstracting Journal of VINITI. The depositing section learns in which of the 173 parts of *R.Zh.* the abstract of a paper accepted for depositing is published, from a printout prepared at a computer centre. This is based on data obtained from scientific departments on the publication of abstracts of manuscripts in *R.Zh.* From information obtained from the printouts, authors' references are filled out and these are then sent to the submitting organizations. The average time for an abstract to be published in *R.Zh.* is four months. Once users have obtained information on a deposited manuscript from *R.Zh.*, they can order a photocopy or microform of it. For this, they send an order to the Information Enquiry Centre (ISTs) of the Production and Publishing Group (PIK) of VINITI, giving the registration number of the manuscript, the names of the authors, the title of the manuscript, and the page numbers, if the required article is from a collection.

In 1972, ISTs received orders for copying 3857 manuscripts, and, in 1973, 7029 manuscripts. Correspondingly, in 1972 about 220,000 photocopies and microforms were made of manuscripts deposited in VINITI, and in 1973 more than 362,000. At present, an analysis is being carried out in VINITI of all orders placed for copies of manuscripts kept in its stock.

The time taken for making copies of a deposited manuscript is not more than one month. A completed order is sent to the user for cash on delivery. At present, the Section for the Theory and Practice of Depositing Scientific Papers does the work in cooperation with the depositories who send abstracts of manuscripts with them for publication in *R.Zh.* The Section works out and distributes to all these organizations special rules for drawing up abstracts. Abstracts take the same path in the depositing system as abstracts of manuscripts deposited in VINITI. In a number of the depositories the work with deposited manuscripts is well established. A more detailed analysis merits a special article. Information about the more active depositories is presented in Table 1.

Table 1

Receipt of abstracts from depositories by VINITI

Depositories	Number of abstracts	
	1973	1974 (1st half-year)
ONIITEKHim (Cherkassy)	120	131
TSNIIEIugol	102	103
OVNIIEM	81	34
TSNIITEIPriborostroeniya	53	42
VNIPIEILesprom	54	41
TSNIITEI MPS	46	30
KazNIINTI	26	3
LitNIINTI	18	10
UkrNIINTI	6	13

Of particular note is the depository in the Department of the Scientific Research Institute of Economic Research (ONIITEKHim in Cherkassy). In the Department a section for depositing was established which carried out a great deal of work with submitting organizations. They were given detailed instructions on deposited manuscripts and a bibliography of deposited papers.* In all, VINITI dealt with 2741 abstracts from depositories for publishing in *R.Zh.*: 251 in 1972, 790 in 1973, 1700 in 1974.

The Section accepted 1389 manuscripts for depositing in 1972, 2658 in 1973 and 2019 in 1974 (January to June). It should be mentioned that in this two and a half year period the Section accepted 6066 manuscripts; that is 1033 more than the total number, 5033, accepted by the Institute from 1962 to 1971. The average length of the manuscripts was 12-13 pages; manuscripts of greater length than 50 pages were comparatively few. In 1974, up to May, 28 long papers were received. Fig. 3 shows the distribution among the branches of science and technology of the 1253 abstracts published in *R.Zh.* of manuscripts accepted for depositing by VINITI in 1974 (January to April). Fig. 4 shows the distribution among the branches of science and technology of the 426 abstracts published in *R.Zh.* of manuscripts sent by other depositing organizations in 1974 (January to April).

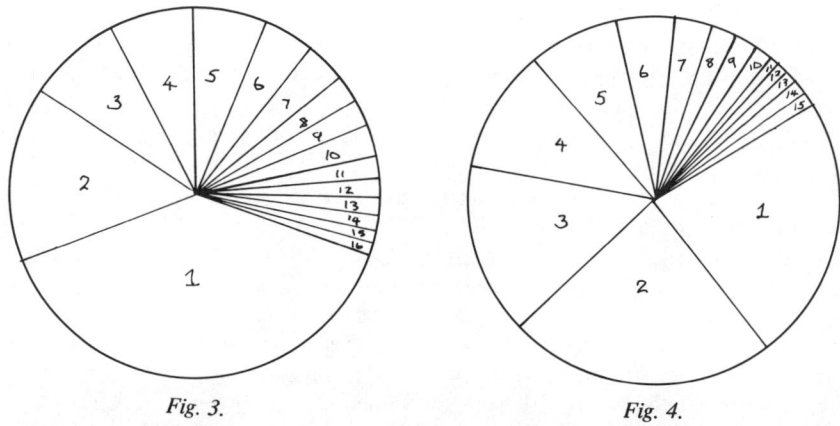

Fig. 3. Fig. 4.

Fig. 3. Distribution of abstracts of manuscripts accepted for depositing by VINITI among the branches of science and technology

1 - Chemistry - 38.8%; 2 - Physics - 14.2%; 3 - Mechanics - 8.8%; 4 - Mathematics - 8.7%; 5 - Biology - 7.8%; 6 - Metallurgy - 4.2%; 7 - Geology - 3.8%; 8 - Mining - 2.7%; 9 - Electrical and power engineering - 1.9%; 10 - Mechanical engineering - 1.8%; 11 - Geophysics - 1.8%; 12 - Astronomy - 1.5%; 13 - Automation and electronics - 1.3%; 14 - Industry - 0.4%; 15 - Scientific and technical information - 0.2%; 16 - Transport - 0.1%.

Fig. 4. Distribution of abstracts of manuscripts on branches of science and technology sent from the depositing organizations.

1 - Chemistry - 23.3%; 2 - Mechanical engineering - 22.7%; 3 - Mining - 13.7%; 4 - Electrical and power engineering - 11.1%; 5 - Metallurgy - 8.4%; 6 - Mechanics - 5.5%; 7 - Automation and electronics - 4.4%; 8 - Industry - 3.1%; 9 - Transport - 2.9%; 10 - Biology - 1.7%; 11 - Geology - 0.9%; 12 - Physics - 0.9%; 13 - Mathematics - 0.6%; 14 - Scientific and technical information - 0.5%; 15 - Geography - 0.3%.

*Procedure for preparing and presenting manuscripts for depositing in the chemical industry. Cherkassy 1973 15pp. Depositing manuscripts in the chemical industry during 1973. Annotated bibliography, No. 1., Cherkassy, 1974, 78pp.

Having analysed the distribution of abstracts among the branches of science and technology, we must take account of the fact that VINITI accepted from academic institutions manuscripts in the technical sciences also, and that individual abstracts of manuscripts deposited in VINITI or other institutes might be distributed over two or three branches of science and technology.

Special attention must be given to the submitting organizations. If we take account of the fact that every year papers by several thousand authors are published by the method of depositing in VINITI, then it is clear why the Section for depositing can carry out the work only with the submitting organizations that send manuscripts for depositing, and not with the authors. A manuscript is returned to the submitting organization if it does not satisfy the requirements of the Instruction, a letter is sent with information about the receipt of the manuscript for depositing, and information about the author is sent.

It is therefore important that submitting organizations should have a clearly defined relationship with their authors. Since 1974, the Section has sent a model letter to submitting organizations with a request for a nomination from each of its collaborators responsible for depositing, to whom the Section could render systematic assistance. The person responsible for depositing must verify that the manuscript obeys the regulations in accordance with the Instruction on depositing, before sending it to VINITI. This practice significantly reduces the number of manuscripts sent back for reworking and speeds up the process of depositing. For example, in 1974 (up to July), 19 manuscripts were received from the Institute of Metallurgy of the USSR Academy of Sciences and all were accepted for depositing. From the editorial office of the Journal of Physical Chemistry 209 manuscripts were received during this time, and 10 were returned. The data in Table 2 show that the proportion of returned manuscripts in 1974 was reduced by almost half compared with 1973.

Table 2

Analysis of manuscripts received for depositing at VINITI

1st half-year	Number of manuscripts			
	Total	Accepted	Returned	Proportion of returned manuscripts in %
1973	1799	1073	726	40.0
1974	2608	2019	589	22.6

In our view, an analysis of submitting organizations helps to present more vividly the picture of the position of depositing and a perspective of its development (Table 3).

In the first half of 1974, organizations sent 522 manuscripts to VINITI for depositing; if we take into account the fact that in 1971 there were only 110, it is obvious that their number has increased nearly fivefold during the last two years.

Table 3 also gives information on the permanent submitting organizations, that is, organizations that send manuscripts at least twice a year, and also on other submitting organizations that send manuscripts once a year. From Table 3 it is obvious that of the total number of submitting organizations (522) nearly half (212) are permanent. In addition, a significant increase in the number of non-academic institutions can be seen. Despite the fact that most manuscripts are received from

Table 3

Quantitive analysis of submitting of manuscripts to VINITI

Submitting organizations	Number of organizations					Number of manuscripts received	
	Total		Permanent	Others			
	1973	1974 (1st half-year)	1973-1974	1973-1974		1973	1974 (1st half-year)
Editorial boards of journals of USSR Academy of Sciences	22	24	17	7		692	378
Editorial boards of journals of union republic Academies of Science	26	26	21	5		847	393
Editorial boards of journals of other departments	20	25	11	14		298	323
Institutes of the USSR Academy of Science	59	73	35	38		641	311
Institutes of union republic Academies of Science	41	55	21	34		478	197
Institutes of other departments	185	285	84	201		886	664
Universities	31	34	23	11		318	342
Total	384	522	212	310		4160	2608

academic institutions, it should be noted that the proportion of manuscripts accepted from non-academic institutions is increasing. Thus, in 1973, manuscripts accepted from non-academic institutions amounted to 27.8%, and in the first half of 1974 to 45.3%. From January to June 1974, 1329 manuscripts were received from non-academic institutions and 1279 from academic institutions.

Table 4

Number of manuscripts accepted for depositing at VINITI from editorial offices of journals

Name of journal	Year	
	1973	1974 (1st half-year)
Journal of Physical Chemistry, USSR Academy of Sciences	435	209
Uzbek Chemical Journal, UzebekSSR Academy of Sciences	245	119
Proceedings of Higher Educational Instutions: Chemistry and Chemical Engineering	76	83
Moscow State University Herald: Chemistry Series	68	38
Biological Journal of the Armenian Academy of Sciences	40	41
Proceedings of Higher Educational Institutions: Physics	14	90
Total	878	580

Table 5

Number of manuscripts accepted for depositing from the most active submitting organizations

Submitting organizations	Number of manuscripts	
	1973	1974 (1st half-year)
Institutes of the USSR Academy of Sciences		
Institute of Metallurgy	40	19
Institute of Mathematics and Mechanics	39	6
Institute of Biological Physics	33	8
Institute of Geophysics	29	5
Institutes of union republic Academies of Science		
Institute of Mining, Kazan Academy of Science	48	36
Institute of Metallurgy and Concentrates, Kazan Academy of Science	27	16
Institute of Zoology, Kazan Academy of Science	21	11
Institute of Geotechnological Mechanics, Ukraine Academy of Science	21	9
Institutes of other departments		
All-union Scientific Research Institute of Nuclear Geophysics and Geochemistry of the Ministry of Geology	21	11
Tomsk Polytechnic Institute	17	15
Moscow Chemical Engineering Institute	8	31
Universities		
Moscow State University	66	27
Dnepopetrovsk University	17	9
Voronezh University	17	7
Total	404	210

Table 4 gives information on manuscripts accepted by the Section from the most active editorial boards of journals, which are included in the permanent submitting organizations. In 1973 there were 384 submitting organizations (148 academic and 236 others), and in 1974, 522 (178 academic and 344 others). Of the 178 academic submitting organizations, 94 were permanent, and of the 344 non-academic 118 were permanent. Among the 212 permanent submitting organizations we can distinguish the 20 most active (Tables 4 and 5).

We should particularly mention editorial offices of journals as the most significant submitting organizations. In 1973, half of all accepted manuscripts received at VINITI were from such sources. Unfortunately, by no means all journals use the method of depositing. Even amongst the 208 academic journals (we are counting journals in the social sciences), only a quarter are engaged in depositing.

In an editorial in *Pravda* on 31 March 1973 "Scientific journals and the five-year plan" (4) it was noted that depositing of articles opens up the possibility of considerably accelerating the circulation of knowledge. A number of journals successfully use this method, but although experience warrants it, many editorial offices are slow to introduce it, in spite of the fact that they are overloaded with material. It seems to us that the reluctance of editorial offices to adopt the method of depositing is explained by their psychological inertia; they still do not realize the advantages of depositing. Depositing allows the possibility of extending the information capacity of a journal, regulates the editorial load and significantly speeds up the time of publishing articles in the journal itself. However, it is necessary that information on deposited manuscripts should be drawn up in the same way in all journals and isolated in a section on "Deposited articles", and that a registration number should be given under which the manuscript is stored in the depositing organization.

At present, VINITI publishes a "List of the main information publications in the USSR" (1974). It should become a basic reference book, both for depositories and for all submitting organizations. Using this list, submitting organizations can correctly direct manuscripts to those depositories whose subjects correspond to those of the manuscripts. Unfortunately, in the meantime, both VINITI and other depositories have to redirect many manuscripts sent to the wrong organization.

We cannot agree with the opinion of some authors who think that, because it is impossible to reflect the whole content of a paper in an abstract, presenting every aspect, depositing does not achieve its aim, since the paper itself does not reach the user. An abstract that is well-prepared by the author can give the essence of a paper; nearly all deposited manuscripts have extensive informative titles and without fail are supplied with a classification. With reference to deposited papers, it is sufficient to inform abstracting and scientific journals, catalogues and indexes of deposited manuscripts published by the depositories. Moreover, bibliographic references to manuscripts and abstracts of them must be included in the traditional search patterns of various libraries and organs of information. In *R.Zh.*, abstracts of deposited manuscripts are marked with the sign "Dep".

Depositing is an effective and economic method, and the fact that, with its help, the papers of more than 10,000 authors have already been published testifies to its popularity. The number of submitting organizations and the number of manuscripts accepted for depositing is increasing. It must be emphasized that "... the truth should be learned: abridging and depositing do not discriminate against a given paper. They are only means of speeding up information and provide a more rational transmission through the necessary channels" (1). A positive side of depositing in the USSR is the centralization of the network. Users can be confident that, by regularly looking through the abstracting publications of the five organs of information mentioned earlier, they will get to know of all deposited scientific papers of a specialist character.

Abstracts of deposited manuscripts in the abstracting journals and catalogues are supplied with a standard bibliographic description, and the title lists are drawn up in the same way by all authors, according to a model described in the Instruction on the procedure for depositing scientific papers (3). All this makes it possible, without special complications, to introduce information about deposited manuscripts to organs of information and libraries. On the possibility of replenishing library stocks by deposited manuscripts, *Pravda* (9 September 1972) published a leading article "The scientific and technical library". In this connection, we must dwell a little on the role of libraries in depositing. It seems to us that a deposited manuscript, like any published paper, should have wide potential use by a reader. At present, a user who knows about a deposited manuscript can order a copy of it, or can become acquainted with it through the second copy which is stored in the depository. However, stocks of the depositories are less accessible to a wide readership than stocks of public libraries, and the problem of storing resources in them is felt more sharply. Thus, on the agenda of VINITI there stands the question of storing more than 10,000 second copies of deposited manuscripts.

In our opinion, a more appropriate way out of the present position would be the setting up of the following procedure. All the depositories should, on a regular basis, within a year of accepting a manuscript for deposition transfer a second copy of it for a specified period, say five years, to the stock of a certain large public library (for example the State public scientific and technical library of the USSR). In the reading rooms of this library, readers could familiarize themselves with any manuscript of a scientific paper deposited in the scientific research institutes of the state system of scientific and technical information. After the given time has elapsed, the public library should give this copy of the manuscript back to the special library depository. A resolution of the Central Committee of the Communist Party of the Soviet Union "On the increasing role of libraries in the communist education of workers and in scientific progress" (5) has stated that, in the near future, a list should be approved of library depositories of all-union, republic and regional importance, in which it is proposed to store little-used literature for all the years of publication. The remaining libraries should hand over little-used literature to the library depositories, and obtain it, if necessary, in the original, or a copy through inter-library loan. At present there can be no doubt of the importance of the future extension of the method of depositing manuscripts of scientific papers, since it contributes to the operational transmission of information to the user.

CONCLUSIONS

1. Depositing of manuscripts of scientific papers on specialist topics has existed for 13 years. At present, 49 institutes of information have the right to accept manuscripts for depositing.
2. In respect of the variety of subjects of manuscripts accepted for depositing and the volume of work, VINITI takes a leading part among depositories. During 13 years, the Institute has accepted more than 11,000 manuscripts. Most of these deal with chemistry, physics, mechanics, mathematics and biology.
3. Other depositories send to VINITI abstracts of manuscripts accepted by them for publication in the corresponding editions of *R.Zh.* Altogether, VINITI has dealt with 2740 abstracts from depositories. Most of these abstracts deal with chemistry, mechanical engineering, mining, electrical engineering, power engineering and metallurgy.
4. At present, there is an increase in the number of submitting organizations. compared with 1971, their number has increased fivefold. Nearly half of them

are permanent. The growth in this number is mainly due to non-academic institutions.
5. Editorial offices of journals are the most significant submitting organizations. Depositing allows the possibility of widening the information capacity of a journal, of regulating the editorial load, and of significantly reducing the time taken to publish material in the journal itself.
6. Scientific libraries need to include more information on deposited manuscripts in the catalogue and to widen their stock with copies of deposited manuscripts.
7. Extensive introduction in practice of depositing depends in many cases on improving the organization of work with manuscripts in both the depositories and the submitting organizations.

REFERENCES

1. E.S. Likhtenshtein and A.I. Mikhailov. Editing of scientific and technical literature and information, *High School*, Moscow, 1974, 311pp.
2. Instruction on the procedure for depositing manuscript papers on the natural, technical and social sciences, Moscow, 1971, 13pp.
3. Instruction on the procedure for depositing scientific papers in VINITI, Moscow, 1973, 15pp.
4. Scientific journals and the five-year plan, *Pravda* (editorial), 31 March 1973.
5. The increasing role of libraries in the communist education of workers and in scientific progress: Resolution of the Central Committee of the Communist Party of the Soviet Union, *Pravda*, 26 May 1974.

Received by the Editors 21 February 1975.

Key to Fig.2(P.260).

— · — · ·	manuscript accepted for depositing
—x—x	manuscript returned to the submitting organization
— ·· —	manuscript of abstract
═══	letter reporting reception of manuscript
— · — · -	data for authors' references and selfreferences
= = =:	manuscript issued to *R.Zh.*
OPNOL-	Department of preparatory mechanical treatment of literature
OOREM-	Department of mechanical treatment of manuscripts and exploitation of means of mechanization

7 THE FUTURE OF THE SCIENTIFIC JOURNAL

7. THE FUTURE OF THE SCIENTIFIC JOURNAL

The scientific journal in its traditional form will continue into the foreseeable future. Nevertheless, external pressures (especially financial) and continuing developments (especially in terms of computer access) are likely to encourage new initiatives in the presentation of research results. The recognition of such trends has led in recent years to a re-examination of the purposes that journals serve.

The problem of replacing the journal is that it fulfils a number of different objectives simultaneously. In the first place, it provides a current awareness service, alerting readers to the existence of new research. Secondly, journals have an archival function, storing research so that it can be made available whenever required in the future. Finally, journals serve a social function − for example, by certifying through publication that a piece of research is acceptable to the scientific community. If it is to be successful, any new mode of communication that aims to replace the journal must therefore also be capable of sustaining a series of roles.

On the other hand, the multi-purpose nature of the traditional journal makes it only a moderately efficient transmitter of information. We noted in the introductory material to Section 3 that few readers of a journal look in detail at more than a very small proportion of the papers it publishes. Hence, from the point of view of any individual reader, much of each journal is simply waste paper. New methods of disseminating research need therefore not only to try and retain the advantages of the traditional journal, but also to try and reduce its disadvantages.

In this section, I have not attempted to cover all the possible innovations that have been tried out, let alone all those suggested. (For example, some interesting experiments in the repackaging of journals have already been made, but are not dealt with here.) Instead, I have concentrated on just two innovations which are currently attracting a good deal of attention − the synopsis journal, and the electronic journal. I begin, however, with the most elderly extract in this whole volume − a suggested deposit scheme for scientific manuscripts, which appeared thirty years ago. The purpose of including this is to illustrate that 'new' methods are not necessarily new; approaches which are now the subject of experiment were often first suggested years ago. The problem always lies in the full-scale implementation, rather than in the initial formulation.

The next paper discusses the synopsis journal, which represents an attempt to separate out the current awareness and archival functions of the scientific journal. It provides what might be called an evolutionary approach to the development of the journal. The synopsis part continues to be print-on-paper, though the back-up is as likely to be microform as hard-copy. In contrast, the final paper − on the electronic journal − presents a revolutionary development. In this case, the material is entirely stored and transmitted by computer, so that paper no longer forms an important element in the communication system. A number of synopsis journals are already in existence, but the electronic journal is only just approaching the experimental stage.

During its long history, the scientific journal has become part of an integrated system of communication. Any transition from the traditional journal to some new form of communication will produce changes throughout the system. We can illustrate this point by an example. We have noted in the introduction to Section 1 that abstracts journals appeared as a necessary reaction to the continuing growth of science. But what will happen to abstracts if the synopsis journal becomes common? Even more, what future is there for abstracts journals if the electronic journal is widely accepted?

We must recognise that changes in the scientific journal may lead to drastic consequences at other points in the information network. The interconnectedness of science and the scientific journal, with which I began this book, is also the point which I would emphasise in concluding it.

PROVISIONAL SCHEME FOR CENTRAL DISTRIBUTION OF SCIENTIFIC PUBLICATIONS

By Professor J. D. Bernal, F.R.S.

This paper sets out extremely briefly the outlines of a scheme to secure more effective distribution of scientific papers. The chief objectives aimed at are those of securing that every scientific worker receives as rapidly as possible and with the least expense those papers in which he is most interested. From a perusal of the scheme it will be seen that this is to be effected not by radical reorganization of the methods of presentation of scientific papers, but the existing machinery of the scientific societies is to be supplemented by a distributing body functioning as the agency of the societies and in no way interfering with their editorial functions. More detailed descriptions of the steps which have led to the formulation of such a scheme are to be found in *Nature*, vol. 160, p. 649, 8 November, 1947, and the Report of Proceedings of the

Twentieth Conference, 1945—Association of Special Libraries and Information Bureaux.

The general character of this scheme is one based on natural developments in the field of scientific publications in the last few decades incorporating a number of methods which have separately been found useful by different journals but which have not been welded together in any kind of comprehensive service. It presupposes the existence of a certain small number of central organizations for the distribution of papers, referred to as the National Distributing Authorities (N.D.A.), which are considered to be combined with abstracting organizations so that the whole of scientific publication and distribution operates together as one unit. The N.D.A. would be primarily distributive and clerical in function, all matters which require scientific judgment being referred to panels appointed by the various scientific societies who would, in fact, function very much as they do at present, except that the clerical and financial burden that now rests upon them in respect of publications would be removed. The functioning of this organization is most easily described by tracing the progress of a scientific paper from the time that it is completed by the author.

1. The paper would be sent to the N.D.A., either as at present, or more probably in somewhat shorter form, together with an author's abstract. In addition to sending the paper, the author would indicate whether he wished to submit the full experimental details to be available for selective distribution as indicated below (5).

2. The paper would be referred immediately by N.D.A., in accordance with the pre-arranged agreement between societies on the subject, to the panel of the appropriate society for acceptance. Acceptance would follow existing practice of consideration by an editor or independent referee. In this way scientific control of publication would be secured and the valuable and personal services of editors would not be interfered with. It would be desirable, however, to accelerate this procedure and to secure at least acceptance, rejection or refer back within a week. Immediately acceptance is decided, the title of the paper is put on a weekly list of *notices* of titles of forthcoming papers, together with the appropriate U.D.C. number.

3. The paper would be at once printed by the N.D.A. and, after proof correcting by the author, would be published in the first place as a preprint.

4. A preprint would be distributed immediately according to the following scheme:

    4.1 Individually by post (signed by the author if desired) to listed persons indicated by the author.

4.2 Individually, or in batches at weekly intervals, to all subscribers previously indicating their desire to receive papers in that detailed field.

4.3 Individually, as specified by U.D.C. category, to all those who have requested any paper, having seen its title on an indicative abstract previous to publication.

4.4 Bound together as numbers of journals to individuals or libraries desiring them in this form.

4.5 In batches to Commonwealth and foreign N.D.A., if this system is extended to cover them, for distribution by them in their countries.

5 If the author has sent in a fuller paper, this would be reproduced by some photographic or microfilm method and distributed—

5.1 To a list of individuals whose names are supplied by the author ;

5.2 To all those making special requests for it ;

5.3 To general libraries, possibly only to national libraries, covering the field of the paper if they so request ;

5.4 To special libraries covering the field of the paper if they so request.

6 For more permanent record it may be desirable to print some or all papers as at present in journals, but these journals now only need appear at longer intervals, annually or quarterly at most, and they could be printed, distributed and sold as *bound volumes*. This would ideally be preferable for works considered by the author or the societies as likely to be of lasting importance.

7 The N.D.A. would be central agencies for the provision of scientific information of the more technical kind and here might to some extent be merged with some of the functions of bodies such as Aslib.

8 FINANCE.—The main value of this scheme should lie not only in its speed, convenience and comprehensiveness, but also in its economy. This is expected to be achieved along the following lines ; and it is hoped that some estimate can be given at the Conference of the actual monetary saving. The financial provisions of the scheme would be essentially that the total costs would be borne in the first place by the N.D.A., but that these would recompense themselves by charges from subscribers based not on receipts on individual publications which would involve complicated bookkeeping, but on a block subscription based on a unit subscription allowing for the annual receipt of some two hundred separate papers as well as all the Lists of Titles and Abstracts ; and

each additional block will be provided for a half this initial amount. Individual subscribers would usually be satisfied with one unit which might, say, be equivalent to £3 per annum. Institutions, libraries and industrial enterprises would probably take a number of units equivalent to their intake. It would be very desirable if it were possible to arrange in each country for an amalgamation of societies on the financial side, a subscription to the N.D.A. giving the subscriber the privilege of belonging to all the societies which were willing to elect him into their fellowship either at a reduced subscription or for no subscription at all. In the latter case, the N.D.A. would refund to the societies an agreed amount of the subscriptions received.

8.1 *Economy by the Reduction of the Number of Journals Separately Published.*—Certain amalgamations of journals with the co-operation of the societies, as is already taking place with many local societies, would go far to reducing general overhead costs.

8.2 *Reduction in the Size of Journals.*—By the shortening of papers and, particularly, by the relegation of long or detailed papers to special methods of reproduction, the amount of printing or other reproduction required would be much reduced.

8.3 *The Reduction in the Cost of Paper.*—By limiting the distribution of papers as indicated above to the persons or institutions really in need of them, the actual amount of paper consumed would be very much reduced, possibly to one-quarter or less. This would simultaneously relieve many libraries of their storage problems.

8.4 *Reduction in the Cost of Preparation.*—By concentrating all the actual clerical work of publishing in a small number of centres, it should be possible to provide a much better and more rapid service at a reduced cost owing to the steady volume of work which would then be possible. Overheads would certainly be reduced and probably publishing staff as well.

8.5 *Reduction of Cost of Distribution.*—The centralization of distribution and the obvious possibility of using mechanical means for addressing and sorting would considerably reduce the costs of distribution.

9 A scheme along these general lines should overcome the major disadvantages of the present system of publication and provide for a more rapid, cheaper and more rational system of distribution of scientific literature. It is recognized that this will not mean that an individual scientific worker will have actually more scientific literature, but

what he does receive is more likely to be of use to him, and he will be able to obtain it with expenditure of far less effort.

10 STEPS TO REALIZATION OF THE SCHEME.—If it is agreed in principle that large changes are needed, then it is essential that these changes should be carried out as a planned operation, in stages determined beforehand, so as to produce a minimum breach in continuity and dislocation of existing organizations. The phases which might be adopted are as follows :—

10.1 *Preparatory.*—An initial skeleton organization might be set up on a whole-time basis with the object of exploring the field and drawing up a detailed scheme on the lines determined by the Conference, including full financial provisions and carrying out the separate negotiations with the different societies, with institutions and Governments. At this stage these negotiations could be carried out through UNESCO to see if it is possible, as it is certainly desirable, to introduce a united scheme which would achieve full international acceptance.

10.2 *Introduction of Commonwealth Scheme.*—On completion of this work, the agreed date could be set for the beginning of the Commonwealth scheme ; but this need not be taken too rapidly, as it might overload the organizations to start over the whole field at the same time. Those organizations which are willing or able to co-operate might initiate the scheme at a slightly earlier date than the others, and their experience might be valuable in modifying the scheme conditional on its acceptance by all publishing organizations. Its advantages should be so patent that bodies which in the first place do not join it would gradually be drawn in. At the same time in this phase the more detailed negotiations for fuller international organization could be carried out.

10.3 *Introduction of World Scheme.*—The third stage would involve the setting up of a complete world organization for scientific publication and distribution. This would not, however, be considered a final objective, but would, it is hoped, carry within itself a section specially charged with the study of the working of the scheme and with the introduction of modifications from time to time in an orderly way.

Note added after Conference :

On account of the misunderstandings about the status, nature and scope of these proposals, some of which are referred to in

Paper No. 35, it seems desirable to put on record the reasons that led the author, in his personal capacity and not as Editor of Section I, to propose that they be not discussed at the Conference.

The essential reason was that the results of the questionnaire (*Paper No.* 46) showed that the distribution of papers to individuals, whether by journal, reprint or other method, played such a small part in scientific communication that it would be a waste of time at this stage to attempt to reform it. As only 6 per cent of papers studied were found in journals taken by the research workers as against 12 per cent from reprints and the rest from libraries, it seemed much more profitable to concentrate on improved library systems and on the possibility of copies of papers through libraries rather than from the original publishing body. The scatter of references in journals also revealed in the survey, though it could be greatly reduced by good grouping, could never from the very nature of science be altogether eliminated. As a consequence an ideal system would be one which would (*a*) Ensure a wide and rapid spread through all libraries of papers from the few great common journals; (*b*) Use special libraries to distribute copies on request of papers in the middle rank of special journals whose numbers at present only run into hundreds; (*c*) Provide a service from central libraries in conjunction with abstracting agencies and special research institutions of papers from the many thousand small, local or highly specialized journals.

Such a scheme would require much consultation and thinking out. It is closely linked with all the other proposals contained in the resolutions of the Conference and needs to be integrated with them at every step.

EVALUATION OF A DUAL JOURNAL CONCEPT

Seldon W. Terrant and Lorrin R. Garson

INTRODUCTION

Publishers of scientific and technical information are faced with a number of problems and needs. Two of the most important are (a) the need to remain economically viable and (b) the need to develop systems that will deliver information, via suitable media, in formats and packages that are useful, convenient, and affordable. The principal method used today to disseminate primary scientific and technical information is traditional journal publication. The present journal system has several important characteristics; first, journal articles are normally composed and typeset prior to printing, and second, the articles usually contain all of the information provided in the authors' manuscripts.

The objective of the present study was to evaluate the concept of a dual journal system . . . . a system whereby scientific articles might be published in two companion journals . . . . in a summary version intended for individual subscribers, and in an archival version intended primarily for institutional (library) subscribers. The summary journal would contain short articles (approximately two typeset pages) in which the key information would be presented. At least two possibilities exist for the content of the archival journal. In one form, the journal would contain the same summaries plus any additional material furnished by the authors. The additional material would not be composed and typeset; instead, the authors' typed manuscripts would be used as camera-ready copy at slightly reduced size. An alternate form of the archival journal would contain full articles (printed via camera-ready copy of reduced-size, typed manuscripts) and the corresponding typeset summaries of the articles.

The investigation was initiated because it was expected that a dual journal system would improve the economics of journal production through reduced composition costs and that it might better serve the information needs of scientists. It was desired to obtain detailed, quantitative information about the potential impact of such a system upon both the producers and users of primary scientific and technical information.

BACKGROUND

One of the obvious results of the rapid expansion of published scientific and technical information has been the significant increase in the number of journal pages composed and printed. This increase, along with the rising costs of each component in the production and distribution stream, has made it necessary to reassess the traditional journal publishing process in a search for more efficient, less costly means of supplying readers with information. A large portion of the total publishing cost results from the composition steps; thus, economies have been sought in this area. Some major cost reductions have been realized in recent years through changes from hot metal composition to computer-controlled photocomposition and from sheet-fed to web offset presses in the printing step.

A slight decrease in the number of pages per article has been accomplished in some journals by the efforts of authors and editors to limit the length of articles to that required for an adequate explanation of the work being reported. The savings realized have not been significant. Thus, a number of alternatives have been investigated and adopted; e.g., the use of "miniprint" (reduced-size print) for portions of articles, and microfiche for supplementary information . . . . in most cases, data that assists in detailed understanding of the article, but is not needed by the general reader.

Another factor that not only impacts the economics of journal publication, but also the utility of (and audience for) the information, is that much more material is provided to the subscriber than is needed or can be used within an acceptable time frame. Journal users require specific, discipline-oriented information and also information of general interest to them. The more specialized the information is in a journal, the less the potential audience (for detailed information) becomes. Thus, the cost per unit of detailed, specialized information to an individual subscriber is high. The same specialized information may be of general interest and relative importance to many (both within and outside of the discipline), but only from the standpoint of the main thrust of the work and the conclusions. It would appear that a system capable of serving both kinds of information needs should probably be based upon presenting and packaging the information in different ways.

Investigation of such systems has been in progress for a number of years and a variety of approaches have resulted. The feature common to most of these systems is the use of short or abbreviated versions of the total information, variously described as extended abstracts, summaries, synopses, etc. Usually, the full accounts or articles have been provided by the publishers only on request, sometimes as hard copy and sometimes as microfiche. In addition to the potential economic advantage offered by a dual journal system, it was the conviction that full articles should be published and made readily available that stimulated the investigation of the dual journal concept by the American Chemical Society.

PURPOSE AND OBJECTIVES

It was expected that adoption of a dual journal system for the publication of the JOURNAL OF THE AMERICAN CHEMICAL SOCIETY (JACS) would permit potential savings of 25–30% of the production costs. This estimate was based upon several assumptions; first, that the ratio

---

Reprinted from SUMMARY REPORT, National Science Foundation, Division of Science Information, March 1977, p. 6-14, by permission of the authors. Similar information appears in *Journal of Chemical Information and Computer Sciences*, vol. 17, no. 2, 1977, p. 61-7. Copyright 1977 by the American Chemical Society.

of individual to institutional subscriptions (approximately 10,000 and 6,000, respectively) would remain about the same and, second, that individuals would want to receive the summary journal and institutions would subscribe to the archival journal.

It is generally believed that most scientists read only a small percentage of the total number of articles published in scientific and technical journals, even in those covering their own fields of interest. Further, of the articles "read", only a few are read in their entirety. It was therefore postulated that a dual journal system might better serve scientists' information needs by providing just the key information in the summary version, yet making all of the details available, to those needing them, in the archival version.

JACS was selected for the experiment because of its general interest articles and broad readership. The findings of the evaluation study should thus be applicable to the production and use of similar scientific and technical journals.

The objective of the investigation was to obtain an organized body of information on the potential impact of a dual journal system upon producers as well as users of primary scientific and technical journals. In addition, it was desired to accumulate background information concerning the attitudes, perceptions, and behavior of people involved in the present, traditional journal system. Some of the key questions to which answers were sought include the following. If a dual journal system were adopted for JACS: (a) Would authors continue to submit manuscripts and reviewers continue to referee them? (b) Would present subscribers continue their subscription? (c) Would nonsubscribers begin to subscribe? With respect to the present journal system: (a) How do readers use JACS? (b) What elements of the journal's contents are useful? important? (c) What perceptions do subscribers, and nonsubscribers, have of journal value versus cost?

METHODOLOGY

Evaluation of the dual journal concept included: (a) illustration of the concept via three sample issues of the JOURNAL OF THE AMERICAN CHEMICAL SOCIETY (JACS), prepared from author-furnished summaries and article redrafts, that were published concurrently with the corresponding regular issues of the journal (3,000 sample sets for each of the three issues), (b) obtaining of reaction to the concept via correspondence, meetings, discussions, face-to-face and telephone interviews, and by means of mailed questionnaires (including pilot, full-scale, and follow-up surveys), and (c) dissemination of the results of the study by presentation of papers, seminars, and a final report (journal article publication is also planned).

Preparation of the JACS sample issues required the assistance of authors whose manuscripts had been accepted for publication. Response to the request for help by the Editor, Dr. Cheves Walling, was excellent. Those authors who agreed to participate in the experiment were asked to choose one of two approaches.

In one approach, an author prepared a summary of his work (to be typeset) and also a separate write-up that included the remainder of the information he wished to communicate. The additional information (author's typed manuscript) was used as camera-ready copy, arranged and photographically reduced so that four pages of typed material resulted in one page in the sample journal. This approach produced a summary journal, containing the typeset summaries, and an archival journal containing the typeset summaries and the corresponding typewritten material, which had been processed as just explained.

In the second approach, authors were only asked to prepare summaries of their work. These were typeset and used in the summary journal. Typewritten manuscripts of the corresponding full articles were used as camera-ready copy, as previously described, and included in the archival journal along with the typeset summaries.

The first approach produced an archival journal designated "Type A" and the second approach resulted in a "Type B" archival journal (see the schematic on the inside back cover of this report). It should be noted that "Communications to the Editor" and "Book Reviews" are published regularly in JACS. The sample issues also contained these features, since it was expected that they would be included if a dual journal system were adopted. Two Type B sample issues, dated February 4 and March 3, and one Type A sample issued, dated February 18, 1976, were published.

Since scientific and technical journals serve a variety of functions and audiences, it was considered essential to obtain reactions to the dual journal concept from all concerned with the use of journals. Thus, included among those contacted were authors, reviewers, editors, librarians, and readers (both JACS subscribers and nonsubscribers). One of the techniques used in soliciting reaction to the concept was to hold small, panel discussions involving groups of five or six people. Separate discussions were held with authors, readers, and librarians. Each session was conducted by a trained discussion leader and tape recorded.

The bulk of the quantitative data gathered during the evaluation project was obtained by means of surveys. These surveys were based upon careful identification and selection of representative samples of each of the journal-using groups mentioned above. Standard techniques (interviews and mailed questionnaires) were used and the surveys were conducted by an experienced professional organization, Strategic Futures, Inc., under a contract based upon competitive bidding. The questionnaires were tailored for each group and the data tabulated so as to preserve the identification of group responses (from authors, from reviewers, etc.). Editors were surveyed by the ACS project staff, as were the authors who provided the summaries and articles for the JACS sample issues.

The major data-gathering operations were, in the order shown: (a) about 40 personal interviews, (b) an extensive mail survey, involving a total of approximately 3,000 questionnaires, conducted in three stages: a small pilot mailing, a large-scale mailing of modified and improved questionnaires, and a follow-up (second) mailing to nonrespondents, and (c) approximately 90 personal interviews. It should be noted that a telephone survey was done among those who did not respond to either the first or follow-up mailing. About 160 telephone interviews were conducted to determine whether or not any bias existed between the mail survey's respondent and nonrespondent groups. Based upon accepted research and statistical methodologies, it was apparent that no bias existed that would invalidate the conclusions drawn from the survey. A few details of the conduct of the survey are given below.

After the potential survey participants had been selected, letters were sent to apprise them of the dual journal concept evaluation and to request their cooperation in the mail survey. About two hundred people were selected at random from the total list (approximately 3,000) and included in a pilot survey. They only received the first of the three sample issues of JACS; questionnaires and explanatory cover letters were sent to them several weeks later. A review and analysis of the returned questionnaires permitted modifications and improvements to be made in both their contents and wording. Those people who were not included in the pilot survey received all three sample issues of JACS. They were sent the modified questionnaires and explanatory cover letters after they had received the last sample issue. It was necessary (and planned) to follow up with a second mailing to nonrespondents. The combined mailings resulted in an excellent response (58% return).

The categories within the journal-using community that were contacted in both the pilot and large-scale surveys included the following: authors who had published in JACS in 1975, reviewers of manuscripts submitted to JACS editors, librarians employed in both industrial and academic institutions, faculty members, graduate students, both industrial scientists and managers/administrators, and ACS members who were not JACS subscribers. All except those in the last category were JACS subscribers; all were domestic (U.S.) subscribers except for one group of foreign faculty members and one group of foreign industrial scientists. It was desired to compare the reactions to and perceptions of the dual journal system by those who had access to only one version of the journals with those who could see both versions. Thus, one group of industrial librarians was sent only the archival journal sample issues and another received both versions. Similarly, one group of faculty members received the summary journal samples only and another group received both versions.

SUMMARY OF FINDINGS

It must be stressed that the information obtained during the evaluation project is detailed and complex. Attitudes and perceptions in some cases covered wide ranges, in others they were remarkably uniform. There were no universally applicable answers to some of the questions asked.

Some highlights of the study findings are provided in the following tables* and explanatory text. Although most of the information given here was obtained from the large-scale mail survey, the inferences and conclusions derivable from these data are in general agreement with those based upon the discussions and personal interviews mentioned in the methodology section of this report.

Present Journal System

A number of questions were asked concerning the present journal system .... on attributes, advantages and disadvantages, use patterns, etc. The replies provided some background against which perceptions of a dual journal system could be compared and judged.

Informational Benefits

The four informational benefits listed in Table 1, derived from the use of scientific and technical journals, are all important to readers, authors, and reviewers. General awareness of current developments is the leader in being very important to all groups, whereas in-depth understanding of specific topics trails, though not by much, and is still considered to be very important by a

*In some cases, the figures do not total 100% since some respondents did not answer all of the questions.

Table 1: Informational Benefits of Journals Considered Very Important

	Readers		Authors	Reviewers
	Sub.	Nonsub.		
Current Awareness	69%	57%	57%	82%
In-depth Understanding of Specific Topics	45	38	43	69
Stimulation of Creative Thinking	58	45	47	79
Subsequent Reference or Referral	48	39	50	71

sizable proportion of respondents. Reviewers attach more importance to all of the benefits than do the others, which might be expected, since they are critical of the lack of them in the journals for which they review.

Useful Journal Features

Individual subscribers view the Table of Contents and Communications as most useful among the components of a journal, with over 60% considering them very useful. Within an article, the majority feel that both abstracts and structures are very useful, with somewhat less enthusiasm for the usefulness of citations (references) and tabular data (Table 2).

Reading Behavior (JACS Issues)

Information was sought on the way in which subscribers and nonsubscribers read JACS issues, with particular emphasis on articles (approximately 40 articles per issue). As can be seen in Table 3, there are some differences apparent in the reading behavior of the two groups. Further, the data help to substantiate the oft stated view that scientists, in general, read only a small proportion of the total number of articles published, even in journals covering their own fields of interest. Also, that of the articles "read", only a few are read in their entirety.

Approximately three fourths of the subscribers claim to read thoroughly one to three articles per issue. An additional handful or so of articles are scanned and about the same number noted or marked for future reference. Nonsubscribing readers infrequently read articles. Most typically, this group reads thoroughly about one article per issue, scans three to five more, and notes for future reference one or two more.

JACS Subscriber/Nonsubscriber Comparisons

Information about several personal characteristics and academic degrees was obtained from both subscribers to JACS and nonsubscribers. Nonsubscribers also indicated whether or not they read JACS. The data are helpful in interpreting the use or nonuse of JACS. The age distribution of nonsubscribing readers is quite similar to that of subscribers, but the proportion of Ph.D.'s is markedly lower, as is a primary interest in organic chemistry. Among the non-readers, interest in organic chemistry drops to the level of interest expressed in other fields, and the non-reader group is appreciably older than the reader group (Table 4).

Dual Journal System

The major portion of the data obtained during the evaluation concerns the dual journal concept. The opinions on conversion of the present journal system, some anticipated effects of the conversion, potential subscription behavior, and other topics are discussed in the following sections.

Opinions on Conversion of JACS to a Dual Journal

A key question, of obvious importance in the overall evaluation of the dual journal concept, concerned the feelings of those contacted toward converting JACS from

Table 2: Journal Components Considered Very Useful By Individual Subscribers

Component	Subscribers
Table of Contents	68%
Communications	61
Book Reviews	11
Full Articles	44
Abstracts	53
Structures	58
Tabular Data	25
Citations	42

Table 3: Reading Behavior (JACS Issues)

	Read Thoroughly		Just Scan		Note For Reference	
	Sub.	Nonsub.*	Sub.	Nonsub.*	Sub.	Nonsub.*
None	7%	12%	–%	1%	6%	9%
One	24	39	2	5	12	17
Two	29	18	9	17	17	20
Three	21	13	16	28	19	11
Four or Five	10	5	33	28	20	18
Six to Nine	2	–	19	7	7	4
Ten or More	1	–	17	3	4	1

Question: In a typical issue of JACS, how many articles (not communications) might you . . . . .
*Refers to nonsubscribers who say they "read" JACS

its present format to the dual journal system of a summary version and an archival version. A six-point verbal scale was used (Table 5), with no "neutral" response permitted in order to "force" commitment, short of failure to respond.

Individual JACS subscribers, authors, and journal editors are favorable to conversion by a small margin, whereas over three fourths of individual nonsubscribers are in favor. The strongest opposition to conversion of JACS is found among reviewers, closely followed by librarians.

The attitudes of different subscriber groups toward conversion of JACS, as given in Table 6, vary only slightly. This consistency of attitude is somewhat surprising, considering the diversity of the groups, as defined by occupation, age, primary technical interest, as well as domestic versus foreign in some cases. There are general tendencies toward favoring or opposing conversion. U.S. faculty subscribers are more opposed than are foreign faculty. In fact, U.S. faculty subscribers make up the only group among individual subscribers in which those opposed outnumber those in favor of conversion. Age is a factor that affects attitude toward the dual journal concept. This is apparent in the age group as well as faculty versus graduate student comparisons, with younger people more in favor of conversion than older people. No striking differences are apparent among those having various primary technical interests. It should be noted that perception of the dual journal concept was apparently not influenced by receipt of only the summary version of the JACS sample issues (instead of both versions), since both U.S. faculty groups involved have the same opinions about the conversion of JACS.

Table 4: JACS Subscriber/Nonsubscriber Comparisons

	Nonsubscribers		Subscribers
	Non-readers	Readers	
Ph.D. Degree	51%	54%	82%
Age			
Under 30	6%	23%	19%
30 to 45	41	45	51
46 and over	51	32	29
Primary Technical Interest			
Analytical Chemistry	24%	18%	7%
Biochemistry	13	15	11
Chemical Engineering	13	9	2
Inorganic Chemistry	4	11	13
Organic Chemistry	18	45	71
Physical Chemistry	11	13	13
Other	23	20	7

Table 5: Opinion On Conversion of JACS To A Dual Journal

	Readers		Authors	Reviewers	Librarians	Editors
	Sub.	Nonsub.				
In Favor						
Strongly	18%	33%	18%	11%	10%	8%
Moderately	24	28	22	17	16	35
Slightly	11	17	15	4	17	12
Opposed						
Slightly	9	4	11	12	12	19
Moderately	13	6	15	18	16	8
Strongly	18	7	18	36	29	15
Total In Favor	53%	78%	55%	32%	43%	55%
Total Opposed	40	17	44	66	57	42

Options to Best Serve Information Needs

When asked to select the one option that would best serve the information needs of the chemical community, high percentages of all concerned chose something other than the current journal alone. The responses naturally bear a strong resemblance to the personal preferences expressed about conversion of JACS to a dual journal. Data in Table 7 show that combinations of a summary journal and the current journal or of a summary journal and either of the two archival journal formats are considered the best option by about the same proportion of each group as favored conversion to a dual journal system. Considered in another way, the data also show that (except for nonsubscribers) 54–71% of the journal-using community responding believe that it is desirable and necessary to continue the current journal format as part of any journal system developed.

Archival Journal Format Preference

Two kinds of archival journal formats were used in the dual journal evaluation, as noted previously: the Type A (summaries plus additional information provided by authors) and the Type B (summaries plus the corresponding full articles). There is a general agreement that the Type B format is preferable, although to varying degrees (Table 8). The negative aspect of the Type A format most frequently mentioned by readers is their inability to find a continuous report of the work in one place in the archival journal. Authors and reviewers who prefer the Type B format feel that the Type A format presents more potential writing and refereeing difficulties.

Summary Article Content

There is general agreement among readers, authors, and reviewers on the kinds of information that are "very important" to include in summary articles. Some comparisons of readers' and authors' concerns about the content of summaries are given in Table 9. The data clearly indicate the correlation between attitude toward conversion to a dual journal and the importance of some of the types of information. In all cases, a higher proportion of those opposed, than in favor, feel that the content elements given in the table are very important in the summaries.

Table 6: Subscriber Characteristics And Opinions On Conversion Of JACS To A Dual Journal

	Total	Mgrs.	U. S. Faculty			Foreign Faculty	U.S. Scient.	Foreign Scient.	Grad. Student
			Total	Both*	Summary*				
Favor	53%	56%	44%	43%	44%	59%	55%	54%	60%
Oppose	40	33	54	53	55	30	41	35	37

	Age				Primary Technical Interest**				
	Under 30	30–45	Over 45		Bio.	Org.	Inorg.	Phys.	All Other
Favor	59%	53%	48%	Favor	53%	52%	50%	48%	58%
Oppose	38	40	43	Oppose	38	42	45	45	30

*Both (saw both summary and archival); Summary (saw summary version only)
**Biochemistry, organic chemistry, inorganic chemistry, physical chemistry, and all other fields (analytical chemistry, chemical engineering, etc.)

Table 7: Option That Would Best Serve Information Needs

	Readers		Authors	Reviewers	Editors	Librarians
	Sub.	Nonsub.				
Current Journal	32%	13%	35%	56%	19%	40%
Summary + Current	23	20	19	15	43	14
Summary + Archival Type A	13	23	14	10	10	8
Summary + Archival Type B	21	29	23	13	19	22
Archival Type A Only	2	5	1	1	–	1
Archival Type B Only	3	1	4	–	5	7
Other	2	3	1	5	–	2

Anticipated Effects of a Dual Journal

■ Authors and Reviewers

Voluntary submission of manuscripts by authors and participation by reviewers are vital to the existence of most journals published by scientific societies. It is therefore absolutely essential to consider the impact upon authors and reviewers of any potential change in the traditional journal system. Authors and reviewers were asked about the effect of conversion of JACS to a dual journal upon the probability of their continuing to submit manuscripts and to review articles (Table 10). Both authors and reviewers believe that conversion to a dual journal system, as illustrated by the sample JACS issues, would affect contributions to and voluntary participation in such a system. The extent to which the conversion is expected to affect participation is influenced by how active people are in the present journal system. The greater their participation, the less likely authors and reviewers would be to submit and review articles, respectively. However, the potential impact is difficult to assess, since much of the reluctance to continue efforts within a dual journal system is based upon a perceived probable loss of prestige and audience for the journal if such a system were adopted. If the quality and prestige of the journal were to continue at the present high levels, then authors and reviewers would be only slightly less inclined to submit and review articles. Another point can be made. Since younger scientists are more in favor of conversion of JACS than are older scientists, the likelihood of their contributing to a dual journal is also greater. Thus, the authors of tomorrow will probably be more receptive to alternative journal systems than those of today.

■ Readers

Attitudes concerning the effects of having a summary journal available reveal that authors and reviewers are somewhat more optimistic than are subscribing readers as to the increased current awareness effect of a summary version, but so are nonsubscribing readers (Table 11). A higher proportion of authors and reviewers believe that readers will need access to a library copy of the archival journal than do the readers themselves, particularly the nonsubscribers. There is obvious agree-

Table 8: Archival Journal Format Preference

	Readers		Authors	Reviewers	Librarians
	Sub.	Nonsub.			
Type A	26%	34%	24%	31%	22%
Type B	53	42	61	52	60

Table 9: Information Content of Summary Articles

Very Important To Include In Summary Articles	Individual Subscribers*			Authors*		
	All	In Favor	Opposed	All	In Favor	Opposed
Experimental Details	32%	18%	51%	12%	4%	22%
Chemical Structures	57	51	67	46	35	60
Tabular Data	24	16	35	17	7	30
Extensive Citations (References)	39	29	52	30	14	49

*"In favor" or "opposed" refer to feelings about conversion of JACS to a dual journal; "all" refers to the total response

Table 10: Potential Effect If JACS Were Converted To A Dual Journal

	Submission of Articles by Authors Who Publish		Review of Articles by Those Who Referee	
	Frequently*	Occasionally	Frequently**	Occasionally
Definitely Less Likely	22%	5%	24%	7%
Probably Less Likely	22	15	24	13
Equally Likely	54	76	52	76
Probably More Likely	–	1	–	4
Definitely More Likely	3	1	–	–

*Five or more articles published in JACS in the last five years
**Thirty or more articles reviewed for publication in JACS in the last five years

ment on the saving of time for the reader. It is expected that a summary journal would not only permit a reader to be able to read less, but also that what he read would be more pertinent to his interests.

■ **Library Operations**

The adoption of a dual journal system could be expected to have quite different effects upon librarians (and library operations) than upon editors, authors, reviewers, and readers. Data on some of the potential impacts considered likely by librarians are given in Tables 12 and 13. Of those developments listed in Table 12, the need for increased storage space and the potentially higher cost to libraries are seen as more likely.

About half of the librarians who responded would expect some added difficulty with referencing and with interlibrary loans. Fewer foresee increased difficulty with either acquisition or cataloging operations. Those librarians employed in industrial libraries who saw only the archival version of the JACS sample issues tend to expect more problems and difficulties with a dual journal system than do their counterparts who saw both versions.

Journal Format Preference and Subscription Price Effect

Conversion of JACS to a dual journal would pose some subscription choices for both present subscribers and nonsubscribers. An estimate of subscription patterns

Table 11: Anticipated Effects Of A Summary Journal

	Readers		Authors	Reviewers
	Sub.	Nonsub		
Save Readers' Time	73%	76%	75%	73%
Increase Current Awareness	49	69	71	62
Would Require Use of Library Copy of Archival Journal	47	25	65	87

Table 12: Developments Considered Likely If A Dual Journal Were Adopted*

	Libraries			
	All	Academic	Industrial**	
			Both	Archival
Greater Demand for Librarian's Guidance	49%	47%	42%	55%
Greater Demand for Library Copy of JACS	56	47	50	67
Increased Use of Copy Machines	50	43	50	54
Increased Storage Space Required	62	65	59	66
Higher Total Cost to Library	73	75	72	73

*Opinions of librarians employed in types of libraries noted
**Both (saw both summary and archival); Archival (saw archival only)

Table 13: Expected Increased Difficulty In Library Operations If A Dual Journal Were Adopted*

	Libraries			
	All	Academic	Industrial**	
			Both	Archival
Acquisition	30%	35%	26%	31%
Cataloging	16	25	12	13
Referencing	49	52	44	49
Interlibrary Loans	44	46	38	47

*Opinions of librarians employed in types of libraries noted
**Both (saw both summary and archival); Archival (saw archival only)

was sought by presenting a number of format and subscription price combinations to respondents. They were asked to indicate their probable choice within each of the combinations offered. Table 14 shows the format preferences and probable subscription behavior of ACS member subscribers (the member subscription price for JACS in 1976 was $28). The alternate pricing schedules offered to nonmember subscribers, represented by libraries in the study, and their reactions to them are given in Table 15 (the 1976 nonmember subscription price was $112).

Some indications of behavior can be deduced from the combinations offered to member subscribers. Of present subscribers, 17–28% prefer something other than the current JACS; a small percentage (3–6%) do not appear to favor JACS in any form at $28. At the same price, those choosing the archival format over the current journal must want the summaries, since both forms contain all of the information provided by the authors. At the same price, with just two choices, about the same proportions appear to want "all" of the information (archival) and "not all" of the information (summary). The summary journal becomes more attractive at a $13 price advantage over the current journal, or a $10 advantage over the archival journal. Perceived disadvantages of the archival journal (separation of information and/or use of typewritten material at reduced size) appear to be compensated for by a price advantage of $17 over the current journal.

The choices offered to librarians (nonmember subscribers), represented in Table 15, were gauged to detect demand and price sensitivity in addition to preference for journal formats. The archival journal alone would be subscribed to by 41–47% of the libraries at the same price as the current journal. Another 24–39% would subscribe to both versions at the prices shown in the table. There is only a slight difference evident between academic and industrial libraries; more industrial libraries would subscribe to both versions. Reaction to the lower subscription price for the combination of both versions indicates only slight price sensitivity.

Price and Nonsubscriber Subscription Behavior

As noted previously, one of the key questions about conversion of JACS to a dual journal was whether or not individual nonsubscribers would want to subscribe to a summary version (about three fourths favor the conversion to a dual journal system). As background and as a reference point, they were asked whether or not the price of a JACS subscription ($28) is the reason that they do not subscribe. As can be seen in Table 16, 67% of all respondents (about half of those who read JACS and over three fourths of those who do not) state that the subscription price is not the reason. Thus, other reasons are involved; for example, the subject matter may not be of interest, the format or amount of material in the journal may be a deterrent, etc.

A range of potential subscription prices was offered for their consideration to provide an estimate of the

Table 14: ACS Member JACS Subscribers' Format Preference And Price Sensitivity

Same Price ($28)		Current $35, Summary $22	
Summary	28%	Summary	41%
Current	62	Current	49
Neither	3	Neither	5
Same Price ($28)		**Current $45, Archival $28**	
Archival	17%	Archival	41%
Current	67	Current	23
Neither	6	Neither	24
Same Price ($28)		**Summary $22, Archival $32**	
Summary	36%	Summary	49%
Archival	38	Archival	27
Neither	17	Neither	15

Table 15: Nonmember JACS Subscribers' Format Preference And Price Sensitivity

Subscription Option*	Academic Libraries	Industrial Libraries
Archival Only at $112	44%	47%
Summary Only at $88	.7	6
Both Versions at $200	25	33
Would Not Subscribe	13	8
Archival Only at $112	44%	41%
Summary Only at $88	7	5
Both Versions at $175	24	39
Would Not Subscribe	13	8

*Price for "Both Versions" is the difference between the options

Table 16: Subscription Price Versus Subscription Behavior
JACS Nonsubscribers (ACS Members)

Reply	All	JACS Readers	JACS Non-readers
Yes	26%	45%	9%
No	67	51	82

Question: Is price ($28) the main reason you do not subscribe?

Price	All	JACS Readers	JACS Non-readers
$24	1%	1%	–%
$22	–	–	–
$20	4	6	2
$15	26	39	14
N.I.*	61	47	74

Question: Would you probably subscribe to a JACS Summary Journal at the following price?
*N.I. means "not interested in JACS Summary Journal subscription at any price"

potential market for a JACS summary journal and to gauge the price sensitivity. The results of the inquiry (Table 16) indicate that about 30% of the respondents would subscribe to a JACS summary journal if the subscription price were $15–20. Of course, the proportion of those expressing an intent to subscribe who would actually carry out that intent is subject to a number of factors (e.g., the intensity of a promotional campaign). However, even a drastic reduction in the percentages indicated would translate into thousands of subscriptions if the survey results can be projected to the total ACS membership not subscribing to JACS (approximately 100,000).

Production Economics

It was stated in the Purpose and Objectives section of this report that adoption of a dual journal system for the publication of JACS would be expected to result in savings of 25–30% of the production costs. This expectation was verified during the publication of the three sample issues of JACS by a comparison of the costs for the dual journal samples and the regular journal issues published concurrently.

FUTURE PLANS

Although no "mandate" is apparent for conversion of JACS to a dual journal, as exemplified by the sample issues, strong evidence has been obtained of an interest in, and need for, a summary journal. There are no plans at present to publish JACS by the methods used to produce the sample archival journals. However, it is planned to investigate the potential of a summary journal that would be a companion to the current, conventionally published JACS (or to other ACS journals), as well as other alternatives to the present journal system. Potential variations might be (a) a summary journal plus a microfiche version of the regular journal, (b) a summary journal plus requested articles, (c) a summary journal that would contain summaries of articles from more than one journal. It is possible that favorable reaction to one or more of the schemes might permit an experimental journal system to be tried for a year or two.

An On-line Scientific Journal
JOHN SENDERS

Increases in the costs of raw materials and energy, and delays in printing and posting, together with increasing difficulty in identifying and retrieving scientific information will lead to the demise of the printed scientific journal and its replacement by a wholly electronically operated system. Even without marked improvements in or radical alterations to the presently available communications systems for handling digital information, the cross-over time when electronic alternatives become cheaper than the conventional printed journal will be within the next 10–15 years.

Introduction

Scientists exchange ideas proximally by talking and distantly by sending letters. When it became necessary to send letters to relatively large numbers of people, a protojournal came into being. The protojournal still consisted of ideas, but it also acquired a physical nature because it consisted of bundles of paper. In due course, as a result of the need to be able to find the ideas which the paper contained, identifications of the bundles by name, and by number and date became necessary. Thus the journal was born. The journal, having acquired a life of its own, continues to exist, although the mechanism for transmitting ideas has altered significantly since its birth. Not only is it possible to speak to many people at the same time via telephone communication, but it is also possible to transmit to many people quantities of readable information through television or its computer-driven equivalent. The equivalent can be in either permanent form, that is to say locally printed on a 'typewriter', or ephemerally on a 'television' screen. The necessity for *simultaneous* transmission and reception via telephone or teletypewriter has long since been obviated by the availability of storage mechanisms which make it possible for individuals to impress either spoken or written material into a memory to be extracted by a listener or reader at some other time.

The journal, then, in its printed bound form has an existence which is unjustified, except as a consequence of habit. The principal idea of a journal is the idea, the information that it contains, and the thought which lies behind the statements of the author. Given modern technological devices, it is possible to conceive of other ways of communicating ideas from a single writer or thinker to a large number of other persons, and it is one of these in

Reprinted from *Information Scientist*, vol. 11, no. 1, March 1977, p. 3-9, by permission of the author and publisher.

particular that we will examine here: the computer based, visually displayed 'electronic journal'.

There are five basic questions about the electronic journal. The five questions deal with conceptual, technological, economic, psychological, and prophetic matters.

The on-line journal defined

The conceptual question is: What is an on-line or electronic journal? It is best exemplified by describing a brief scenario. The author, in this case myself, sits down and writes a paper. (I usually write papers either by dictating into a tape-recorder and having it transcribed by an expert of one sort or another, or sitting down at a typewriter and typing directly.) In this particular case I sit down at a typewriter connected to a computer—a text editor. The text editor can be conceived as a mechanism for taking a sequence of alphanumeric characters (and certain other symbols), expressing it as a tape of indefinite extent, and giving the writer the power to cut, insert, remove or relocate anything, anywhere, from a single character to the entire text. This brief description encompasses nearly all the functions that a good text editor will do. When I am satisfied with this long stream of characters I ask my colleagues for comment. They dial up my number on the computer and look at what I have done and make their comments in a copy of my indefinitely long tape. When I dial up from my terminal and look at what they have done, I may rewrite, I may call them up and argue about it, or do whatever one usually does. In other words, the traditional process of the preparation of a scientific paper has not really altered in structure, only in the particular methods or mechanisms that one uses. When I have satisfied myself and my critics, I send the telephone number of the computer, the log-in number and the identification code of the document to an editor.

In an ideal system I would type in a code which, through the message handling capability of the computer network, would cause a signal to appear on the local store of an editor whom I have selected. The editor, when he or she comes in in the morning, turns on the machine and sees that a paper has been received from J. Senders. He may reject it summarily on the grounds of its author; he may decide to read the abstract; or he may decide to read the whole text. Whatever he wants to read he calls for, because the text editor allows one to identify and call out certain sub-sets (such as the bibliography, the figures, the tables, the abstract, the introduction, or what have you). If he decides that he likes it as a possible part of what I will loosely call his journal, he will then direct it by the same message capability to a referee or a group of referees. In no case has the document ever gone anywhere. It stayed, in all probability, in my computer. All the editor does is to direct to these various other people the information needed to access it. The referees look at it, discuss it, argue about it among themselves or with me and with the editor, decide that they don't like this or they do like that and so on. Eventually in the course of an interactive process, which goes on on-line, the arguments and disagreements are resolved, and, assuming that this is the right journal and this is the right editor, the editor accepts and publishes the document. Now, when he publishes it, what he does is merely transfer it from a private file to a publicly accessible file in what I'll call the 'central computer'. The central computer isn't central and it isn't a computer, but rather is a distributed memory, part of which may in fact be in my laboratory; it is just that now access to the file containing that particular published content is available to people who are 'subscribers' to the journal. The subscribers are people who have paid to participate in the activity of the journal. Those subscribers for whom that document is relevant, who have put down their individual 'profiles', may automatically receive the title, the author, the abstract, possibly the conclusions, whatever they have specified. When they wish, they can call for the whole text or for any part. Those who have not specified an interest profile may merely ask what has been published since they last called. They will get a list of titles and can call for whatever they want. Meanwhile, the 'document' has gone into the bibliographic search and retrieval systems (which already exist) and can be retrieved by anyone merely by searching with keywords or search terms which may appear in the text or be attached to it.

Technological feasibility

The technological question is: Can these things be done? The answer is 'yes' because text editors, message switching capabilities, telephone accessible ports, soft and hard copy terminals, and bibliographic search and retrieval systems exist today. Indeed all of the components I have described exist today. Some of them are inefficient, there are some problems of compatibility, some of them are slow, some of them are expensive and so on. Nonetheless, it is indeed possible at this time to create such a journal. One of our reports was delivered to the National Science Foundation on Monday 13 May 1975, in Washington. I completed the editing of it on Saturday, 11 May in London, England through the use of the IP Sharp network which has its headquarters in Toronto. My two associates and co-authors, Michael Anderson and Christopher Hecht of the University of Toronto, had dumped from the text editor system into the Sharp network with minor linguistic transformations. I pulled it out in London from the Sharp network terminal, read the document, made editorial comments (with a small program we had written to accept these comments) and sent it back into Sharp. On Sunday Hecht and Anderson pulled it out and directed the computer to type out a final copy which was then bound in a spring holder and delivered to Washington the next day. The total cost of this operation was about $50. In other words it was much cheaper than writing letters back and forth across the Atlantic, and certainly far cheaper than attempting the same thing by ordinary telephone communication.

Economics

The next question, and one that excites much discussion, is economic. Would it cost so much to create such journals that it will not be done? The answer is 'no'. Christopher Hecht constructed some very flexible dynamic models of the economic structure of conventional and electronic alternative forms of scientific publishing.[1] He then used a variety of initial conditions and assumptions from which to generate cost projections from 1976 to the year 2000. In brief what he found was as follows: the cost of paper publishing is rising at a faster than uniform exponential rate. This stems from the joint effect of the increasing costs of labour, paper, postage and overheads. The rapidly increasing costs cause the price of journals to be a significant component of the incomes of journal readers. Because of the increase in the population of the world and the continued increase in standard of living in the paper consuming part of the world, and because of the finite number of trees in such countries as Canada and the United States and Scandinavia, which supply a majority of both timber for construction and of pulp for paper, the cost of paper has gone up at more than the inflationary rate. The postage system has over the years, at least in North America, been subsidizing the scientific distribution system. The United States Post Office is in the process of phasing out the subsidizing of special rates on books and scientific journals, which are to be eliminated by 1983, and it is expected that this will raise the cost of subscriptions by as much as 100 per cent. Lastly, overheads—the printing, binding, bundling and mailing of paper, as well as the storing of paper in buildings, all have implicit in them a hidden cost which must be added to the cost of producing a paper. The mere fact that this paper exists costs money because it has to be kept in a space and kept in good physical condition.

Hecht's analysis showed roughly the following: that for an initial investment of approximately £100,000,000 this year, we could effectively substitute an electronic system which would be almost identical in cost to the present paper publishing systems. The capital costs would be spread over five years.

The actual cost in the first year would be close to £7 or £800,000,000, which is a very small figure in comparison to the overall actual cost of distributing the world's scientific literature. If we try to make electronic a small journal of about 900 pages per year with no more than 2,500 subscribers, both private and institutional, the economics of the situation indicate a crossover point in the middle or late 1990s. However, if we set up a system to handle the entire body of English language scientific publications at once, the crossover point has already been passed. This is true even though we assume an enormous initial investment for the supplying of terminals to scientists in sufficient numbers to ensure that access can be had by all.

None of the above cost figures take into account the value of saving time. The delay in publication implicit in the electronic system is the editorial processing time, which runs about six weeks for most of the North American journals. The average lag in publication for the North American journals is about one year, and in certain of the social sciences and humanities, as much as two years. No one seems to be able to equate dollar savings with time savings, but there seems to be some correspondence. This would suggest that the crossover points actually occurred some time ago. My original estimate of the crossover for the North American corpus of scientific information, based on a comprehensive model of costs, was around 1971.

Acceptability

The next question is the psychological one: Will people accept it and use it? It is more difficult to give an unequivocal answer; one is easily convinced that it will be accepted in due course. The objections to the electronic journal system fall into a number of classes. One is that without cost-dictated page limitations the system becomes a means of "transferring garbage from one desk through a sewer to another desk".[2] The answer to this objection is that, in general, with present trends in mass storage capacities, computer speeds and component costs, it will become economically feasible at some time in the near future to store infinite quantities of sewage at infinitesimal costs per unit—but, one does not have to look at it. A second complaint is that many busy people do their reading outside of their laboratories or offices, on the train or the plane for example, and thus require their reading material to be portable. I predict that within some few years (say by 1984) a mechanism will be available that will be approximately the size of a small tape recorder and shaped like a book which will have a display system like that of a compact electronic calculator. Another common objection is that a bound journal, that one can hold in one's hand, feels right. Most of the expressed concern stems from familiarization and habituation. Perhaps users' acceptance will have to await the retirement of the older scientists.

Will it happen?

The last question is the prophetic one. Will an electronic journal be published? The answer to this varies in its degree of certainty almost from day to day. At the present time the answer is 'Yes, it will happen'. It is in the process of being put together now.

The electronic journal has three parts: the writing, the editing, and the retrieval. In a sense, the distribution to the readership is a trivial extension of the retrieval system. The author produces information and clarifies it with his local editing process. He then sends the material via electronic communication to an editorial processing centre.[3] An EPC accepts the document (if it is not in computer readable form, it will be keyboarded into the computer), and from that moment on it stays in the computer. At the end of the editorial process the EPC puts out a tape which operates a computer controlled typesetter. An electronic journal would merely take the output of the EPC and enter it into a searchable store, which in a sense *is* the published journal. Once it is there, it is accessible by the users. The electronic journal then, will exist in a computer, accessible to subscribers with terminals from computers, and the material in the journal will be coalesced in a bibliographic search and retrieval system. (Search and retrieval systems are also funded by the National Science Foundation for a variety of academic and scientific disciplines—psychology, linguistics, biology, chemistry and so on.) *The On-line Journal*, first edition, volume one, number one is expected to open its electronic ports around the end of 1976.

The On-line Journal is not going to make a profit in its first year, and probably won't for some time. However, since there exists in North America a sufficiently large community of well endowed investigators who have computers and terminals in their laboratories, we don't have to provide the initial funding in order to get a body of possible readers and users of the system. Our only task here is to select some discipline or area of research, sufficiently dynamic that there is a large group of interested persons. The only people we will have to provide with terminals and the associated equipment are those without them who are members of the Editorial Board or the Editorial Staff, in order that there will be a communication network for the refereeing of articles.

In summary, then, it is possible to describe a feasible system, without a requirement for future developments or improvements; a system which is economic today, if it is done on a sufficiently large scale; a system which will, in the course of time, be accepted by the majority of potential users because of their continually increasing familiarity with the use of on-line computers; and lastly, a system which can be forecast as being an almost inevitable consequence of economic and technological change.

References

1. Christopher Hecht. Interactive dynamic models of the economics of scientific journal publishing. Unpublished M.A.Sc. thesis, University of Toronto, 1976.
2. A. P. Melton. Personal comments, 1973.
3. Sarah N. Rhodes and Harold E. Bamford, Jr. Editorial Processing Centers: a progress report. The American Sociologist, vol. II, August 1976, p. 153-159.

SUGGESTED FURTHER READING

The references attached to the papers reprinted in this volume form an excellent introduction to the basic literature in each section. The purpose of this reading list is simply to suggest a few general references for introductory reading, and to comment briefly on the literature. Two books that contain material relevant to a number of the sections are:

> HOUGHTON, Bernard. Scientific periodicals: their historical development, characteristics and control. London: Bingley, 1975.
>
> MEADOWS, A.J. Communication in science. London: Butterworths, 1974.

A very useful listing of the literature on scientific journals up to the early 1970's is provided by:

> HILLS, Jacqueline. A review of the literature on primary communications in science and technology *(Aslib Occasional Publication No. 9).* London: Aslib, 1972.

Section 1

The most important reference on the history of the scientific journal is:

> KRONICK, David A. A history of scientific and technical periodicals: the origins and development of the scientific and technical press, 1665-1790. 2nd ed. Metuchen: Scarecrow Press, 1976.

A new volume on *Science Publishing in Europe*, concentrating on the nineteenth and twentieth centuries, is due to be published in 1979.

Section 2

As is mentioned in the introduction to this section, a number of studies which touch on the economics of journal publication are currently appearing in the United States. Of these, the entire King Report (part of which is extracted in this section) probably represents the best current source of information. A report on the economics project headed by Professor F. Machlup at Princeton University has recently appeared: MACHLUP, F.E. and LEESON, K. Information through the printed word, 1978. A short survey of the current economic situation in the UK can be found in:

> MEADOWS, A.J., and WHARMBY, E. Current trends in scholarly journal publishing. In: Peter Lea, ed. *Trends in scholarly publishing* (BLRDD Report No. 5299). London: British Library, 1976. pp. 33-34.

Section 3

Since this section covers a wide variety of topics, it is difficult to find a general reference that is entirely relevant. However, one basic text dealing with problems in communicating science is:

> PRICE, Derek J. de Solla. Little science, big science. New York; London: Columbia University Press, 1963.

This provides a good foundation for subsequent study of the journal literature.

Section 4

There is an interesting discussion of the role of refereeing in:

> ZIMAN, John. Public knowledge. Cambridge: Cambridge University Press, 1968.

The most recent detailed study of the subject can be found in

> GORDON, M.D. A study of the evaluation of research papers by primary journals. Leicester: Primary Communications Research Centre, University of Leicester, 1978.

Section 5

A great deal about the development of citation studies of journals can be gathered from:

> GARFIELD, E. Essays of an information scientist (2 vols). Philadelphia: ISI Press, 1977.

An enlightening analysis of scientific development over the past century on the basis of studies of the literature is provided by

> MENARD, H.W. Science: growth and change. Harvard University Press, 1971.

Citation studies appear in a number of journals, but some particularly interesting articles have been published in recent years in *Social Studies of Science* (previously *Science Studies*). A new journal, *Scientometrics*, has also begun to publish papers in this field.

Discussions of the scattering of research papers across journals have mainly been published in the journal literature. A good survey of developments in this field can be obtained by browsing through past volumes of the *Journal of Documentation*.

Section 6

The Russians have published a good deal on various aspects of 'informatics', but little of this material is available in English. Some insight into the progress of Soviet work on journals can be obtained from the translated papers presented at international meetings.

Section 7

The literature on current and future changes in the scientific journal is large, expanding and liable to be published in unexpected places. The best introduction to this general topic is probably:

> AITCHISON, J. Alternatives to the scientific periodical. (OSTI Report No. 5190). London: OSTI, 1974.

This report reviews new methods of approach that have been discussed in the literature.

AUTHOR INDEX

Page numbers in bold type refer to papers reprinted in this volume. All others refer to entries in the *Further Reading* Section.

AITCHISON, Jean 298

BARINOVA, Z.B. *and others* 223
BASOVA, I.M. *and* KUZNETSOVA, I.F. 256
BERLT, Nancy C. (NARIN, Francis, CARPENTER, Mark *and*) 163
BERNAL, J.D. 273
BROADBENT, Margaret **71**

CARPENTER, Mark (NARIN, Francis, CARPENTER, Mark *and* BERLT, Nancy C.) 163

FLORENTINE, Harry **56**
FRY, Bernard M. (WHITE, Herbert S. *and*) **50**

GARFIELD, Eugene 298
GARSON, Lorrin R. (TERRANT, Seldon W. *and*) **279**
GARVEY, William D., LIN, Nan *and* TOMITA, Kazuo **73**
GORDON, M.D. 298

HILLS, Jacqueline 297
HOUGHTON, Bernard 297

KENDALL, M.G. **151**
KING, D.W., LANCASTER, F.W., McDONALD, D.D., RODERER, N.K., *and* WOOD, B.L. **29**, 297
KRONICK, D.A. 297
KUZNETSOVA, I.F. (BASOVA, I.M. *and*) 256

LANCASTER, F.W. (KING, D.W., LANCASTER, F.W., McDONALD, D.D., RODERER, N.K., *and* WOOD, B.L.) **29**
LIN, Nan (GARVEY, William D., LIN, Nan *and* TOMITA, Kazuo) **73**

McDONALD, D.D. (KING, D.W, LANCASTER, F.W., McDONALD, D.D., RODERER, N.K., *and* WOOD, B.L.) **29**
MACHLUP, F. 297
McKIE, Douglas **7**
MANHEIM, Frank T. **99**
MARTYN, John **68**
MEADOWS, A.J. 104, 297
MEADOWS, A.J. *and* WHARMBY, E. 297
MENARD, H.W. 298
MERTON, Robert K. (ZUCKERMAN, Harriet *and*) **112**

NARIN, Francis, CARPENTER, Mark, *and* BERLT, Nancy C. **163**
NOVIKOV, Yu. A. 248

OSGOOD, Charles E. (XHIGNESSE, Louis V. *and*) **172**

PRICE, Derek J. de Solla **157**, 297

RODERER, N.K. (KING, D.W., LANCASTER, F.W., McDONALD, D.D., RODERER, N.K. *and* WOOD, B.L.) **29**

SENDERS, John **289**
SHEPHARD, David A.E. **88**
SINGLETON, Alan **186**

TASK GROUP ON THE ECONOMICS OF PRIMARY PUBLICATION **23**
TERRANT, Seldon W. *and* GARSON, Lorrin R. **279**

TOMITA, Kazuo (GARVEY, William D., LIN, Nan *and*) 73

WHARMBY, E. (MEADOWS, A.J. *and*) 297
WHITE, Herbert S. *and* FRY, Bernard M. 50
WOOD, B.L. (KING, D.W., LANCASTER, F.W., McDONALD, D.D., RODERER, N.K. *and*) 29
WOOSTER, Harold 63

XHIGNESSE, Louis V. *and* OSGOOD, Charles E. 172

ZIMAN, J. 298
ZUCKERMAN, Harriet *and* MERTON, Robert K. 112